Praise for *Facing toward the Dawn*

"*Facing toward the Dawn* is an important book, an act of recovered memory, that says much about regional life at the dawn of the twentieth century, when the future seemed more open than it does now."

— *New Politics*

"Lenzi's cultural and political history of the New London anarchists is a valuable addition to the history of US radicalism. Simultaneously local and international in its scope, *Facing toward the Dawn* broadens the reader's understanding of early twentieth century immigrant life in the United States while adding some important context to the popular history of resistance to American capitalism."

— *CounterPunch*

"*Facing toward the Dawn* is unlike anything in the literature of local history. It's the biography of a place built and sustained on shared beliefs at an extreme end of the political spectrum."

— *The Day*

FACING TOWARD THE DAWN

SUNY series in Italian/American Culture

Fred L. Gardaphe, editor

FACING TOWARD THE DAWN

THE ITALIAN ANARCHISTS OF NEW LONDON

RICHARD LENZI

Published by State University of New York Press, Albany

© 2019 State University of New York

All rights reserved

No part of this book may be used or reproduced in any manner whatsoever without written permission. No part of this book may be stored in a retrieval system or transmitted in any form or by any means including electronic, electrostatic, magnetic tape, mechanical, photocopying, recording, or otherwise without the prior permission in writing of the publisher.

For information, contact State University of New York Press, Albany, NY
www.sunypress.edu

Library of Congress Cataloging-in-Publication Data

Names: Lenzi, Richard, author.
Title: Facing toward the dawn : the Italian anarchists of New London / Richard Lenzi.
Description: Albany : State University of New York Press, [2019] | Series: SUNY series in Italian/American culture | Includes bibliographical references and index.
Identifiers: LCCN 2018009434 | ISBN 9781438472713 (hardcover) | ISBN 9781438472706 (pbk.) | ISBN 9781438472720 (ebook)
Subjects: LCSH: Italian Americans—Connecticut—New London—History. | Anarchists—Connecticut—New London. | New London (Conn.)—History.
Classification: LCC F104.N7 L46 2019 | DDC 974.6/5—dc23
LC record available at https://lccn.loc.gov/2018009434

10 9 8 7 6 5 4 3 2 1

For the Future—
Arya, Bella, Brooke-Lyn, Jonathan, Josh, and Layla

We work for the emancipation of the proletariat, for the coming of a free society, in accordance with our weak forces, but without weakness and compromise, today as with tomorrow . . . and with equal if not better activity and ardor—and we have no other ambitions.

—Gruppo L'Avvenire, New London, Connecticut
January 2, 1909, *Cronaca Sovversiva*

Q: Do you believe in Anarchy?

A: I believe in all which is good.

Q: Do you believe that the government of any country should be overthrown by force?

A: That depends on what kind of position they are in.

Q: Do you believe that the government of the United States should be overthrown by force?

A: I never tried it.

Q: Are you an Internationalist or a Nationalist?

A: I am a citizen of the world.

Q: You don't regard yourself a citizen of Italy?

A: I like everybody in the whole world.

—Paolo Rinaldoni, active in the New London anarchist movement, 1920–1956; from an interview by the Bureau of Investigation on September 15, 1918

CONTENTS

Preface — xi

Acknowledgments — xix

Introduction — 1

Chapter One
From Fano to New London — 7

Chapter Two
Italian Revolutionaries in a Yankee State — 23

Chapter Three
Birth of Gruppo L'Avvenire — 35

Chapter Four
A Night at the Opera House — 55

Chapter Five
Toward Galleanism — 65

Chapter Six
Breakdown — 73

Chapter Seven
Rebuilding — 91

photo gallery follows page 104

CHAPTER EIGHT
Solidarity Neighborhood					105

CHAPTER NINE
Anarchists at War					123

CHAPTER TEN
Facing the 1920s					145

CHAPTER ELEVEN
They Fought the Law					161

CHAPTER TWELVE
"The 12th of October in New London"			173

CHAPTER THIRTEEN
Allies and Enemies					191

CHAPTER FOURTEEN
From New Deal to World War				213

CHAPTER FIFTEEN
"Tested by Attacks of Time and Illness"			225

CONCLUSION						235

NOTES							243

BIBLIOGRAPHY						273

INDEX							285

PREFACE

Bulldozer crews did their work well—one strains to find even a trace of brick or mortar in the Fort Trumbull neighborhood of New London, Connecticut. It has been over a decade since the completion of the mission begun years before of removing any sign of human habitation from this locale. Fort Trumbull now looks close to what it did in 1852—minus the trees—when it had been laid out by Yankee landowners as a grid of rutted tracks that they called streets, ready to receive successive waves of working-class immigrants. Stubborn sewer grates and telephone poles now intrude on the vacant lots, unwanted reminders of a distant past in a new, flattened world. Fort Trumbull is a ninety-three acre expanse broken only by rock outcroppings. One building has survived the combined drive of government and corporate power: the Italian Dramatic Club (IDC) hall.

In the late 1990s the IDC hall became a minor focus of controversy in the dispute over the use of eminent domain known as *Kelo v. City of New London*, which began as a local conflict and eventually gained massive national media coverage as it wound its way through the court system. The confrontation revolved around the issue of whether the government could seize private property, not for building a highway or school, but for the advantage of other private interests, in the name of "public benefit." A previously defunct quasi-public entity called the New London Development Corporation (NLDC) had been given the responsibility of finding parties willing to finance development schemes in the city, the idea being to revamp New London's extensive waterfront areas by attracting new upscale businesses. Pfizer Corporation, with its headquarters across the Thames River in Groton, early on expressed interest. They would secure commercial and federal government land to expand their research facilities, but with the stipulation that the adjoining neighborhood of private homes in Fort Trumbull be leveled to make room for a projected world-class hotel, health club, and condominiums. The NLDC and the city government initiated a seven-year-long campaign to gain control of the neighborhood through the vehicle of eminent domain. Aimed at a handful of recalcitrant homeowners who refused to leave, the battle ended in the US Supreme Court in 2005. The decision came in against the homeowners and in favor of the NLDC. Wrecking crews completed their task; Pfizer then reconsidered its development plans, and in 2009 announced that it was closing its existing New London facilities and moving back across the river. Fort Trumbull awaits its future, with few buildings and fewer people.[1]

Through it all, the Italian Dramatic Club became a target of ridicule and derision. Very early in the battle, an agreement had been reached to leave the IDC hall untouched. Critics cited its political connections, calling the club a "watering hole for politicians" because of numerous fund-raisers held there as the reason for its survival. Supporters of the Coalition to Save the Fort Trumbull Neighborhood understandably did not view the Club as a possible ally. The hall was seen as an empty shell, a relic way past its day, which stood only as a reminder that the Italian Americans who built the neighborhood in the early years of the twentieth century had long passed from the scene.

The IDC hall, in fact, does stand as a monument to the accomplishments of the Italian community of Fort Trumbull. It has seen more than its share of dances, weddings, parties, meetings, *festas*, and, of course, theatrical performances, since its construction in 1922. That year anarchists of Gruppo I Liberi—"the free"—built the hall for their circle to hold social and political functions. If the hall now stands as a sentinel to empty urban space, it represented at one time a tangible symbol of a revolutionary movement that touched the lives of hundreds of New Londoners. It stood as the antithesis of conventional deal-making politics that rose across the country just as waves of immigrants appeared on our shores.

By coincidence, I became intrigued with Fort Trumbull at about the same time the razing of the neighborhood had been decided on. Chance, or luck, brought us together. I had a long-standing interest in the history of labor and radicalism in the United States, especially Connecticut, and had published a few articles and written even more papers that remained in my file cabinets. In 1998, I happened upon Paul

Avrich's *Sacco and Vanzetti: The Anarchist Background*, a well-researched, succinct little book.[2] It proved to be an excellent introduction to the vibrant Italian American anarchist movement that existed between the 1880s and 1920s. My hometown of New Britain, I learned, had hosted several Italian anarchist and syndicalist groups. This led to my eventual viewing of reels of microfilmed, long-extinct newspapers as I entered a hitherto unknown realm. I found that a "Lenzi" from New Britain, probably my grandfather, had been a one-time subscriber to the militant *Cronaca Sovversiva* in 1916. My initial research resulted in a modest paper for a history course. But while digging through the Italian radical press, I came across far more hits on New London than any other locality in Connecticut. It became clear that the city had more than held its own during the heyday of the Italian American anarchist movement.

Through some preliminary research I discovered the salient character of New London's anarchists: they had been concentrated in Fort Trumbull and most had come from the town of Fano, in the Pesaro province of the Marche region of Italy. I traveled to New London a few more times, talked to librarians and communicated with the author of a neighborhood study, but for the most part the accumulated information joined my jumbled pile of research.

The parties involved in the eminent domain clash over the fate of the remaining homes had overlooked the unique history of the Fort Trumbull neighborhood. Those fighting to preserve the neighborhood had rightfully focused on the needs of the affected residents rather than on ghosts of the past. But I never stopped feeling that my initial probes into Fort Trumbull had been left unfinished. In early 2015, I decided to rifle through my file cabinets and proceed from there; here is the result.

Public histories of Fort Trumbull are not lacking, and some have peeked into the unique heritage of the neighborhood. These accounts include articles in the *New London Day* based on the reminiscences of former residents. In 1998, the Oral History of Italians in New London Project resulted in the deposition at the University of Connecticut's Dodd Research Center of videotaped interviews that included a number from Fort Trumbull.[3] Narrators and interviewees alike describe traits of the neighborhood such as the unity of its residents, the long-standing practice of mutual aid, and differences with Italian migrants from other regions. In one interview, a third-generation descendant teasingly remarked, "It was like an early commune." A student at Connecticut College wrote a very helpful account in 2001 that used the A word: "While they (members of the Italian Dramatic Club) were not politically oriented, they were referred to throughout the neighborhood as anarchists." She interviewed a descendant who said simply, "The people who started this one (the IDC) were anarchists—they didn't believe in God."[4]

Fort Trumbull emerges from these accounts as a fascinating, independent-minded neighborhood well deserving of having its story told, even leaving politics aside. Fort Trumbull's narrators usually hint at what lies off-stage: a neighborhood with a passionate hatred of fascism; a community with an enduring indifference, if not hostility, towards organized religion; one in which residents allegedly wore silver ribbons on the workers' holiday of May Day, and attended the Sacco and Vanzetti trial. After having the door opened to a radical past, however, discussion proceeded no further. This book is an attempt to complete the narrative, to bring to center stage the revolutionary commitment of so many of the Italian residents of the neighborhood.

A number of works have been published on Italian American radicalism in the last two decades on such topics as the syndicalist movement, women's activism, anarchist roots of the Sacco and Vanzetti campaign, transnationalism of Italian anarchists, Italian radical subculture, as well as a biography of anarcho-syndicalist leader Carlo Tresca. A few discuss the anarchist movement in a particular geographical area, such as Paterson, New Jersey, the national center of Italian anarchism in North America. These works provided the scaffolding necessary for me to write this history, by pointing the way to research sources and by making sense of a complicated, not-easily-categorized movement.[5]

Anarchist activity in Fort Trumbull usually escaped public scrutiny. In 1900, the New London Day warmly welcomed an upcoming "opera performance" that caused much excitement in the local Italian community, unwittingly providing free advertising for a rendering of anarchist Pietro Gori's play *Primo Maggio*. Italian anarchist communities in the United States fit the category usefully described by Davide Turcato as an "opaque society." Turcato unearthed the phrase from the classic work of E. P. Thompson, *The Making of the English Working Class*. Thompson employed it to describe the activities of the Luddites, a clandestine workers' group at war with the job-stealing technology of the textile loom system. Turcato compares the seeking of information on this early insurrectionary movement with researching the anarchist movement: the necessity of combining "reliable, but typically reticent" anarchist sources with "more readily available" but "unreliable and distorted" police accounts.⁶ Fort Trumbull's anarchists often remained out of the public eye to avoid the attention of the authorities, perhaps to be expected because of the militancy of their politics. This created a contradiction for a movement that sought to educate the working class for revolution while remaining in the shadows.

Several months into research in 2015, I discovered the website of the Fano-based Enrico Travaglini Archivio/Biblioteca, an organization dedicated to preserving the history of the region's anarchist and workers' movements, and with attention to those who emigrated. An email brought me in touch with historian Federico Sora, the principal researcher and keeper of the archives. He was very aware of New London being the destination of so many of the Fanese anarchists, so he was as pleased as I was to establish contact. We began a serious and fruitful collaboration. Federico, who has also written histories of the Fanese labor movement, began to compile biographies of the local anarchists based on the files that the Italian government kept on dozens of New London anarchists at the Casellario Politico Centrale in Rome, and from local and regional police and court records as well. In addition, he and another historian, Luigi Balsamini, had assembled in a single volume all of the anarchist periodicals published in the Pesaro province from the 1870s until the coming to power of fascism. For my part, I sent Federico biographies of 170 names of New London anarchists gleaned from North American sources. In March 2016 my wife and I visited Fano to cement the relationship, eat local cuisine, and drink a lot of wine. While there, our hosts showed us the splendid main piazza in the center of town, along with the typical *passagiata* for evening strolls and the second-century Arch of Augustus. I thought of inviting them to see New London, but then remembered the empty lot that would await them.⁷

To the old anarchist papers that I trolled through I added Sora and Balsamini's massive volume of Fanese journals, which I lugged home from Italy; it allowed me an invaluable transatlantic vista into my subject area. Federico also digitally sent many issues of other papers, some of which would have been inaccessible to me.

The title of this book partially derives from a stanza in the oft-quoted anarchist hymn "Inno del Primo Maggio" ("Hymn of May 1st") by Pietro Gori, written in 1892:

> Give flowers to the fallen rebels
> With a glance turned toward the dawn.⁸

Gori toured the United States in 1895, speaking hundreds of times. I have not found evidence of his appearing in New London. He might have, but the grouping that formed the city's movement in 1898 had no recollection. The New London anarchists often used the imagery of the dawn—as well as of light, awakening, redemption, rejuvenation, spring, and so on—to bring closer to realization the ultimate victory, to make worthwhile their hardships and struggles. In a 1906 article concerning the need for more effective anarchist propaganda, New London's Gino Cordiglia forecast "the glorious dawn of humanity, of brotherhood and liberty." The New London anarchists' reverence for the rising sun of a future society is best shown in their frequent naming of daughters "Alba" and "Aurora."[9]

New London's Italian anarchists, or a parody of them, made it to the written page in 1940, when Eugene O'Neill began writing a play titled *The Visit of Malatesta*. Its setting was a fictional New London, where O'Neill had spent his boyhood and much of his formative period. Set in the 1920s, the cast of characters who had been anarchists back in Italy now led corrupt, selfish lives in exile. Malatesta, called Cesare rather than the real-life Errico, leaves prison and comes to New London, where he finds his former comrades have abandoned the anarchist movement.

Errico Malatesta did come to the city, but in 1899. As far as I know, no evidence points to O'Neill having any connections with Italian anarchists in the city. He did not speak Italian, but he considered himself a philosophical anarchist and knew Emma Goldman. Goldman had visited New London in 1900, and had spoken to "the Italian group." Did O'Neill, in his sojourns through Bank Street taverns, pick up ideas for the play from stories about true-life characters? It is possible, but will probably never be known for certain. O'Neill gave up on the play in the face of the cataclysmic events of World War II, with the comment that "trouble is too many ideas."[10] That he never finished the play is probably as it should be, since the anarchists would not have come off well. A former professor of mine suggested that O'Neill's play might make a good "hook" into the book, but after some reflection I decided against it. The O'Neill connection arouses my curiosity, though, and he pops up in a few places here.[11]

Researching this study required a self-education in anarchist history and theory. I grew to respect the rank-and-file militants who composed the core of New London's movement: they were self-educated workers and artisans dedicated to their cause, idealists attempting to forge a better future. They had faults and often stumbled on the road they had chosen; they committed mistakes. New London's movement sprang from the same insurgent wave that rejected the worldwide capitalist order and sought to fundamentally rebuild society from the ground up. Long after the heyday of classical anarchism, the comrades of the Fort Trumbull neighborhood held their group together.

The question of violence and terrorism comes to the fore, since the movement to which the New London militants adhered was not motivated by pacifist principles. They did not shun the force of arms in their ideology and in some of their actions. They must be viewed in the context of the time in which they lived. For much of the late nineteenth century and beyond, in both the United States and Italy, the forces of order habitually mowed down workers who asserted their rights. In the United States, armed militias formed by corporations and labor unions confronted each other on more than a few occasions. In Italy, a number of respected liberals supported the thuggery of the fascist movement as an answer to a radicalized workforce. The anarchists' support for "propaganda of the deed" sprang from several sources, not least the insurrectionary republican traditions of Garibaldi and Mazzini. Their actions partially came as a response to government repression. But they also made the conscious choice to take the path they did, and embarked on a journey from which a return proved impossible.

No world development so impacted the New London anarchists as did the coming to power of Mussolini in 1922. At this writing, the nucleus of a fascist movement appears to be making a stir in the United States. Some of the strongest opposition to the extreme right wing has come from anarchists grouped within a tendency called "antifa." They have been criticized widely by liberals and some on the left for meeting the fascists blow for blow in the streets, and even been equated with their Nazi enemies. I have devoted a chapter to the experience of the New London anarchists who similarly faced blackshirts on the streets of their city in 1928. Under the watchwords of discipline, community support, and "united front" in the fight against fascism, I think the lessons of New London decades ago carry forward to the present.

I would like to bring attention to the structure of this book. Two chapters, 8 and 13, are not arranged chronologically, but are of an "overview" nature. Chapter 8, "Solidarity Neighborhood," discusses the critical importance that the anarchists placed on building a community that would resist greater society's values and provide a climate of mutual support in which to live. Chapter 13, "Allies and Enemies," deals with three subjects: the role of women, nearby Italian anarchist circles in Connecticut and Rhode Island, and the relationship of the *prominenti*, or prominent ones, to the New London anarchists. It has a deliberately ambiguous title. The position of women in the anarchist movement proved a challenge to the male-dominated group from its inception. The New London anarchists developed strong ties to other Italian groups in their region that often did not share their ideological orientation. Their relationship with the *prominenti* would prove complicated, defying an easy categorization.

Finally, in researching New London's anarchists, I unexpectedly came across material that may shed new light on the "anarchist background" of the Sacco and Vanzetti case and on the relationship of a wing of the anarchist movement with bootlegging and social clashes during Prohibition, showing at least that one never knows what might be unearthed in digging even at the local level of history.

ACKNOWLEDGMENTS

I have mentioned my indebtedness to Federico Sora in the preface; without his help this work would not exist in anything like its present form.

Years ago, Gene Leach, professor of American Studies at Trinity College, took the trouble to read my early labor and radical history research on Connecticut. More than any other person, he encouraged me to stay on the course that led me here. Later, his graduate studies classes provided a stimulating environment for looking deeper into the hidden byways of US history. Thanks, Gene.

Staff at the New York, Boston, Paterson, and New London public libraries, as well as the Connecticut State Library, proved unfailingly helpful and courteous in responding to all my obscure requests.

Fred Paxton, professor of history at Connecticut College gave me invaluable assistance by opening doors in New London for my research. Fred has a reputation for unselfishly helping local and student researchers with their projects—it is well deserved.

Robert Dowling, Central Connecticut State University professor and Eugene O'Neill biographer, pointed me in the right direction on O'Neill's unfinished play on Malatesta in New London.

Kristin Eshelman of the Special Collections Department of the Thomas Dodd Research Center at the University of Connecticut consistently provided me with some of the most vital material throughout my research.

Benjamin Panciera, whose family name has more than a few links to the radical Italian community in Mystic, assisted me as Special Collections director at the Linda Lear Center of Connecticut College.

Laura Natusch of New London Landmarks Society guided me through the files of her organization that has carefully archived precious New London history.

Barbara Tucker and Anna Kirchmann, two of my professors at Eastern Connecticut State University, gave me encouragement and great advice throughout.

Jennifer Guglielmo, Kenyon Zimmer, and Gerald Meyer—all scholars in the field of Italian American radicalism—also offered encouragement as well as helpful suggestions and good leads on sources.

Both anonymous reviewers for SUNY Press saved me from embarrassing errors and provided necessary criticism that strengthened the book.

All the folks at SUNY Press—Amanda Lanne-Camilli, Chelsea Miller, Ryan Morris, and Anne Valentine—efficiently and smoothly guided the process along.

John B. Coduri, historian of the granite industry of Westerly, Rhode Island, graciously took the time to meet with me and share his photo collection and knowledge of his family in the area.

Shirley Mencarelli and Luisa Mencarelli contributed tremendous insight into New London's complicated Italian past and present, shared family photos and material, and provided great company along the way.

And in the end of course, any errors or miscalls in this book are mine alone.

Finally, I need to thank my wife Luisa. She not only encouraged me in my project but accompanied me on numerous field trips. Most of all she had to listen to my endless, boring harangues while I put together plans for a book. Thanks, Lulu.

INTRODUCTION

During the 1880s and 1890s, immigrants from the Pesaro province of the Marche region in north central Italy—and in particular from the city of Fano—began to settle the bulge of land located to the south of downtown New London, to the east of the city's main thoroughfare and along the Thames River. The Italian community of Fort Trumbull, also called Fort Neck, gradually displaced the original working-class Irish inhabitants, and by 1920 the neighborhood was overwhelmingly Fanese or Marchegian in composition. It occupied a pronounced geographical position, nestled close to an imposing naval installation from which it derived its name, as well as being securely positioned within the city's port and shipbuilding facilities.

Anarchism, not geographical location, however, defined the Fort Trumbull neighborhood. Between 1900 and 1910, anarchism became the dominant system of belief of its inhabitants, and would occupy that position for decades after; not a "philosophical" variety of anarchism along the lines of Henry David Thoreau, but one that adhered to the most militant wing of the movement. Fort Trumbull residents became supporters of the Italian anarchists Errico Malatesta, Luigi Galleani, and others who advocated social revolution and rejected all accommodation with the ruling powers of society.

The Italian anarchist movement at the end of the nineteenth century reflected the influence of the two figures whose writings and activities established anarchism as a worldwide revolutionary movement: Mikhail Bakunin and Peter Kropotkin, both scions of aristocratic families. Their doctrine of anarchism differed with preceding antistatist thought in its orientation toward the "popular" classes, the workers and peasants. Pioneering figures such as Pierre-Joseph Proudhon had taken part in revolutionary events such as the upheavals that shook Europe in 1848–49, and issued programs to help guide the struggle to overturn the existing order. Proudhon's ideas would continue to influence the movement. Bakunin and Kropotkin helped to establish anarchist circles and groups across the continent. Anarchism attained mass influence in Spain and Italy, and commanded the support of workers and artisans not only in European countries like France, Germany, and Belgium, but across Latin America and Asia as well. Paris contained numerous anarchist groupings and journals, while London became the center for several thousand anarchists fleeing repression in their home countries.[1]

The anarchist movement contained a variety of currents, from supporters of individual terrorism who advocated and used dynamite for bombings to those who preferred to work in mass movements. The trend that favored "propaganda of the deed," or expropriations and individual terrorism, received a boost with the founding of the Anti-Authoritarian International, or Black International, in London in 1881. While this body succeeded in diverting much anarchist energy to the advocating of attentats, most anarchists—and even the Black International itself—kept their focus on establishing or working within trade unions. As will be seen, these factions often overlapped, with doctrinal collisions ever-present.

A few basic principles of the anarchist movement can be stated, although at heavy risk of oversimplification. At the core of revolutionary anarchist doctrine are several elements that distinguish it from the Marxism on which social democratic parties of the late nineteenth century based themselves. Anarchism places the role of the individual as crucial for revolutionary activity, and proceeds from there to engagement with the masses. The anarchist movement rejected social democratic prioritization of parliamentary activity and instead focused their efforts on building a revolution from below, involving sections of the working class outside of the existing trade unions. Anarchists stood as "anti-authoritarians," and while some supported the forming of anarchist-led organizations, they criticized "professional" revolutionaries for attempting to gain leadership of the working class. They did not seek to replace the bourgeois state with a workers' state, as they regarded all government authority as inherently oppressive and corrupt; in the anarchist vision, a social revolution of the working masses would quickly bring about a society based on self-directing associations of the populace.[2] Nicola Sacco, while in prison for his alleged role in the South Braintree payroll robbery of 1920, offered the goals of anarchism as follows: "no government, no police, no judges, no bosses, no authority; autonomous groups of people—the people own everything—work in cooperation—distribute by needs—equality, justice, comradeship—love each other."³ Some anarchists like Kropotkin saw the need to "realize communism without delay," and even that "existing societies . . . are inevitably impelled in the direction of communism." Kropotkin tended to minimize the potentially fierce resistance to socialism by defenders of the old society, while Italians such as Errico Malatesta and Luigi Fabbri were quite cognizant of the possible danger ahead.⁴

Anarchism crossed the Atlantic during the early 1880s. Immigrants, especially Germans, provided the base for the profusion of clubs, circles, and newspapers that sprouted across the American Northeast and Midwest. Anarchism as a revolutionary mass movement may have reached its height in the Chicago area, with its leaders assuming the leadership of the struggle for the eight-hour day. The Haymarket bombing and subsequent repression of the movement forced the anarchists to adapt to new conditions as thousands of immigrants arrived to fill their ranks.⁵

If anarchism in the present day brings to mind disaffected middle-class youth, counterculture, and pacifist currents in the antiwar movement, it historically had been a working-class movement; in France, for instance, it gained a foothold in the Parisian workers' suburbs such as Belleville that had provided the base of support for the Paris Commune in 1871. Anarchism became the dominant revolutionary current among workers in the industrial metropolis of Barcelona, representing a deeply rooted movement that lasted until the triumph of Franco's forces in 1939. The meetings, debates and social activities these anarchists organized did not differ much from those of their compatriots throughout the rest of Europe and the Americas.⁶

A significant portion of Fort Trumbull Marchegiani brought with them this anarchist doctrine that had found a welcoming home in their province's long history of insurrection and popular revolt. Along with their carpentry, masonry, and maritime skills, seasoned militants carried to the United States the experience of having participated in one of the most important sectors of Italy's revolutionary movement. Many more were radicalized here on the shores of the new continent. The clubs that they created, first known as Gruppo L'Avvenire, would last for over seventy years. They would anchor Italian American radicalism in southeastern Connecticut and play a considerable role in their nationwide movement. Galleani, the most prominent as well as one of the most militant of the Italian transplants on American soil, would describe his New London comrades on more than one occasion as "among the best" of the movement. Fort Trumbull anarchists interacted with the greater New London working class community, participated in workplace protests and strikes, and tried to construct a "solidarity culture" in their neighborhood. They hosted mass meetings and carried on a relentless struggle against their many opponents on the left as well as the right.

The title of a recent collection of essays on the Italian left in the United States aptly captures the disappearance of this revolutionary movement from popular memory: *The Lost World of Italian-American Radicalism*. Marcella Bencivenni ends her study of the cultural movements of the Italian American *sovversivi* (subversives) with a mournful final paragraph on aging Italian radicals unable to transmit their ideas to their offspring and condemned to live in ever-smaller circles until they passed from existence.[7] But for a considerable time the anarchists of New London played as significant a role in shaping the Italian community of their city as did the church, major political parties, and the rising *prominenti*. What follows is how they contended with these forces and developed a vision quite at odds with the values of the emerging American mainstream.

Historians have increasingly applied the concept of transnationalism to the migration process of Italian radicals. Donna Gabaccia defined this general term as "a way of life that connects family, work and consciousness in more than one national territory . . . Family discipline, economic security, reproduction, inheritance, romance, and dreams transcended national boundaries and bridged continents." She also offered a simple definition: the immigrants lived in both worlds.[8]

Applied to Italian anarchists, historians have focused on, in the words of Travis Tomchuk, "a system of networks—a form of anarchist migration process." These networks "laid the groundwork for a global movement." As Davide Turcato observed, "Italian anarchism is best analyzed as a single movement stretching across the Mediterranean Sea and the Atlantic Ocean." This transnational perspective, according to the editors of a collection of essays on this subject, requires historians to keep anarchism's transnational character in view when studying the movement in a particular geographical place. From this migration process, anarchism drew its strength because, again in the words of Tomchuk, it became "difficult for a state or states to destroy autonomous groups spread across wide geographical spaces." Turcato points to the resilience of the anarchist network in his study of Malatesta's activism between

1889 and 1900, from his refuge in London, founding of a journal in Nice, escape from Lampedusa Island to his ability to remain connected with developments whether in the Americas or in prison. His book ends with an extended discussion of the "transatlantic organizational integration (that) characterized Italian anarchism."[9]

This book is an attempt to discuss the history of Italian anarchism in a small port city in Connecticut within this framework and hopefully contribute to the growing field of anarchist studies. Its focuses on the rank and file movement in New London: how they built their anarchist circles, how they lived their lives, and why they stayed around so long. While these anarchists may have traveled across the Atlantic as part of a migrating network while never out of touch with comrades left behind, they nevertheless fought nearly all their battles in one region of Connecticut, one city, and, in the end, one neighborhood.

CHAPTER ONE

FROM FANO TO NEW LONDON

The Marche region of Italy on the Adriatic coast, lying due east across the Apennines from Tuscany, became an epicenter of insurrection and rebellion during the latter part of the nineteenth century. Its principal city of Ancona developed into the capital of Italian anarchism by the late 1890s, the socialist paper *L'Avanti* calling it a "den of rebels." So strong was anarchism's influence that Errico Malatesta, the Italian revolutionary who made Ancona his base in 1897–1898 had, according to the police, morally shamed the criminal underworld into curtailing their activities. The police complained of having little to do. Regardless, a liberal English weekly in 1906 luridly characterized Ancona as a center of plots and murder for having "old and dreaded traditions in anarchism." The Marche is perhaps the only region of Italy with a real estate website that mentions its anarchist history along with beautiful beaches, rolling hills, and medieval towns as a selling point to potential customers.[1]

Fano rests on the northern Marche coast midway between Pesaro to the north and Ancona to the south. Established as a Roman garrison town in 2 AD, Fano can be reached by following Route SS3 northward from Rome along the ancient Via Flaminia to arrive at the Arch of Augustus. For motorists, signs for Fano appear along the roadside in the Lazio region; not a large town by any means, it now unabashedly draws tourists as a popular seaside resort. The town had few tourists in the 1890s but plenty of disgruntled citizens. What would develop in its sister towns quickly found an echo here. One of the first Italian sections of the International Workingmen's Association (First International) arose in Fano in 1872, as well as a revolutionary newspaper, the *Communard*. Fano was represented at the founding meeting of the IWA in Rimini in the Romagna, and later provided a participant, a student of about twenty years of age named Napoleone Papini, to La Banda del Matese, a group of militants attempting to initiate guerrilla warfare outside Naples in 1877. The first socialist circle emerged in 1881 with a Bakuninist tinge to it. The town gave birth to a revolutionary consciousness that would only grow in intensity as the twentieth century approached.[2]

In common with the rest of the Marche, Fano possessed none of the growing industries or large metropolises that characterized the regions of Italy to the north. With 20,000 inhabitants by the time of the country's unification, its economy rested on handicraft and artisan production. Sixty per cent of its population lived in the nearby countryside; crops and domestic animals continued to consume much of the time of the growing working classes. Some Fanese worked in occupations that blended countryside and city, premodern and industrial modes. One of these, a carter, owned a horse and cart to transport building materials and lived on the outskirts of Fano. His biographer (for he had been a figure in the Sacco and Vanzetti case) describes his vocation as not "artisan, peasant or worker." The very character of Fano's arrested economic development impelled vigorous social movements of protest. Italy's unification, seen by many as being driven by the interests of a narrow northern elite, solved none of the country's overwhelming social problems. Questions of land ownership, religious power, taxation (to fund the needs of the rising national state) and compulsory military service combined with the rising political consciousness of the working classes produced the explosions of the 1880s–90s. The land cultivation system of the countryside of the Marche had its roots in the fourteenth century; the *mezzadria*, or sharecropping system, had placed tenant farmers in the onerous grasp of landowners who lived mostly in the towns. Abuses were common under the system, with the country dwellers mocked by the towns as *schiavi*— slaves. Unlike in the nearby Romagna, the Marchegian countryside did not foster radical currents; almost all class-based movements would have their origin in the region's "honeycomb of urban cores."[3]

Fano's largest industries were silk mills—one mill employing five hundred workers—and the fishing commerce, with the rest of the working classes spread out among olive mills, a match factory, brick-and-chalk furnaces, and other one-owner establishments. The construction trades also employed considerable numbers, with masonry probably predominant.

As a port city, considerable numbers worked in the nonfishing maritime industry. Because of the laggard economic and social structure of Fano, as an historian of the local labor movement has written, the trade union movement dragged in its wake the growing demands of the populace. If the cobblers, blacksmiths, masons, carpenters, and tailors could not form strong labor organizations that could stand alone, they could at least act as effective mouthpieces for the insurgent citizenry. In 1879 the maritime workers of Fano had formed a Società di Mutuo Soccorso, or Mutual Benefit Society, as had workers across Italy; others formed the Società Democratica Artiziana, or Democratic Artisans' Society.

Throughout northern Marche, workers clubs and societies proliferated after Italy's unification. Many of these groups had been composed of different classes and at first were dominated by monarchists and the clergy; fierce battles broke out as new political forces arose to contest their leadership. Republicans and "Internationalists," as the anarchists were known, made up the radical representation of the popular classes of the cities. Even though they shared an anti-oligarchic and anticlergy orientation, these two groups soon locked in fierce battle for leadership of the working classes. Artisans and small businessmen predominated, with the former eventually taking the reins of control. Artisans occupied a higher position than unskilled categories of workers such as day laborers in the urban social structure of Marchegian towns like Fano, but their position was precarious, and they lived with "much difficulty, on the margins of survival." They often faced opponents in the small shop owners for which many masons, stonecutters, and carpenters worked, while at the same time viewing with some apprehension the approach of industrialism. Marchegian artisans in towns like Fano produced goods for the sharecropping households and thus, "depended for their livelihoods in no small part on the good opinion of the landlords."[4]

Revolutionaries won the ideological war in the workers' movement of the Marche, as an historian remarked, "in consonance with the characteristics of a region perhaps tending to 'extremisms.'" The artisanal and craft-based economy of the region shaped the nature of the revolutionary movement for decades. Anarchists repeatedly urged their fellow Fanese artisans to look beyond immediate gains and bargaining with the bosses, to strive toward the social revolution that alone could redeem their lives. A leading Marchegian socialist, Domenico Baldoni, noted the contradictory status of artisans, who often were small businessmen that hired workers on their own. Artisans, he said, were merely envious of the bigger bosses, and viewed capitalism as "an invisible enemy far from their experience." A Fanese communist paper commented in 1921 on "the artisan, of the small industry, of the sharecropping, of the small businesses, of the salaried white collar employees of the area" who sought to construct "the reformist cooperative of production and consumption and contracts for small businessmen and the business of a few shopkeepers under a red bough," rather than revolution. The anarchists, and later the communists, confronted the tendency of their supporters to concentrate on building up "their" institutions, to improve the standard of living in the here and now. Regardless of these obstacles and contradictions, the Fanese anarchist movement in the late nineteenth century strove mightily to create a capable training ground for the younger revolutionaries who later would leave for the North American continent.[5]

Fanese anarchists founded the journal *In Marcia!* (On the March) in 1885, which would survive between alternate periods of rebellion and repression for two decades, and they formed the Circolo di Studi Sociali around the same time. The anarchist press until suppressed by Mussolini provided the movement with a means of transmitting their values to the greater population, helped in the political/cultural education of militants and established a method of class identification for the workers and artisans of the region.[6]

Ettore Antonelli, the first editor of *In Marcia!*, epitomized the generation of young idealists attracted to the rising anarchist movement. Probably of middle-class origin, Antonelli had interrupted his studies at the University of Bologna to throw himself into the revolutionary movement; his comrades described him as "young of sharp intelligence, of gentle and enthusiastic spirit, supporting strongly his ideas in congresses, circles, journals," a true "gentle flower of Fanese youth." Under Antonelli and others that followed him, the anarchist papers of Fano and the provincial capital of Pesaro raised a number of agitational issues that sought to rouse the broad layers of the population; in a local news column, they took sides on infanticide committed by poor women, the dalliances of priests, and the hypocrisy of the authorities' treatment of paupers. *In Marcia!* and other papers took positions that urged workers to defend their mutual benefit society, to "drive away from their very strong bulwark the profiteers . . ." The anarchists called on tenant farmers not to be content with simple improvements in labor contracts with landowners, but "to sing in chorus the fateful emancipatory cry: Land to those who work it."[7]

Many articles focused on the important fishing sector of the local maritime industry, and covered developments in the anarchist-inspired associations of Fano fishermen. The mutual benefit society had fought for the interests of fishermen against the owners of the fishing boats, fish vendors and city authorities, agitating for the correct weighing of fish, a better share in profits from the catch and the right to refuse to set sail during dangerous weather. (The maritime registration book of a future New London anarchist shows all of his terms at sea between 1904 and 1907 undertaken during winter months, when the Adriatic is at its coldest and stormiest.) In 1913, anarchists helped form the Lega di Resistenza dei Marinei, the first formation of fishermen with an exclusively working-class membership. The Lega developed a close relationship with the syndicalist Unione Sindacale Italiana and took a leading role as a vanguard organization in the struggles of Fano's working class.[8] In an 1890 *In Marcia!* article of not a little prescience, Fano anarchists sounded the alarm on the coming tourist wave, bemoaning the construction of a bathing establishment near the beach. A local bourgeois paper promised "that for its elegance and convenience it will bring an extraordinary influx of foreigners." The anarchists were "nauseated by the squander earned by our sweat to the welcome given to these people." (Fano's fishing port is now hemmed in on both sides by tourist-laden beaches.)[9]

From 1897 to 1898, Marchegian anarchists drew on the presence of Errico Malatesta, one of the most capable leaders of the movement. A member of the original First International in Italy who had worked with Bakunin, Malatesta developed strong ties with the French and Spanish anarchist movements, and spent exile years editing journals and spreading the word in Argentina and London. Malatesta had stolen back into Italy and began to edit the journal *L'Agitazione* in Ancona. He also spoke frequently in neighboring towns, undoubtedly including Fano.[10]

The anarchism that grew to dominate the revolutionary movement in the Marche reflected the influence of Malatesta, who called both for more effective organization of anarchists and their deeper ties to the working classes. The local social movements drew in democratic and republican elements from the earlier Mazzini currents, to produce remarkable explosions of struggle from the 1870s to the close of the century. Demands concerning the rising cost of living, unfair taxes and wage issues of the proletariat coalesced into a movement whose leadership gained a high level of political sophistication. Concessions from employers and politicians failed to dampen the growing revolutionary consciousness of masses of workers, artisans, and peasants. General strikes shut down all commerce in Fano at different intervals and increasingly violent confrontations with the police occurred.[11]

These conflicts culminated with the *Fatti di Maggio* (May events) of 1898 that brought unprecedented social explosions across Italy. Ancona led the way with attacks on government buildings that resulted in military occupation of the city. In Fano, sailors and maritime workers, who took an increasingly important role in the local labor movement, initiated agitation for their demands. In May a group of revolutionary youth attempting to stage a noisy demonstration in the city met with arrests. After a brief period in which the authorities seemed to hesitate in responding to the mass movements, they decisively acted to repress the workers' organizations. The unprecedented clampdown in the Marche and across Italy resulted in hundreds of deaths and thousands jailed. These developments landed many Fano activists in jail and induced others into emigration and exile. Among those arrested were Malatesta and a number of dedicated Marchegian anarchist leaders around him. Thousands of radicals were arrested across Italy. Many of these militants were forced into permanent exile. After his release from prison, Malatesta faced five years of *domicilio coato*, or house arrest. "The advances he and his associates had struggled so hard to attain during the previous two years," wrote Nunzio Pernicone, "were completely eradicated and the movement nearly paralyzed."[12]

These events provided an impetus for the departure of a number of Fanese workers and artisans who had been active in the local movements, thus supplying part of the nucleus of the anarchist movement that would arise in New London. Fanese anarchists were aware from an early date of the possible effects of the developing Italian mass emigration wave on the workers' movements of Italy. The ruling class

> looks with satisfaction on the trend of the disinherited classes to abandon Italian soil, because they think this enormous mass of emigrants have the strength for the much-feared day of social revolution. And at the same time as the pauperization of the population comes like a flow of blood from the open veins of Italy, the ruling classes in immense indifference continue to smile in lasting and cheerful dreams.[13]

In Marcia! heartened at the likelihood that their politics would "extend to all the world," to improve on "the ideal of solidarity among men, ideals now limited (to) narrow doors of nationality." They called on the emigrants heading to America "with the hope of a better world" to take on the exploiters in their new homeland, and build also a "new world." "Why Emigrate?" the title of another article asked, as "workers of the countryside, the workshops and the sea affected by pellagra, tuberculosis, malaria, and hunger are forced to emigrate to faraway lands, abandoning their parents, spouses, children—all that is dear to life; and often those lands (become) our tombs." The saving grace, again, would for them not to forget to fight the oppressors, to gain redemption and emancipation for the proletariat, to confront the "charlatans with their parliamentary chatter."[14]

Deteriorating social and economic conditions in Italy were the primary cause for the waves of Fanese landing on American shores, but it is impossible to separate the political motives of the exiles from their desires to improve the living conditions of themselves and their families. The pages of the local anarchist papers and police files in Fano, Pesaro and Rome are filled with accounts of the young rebels of Fano confronting the authorities and employers, often ending up in jail, under house arrest, or at the least under constant surveillance. The cycles of insurgence followed by repression, during which political activity became difficult if not impossible, made attractive the idea of transplanting the anarchist ideal across the Atlantic Ocean.

Italian immigrant radicals brought with them the experiences and ideological perspectives gained from exposure to social movements in the country of their birth. Differences that originated in Italy between these revolutionaries strongly affected the nascent radical formations in the United States. The most important, and at times paralyzing, schism among Italian anarchists (and one that would greatly impact the movement in New London) was that between "organizationists" and "anti-organizationists."

The split between the two branches had deep roots in anarchist history, receiving a strong impetus from the Saint-Imier international anarchist congress in 1872, and gaining further traction from the London congress of 1881.[15] Organizationists believed that anarchists had to build political parties, trade unions and federations in which to fight for their revolutionary goals. While they abstained from the electoral process, which they believed was useless to the struggle, they advocated finding practical means to reach and integrate themselves with the working class. Malatesta called for anarchists to "profit from all the methods and all the possibilities that we find in the actual environment" to raise the consciousness of humanity to make possible the social revolution that will bring an anarchist society. "Workers will never be able to emancipate themselves," he wrote, "so long as they do not find in union the moral, economic and physical strength that is needed to subdue the organized might of the oppressors." During the period in which he functioned as revolutionary agitator in Ancona prior to the *Fatti di Maggio*, Malatesta relentlessly urged anarchists to deepen their ties to the working class, participate in the labor movement and to build leagues of resistance against governmental authorities.[16]

Anti-organizationists shunned any form of organization above the small anarchist group or circle, believing that such a course would weaken and corrupt the working class' revolutionary struggle to overthrow the state and class society. While organizationists would initiate and help build trade unions to both strengthen them and raise revolutionary demands, the antis typically saw them simply as vehicles in which to advocate for social revolution; a short-lived paper from Fossombrone, a town close to Fano, declared in 1892 that "Organization always instills authority," and will create a target for the state. Both sides fought for influence in the Pesaro-Ancona region, though the organizationists were dominant by far. The fight would follow Italian radicals as they reached the shores of North America.

By the time the "new immigrant" wave hit New London from the 1890s, the town had fallen from its perch as a major whaling center. Old money was still there, but looking for new places to be put to use. Immigrants from Fano and other regions of Italy found a city strenuously trying to change its course. When past methods to accumulate wealth and develop New London as a major center of economic endeavor had to be abandoned, such as the whaling industry, or when dreams of the city's becoming a transatlantic destination for steamships and ocean liners could not be realized, the local entrepreneurial class frantically sought viable substitutes. The stubby, semipeninsula known since Revolutionary times as the Neck, or Fort Trumbull, early on would serve as a target for their schemes of economic development.

During the 1890s, local commercial interests decided that New London's next wave of prosperity would come from its important position as a rail hub between major metropolitan centers, as well as its being a port city. The need to move goods from dock to consumer required massive investment in the rail facilities that existed in New London at the time, and in 1891 a great debate ensued about the need for spur lines in Fort Neck. These would cross a few streets in the neighborhood, imperiling local children perhaps, but were necessary to make the grand plan work—as well as connect the numerous, medium-sized manufacturers that had sprung up on the outskirts of the neighborhood. Property owners in Fort Neck with names like William English, John Keefe, and John Robinson raised objections, saying they wouldn't be able to rent their tenements because people were already threatening to move out. Others countered by saying that the neighborhood could use an uplift, literally: "At present Walbach Street is a mudhole and would be improved by raising it if a spur track crossed it." A property owner named Peleg Williams argued against his comrades, saying that property values would rise like they had when all the manufacturers had come in: "There was a barn and an office on the property, and now there are over 100 houses occupied principally by the employees of the several manufacturers in the vicinity." In the end, the railroad commissioners decided on a raised bridge instead of a spiderweb of tracks through the neighborhood.[17]

A decade later they were at it again. Plans were afloat to relocate Union Station from downtown to squarely in the middle of Fort Neck. "Real estate men have their eyes centred (sic) in the Fort Neck section this season. It is no difficult matter to see a dozen of them going or returning from the vicinity of Pequot avenue and Trumbull streets most any day." These interests intended, basically, to demolish the Neck as a neighborhood: "Already there are signs of marked changes in this locality. The big lumber shed and saw mill on the Bentley estate are rapidly being demolished and signs are posted on the property which indicates that speculators looking for cheap houses or kindling wood should apply."[18]

These plans obviously were never realized, since a future Fort Trumbull neighborhood would have been impossible. The partially settled Neck would have met its fate, and its nemesis, the bulldozer (or perhaps more accurately the steam shovel) would have won out a century earlier than it did. Opportunities presented themselves through the years to chisel at the edges of Fort Trumbull, part of the recurring cycle in which someone felt they knew a better way to put to use the Fort's coveted land. Fort Trumbull never lost its place as a stepchild neighborhood. A domestic altercation in the neighborhood was described as having occurred "in an Italian place on Fort Neck," as if it had taken place on an island. The most direct route from the Fort to downtown New London was across Shaw's Cove footbridge that ran alongside the railroad tracks. The neighborhood did not become completely connected with the city's transportation system until 1927, when a bus service began to run between Walbach Street and Union Station.[19]

The railroads that so threateningly tried to spread their tentacles across Fort Neck had in fact been responsible for the first settlement of the area, the construction of the New Haven and New London lines in 1852, bringing Irish immigrants to the neighborhood. Later a clatter of varied manufacturers sprang up along the neighborhood's northern and southern perimeters: the Brown Cotton Gin Company, Standard Keystone Target Company, Hopson & Chapin Company, Whiton Machine Company, a machine tool manufacturer, a steam saw mill, a silk mill owned by Brainerd & Armstrong, as well as several shipbuilding yards. These nearly completed a ring around the neighborhood, as Fort Trumbull itself, the already-obsolete military installation, separated the grid of city streets from the banks of the Thames River.[20]

The sea remained a constant and vital factor for Fort Trumbull even if New London's whalers had nearly disappeared by the turn of the century. With its banks sprouting shipbuilding and repair firms, the Thames River swarmed with a variety of vessels—steamships, barges, revenue cutters, and yachts. The city possessed a substantial fleet of forty to fifty fishing vessels. This maritime mix provided an added draw for the inhabitants of an Adriatic Italian town long accustomed to earning a living from the ocean.[21]

Some proponents of economic progress held that New London could become a magnet for well-to-do tourists during the summer season. Their plans moved mightily forward with the construction of the massive, modern Griswold Hotel on the banks of the Thames River in Groton, where it perched for all in the bay to marvel at. Summer estates multiplied elsewhere, including on Fishers Island. Old money celebrated, as the flow of capital into this arena generated both excitement and smugness. It all eventually brought to the fore the "live-wire mayor" Bryan F. Mahan who managed to convince the Connecticut legislature—normally insufferable tightwads—to provide a one million dollar grant to refurbish the city's docks in order to supplant New York as the country's major East

Coast port. Mahan, according to one New London historian, won the support of both Democrats and Republicans "by latching onto the one thing both parties had in common: the craving to get rich and put New London on the map again." The social climate drove Eugene O'Neill, growing up in his boyhood home on Pequot Avenue on the river, to distraction: "I certainly would rather be thrown down the sewer than be planted in New London."[22]

Whatever economic plans came to fruition, and whether railroad facilities, piers, or hotels were built, labor power and muscle were needed. While not an industrial center like Waterbury or Bridgeport, New London's significant manufacturing base and infrastructure attracted a workforce composed of Yankees, Scots, and Irishmen and women. They were often of a mind to organize in defense of their rights from an early period. The city's tradition of trade unionism dated at least from the Knights of Labor, an organization whose national membership peaked in the mid-1880s. In 1890, the Granite Cutters' and Paving Cutters' unions of the American Federation of Labor had combined with the Knights of Labor to present the city with its first Labor Day parade that proudly marched through the streets of New London with a platoon of police at its head. The unionists proudly observed that "along the line of march were noticed a liberal display of flags and bunting, and the compliment was acknowledged with hearty cheers" to produce a "very creditable appearance."[23]

The leadership of the Knights of Labor, eschewing radicalism of any kind, found a fairly warm reception from local business interests. The *Day* felt that Grand Master Workman Terrance Powderly of the Knights wished to "close the breach between capital and labor." Revolutionaries, on the other hand, were certainly not welcome. In the aftermath of the violent clash between police and striking workers at Haymarket Square in Chicago in May 1886, the newspaper editorialized: "The best way to deal with the dynamiters and anarchists is to string them up. They are the worst enemies of society and the most dangerous enemies of honest labor, which has no sympathy whatever for them."[24] In 1885, leaders of the Granite Cutters union on strike at Millstone Point in Waterford, only a few miles from downtown New London, employed conservative language in appealing for support, having denounced their employers as the worst form of "labor agitators . . . endeavoring to foment discord between employers and employees," and compared them to the anarchist Johann Most.[25]

The large influx of immigrant workers into New London brought about a steady increase in the geographically small city's population, from 19,659 in 1910, to 25,688 in 1920, and 29,794 in 1930. Nineteen percent of New London's inhabitants were foreign-born by 1930, while the Italian population had increased from 150 to 1,169 over the same period.[26]

Not really wanted, but nonetheless necessary, were the hundreds of immigrants arriving from Southern and Eastern Europe to provide the underpinning for New London's economy. Italians comprised a large portion of this incoming wave. Unlike Russian Jews, said the *New London Day* in an editorial, who were undesirable because they could not perform manual labor, Italians were at least useful "in constructing railroads or laying sewer pipes." Though useful, these Italian laborers remained an undefined lot—when two men working for the Coast and Lake Contracting Company on the Thames River received severe head injuries, they could not be identified, as they were "known only by the numbers on their pay checks." Labor gangs of Italians passing through New London in the early 1890s became news stories, even though no mention is made of an Italian community as such. Two of the first Italians to settle in the city are listed in the 1880 census as "hucksters," or sellers of small wares; another is a confectioner. This small embryo of a colony lived in the downtown area around Bank and State Streets. By 1892 about a dozen Italian fruit sellers did business in the Bank Street area and comprised a base for future growth.[27]

Italians, including Fanese, began arriving in New London during the 1880s and 1890s to establish businesses in the downtown area; the names of Benvenuti, Menghi, Ballestrini, and Gentili show up early, although no Italian names appear in the Fort Trumbull neighborhood in the 1880 census. Most of these individual immigrants would have their families over to join them by 1900. In an interview from the 1990s, Fort Trumbull descendants relied on the memories of the neighborhood, recounting one young Marchegian "getting work on Irish construction gangs as a water boy and eventually working as a gardener on a private estate." A typical manner of immigration is probably shown in the example of Alessandro Secchiaroli (although he arrived somewhat later in 1904). He left the town of Pesaro in the Marche with two companions and landed in New York. According to the ship's manifest, they had a connection with someone in New London, through whom they probably found employment on Plum Island in the construction of Fort Terry. After living on the island until 1908, Secchiaroli relocated to

Walbach Street in Fort Trumbull. Within months he married a woman who had arrived from the Marche the year before. Immigration from Fano proceeded by word of mouth—"usually the men came first"—and then would begin the process of getting the family over, sending money back and sometimes making several trips back and forth. In the case of Luigi Valentini Mei and Antonina Cerminezi, the period of courtship to marriage lasted twenty years. Childhood sweethearts, Luigi left Fano for New London to find a job as a trolley track inspector for the Connecticut Company. He worked for years to save money to eventually send for Antonina, though he had only known her in person when she was a child. When he had saved enough, Antonina came over accompanied by Luigi's brother in 1913, her in second class and him in steerage. The couple married in Groton.[28]

By the 1900 Census, a large group of Fanese immigrants had settled in the heart of the Fort Trumbull neighborhood on Smith Street. They had moved into a fairly stable working-class neighborhood of people with occupations such as laborer, silk mill worker, railroad gate tender, nurse, molder, and machinist—generally one step up from the arriving Italians. Many were Scottish, Irish, and a few Portuguese, most with earlier immigration dates from the 1870s, and a number of "indigenous" Connecticut-born residents. Marchegiani gradually took the place of the earlier occupants; by 1910 the neighborhood was 60 percent Italian.[29]

The first wave of Marchegian immigrants generally arrived between 1883 and 1899, most husbands and wives being in their twenties and thirties, and the men for the most part coming first as laborers. The Ballestrini family at 52 Smith Street, with their eight children, apparently came in 1887, a year after Augusto, the head of the household. Two widowed women, with both intriguingly listed as "day laborers," headed two families. One, Mary Silva, had four children, her fourteen-year-old son working in a silk mill. The second, Louisa Pallus, had two older sons who were working, and four boarders. One married couple with the Americanized names of George and Mary Nelson, him a laborer and renting from an Irish family at 54 Smith Street, have the earliest immigration dates—1872—of all the Italians.

Of these names, not all of them necessarily Fanese, the most notable might be the Ballestrinis. From the Marche, Augusto Ballestrini, a laborer, displayed an early knack for accumulating property. He may have established a business on Bank Street where, in November 1890, locals who called them "hard names" accosted him and a group of other

Italians. An ensuing confrontation led to one of the antagonists named Smith being hit by a brick and badly injured. Ballestrini and another Italian were arrested and the case generated attention, as it seemed that the defendants would be prosecuted to the full. But the small Italian community, or the Marchegian segment at least, turned out to attend the court hearings, and hired a lawyer and interpreter. After the Italian side was explained in court, made possible by the community mobilization, Ballestrini as the alleged brick thrower was fined seven dollars ($182 in 2017 currency). "A lot of his friends came into court to see the trial and they paid up."[30]

The appearance of Italian labor gangs began to be a common sight in the streets of New London. One such group, thought by city residents to be on their way to a sewer project, turned out to be a gang laying railroad track in nearby Westbrook, and brought into the city by padrones. They crossed into Waterford to demand money owed them from a contractor, earning them a headline in the New London *Day*, "Trouble with Italians."[31] This labor system so commonly used by many Italians, including Sicilians and Napolitanos coming to New London, is never mentioned in relation to the Marchegiani coming from Fano.

Literally across the tracks from Fort Trumbull, streets filled up with immigrants from Naples and Sicily. They would occupy an area referred to as the "Shaw Street neighborhood," and while they shared working-class occupations with the Fanese, many would prove unreceptive to radicalism. They had sailed from the port of Palermo, and almost all came from the towns of Tusa, Caltavuturo, and Cefalù, located in northeastern, north central, and northwestern corners of mountainous Sicily. The greater number came from Tusa, a town known more for religious feasts and annual devotions than labor radicalism; the Tusanese spread throughout eastern Connecticut and western Rhode Island. Caltavuturo in January 1893 had been the site of an infamous massacre in by militia of thirteen peasants who demonstrated in support of the seizure of communal lands promised them by the government. Uprisings across Sicily spurred the rapid growth of the local socialist movement until suppressed by the introduction of thousands of soldiers and martial law. Caltavuturese may have carried rebellious sentiments with them to Connecticut, but there are few indications they retained socialist consciousness.[32]

As an Italian community, Shaw Street presented the most visible target for the authorities and the press. As late as 1922, an article in the *Day* portrayed the neighborhood as an alien preserve in the city:

> The first impression which one gets is that Italy had crossed the ocean. Beginning at Garibaldi Park a motley sight is presented. Everything is disconsolate, stagnant, shriveled, commonplace, routine, neglected—all too neglected. In the streets the gutters are muddy and filled with pools, sewers are clogged, watermelon rinds are scattered about, rubbish is ungathered, dangerous holes and ruts are in the highway. The whole place needs 'policing up.' Corners are knocked out of buildings, foundations rise high above the surface of the ground . . . There are few or no verandas. Window blinds are loose and hanging at angles and on edges. Paint is either flashy or absent. Bricks are missing from chimney tops. Tin smokestacks wave in the wind like reeds or rods. Electric wires enter the stores but not the homes. Wick lamps, not gas or electricity supply lights in the houses.

The article paired the neighborhood inhabitants with their surroundings.

> Knowing only the half standards of life, crowded back into the sordid realities, with no social fitting or educational refreshment, these people have been shoved into the gutters and side eddies of life even though their souls have been 'looking at the stars.'[33]

It did not take long, however, before the neighborhood into which the Marchegiani had filtered would earn the epithet as "the Italian quarters of Fort Neck." Shaw Street and the Fort shared at least one earmark: in neither neighborhood did city services keep pace with the needs of residents. Columns in the *Day* often commented on the "Ragged Dick" versus "Cinderella" contrast between Shaw Street and Fort Neck and the more prosperous neighborhoods: "The Fort Neck streets are, I am convinced, quite the worst in any city of the world with the possible exception of Foo Chow, China." Another columnist drew attention to the lack of sidewalks in Fort Neck in 1916, using hyperbole to make his point: "And then look at Fort Neck. Honestly, if I lived on Fort Neck I should be an anarchist, I know.[34]

CHAPTER TWO

ITALIAN REVOLUTIONARIES IN A YANKEE STATE

In early 1909, an unemployed Italian immigrant named Bartholomeo Vanzetti boarded a ship in New York that took him up the Connecticut River as far as Hartford, where he disembarked to search for work. Finding no luck in the surrounding towns and countryside, he eventually landed a job in a brickyard in Springfield, Massachusetts, where he remained for ten months. His travels then led him southward back into Connecticut, where he successfully found work in a stone quarry in the city of Meriden. Here he stayed for two years while living in the midst of a colony of his countrymen who, like himself, were from the northern part of Italy.

Until this point his story is a far from remarkable account, one that is only typical of the experiences of tens of thousands of Italian workers in New England who comprised the labor gangs that built roads and reservoirs; laid tracks for trains and trolley lines; and toiled in quarries, brickyards, and freight terminals, as well as on the docks and construction sites of the region. His biography began to shift from the routine during the time he labored in the quarry and brickyard, as he began to question the social ills that engulfed the lives of all the working people with whom he came into contact. By 1912, after meeting anarchists in Worcester, Massachusetts, he had cast both his identity and fate as a dedicated member of the most militant wing of Italian anarchism in the United States, and on the path toward a courthouse in Dedham.[1]

The Bartholomeo Vanzettis among Italian immigrants provided the most receptive audience for the profusion of radical doctrines—the thousands of unskilled and mostly single male workers who existed from job to job by their raw labor power alone. Eastern and Midwestern industrialized states attracted the bulk of these immigrants. Connecticut ranked seventh in total numbers of Italians by 1920, with 127,000, and this population was highly urbanized: 45 percent lived in the state's four largest cities. Ten years later, first- and second-generation Italians constituted one-fifth of the state's population as well as its largest ethnic group. Of these, two-thirds were from the underdeveloped central and southern regions of Italy; the majority was unskilled laborers. Contractors recruited these workers on a temporary basis in urban centers such as New York and Boston and provided transportation to the job site and lodging until the completion of the project. The padrones often organized the work system by directly furnishing the laborers to contractors, providing for their living quarters and recruiting the workers for the next job. They took a substantial cut of the laborers' pay, and abuses were common. Small groups of these Italian laborers, rather than returning to the big city, remained in hinterland areas throughout Connecticut and Massachusetts, obtaining work as laborers in local industries. Once they put word out to friends and family in Italy of the promises offered in the newfound locations, a stream of immigrants might have followed.[2]

Italian colonies grew in widely dispersed areas of the state. In the smaller towns, these formed around particular industries: lime quarries in Canaan; textile factories in Stafford Springs; granite quarries in Stony Creek, Leete's Island, and Waterford; trap rock quarries in Meriden; and brickyards in Berlin. In the larger cities, Italians filled a variety of occupations, invariably as unskilled laborers. In Hartford they found work as day laborers, freight handlers, on railroad section gangs, and as street laborers. Large numbers hired on for railroad track maintenance work; according to the Italian consular agent in New Haven in 1908, the NY-NH-Hartford Railroad employed as many as ten thousand Italians at different intervals each year. Hartford's Italian laborers were the city's poorest-paid and highly vulnerable to industrial accidents. When Italians entered factories, they seldom found work as machinists, but as polishers, buffers, or in the general category of "shop hands."[3]

New Haven Italian men labored at similar occupations, as street laborers and dockworkers. Their role in unskilled occupations far exceeded that of other nationalities in the city. Italians lived in close proximity to the industrial districts and thus inhabited the neighborhoods in which conditions were poorest: crowded tenements, shabby boarding houses, and dirty streets. As in Hartford, a number of Italians had found jobs in New Haven factories, with 1,500 at Sargents alone—these again concentrated in the polishing department. Waterbury Italians worked as construction laborers, in the clock factories, and as laborers in the massive brass mills.

Important exceptions existed to these occupational trends. In Hartford, New Haven, and other cities, Italians in the masons' trade represented a far larger proportion than their numbers in the workforce. A researcher found that 26 percent of Italian workers in New Haven classified as skilled between 1890 and 1920. In the smaller towns, Italians worked as highly skilled stonecutters along the Connecticut coast and as skilled weavers in the Cheney Mills in South Manchester.[4]

Each Italian community in Connecticut formed in a distinct manner. What they had in common was their origin in the immigrants' relentless search for employment. Four of these localities—New Britain/Kensington, Wallingford, Stony Creek, and Stafford Springs—shared something else: each would come to host a sizable radical movement among its Italian workers. The first Italian "community" in the Hardware City, as New Britain was known, may have been a camp of dugouts and shanties constructed for laborers digging the Shuttle Meadow reservoir in 1892, which attracted curious middle-class New Britain residents for a Sunday outing tour. Nearby Kensington's brickyards, because of their large scale, drew a number of Italian laborers. The brickyards functioned as something of a conduit for Italians gaining jobs in New Britain. When Italians moved into the city in numbers, they took jobs in the hardware shops (my grandfather among them), not as machinists or machine operators but as laborers, a category that included sweepers, parts movers, loading dock workers, and construction gang members.[5]

Male boarding house residents who worked in a trap rock quarry near the Durham line composed Wallingford's first Italian community, which expanded and took root in the east end of town near large silverware factories. While these shops provided an important anchor for Italian employment in the area, large numbers continued to work on the many truck farms in the region. Northern Italians predominated initially but large numbers of southerners soon joined them; at least six different regional dialects could be heard on Wallingford's streets by 1920.[6]

Granite quarries drew Italian stonecutters to Connecticut's coastal region east of New Haven. A union journal makes mention of Italian members as early as 1888 in the Leete's Island (Guilford) branch of the Granite Cutters, and they probably arrived in Stony Creek at about the same time. They were part of a wave of Italians entering the New England quarries who came from the Carrara region, a marble center in Tuscany, and then from the provinces of Como, Novarra, and Trento in the Italian Alps. The overwhelming majority of Stony Creek Italians came from the north, with the North Italian Society gaining over a hundred members. These workers found their way to the numerous coastal granite quarries, making their way to Groton, Waterford, and Niantic in Connecticut and Westerly in Rhode Island.[7]

Italians in Stafford Springs followed yet another route. Rather than initially being consigned to pick and shovel work, they entered the town's ten or so woolen textile mills on arrival, often in skilled occupations. The Italian population exploded in the first decade of the twentieth century, as the group grew to become a critical component of the labor force like it did in other New England textile towns, including Lawrence, Massachusetts and Thompsonville, Connecticut. The Italians of Stafford Springs came from the northern Veneto region, especially the Val di Zoldo, with a smaller number from the far-northern Austrian-held province of Tyrol. The Veneto was one of Italy's principal textile producing areas, with some of the mills at the cutting edge of the industry's technology and management techniques. The textile workers who found their way to Stafford Springs did not have the same economic motives to emigrate, as did their countrymen and countrywomen of the desperately poor south. These northerners often had political reasons for leaving Italy that stemmed from their roles in the labor and radical movements. It is beyond a doubt that a number of these class-conscious workers and artisans brought their politics with them to the unlikely place of a small, somewhat isolated textile town in the far northern reaches of Connecticut.[8]

Employers often greeted Italians initially as an industrious but pliant workforce, as did the Connecticut Bureau of Labor Statistics in 1885: "The Italian's object in coming to this country is simple. He wishes to stay here until he can save two or three hundred dollars, and then go home . . . Staying here for the short time that he does, the Italian has little or no inducement to learn English, and still less to change his habits or methods of living." Italian workers, however, wasted no time in addressing their immediate wage and working conditions. That same year, Italian laborers on water works in Willimantic struck for a wage increase. The contractor refused to pay the $1.50 a day ($32 in 2017 currency) sought by the workers and threatened to bring in a "gang of Italians" from New York as strikebreakers, resulting in the strike's collapse. That no strikebreakers were available locally may have been the result of the following notice in English posted near the site of the walkout:

> Notice—Fellow citizens and laborers, you are hereby notified by the laborers resident in Willimantic, not to work on the water work, for any of the contractors, for less than $1.50 per day.
>
> Any resident laborer offering his service for less, shall be boycotted, not only by his fellow workmen but by the community at large. Per order,
>
> Labor Committee[9]

A local Knights of Labor assembly had probably issued the notice, since the order was near its peak of strength at the time, and the boycott was one of the Knights' favorite weapons against recalcitrant employers. It represents a significant but probably seldom practiced display of solidarity with generally ignored immigrant workers.

The mostly single-male Italian immigrants in Connecticut began to show an extraordinary capacity for rebellions, strikes, and other acts of resistance on the job. State newspapers and reports of the Bureau of Labor Statistics contain numerous examples of these occurrences; in the latter's "Strikes and Lockouts" section from 1902, the only ethnic reference on the list is "Italian laborers." The Italians' strikes, often ending in defeat similar to the early one in Willimantic, continued to erupt well into the next century. Few industries that employed Italians remained unaffected: railroad laborers in Plainfield, construction laborers in Windham, and trolley laborers in Willimantic and New Britain, all in 1902; lime quarrymen in East Canaan in 1907, and brickyard workers in Berlin and Kensington between 1905 and 1912. Implied threats of violence sometimes accompanied the strikes.[10]

The strikes were invariably of short duration because of the Italians' susceptibility to loss of income and the usually hostile response of local authorities. Initially they were spontaneous actions and involved little evidence of organization. But most of them seemed to erupt when the employers were most vulnerable and thus necessitated a degree of planning on the part of the "organizers." As Italian communities took root across Connecticut, working-class organizers employed tactics both sophisticated and suited for the nature of the Italian workers' job market.

In 1902, one such struggle erupted in New Haven, a city that occupied the position of Connecticut's Italian cultural and political center, with one-third of the state's Italian population. At the important metalworking firm of Sargents Company, Italian members of Local 205 of the International Metal Polishers, Buffers, Platers, and Allied Workers Union struck against injustices of the piecework system. The Italian Labor Hall, a socialist-led institution modeled on the Italian Camere di Lavoro, supported them. As the author of a study of this significant strike has observed, the Sargents' walkout symbolized both the Italian workers' ability to utilize collective action at the workplace as well as ethnic solidarity that crossed class lines in the community.[11]

Included in the earliest waves of Italian workers to arrive on American shores in the 1880s were a significant number of radicals—socialists and anarchists—who, like their fellow Italians, may have planned only a short stay in the United States. Many of the most well-known participants in the Italian left migrated or were exiled this country at the close of the nineteenth century, including Giacomo Serrati, Pietro Gori, Francesco Merlino, Errico Malatesta, and Luigi Galleani. Most, if not all of them, launched speaking tours through Connecticut. Many of them educated men, they immediately started a series of radical newspapers to reach the growing Italian workers' colonies in the new world, including *La Questione Sociale* in Paterson, New Jersey in 1895, a city destined to become the bastion of Italian anarchism in this country. The year 1899 saw the birth of *L'Aurora* (The Dawn), published at first in West Hoboken, New Jersey by Guiseppe Ciancabilla, who had formerly been active among anarchist exiles in Paris. Here he had been won to the rising current of anti-organizational anarchism. The principal Italian socialist paper, *Il Proletario*, began publication in 1896, and became the organ of the Federazione Socialista Italiana (FSI), that would form in 1902.[12]

From the beginning, Italian radicals in the United States imported organizing techniques they had developed in their homeland. To compensate for the massive illiteracy of Italian workers and peasants, socialists, anarchists, and trade union organizers used traveling propaganda tours with speeches and lectures by renowned spokespeople for their respective political viewpoints. Lack of ability to read did not prevent the scores of radical publications from influencing tens of thousands: group readings of newspapers and political materials were organized wherever radicals established nuclei. Most significantly, the radicals also integrated Italian cultural traditions—peasant folklore, ceremony, and theater—into their political activities.[13]

The majority of Italian-American radicals stood on the revolutionary wing of the sprawling, variegated American left from 1900 to 1920. Their politics reflected the early strength of anarchism—Mikhail Bakunin had made Italy a principal theater for his activities and had nurtured the country's movement—that only slowly lost its character of staging violent, episodic revolts against the oppressors. Workers in northern cities joined a movement with an anarchist, and later syndicalist slant. This militant orientation crossed the Atlantic and showed its influence in the building of circles, groups, locals, and sections among an immigrant proletariat to a certain degree resting on gangs of mobile manual laborers, a class undoubtedly difficult to organize, but also a class not prone to moderate electoral politics or the civic reform efforts of the period. The FSI throughout its history remained independent of the American Socialist Party, which it viewed as hopelessly reformist, and affiliated instead with the revolutionary Industrial Workers of the World (IWW), which attempted to organize the unskilled workers in basic industries rather than the skilled craftspeople preferred by the American Federation of Labor (AFL). Another trait of the Italian movement to cross the Atlantic would have unfortunate consequences. Despite the common thread running through the different groups, tendentious—and sometimes violent—conflict became an ever-present factor in the radical movement. Conflict occurred between and among the socialist and anarchist groups. No faction refrained from bitterly hostile attacks against their rivals, charges that were often personal in nature. At times they expended as much energy in the feuds with one another as they directed at the class enemy.[14]

Italians were not the first immigrant anarchists to settle in Connecticut. In the early 1880s, a group of German anarchists formed a branch of the International Working Peoples' Association in New Haven. Led by cigar maker Frederick Siebold, the branch published *The Beast of Property*, an important pamphlet by Johann Most. Most, a recent immigrant from Germany, adhered to a program of dynamite and insurrection. The New Haven Germans held picnics and put on plays, and conducted themselves as did their comrades throughout the country at the time and met regularly until at least 1901. In 1885, future

Haymarket martyr Albert Parsons had toured Hartford, where he "made many converts and won a large number of sympathizers." German and Russian Jews most likely composed his audiences. Immigrant Russian Jews probably constituted an early base of anarchist support in Naugatuck Valley towns like Ansonia.[15]

Connecticut's location between the urban centers of Boston and New York, as well as its large Italian population, ensured constant speaking tours by radicals; the left-wing Italian newspapers show early participation of workers in Connecticut in the budding movements of anarchism and socialism. Some of the first Italian sections of Daniel DeLeon's Socialist Labor Party of the 1890s were in the Nutmeg state, and these mostly moved into the FSI. By the close of the first decade of the twentieth century, FSI sections had been established in most urban centers in the state, including Bridgeport, New Haven, Hartford, Waterbury, New London, Middletown, Meriden, and New Britain.[16]

One FSI/SLP section in North Haven arose from a group called the Union and Brotherhood of North Haven. Almost exclusively workers from Emilia Romagna, they sought "to change our name at present to form a socialist circle affiliated with the SLP." They also formed the League of Resistance of Brickyard Workers, apparently modeled on similar groups in Italy, and which grew to at least 150 members. Manufacturing towns north of New Haven continued to be centers of agitation for Italian syndicalists, socialists, and anarchists for decades.[17]

Italian anarchism gained a Connecticut foothold mainly after 1900, partly as the fruit of the speaking tours by its principal figures. The majority of these anarchist groups eventually gravitated to the wing of the movement represented by Luigi Galleani, who would become the foremost figure in the Italian American movement. Galleani was born into a middle-class family in 1861, in the Piedmont region in the north of Italy. He studied law at the University of Turin but soon became immersed in the anarchist movement to which he would devote his entire life. After his anarchist agitation forced him to flee Italy, Galleani was expelled from France, and on return to Italy was arrested on conspiracy charges and jailed for five years. On escaping, he lived briefly in Egypt, then London, until finally, in October 1901, he landed in the United States, where he would remain for the next eighteen years. Galleani plunged into anarchist activity as both agitator and editor (of *La Questione Sociale*) while living in Paterson; here he faced indictment on inciting-to-riot charges after an armed confrontation in 1902 between striking silk mill workers (whom he was leading) and police. Kenyon Zimmer points out that Galleani had only recently moved away from the organizational anarchism of Malatesta and toward the perspective of Ciancabilla. The defeat of the strike in question served to deepen his cynicism toward trade unionism: "He now gave full expression to the doctrines of the *antiorganizzatori* and severed his relationship with *La Questione Sociale*."[18] In the wake of the incident, Galleani went into hiding, moved to the Italian stonecutters' colony in Barre, Vermont, where, in 1903, he commenced publication of *Cronaca Sovversiva*, a journal inseparably linked to him and his band of supporters. By 1918 the Department of Justice would refer to Galleani as "the leading anarchist in the United States" (thus eclipsing the far better known Emma Goldman and Alexander Berkman), and labeled *Cronaca Sovversiva* "the most rabid, seditious and anarchistic sheet ever published in this country."[19]

Galleani has been described as one of the most effective speakers of his day, as attested to by someone who heard him in 1903.

> I have never heard an orator more powerful than Luigi Galleani. He has a marvelous facility with words, accompanied by the faculty—rare among popular tribunes—of precision and clarity of ideas. His voice is full of warmth, his glance alive and penetrating, his gestures of exceptional vigor and flawless distinction.[20]

Galleani's uncompromising anarchism equaled his strong public speaking presence. He advocated unequivocally clear, militant insurrectionism, and he adhered to the trend of the movement, as did Malatesta, known as anarcho-communism for its support of collective action, but he also welcomed all individual acts of violence, whether wielding dagger, pistol, or dynamite. Political assassination also fell within the arsenal of accepted tactics for revolutionists. "There are no innocents among the bourgeoisie," he wrote.[21] Week after week, *Cronaca Sovversiva* contained Galleani's recipe for the coming revolution, which included no trading with the enemy: all reform efforts and electoral politics were both useless sops and unacceptable compromises with the hated capitalist system. Trade unions as well distracted the workers from genuinely revolutionary goals and became institutions led by self-serving bosses. No proletarian form of organization above the level of local autonomous circles and groups were acceptable, and these would be guided solely by their adherence to social revolution.[22]

While *Cronaca Sovversiva* never attained more than five thousand subscribers, its influence among Italian immigrant workers extended across the globe. Moreover, it served somewhat ironically as the organizing center of the anti-organizational movement, uniting the scores of Galleanist groups across the country that successively coalesced, formed, and dissolved during the early part of the twentieth century. Many of these local circles rented buildings or halls, formed amateur dramatic groups, and conducted a host of educational and social activities, and in short, strove to construct an alternative culture in opposition to that of the dominant capitalist society.[23] New England became a stronghold of the Galleanist movement, and after *Cronaca Sovversiva* relocated to Lynn, Massachusetts, in 1912, the towns surrounding Boston its epicenter.

Anarchist formations of one type or another rooted themselves in about twenty Connecticut cities and towns between 1903 and 1919, with at least that many more containing individual sympathizers. Groups in Connecticut included Hartford's Circolo Libero Pensiero, New Haven's Gruppo Educativo Pietro Gori, Meriden's Circolo Autonomo, Waterbury's Gruppo La Termite, and Derby's Circolo Michele Bakunin. These groups often first took form, in Connecticut as throughout the country, as a Circolo Studi Sociale, most likely as a means of attracting potential recruits to the atmosphere of a discussion group. As they oriented toward revolutionary anarchism, a *gruppo* would be established, with study circles often continuing to exist alongside the groups, and their names being changed and swapped at will. At times the groups blended anarchism with syndicalism and socialism.

This profusion of Italian immigrant radicalism must be viewed in the context of what historian Paul LeBlanc sees as critical to sustaining the left during this period: the radical labor subculture in the United States that existed from after the Civil War into the 1940s.[24] Almost every town or city, except the Deep South, hosted a layer of working class radicals—socialists, anarchists, syndicalists, and later communists—both immigrant and native-born. They may have been members of parties, clubs, unions and fraternal organizations, or just independent dissidents, who could be counted on to fill audiences for radical speakers, subscribe to left-wing newspapers, fund various causes, and strengthen picket lines during strikes. One example might suffice: in 1946 a team of members of the Socialist Workers Party, a Trotskyist formation, went door-to-door in a housing project in an unnamed industrial city in Connecticut, possibly New Britain, trying to sell subscriptions to their newspaper. They complained in a report of running into old radicals and militants who "were simply dying to pour their hearts out to us," thus impeding their sub drive.[25] The old-timers may have been former Socialist Party members, old DeLeonists, Wobblies, Russian anarcho-syndicalists, ex-CPers: New Britain, like many aging manufacturing towns, had them all. This social layer is long extinct; hardly a trace remains, physically or in peoples' memories, of either them or the hard battles they fought so long ago.

New London possessed this radical subculture. The Socialist Party and Socialist Labor Party had small locals or sections in the city for decades, as would the Communist Party, which had a unit that remained active from the 1920s through the 1940s. These groups held meetings and rallies that often attracted hundreds, at times under the auspices of a union, strike support committee or legal defense formation. Ethnic left groups included the Jewish Workmen's Circle, the Estonian Socialist Federation, the Union of Russian Workers, the International Workers Order, and a Finnish Socialist local. The daily press regularly reported on the doings of the English-language groups and the individuals active in them. The Italian anarchists of New London, while occupying a more extreme position on the left than the others, comprised part of this subculture. If not a mass movement, working class radicalism during the early twentieth century represented far more than an aberration. New London radicals composed part of a small but lively community that attended each other's meetings, if only to note their shortcomings.[26]

CHAPTER THREE

BIRTH OF GRUPPO L'AVVENIRE

Circumstance and design seem to have combined to lay the basis for the transformation of Fort Trumbull into an anarchist bastion. New London had by the late 1890s become an important destination for Fanese workers open to radical ideas. Beginning in 1894, the Italian government began keeping dossiers on roughly 150,000 Italian citizens—socialists, syndicalists, anarchists, and later communists and antifascists—as well as Italian immigrants in all corners of the world. These files, in the Cassellario Politico Centrale in Rome, contain dozens of reports on individuals from the area around Fano who wound up in New London. Few if any non-Fanese radicals immigrated directly to New London. Steamship manifest registrations in the National Archives for approximately 850,000 people arriving in the country before 1900 list 172 hailing from Fano; 22 percent of these listed their destination as New London.[1]

Anarchists among the Fanese arrived with the first immigrant wave from the Marche. The stream of immigrants from Fano and surrounding towns that steadily flowed into Fort Trumbull and its environs would augment the anarchist movement with new recruits. The occupations available to them in New London in the building trades, shipbuilding, and maritime work perfectly fit their skill backgrounds in Fano. A document in the archives of the municipality of Fano from 1897 certifies that a *marinaio*, or sailor, is of "sound moral character" and plans to locate in New London, but during the early years of the twentieth century, the building trades—carpenters, masons, plasterers, and laborers—came to predominate in the Fort.[2]

The earliest Marchegian immigrants found employment mostly as construction laborers in the New London area. In May 1890 the *Day* reported "a gang of 40 Italians went over to Fisher's Island this morning."[3] These laborers comprised what became a torrent of Italian immigrants whose introduction to New London came by way of the nearby islands off southeastern Connecticut's coast.

Significant numbers of them initially found jobs in construction projects on Fishers Island for the summer mansions for well-to-do residents of southeastern Connecticut. Toward the end of the decade, as US military authorities viewed with alarm the European powers' frantic building of large navies, large sums of money were made available to build a series of forts and other installations at the eastern approaches of Long Island Sound. Hundreds of Italian laborers found employment in building these military installations on Plum, Gull, and Fishers Islands. By May 1898, soon after the outbreak of the Spanish-American War, "large forces of workmen . . . mostly Italians," could be found on the islands. Worried about the defense of the installations, the commander of the Corps of Engineers in New London disparaged the laborers as "at best turbulent in disposition and wholly irresponsible and unreliable." A number of anarchists from Fano worked on the construction of Fort H. G. Wright on Fishers Island, officially part of New York State but only a few miles from the mouth of the Thames River.[4]

Here they toiled under abysmal conditions, were paid extremely low wages and were forced to live in tarpaper shacks. Lack of sanitary conditions, described as "high ground water, clouds of dust . . . flies in large numbers, ineffective disposal of excreta, prevalence of diarrhea," later led to a serious outbreak of typhoid fever among the troops stationed near the Fort close to where the Italians worked. Work crews fell under the control of the padrone system. An ex-foreman described the Fishers Island situation: "These Italian padrones are veritable leeches. They ground the poor laborers and get the majority of their wages—if they protest they lose their places." But protest they did, staging an "occasional rebellion" and organizing an unsuccessful strike. While no mention exists of these actions in their press, anarchists would undoubtedly have participated in them. Although most of the workers on the island had been recruited in New York and Philadelphia, New London's Marchegian anarchists probably hired on locally, since a number of fellow immigrants from Fano, including relatives, had already established themselves in the city. Construction of roads, with the necessary blasting, leveling and grading, provided employment opportunities during the early part of the decade for newly arriving Fanese immigrants, but the abominable conditions on the island probably also spurred the rise of the Fort Trumbull building contractors who would specialize in home construction. Three Fishers Island laborers who spent their entire working lives in the construction industry—Augusto Benvenuti, Luigi Camillucci, and Enrico Broccoli—would emerge as key figures in the local anarchist movement.[5]

On April 1, 1898, "almost all the Italians who live here" gathered to form the first anarchist group in New London, the Circolo di Educazione ed Istruzione Sociale. The meeting took place in "the middle of this Italian colony," which would have meant either Bank Street, where Italian fruit sellers and their boarders had set up shop since the early 1890s, or the area of Fort Trumbull, where a small cluster of Marchegiani had already lived. Rafaelle Sommariva, an anarchist from nearby Mystic, where Italian radicals may have settled earlier than New London's, spoke of the need to "understand the necessity of workers' organization to resist capitalist organization," thus placing the group squarely within the wing led by Malatesta.

In July, the Circolo organized an important weekend conference with Catalan-born Pedro Esteve of Paterson as guest lecturer. Esteve spoke on several topics, such as "the present social question," "the practicality of the anarchist ideal," and "women and children in the future family." As an eloquent, multilingual speaker who used simple terms to express complex issues, Esteve was the perfect educator for the new group and who had helped found *La Questione Sociale* in 1895. The meeting was held at 128 Bank Street, the tavern of Fano-born Nazarene Benvenuti, a future building contractor, and a significant "friend" of the local movement. It became a "steam bath" in the July heat and proceedings adjourned to a nearby island.[6]

"It was sublime to see the enthusiasm of these good comrades, the greater part of whom were *operai del mare* (maritime workers)." They had probably worked as fishermen and sailors in Fano, and some continued to find employment in that sector in New London. Gaetano Olivieri, an early member described at his death in 1915 as an "ardent comrade," had immigrated in 1890 and worked as a laborer in New London before returning to the sea to captain a river barge.[7] A number of participants at the meeting appeared new to politics, while others were veterans "who had borne infamous persecutions struggling for the triumph of well-being and equality." One of the early members, Alberico Biagioni, a stonecutter and mason, had worked in a small shop in Fano and already had years of political experience by the time he migrated to New London in May 1898. Arrested at sixteen for "disturbing public peace and resisting" along with some anarchist friends, he still later had to go into hiding after a violent clash in the streets of Fano in 1897.[8] Others had been won from rival political currents.

A sizable minority of Fort Trumbull anarchists would come from Senigallia, a town in Ancona province located about ten miles from Fano on the Adriatic coast. Senigallia was the nearest population center, besides Pesaro, that closely resembled Fano for its demographic makeup as well as its long history of anarchist militance.

Despite the fact that a considerable number of early New London anarchists brought their political experiences from their European homeland, the majority of their recruits became radicalized in the belly of industrial America. Some "fine-tuned" their politics in New London, three of whom gave testimony in the pages of *La Questione Sociale*. Born in Fano in 1868, Enrico Broccoli announced his rejection of Mazzini republicanism and conversion to anarchism in a letter to the paper in 1899, under the title "Progressing":

> Until today I was active in radical parties, believing that the triumph of a republican form of government, inspired by a social tendency, would make it possible to resolve the Social Question. Deep reflection and practical matters finally convinced me that as long as Property, Government and Religion exist in society, true equality and true freedom cannot be established.
>
> I therefore feel convinced to declare myself an anarcho-communist, and as a sincere and devoted soldier, within and part of such a party.
>
> If all the brothers of poverty study and think about the reasons for my evolution, they would be convinced of their soundness.
>
> Health and solidarity to all my comrades of the ideal![9]

Paolo Montanari, born in Pesaro in 1875, attended lectures by touring anarchist speakers and read "the anarchist journals of America and Italy." He came to reject his republican beliefs because "the republic will not be different than the monarchy since changing the musician when the music stays the same always will be."

Another early supporter asserted his newfound scorn for reformist socialism in the pages of the same paper. Charles Coduri was born in the town of Colico in the area of Lake Como in northern Italy in 1872, and worked as a skilled stonecutter in the granite quarries of Waterford.

> Until the last few months I had faith in legalitarian socialism and its tactics, believing it the only way to achieve the emancipation of the proletariat. But experiences and facts have finally convinced me that legalitarian socialism deviates from the true path to socialism, for aiming to increase the number of people who vote for their candidates, rather than to shape their consciousness. I understand that the struggle to win at the ballot box will have no useful result for the cause of human emancipation, but on the contrary will cause damage.

He contrasted the behavior of socialists in Italy who equivocated before military tribunals with anarchists who had refused to "go pale with fear."

> This sympathy for true revolutionaries induced me to read anarchist pamphlets and journals, of these the fine paper *Questione Sociale*, and in these found logic and truth, and not utopia, and convinced me that the only idea, that to fight for true emancipation of the workers, without ambition and interest, is the anarchist-socialist idea, that which I give all my efforts to work tirelessly for its triumph.
>
> Yours for the anarchist idea.[10]

Broccoli, Montanari, and Coduri cited Italian events as the principal factors that spurred their radicalization. At the first meetings of the Circolo, the members also probably made their regional origins evident by sending money to Errico Malatesta's Ancona-based organ *L'Agitazione*, and other funds "to benefit the arrested of Ancona."

While Marchegian laborers predominated in the founding of New London anarchism, the fortuitous arrival in the city of a contingent of anarchist textile workers from Paterson, New Jersey seems to have actually triggered the birth of the Circolo. This move to Connecticut allowed the young movement to benefit from the presence of experienced anarchists, the most important of whom was Vittorio Cravello. Cravello found employment, along with several others, in the Brainerd & Armstrong silk mill in New London as a weaver and almost immediately took an active part in the local movement. The Cravello family came from Biella, in the textile region of the Piedmonte in northern Italy, as did a large number of Paterson's anarchists. His older brother Antonio had led strikes in Biella during the 1880s. Vittorio during his New London hiatus lived in Groton on Church Street with his wife and infant son. His sister Ernestina, soon to become a public figure of some notoriety, lived with him there for a brief period in 1898.

By then a veteran in the movement, and cut from the same cloth as Malatesta, Cravello committed himself to agitation within the workers' movement. While in Paterson in 1897, according to historian Kenyon Zimmer, he served as the "leading spirit" of the anarchist-led Lega di Resistenza fra I Tessitori Italiani (League of Resistance of Italian Weavers), as well as being a member of the important Gruppo Diritto all'Esistenza (Right to Existence), which published *La Questione Sociale*.[11] Cravello spoke at most New London meetings and public lectures and served as correspondence secretary for the group.

From the earliest days, New London anarchists organized public and private functions whose purpose was to spread "the idea," to attract a widening audience for their movement and recruit new members. Their efforts achieved a shot in the arm with two almost simultaneous developments. First, the membership of Paterson's Gruppo Diritto all'Esistenza voted out Giuseppe Ciancabilla, a skilled and talented writer but a supporter of the anti-organizational perspective, as editor of *La Questione Sociale*. Second, Errico Malatesta arrived in the United States to take over this position and the paper immediately began to serialize an important document expounding organizational anarchist principles called *Il Nostro Programma*. Malatesta almost immediately embarked on a speaking tour of the eastern states.

In November 1899 the anti-organizational *L'Aurora* briefly mentioned in a donation column that "meetings" had been held with Malatesta in New London. *La Questione Sociale* reported on September 16 that his tour would soon begin, and in the next issue that New London contributed the earnings from their event to the paper. The subject of Malatesta's speeches in New Haven, Providence, and New London received no attention in either paper; it can be assumed, however, that he spoke about his important, newly elucidated program just published in the paper. During December 1899, on the initiative of anarchists in Barre, Vermont, a nascent "Federation of Anarcho-Socialists" formed based on the document's principles, with Waterford's Charles Coduri serving on the correspondence commission of the group.

By early 1900 Malatesta ended his brief stay in the United States and returned to London. His cothinkers in the United States would miss his absence. Besides profoundly influencing the New London group, Malatesta took with him the names of six local militants in his address book.[12]

On December 24, 1899, probably as a result of the momentum produced by Malatesta's presence in the city, a group of about two dozen predominantly Marchegian laborers, quarry workers from Waterford and Groton, and the contingent of silk mill weavers met to form "Gruppo L'Avvenire" as an anarcho-socialist circle. (Malatesta had characterized his organizational wing with this formulation.) Overwhelmingly but not exclusively male, they possibly contained several Sicilians or Napolitanos. An anarchist correspondent for *La Questione Sociale* spent some time in New London a week after the founding of the group and, under the nom de plume "Il Piccione Viaggiatore" (the wandering pigeon), offered his impressions of the comrades he met and the local scene in general. After offering an odd description of New London as "a citadel with a slightly delightful aspect," he divided the local working class into two parts: the Irish who are devotedly Catholic and want to know about "the straw on which (the Pope) slept," and "the Italian workers (who) are scattered in the various islands in the bay in the construction of forts." He complimented the local anarchist comrades for their "cordial reception," and took a jab—the pigeon was from Tuscany—at their regional origins: "The majority of our comrades here are from the Marche, and with their dialect somewhat broken and their welcoming dispositions, they are recalled with a feeling of cordiality that they left with from their country." He predicted "in this locality we will have soon a good Circolo, because the comrades are convinced of the necessity to unite their forces to make good propaganda."[13]

For at least the first year of its existence, at least two non-Italian anarchists, David and Bessie Levinson, played active roles in Gruppo L'Avvenire. The Levinsons emigrated from Russia in 1886, and moved to New London between 1895 and 1898. With seven children, they owned a store that sold crockery, and later stoves and ranges, on Bank Street. In a subscription list from 1899, a "D. Robinson" and "un Americano" are found, but the Levinsons were the only non-Italians to take an active role in founding the group. Levinson's fluency in English would prove useful.[14]

Historical accident provides another window through which to view the New London Italian anarchist movement as it coalesced in 1900. In July of that year, an Italian anarchist living in Paterson, New Jersey, named Gaetano Bresci, assassinated King Umberto I of Italy in revenge for the latter's role in the killing of demonstrators in Milan in 1898. Bresci's act initiated a period of press fixation with Paterson as a major center of world anarchism, and part of the frenzy revolved around Ernestina Cravello, who had returned to New Jersey from New London by that time, and who was promptly dubbed "Queen of the Anarchists." Much of the attention of newspapers like the *New York Times* drew on her eloquence, dedication to the cause, and physical attractiveness, personal traits supposedly not associated with the stereotype of an anarchist militant.[15]

The *New London Day* became aware that Vittorio Cravello lived in their midst and immediately sought him out at his place of work. He took the afternoon off to grant a reporter the first of several interviews. A week later a *Day* reporter made it to Cravello's door after hearing that Ernestina was in town visiting her brother. "Miss Cravello said she worked in the Brainerd & Armstrong mill two years ago. She went to Paterson and was engaged in a mill there as a weaver. She has many friends in New London and Groton among her own countrymen, and a number of these called during the reporter's stay at Victor Cravello's house. The callers were all respectable looking men who greeted the young woman with enthusiasm." The reporter took in the scene around him, as follows:

> The Groton anarchist's home is a comfortable one. The house the family occupies is near the riverfront, in the rear of Thames street [sic], nearly opposite the fountain. The large parlor is plainly but neatly furnished and pictures of patriots adorn the walls. Mrs. Crevello [sic], the anarchist's wife, who is also according to her own statements a believer in anarchy, is a comely woman, with more than average intelligence. She has a nine-months-old baby, who is a handsome little chap and a pet of the neighbors, who visit with the anarchist's family quite frequently.[16]

When leaving, the reporter found "his pockets were filled with literature" on anarchism. Two weeks later, the *Day* carried rare coverage of an event organized by New London anarchists. Over two hundred Italian anarchists and sympathizers, including Vittorio Cravello, crowded into a performance of Pietro Gori's well-known play *Primo Maggio* (The First of May), at the New London Opera House, which usually hosted burlesque and vaudeville shows. The performers, the paper observed, included local talents, from New London, Norwich, Groton, and Fishers Island, while attendees came from New London, Norwich, Groton, Waterford, and Westerly. "The gathering was orderly and lasted until a late hour," a highlight being the distribution of seventy lithographs of Gaetano Bresci. All proceeds went to Malatesta's *L'Agitazione* of Ancona in the Marche. The group promised to next produce Gori's *Senza Patria* (Without a Country), a play with an equally militant message.[17]

The Cravellos moved from Paterson to New London accompanied by Giovanni and Margherita Barbanet, and possibly Giuseppe (or Giovanni) Ramasco. Giovanni Barbanet and Ramasco worked in Brainerd & Armstrong silk mill along with the Cravellos, and shared a household with the Cravellos in Groton. The Barbanets later moved to 54 Smith Street in the heart of the growing anarchist community in Fort Trumbull. Whether this small group moved for reasons of work or for the spreading of the anarchist idea is unclear, but New London seemed to offer potentially fertile ground for a revolutionary movement. These silk workers were a strong, if temporary, local force for organizational anarchism.

The birth of Gruppo L'Avvenire took place during a heightened period of ideological struggle between the organizational and anti-organizational anarchist trends. Giuseppe Ciancabilla founded *L'Aurora* as a mouthpiece of anti-organizational militancy and soon queried Gruppo L'Avvenire as to its position on these questions. That tensions existed within the group between the trends became evident from a very early date. Luigi Camillucci, who would be a longtime member of the New London movement, reported to *L'Aurora* that while he supported the journals of both wings, most members favored Errico Malatesta's strategy.

> Many comrades in New London said that to make propaganda there needs to be organization, while I say there needs to be more consciousness because the same organizationals were thinking only of one journal. The conscious anarchists that

truly intend to propagate our ideal instead know that two journals are better than one.[18]

A small number of members of Gruppo L'Avvenire leaned towards anti-organizational anarchism. In his interview with the *Day* in 1900, Cravello had remarked that in 1898, "there were a large number of believers here. There have been no meetings held here since then." It is significant that Cravello ignores the local activity mentioned in *L'Aurora*, a paper with which he would have fundamental differences; he certainly knew of the meetings since he subscribed to that paper.[19] In November 1899, when *L'Aurora* noted the appearance of Malatesta in New London, the paper also reported on an organizing meeting for a Christmas speaking engagement with Pietro Raveggi, an anarchist who went by the pseudonym "Evening," recently active in the Italian exile community in Tunis, and a firm anti-organizationist. He would speak at the New London Opera House at 395 Bank Street on the topic "Why We Are Anarchists." We have no report on the speaking engagement, but the planning meeting had taken place at Benvenuti's tavern.[20] *L'Aurora* eventually tired of the balancing act that Gruppo L'Avvenire attempted to maintain between the two camps. Citing the group's agreement with Paterson organizationists on the need of a national anarchist conference and its support of *La Questione Sociale* with a monthly stipend, *L'Aurora* in 1901 refused to publish correspondence from New London.

Anarchists held meetings on Fishers Island, at one point defiantly raising their flag: "We waved over us a black handkerchief with a red cord, and for a moment capitalist oppression was kept out of sight, the appearance of freedom in that countryside to be had forever." The act may have provided temporary uplift, but a dilemma remained: "Our group is not stable," they wrote, speaking about the whole New London movement, "because the uncertainty of work renders us united today, separate tomorrow." Nine months later *La Questione Sociale* received a donation from New London from "the comrades of Gruppo anarcho-socialist L'Avvenire of New London despite everything in this moment, because of the winter season, almost all unemployed."[21]

The contingencies of construction work put much of Gruppo L'Avvenire on the road for extended periods of time. Their jobs included a number of projects located out-of-state or in the far reaches of Connecticut, and they could usually only travel home on the weekends. Families had begun to appear on the scene in Fort Trumbull, either through marriages in New London or with wives and children being brought over from Italy. The prolonged absences put an enormous strain on women in the Fort, since they had to continue earning supplemental income and raise the children by themselves. The difficulties in building a strong anarchist movement were only partially resolved when Fort Trumbull anarchists and others established their own firms and worked closer to home, and when building tradespeople began to find jobs in the local craft unions.

The Italian anarchist groups that spread throughout the United States did not keep membership lists, and in Gruppo L'Avvenire's case the dispersed makeup of its adherents makes an estimate of its size difficult. Twenty-three subscribers to *La Questione Sociale* from Fishers and Plum Islands, for example, sent in their money to New London in June 1900. Others undoubtedly plied their trades closer to the city, with an undetermined number in the granite quarries along the Connecticut coast and with others working on the water. From its beginnings, the New London anarchist movement had a base of supporters and sympathizers that numbered in the hundreds, with an actual membership in the dozens, making it one of the largest Italian radical groups in the Northeast. Other anarchists in New England remarked of the large size of "the group" in New London. The city's movement, unlike other localities where the movement's membership derived from one particular industry, such as quarrying or mining, found employment in more diversified sectors. And despite the havoc created by the comrades' scattered construction sites, the key components of the movement steadily made their way to New London: brothers, sisters, girlfriends, wives and children began to arrive steadily and move into the Fort Trumbull neighborhood. Moreover, they had a birthplace in common; they shared a dialect and social customs that they would transplant in their new home. This would allow the anarchist groups based there to weather crises and political repression and to maintain a strong presence for at least five decades.

Gruppo L'Avvenire, in common with most Italian anarchist formations of the day, had little in the way of organized structure. The most important figure in the group became the correspondence secretary; limited information suggests that the position was elective. Other dedicated positions, at times at least, included one similar to a treasurer, or at least a person who collected donations for an extremely varied number of causes. A press distributor saw that members and sympathizers received copies of anarchist periodicals and sought to gain new subscribers. At times, individuals devoted themselves to propaganda and literature distribution. During slack times, when the efforts of Fort Trumbull's anarchists fell off, correspondence secretaries harshly criticized the comrades for laziness, sloth, and so on, and complained of having to perform multiple tasks. The "leadership" responsibility usually fell to those willing to put in the necessary time, and this did not significantly change for seven decades.

In October 1900, Gruppo L'Avvenire found itself in the thick of an important labor struggle in New London. About 160 freight handlers for the Central Vermont railway in the city's waterfront area struck for better wages and organized an independent union, the Freight Handlers and Laborers' Alliance of New London, Branch No. 2. Facing repeated company attempts to recruit out-of-town strikebreakers, they gained public support and sympathetic press coverage. Members of the local militia reportedly voiced support for the strikers as well, who were predominantly Polish and Slovakian, but also included "Americans," Irish, Norwegians, Swedes, Italians, and Portuguese. They maintained remarkable bonds of solidarity across ethnic lines, ties that did not fail to impress the reporter from the *Day* newspaper.[22]

The most serious initial threat came from padrone-supplied Italian laborers who arrived by ship from New York. After strikers successfully persuaded the first group to exit the pier and leave New London, the company brought in another group and isolated them from any contact with representatives of the strikers. Hopes of winning the Italian strikebreakers over to the cause of the labor movement seemed dim—but then a new force appeared on the scene. "All schemes had failed until Gennero [sic] Foschini, a young barber who keeps a shop at 30 Main street [sic], prepared an elaborate message, explaining the situation in a nutshell and addressed it to the Italians on the pier."

> The message reached those for whom it was intended and caused excitement immediately. Two Italians left the pier and met representatives of the strikers at the rendezvous agreed upon and there the entire situation was explained to the men from New York. The Italians returned to the pier and in a few minutes the strikers saw 'as pretty a bunch of Italians' as their eyes eve met, marching in a solid body, about 110 strong, up Atlantic street [sic]. It was an inspiring sight to the strikers and all hands proceeded to the Union hall, where a jollification meeting was held.

As they marched down the street, *The Internationale* erupted from the crowd. At the hall, according to the *Day*, Foschini gave another speech to explain "the real situation" to the Italians, which another speaker translated into English for the strikers. Unknown to the *Day*, the interpreter was anarchist David Levinson, who explained the meaning of the words of *the Internationale* to the strikers. And Foschini was an anarchist as well—a member of Gruppo L'Avvenire. Victor Cravello followed Foschini with a similar speech. The New York Italians revealed that they had to pay a padrone five dollars each for what they thought would be months of work, and were more than willing to abandon their posts. The *Day* reporter wrote, "every one of them left their trucks and flocked to the standard of the strikers. This is a great victory for the latter and the company may be compelled to give in to them." The union committee, reported *La Questione Sociale*, later met in the house of the Levinsons.[23]

Despite this auspicious beginning, victory proved elusive for the strikers. The company soon brought in African American strikebreakers from New York. While the strikers were able to persuade some to leave their jobs, their efforts proved largely unsuccessful. Although pitched battles broke out in the streets between the two sides, the strike was broken. Employers on the waterfront often pitted ethnic groups against each other; black longshoremen had their own strikes broken in New York by white workers. While the New London strike was defeated, the International Longshoremen's Association eventually organized the docks.

Gruppo L'Avvenire's intervention in the freight handlers' strike strongly resembled the organizing tactics of Paterson's anarchists. Foschini and Cravello concretely aided a labor struggle that mostly involved non-Italians, because in their view a victory for the workers would have advanced the cause of the revolutionary movement by teaching workers to collectively struggle against the employers and to rely on their own efforts to do so. In their participation in the dispute, Foschini and Cravello obviously did not set preconditions that the strike leaders had to meet before getting anarchist assistance. They simply waded into the battle and provided what could most effectively aid the strikers.[24]

Gennaro Foschini had moved to New London only months before the strike from Passaic, New Jersey, where he had been correspondence secretary for an anarchist group. Born in Naples in 1876, he had not left Passaic on the best of terms, having criticized several members there in the pages of *La Questione Sociale*. He immediately took a prominent role in New London, often speaking at functions, contributing articles to the paper, and sharing the task of correspondence secretary with Cravello.[25]

On December 23, 1900, Emma Goldman and Pedro Esteve came to New London and spoke before the group. "Emma Goldman has been to New London, Connecticut where she had the distinction of delivering the first lecture on Anarchism in English, that city ever had," reported the London anarchist journal *Freedom*. The subject of Goldman's address in the afternoon that day at the New London Opera House was "Liberty in the United States." She had been in France when Bresci assassinated King Umberto. Although a supporter of anarchists working in trade unions, Goldman supported Bresci's act: "King Umberto was justly put to death by a brave man who dared to act for the good of his fellow men . . ." She had developed some ties to the Italian movement, having met Galleani in Barre, Vermont a year previous. Esteve spoke that night in Italian.[26]

The anarchists of New London initially cooperated with the efforts of Italian socialists to organize locally. The Connecticut Federazione Socialista Italiana did not have a section in the city at the time, but held a successful May Day event in 1902. Of the twenty-one attendees to appear in *Il Proletario*, perhaps half were also donors to *Cronaca Sovversiva* when it first appeared in 1903, including Luigi Camillucci and Gaetano Lombardozzi.[27]

Their publication of Malatesta's first full anarchist platform, *Il Nostro Programma*, in 1903, defined the group's early orientation. According to an on-line collection of Malatesta's works, the paper had only appeared once before, in *La Questione Sociale* in 1899, and would be published again in Paterson in 1905. Gruppo L'Avvenire's publication of the program reflected its support for Malatesta's openness to building anarchist-led formations to advance the class struggle. For emphasis, the group added an introduction in which the optimism then reigning in the camp of the revolutionary workers' movement shone through: "We as organizational anarchists believe it is useful to present to the people a program that is an exact expression of our principles." To accomplish the goals of freedom and happiness for humanity, "it is necessary to organize ourselves and coordinate our efforts to bring about the fall of the existing system."[28]

Four individuals played key roles in the early years of Gruppo L'Avvenire: Gaetano Lombardozzi, Luigi Camillucci, and Federico and Marta Dondero. Federico Dondero is listed in his Italian government dossier for political dissidents as having been born in Pesaro in the Marche (though his obituary gives his place of birth as Genoa) around

1860. Born into a family of merchants, he immigrated in 1880, first settling in New Haven and then Waterbury, where he opened fruit businesses. A year after his arrival in New London in 1896, he started a similar business at 28 State Street in New London, and by 1900 some type of liquor dealership at 26 Bradley Street in the city's most crowded "slum" area. Four years later he opened a tavern 90 Bank Street, with his residence at 105 on the same street. He maintained the Bank Street business for a decade and a half and also specialized in imported wines. A few years later he broadened his business activities to include that of steamship ticket agent, a field undoubtedly useful in enabling a steady flow of those from the Fano region planning to move to New London.

While living in Waterbury, Federico—always "Fred" in New London—met and married Marta Clementi, who had immigrated that year. Slightly more is known of Marta's political development than Fred's, and her name appears as a subscriber to *La Questione Sociale* before Fred's. Marta, five years younger than her husband, had been born into a poor family in the north of Liguria, and suffered from a lung condition that arose from her early life. Marta grew up fiercely religious—*Cronaca Sovversiva* would even comment on "the buttress of the Apennines that seems to have saved her against all the assaults of freedom that test the old religious faith." She was strong-willed and not afraid to question movement heavyweights. After a lecture by Pedro Esteve in the early period of the group, Marta approached him and "asked if allowing the existence of God was compatible with anarchy, and if it wouldn't be better to propagate our idea without combatting religion." "Marta Dondero," said *Cronaca*, "did not come to us but through a severe and tenacious struggle with herself with old afflictions of hers." She had personal contact with Errico Malatesta and Pietro Gori, and slightly later with Luigi Galleani, and finally "with a lengthy work of analysis and personal reflection," she became a militant anarchist. Her name, not Fred's, is found in Malatesta's address book, although from at least 1903 to 1908 Fred functioned as the group's correspondence secretary. The Dondero house on Bank Street served as the gathering point for comrades and sympathizers in the early period of Gruppo L'Avvenire. Their house served political as well as social purposes, and the Donderos also rented out rooms—to Giuseppe Ramasco, for example, the weaver at Brainerd & Armstrong and an early comrade. An article in the *Day* from 1906 on the possible drowning of an Italian laborer from New London in a stone-laden barge in the Connecticut River strongly suggests that

Fred played a role as contact person between community members and relations in Italy. From their early arrival date, the Donderos most likely staffed a forward outpost for immigrants—especially anarchists—coming from Fano.[29]

Gaetano Lombardozzi may have arrived in New London at roughly the same time as the Donderos. Born in 1860 in the town of Loreto in Ancona province, his occupation is listed as "sailor," and he played a role in this sector of the workers' movement in Fano that was always at the forefront of struggles. In September 1884, Lombardozzi served on a fishing boat that docked in Fano at night. After being refused permission to unload and disembark by an awakened port inspector, he and several other young fishermen influenced by anarchist ideas led a rebellion of the crews. Lombardozzi and his comrades were absolved in court in this first episode of anarchist agitation among the seamen of Fano.[30] He had another run-in with the authorities—for dealing in contraband wine with other sailors—by the time he and several other anarchist comrades disrupted a military band playing in a piazza in Fano on June 3, 1894. They protested in solidarity with the uprising led by Sicilian revolutionary Giuseppe DeFelice Giuffrida; Lombardozzi was accused of shouting, "Long Live DeFelice! Down With [Premier] Crispi! Long Live Revolution!" This led to his emigration, under surveillance by the Italian government that would last for decades. Whether he practiced his vocation in the United States is uncertain, and it is possible that he boarded with the Donderos. Gruppo L'Avvenire would rely on Lombardozzi for his expertise, seriousness, and dedication to the struggle. Younger activists regarded him as a "veteran" and correspondence in *Cronaca Sovversiva* reveals that he had numerous friends and contacts along the coast from Westerly to New Haven.[31]

Luigi Camillucci, a Marchegian stonemason probably from Fano, was born on August 15, 1867. He immigrated to the United States in 1892, and contributed organizationally, politically, and culturally to Fort Trumbull anarchism from its inception; his name appears in the pages of the revolutionary press over a longer and more sustained period than nearly any other New London figure.[32]

Gruppo L'Avvenire's membership maintained its orientation toward the Malatesta wing, with close ties to *La Questione Sociale* that exasperated the anti-organizationists. The group did not shift its allegiance even with the appearance on the scene of *Cronaca Sovversiva* in 1903 and the rise of Luigi Galleani to a position of decisive influence within the Italian anarchist movement in New England. But in 1901 the New London organizational wing began to suffer a string of reverses. On September 6 of that year, Leon Czolgosz, a self-professed anarchist of Polish descent, assassinated President William McKinley in Buffalo, New York. Prior to this, Vittorio Cravello and several others had worked openly as anarchists in the Brainerd & Armstrong Silk Mill. After the assassination, however, the climate changed in New London. Called to the foreman's office within days of the assassination, the whole group found themselves summarily fired. At first, management claimed their work had been "insufficient," then admitted, "they didn't want factory workers who were anarchists and in addition being Italian."[33] Within a month Cravello had left New London and returned to Paterson. He arrived in time to play an important agitational role during a textile strike of that year, a role he shared with Galleani. (Soon after, as mentioned, Galleani began his swing toward full-fledged anti-organizationism.) Cravello later moved to Los Angeles, where he developed strong ties with the Mexican anarchist movement.[34]

Ernestina moved back to Paterson before Vittorio and continued her activities as an important organizer for anarchist women's circles that she had helped initiate.[35] Tragedy had already mercilessly removed the Barbanets from the New London scene. In early June 1900, Margherita, at the age of twenty-two, took ill and died within only a week's time. Utterly despondent, Giovanni began to aimlessly wander the streets of the city. He knelt on her grave two weeks later and fired a bullet from a .38-caliber pistol into the right side of his head. The grievous event made news around the state, although the public remained unaware of the couple's connection to the anarchist movement. The small but important Paterson silk worker grouping in New London had thus disappeared.[36]

Their organizing experience would be missed two years later when two labor confrontations put New London–area trade unionism to the test. Between May and August 1903, Eastern Shipbuilding Company in Groton and Brown Cotton Gin Company on Pequot Avenue in New London locked out over fifteen hundred workers at Eastern and several hundred at Brown in a determined attempt to break the shop floor power of mostly metalworking craft unions among machinists, ship fitters, boilermakers, and others. This occurred simultaneously with a drive of the labor movement to win the nine-hour day at ten-hours pay.

The "open shop" became the objective of both firms, and the *New London Day* stood behind their efforts. In a column by "The Tattler," written by the publisher of the paper, came the following warning regarding

E. T. Brown, head of the cotton gin manufacturer: "It is understood that Mr. Brown is a member of a big steel and iron manufacturers' and has its support in every way. If he needs any help he'll get it. The association is in a position not only to furnish financial aid if needed but to supply workmen." The organization, the Connecticut Manufacturers' Association, had launched a furious crusade against unions during this period, preferring that their workers not organize as the employers had. New London's craft unions maintained perfunctory picket lines, conducted the strike as perfect gentlemen, and went down to ignominious defeat as perfect gentlemen. Italian laborers at Eastern Shipbuilding, though not organized by the unions, had met separately and voted to support the strike. They soon returned to work along with the defeated metal trades' unionists.[37] *Cronaca Sovversiva* briefly covered the strike, urging that the strikers conduct their struggle "as war is war," and rely on their own strength, rejecting politicians, "confusers," and arbitrators.[38]

Gruppo L'Avvenire jumped into the battle to support the striking workers. The group had, through "all our efforts, our words of encouragement spoken in the streets, in the taverns, in the houses of the workers," attempted to deepen and widen the strike. They issued leaflets to the Italian laborers urging them to stick by the strike and called for a general strike that could beat back the attack by the employers. Gennaro Foschini spoke at a meeting at the Central Labor Union and explained the issues involved in labor's fight for a nine-hour workday. Despite the promising beginnings, "discouragement began and took possession of the masses," and soon, "the spirit of resistance is dead, the solidarity spent." The anarchists acknowledged that the question of nationality would have been difficult to surmount, and that many workers saw their agitational work "as belonging to the anarchist sect." An article in *La Questione Sociale* titled "Looking around Bank Street," portrays the demoralization felt by many workers. A worker who had returned to work and appeared among those discussing the strike "was representative of a worker who kneels down to the wallet."

The strike's defeat may have affected the future orientation of the New London anarchists. A comrade who had urged a general strike at a meeting, they reported, was "welcomed by workers with enthusiasm," but leaders of the craft unions worried that such a bold action "could lead to disorder." In June they referred to the conflict as "a great awakening of the proletariat of this city that they have set forth towards their emancipation," while by August the scene had changed to one of a "blessed calm . . . decided on the part of the victory of the capitalists." The showdown between the contending forces had also occurred as Gruppo L'Avvenire prepared to publish Malatesta's *Il Nostro Programma*. The defeat revealed the tremendous obstacles facing the city's anarchists who sought to make the local labor movement an important arena in which to propagate their ideas.[39]

In November 1903, Gruppo L'Avvenire announced in *Cronaca* that their mailing address had changed to "6 rear Maple Avenue," just outside the boundaries of Fort Trumbull, and that "We have in storage the pamphlet of Errico Malatesta, *Il Nostro Programma*, and we will send it for the amount of 5 cents a copy."[40] *Cronaca* listed the pamphlet for sale in its library of social studies. From the inception of *Cronaca*, however, the nuclei of groups and circles that would become the Galleanist subculture insistently claimed Gruppo L'Avvenire as one of their own.

The anarchist movement that formed in New London in the late 1890s reflected political currents that had motivated Fanese revolutionaries in Italy. The group received important contributions from non-Marchegian elements, but these dropped away within a few years. Complex relationships developed between the organizational and anti-organizational trends within the movement. While they cooperated in laying the foundation for an enduring movement in the city, they began to conduct political functions entirely separate from one another. A large part of the membership and sympathizers of New London's anarchist movement may not have fallen into either defined camp. As the group coalesced, the rank and file attended speaking events from both sides and simultaneously subscribed and donated to a variety of anarchist journals. The ideological battles, however, were just getting underway.

CHAPTER FOUR

A NIGHT AT THE OPERA HOUSE

On Sunday, July 9, 1905, hundreds of Italian workers filled to capacity the New London Opera House on Bank Street for a debate between two leading figures of the Italian American revolutionary movement: Arturo Caroti and Luigi Galleani, who represented the socialists and anarchists, respectively. Caroti at the time served as the chief publicist of the FSI and the administrator of its journal *Il Proletario*. Galleani had begun to emerge as the most important figure in the Italian anarchist movement in the United States. The Italian working class of New London would sit through nearly six hours of contentious verbal battle over a key question in their minds: how to overthrow the capitalist order and replace it with a classless society. "It was a true training school in the art of oratory on both our and their part, and for the working class public of New London," *Il Proletario* would write. But Caroti was at a decided disadvantage, and not just because of Galleani's reputation as an able, fierce debater. Anarchists, the socialists conceded, composed the overwhelming majority of the audience. New London, as far as the Italian revolutionary politics went, was clearly an anarchist town.[1]

When the context in which the debate took place is understood, it becomes obvious that a prime target of Galleani's eloquence was not just the Italian socialist movement as such, but the rival organizational wing of anarchism—based in Paterson, but having a strong core of adherents locally. The debate represented perhaps a tipping moment in the political evolution of Gruppo L'Avvenire, where anti-organizationists would attempt to transform it from an "anarcho-socialist" formation to a more strictly Galleanist one. As much as the Opera House battle represented a no-holds-barred confrontation between two major trends competing for influence in the Italian working-class, it also began the settling of accounts within the group itself.

The ideological struggle in New London behind the Galleani-Caroti debate had been several years in the making. Both anarchist trends continued to send their strongest exponents to New London. Pedro Esteve came from Paterson in June 1904 to debate a socialist lawyer by the name of Alfredo Bonucci, whose practice was located at 69 Golden Street. Bonucci represented a relatively small number of Italian Socialist Labor Party members in New London. Arturo Meunier, a social democrat with a more reformist perspective than Bonucci, was also present at the debate. Esteve took issue with what he called socialism's overemphasis on economic factors to the detriment of "morals and idealism," and memorably characterized reformism as *ninnananna*, a "lullaby to serve as wonders to put the people to sleep."[2]

The war between organizationists and anti-organizationists escalated after the founding of *Cronaca Sovversiva*. Luigi Galleani gained strong support from Italian anarchists throughout New England as a result of the growing importance of his Barre, Vermont-based publication and his incessant speaking tours throughout the region. His talents as a speaker as well as his ability to expound his anarcho-communist doctrine of uncompromising militancy proved hard to resist. But even as admiration increased of Galleani for his personal qualities of total dedication and self-sacrifice for the movement, New London anarchists continued to lend their support to the rival *La Questione Sociale*. Shortly after the Esteve tour, a group of anarchists in the city announced in the pages of that paper the appearance of a new formation, Gruppo I Riabilitatori—the rehabilitators. The main figure in the group was Nazzareno Falcioni, a stonecutter born in Fano in 1878, and while apparently not a founding member of Gruppo L'Avvenire, he had been important enough as an anarchist to be under Italian government watch since 1898. The new group formed in open opposition to the Galleanists: "this new group invites all the comrades living in North America, don't believe the gossip of our movement. We find absurd and harmful the campaign that some make against *Questione Sociale*. For about ten years, it has been in the middle of all the storms, has held high the banner of anarchy."[3]

This proclamation is the first and last mention of "Gruppo Riabilitatori." Did the group disappear? Probably not, since *La Questione*

Sociale (*QS*) contained reports of a *festa* to raise funds for six anarchist papers—*QS* received the lion's share, with the rest divided among mostly Italian papers, and no money going to *Cronaca*.[4] The name "Gruppo L'Avvenire" only appears perhaps twice before 1909. Communications to the rival anarchist newspapers are signed by individual names or by "a few anarchists in New London," or by one individual "for the group."

This name changing signified bitter political struggles inside the New London anarchist movement, battles at ground level for influence among the rank-and-file base of Italian American anarchism. While the city possessed a significant number of anarchists and sympathizers, it would have been difficult for two diametrically opposed wings of the movement to exist for long within a neighborhood the size of several city blocks like Fort Trumbull. It was far from being a metropolitan political center such as New York, Philadelphia, or Chicago. Whatever their sympathies for either wing, a number of anarchist comrades in New London attempted a balancing act between the two wings. The activities of Charles Coduri, the Waterford stonecutter, illustrate this nearly impossible undertaking. Coduri gave clear support to the organizationist tendency by signing on to the correspondence commission for Paterson's plans for an anarchist federation. The very idea of an anarchist federation was anathema to the Galleanists, who polemicized against it vigorously. Coduri attended and spoke at a conference organized in Paterson by Gruppo Diritto al'Esistenza to answer charges from Galleanists and other anti-organizationists. But only several months later, Coduri authored an article on a speaking engagement of Galleani in New London that refers to him as "our beloved Pimpino," (a pseudonym while Galleani avoided criminal charges stemming from a strike). The article effusively praises Galleani, the nemesis of the Paterson version of social revolution.[5]

Coduri learned his stonecutting trade in Long Island, moved with his parents and brothers to Barre, Vermont, and then to Waterford, where his father bought a farm. As a former socialist, he embraced his radical beliefs along the way, as did his brothers and father, who all subscribed to various radical papers. He contributed an article from the Waterford quarries in which he asserted that he and his fellow anarchist comrades in the stonecutters union there functioned as a "watchful minority." Remaining single into his early forties, the serious pose in his photos give him more the look of a New England school headmaster than agitator, but one not to be trifled with. He represents the many Italian anarchists who attempted to support the movement as a whole as best they could.[6]

Galleani spoke in the city in February 1905, on "Anarchism and the Political Parties," and answered criticisms leveled by Attorney Bonucci, who was in the audience. According to *Cronaca*, Bonucci gave a weak defense of his party; Galleani explained "how the original revolutionary philosophy (of the socialists) was able to degenerate toward a more opportunistic conservatism." The anarchists in the audience closed the night by breaking into "a vigorous hymn to revolutionary action, to anarchist thought, to the inevitable society."[7]

Then in March the Foschini affair exploded. An article signed by "Gruppo L'Avvenire" appeared in *Cronaca Sovversiva* complaining of the activities of Gennaro Foschini, who had lived in the New London area for about four years, with an address at 5 Goshen Street in the Fort. By early 1905, he relocated again to Providence and had established an alliance of sorts with the FSI there. From there he issued a communiqué to the New London comrades calling for joint activity between anarchists and socialists. For unstated reasons, his personal character came into question; *La Questione* Sociale grudgingly printed testimony from several individuals who defended him. (Two years prior, Foschini had written a very critical piece to the paper for its failing "to understand that the majority of anarchists living in the United States are not professors at universities that can understand certain articles, incomprehensible to people who did not finish elementary school studies.")[8]

It soon became clear that Foschini had both allies and critics within the New London movement that he had made an enormous effort to build. Along with a statement from the Providence FSI appeared a brief note signed by three members of Gruppo L'Avvenire—Enrico Broccoli, Ernesto Ghiglione, and Augusto Peroni—that affirmed their faith in Foschini's integrity, that "every doubt of his ideas in us dissipated . . . for the duty of loyalty, it's as anarchists we want to make this known." While Foschini professed to be an anarchist, the text of his address contained several incriminating phrases in the eyes of L'Avvenire. He saw the need to split the anarchist movement into "cantons" to accomplish his objective and that to attract potential socialist recruits, the anarchists needed to "soften the edges of their ideas.[9]

A communiqué signed "a few anarchists, New London," opened the attack on Foschini, and closed with the pledge to "reaffirm to the *Cronaca* our vivid support." In an article under his familiar pen name "El Vecc." (shortened from "vecchio," the old one), Galleani weighed in, first by prefacing his remarks by tipping his hat to the New London group, which represented "quite a few of the best" of the anarchist movement. Galleani characterized Foschini's address as full of ambiguity and inconsistency. Foschini had previously been a "rabid individualist," and his efforts now were full of "hypocrisy, calculation and of bad faith." His program was "testimony unexceptional," with a "shortage of reliability, convictions and character." Galleani also accused Foschini of ingratiating himself with his "paesani" of Providence, (Napolitanos) a charge of bending to regionalism, and worse, "the paesani are socialists, anarchists are not seen in Providence."[10]

At the end of March, Galleani resumed the attack, this time responding to a full statement released by Foschini. Foschini held that in recent years, anarchists had made great progress but that "we have pushed too much, we need to stop and reflect . . . today the new era socialist is beginning to hold parliament as half-secondary, but to bring about socialism we will need a social revolution . . ." Galleani found the idea of an alliance between socialists and anarchists to be a "nauseating act of contrition," and a "miserable spectacle of irresponsibility."[11]

Finally, the dissenters within Gruppo L'Avvenire came under fire. Charles Coduri weighed in against the three unfortunate comrades, asking why they would "carry the bags of Brother Foschini and make three parts of a comedy," calling them "miserable people" committing "stupidity." Coduri closed by asking of the three group members, "are they impostors or are they imbeciles?" Marta Dondero as well declared her solidarity with Coduri in the fight against the three friends of Foschini. Galleani joined the attack on the three at the end of May, but this time within a new arena. "We have read also the declarations appearing in the newspaper of Paterson (*La Questione Sociale*) to the consolation of Gennariello Foschini, but frankly! we cannot return without being indignant." The argument now appeared in full view of the Italian anarchist public, in the organ of the main pro-organization journal. But Galleani's anger only increased in intensity, and he meant to leave no doubt in this last article on the fracas that he saw absolutely no place for "socialism-anarchism" in the movement around *Cronaca Sovversiva*. Galleani cited recent attacks by leaders of the Socialist International on anarchism, and accused Foschini of being an ally of these leaders who were "kneeling to their creed devoted to the parliamentary struggle and the conquest of political power." Galleani can understand "the enthusiasm and the solidarity of the Socialist Section of Providence," but what of the three New London comrades? he asked. How can they dare to lend a hand to Foschini, "who is persistent in wanting to be a socialist, to soften many edges of our anarchist ideas"?[12]

The debate ended here. We hear no more of Foschini's proposals. The three comrades remained members or supporters of Gruppo L'Avvenire, but whether they adopted the new hard line is questionable. Even though a large number of the group's members were not averse to cooperation between different wings of the radical movement, Foschini probably had crossed the ideological line that separated anarchist from socialist doctrine. "Better disunited than badly united," Malatesta had written in 1897.[13] That unanimity did not exist among the membership would become clear several years later, but for now the Galleanist core of the group had begun to congeal.

These skirmishes set the stage for the Caroti-Galleani debate. By this time FSI supporters were few in New London, even though the organization had begun to grow across the state. Caroti stood for revolutionary socialism and had been active in the rising intransigent faction of the party in Italy. Born in Florence in 1875 and having emigrated to the United States in 1905, he became active in Philadelphia. Accompanying him to New London was his close friend Carlo Tresca, editor of *Il Proletario*. While Tresca attended the debate he did not say a word. He would soon be removed as editor for refusing to strongly attack the anarchists, after which he broke entirely with the faction-ridden FSI. Tresca later developed his own brand of anarcho-syndicalism and edited the well-respected *Il Martello* (The Hammer), which would be the chief "rival" of Galleani in the Italian radical movement.[14]

It would be helpful to at least summarize the argument put forward by the two speakers at the Opera House debate. Galleani's thought came to represent a large number of New London's anarchists for decades. Caroti opened the debate, giving an extended lesson in history and political economy, in the confident tone that characterized the rising forces of socialism around the world. He linked the rise of scientific doctrine and its refutation of religious dogma with the rising class struggle. "With the law of evolution it is possible to studiously follow the course of society in its path." All class societies, from ancient to feudal and then capitalist, would give way to a communal order. To attain this, the proletariat must utilize all weapons at its disposal, including parliament, cooperatives, and the trade union movement. Social development created the need for organization and association among the workers. Violence would probably be necessary because no dying social order departs without coercion of some sort, just as the bourgeoisie overthrew the feudal order.

He drew much of his argument from an Italian context; his promise, for example, to "go down to the piazzas" with the anarchists in confronting the power of the authorities, a phrase developed from the countless insurrectionary movements in his listeners' homeland. But, he said, all anarchists do is talk. They do not build movements. "Tomorrow, calls for mounting the barricades, we will be with many, you with few."

Galleani answered by first urging the audience to dismiss what Caroti had said in terms of science. He said that in "the law of evolution in the camp of social life of men we see first free individual association." The rise of the state in the various class-dominated societies crushed this initial freedom. Galleani rejected the socialist tactics of struggle, because "if the people are educated in trade unionism, in parliamentarism, in cooperativism, their consciousness will become weakened." Socialist members of parliaments cannot serve the proletariat "without assuming responsibility for bourgeois crimes." How to overthrow the existing order? "We need to emancipate ourselves, here and completely." First, with propaganda that "will determine that masses feel an acute state of intolerance for their many obstacles . . . How to overcome it? With violence." We are not anarchist socialists, he said, for that is merely hybridism.[15]

Cronaca Sovversiva drew from Galleani's remarks the following general anarchist goals: (1) labor emancipated from slavery relying on muscles, trusting in the inexhaustible energy of the machine; (2) the family resting on a civil basis and on love, "torn from religious sacraments"; (3) morals that assume the needs of solidarity on the ruins of dogma; and (4) the autonomy of the individual, dedicated to the ruins of every form of authority and for freedom of association.[16]

Arturo Caroti continued his activism within the FSI for several more years before becoming an organizer for several AFL unions in the New York City area. Caroti played a leading role in the strike of 40,000 women garment workers in 1909. He later returned to Italy, ran for office as a Socialist and became a founding member of the Communist Party. Along the way he wrote several novels influenced by the writer Jules Verne. He fled to the Soviet Union after the victory of fascism, dying there in 1931.[17]

Luigi Galleani would speak in New London on more occasions than any other anarchist figure. As if to symbolize the importance of his presence in the area, a national speaking tour of Galleani in October 1906 originated in the New London area. He spent an extended amount of time there, with his mailing address for speaking dates given as "Rfd 1, Waterford," the address of the Coduri family. To believe *Cronaca*

Sovversiva, New London had become a bastion of support for Galleani's interpretation of revolutionary anarchism. But *La Questione Sociale* also contains coverage of anarchist activities in the city during this time. It reported that in June 1906 a Circolo Studi Sociali of New London sponsored a speaking engagement of Ludovico Caminita, the editor of *Questione Sociale*. This might indicate a continued existence of competing anarchist groups in the city. In December, the paper mentioned a joint meeting of anarchists and socialists against an unnamed member of the local *prominenti*. In January 1907, Charles Coduri signed an announcement for the new circle, and in May anarchists held a *festa* in the home of Luigi Camillucci—under the auspices of Gruppo L'Avvenire—to raise funds for only *Questione Sociale*. Neither of the rival anarchist journals reported on the doings of the other in New London, although at times the same individuals organized the activities.[18]

Throughout New London's ideological wars, Fanese anarchist immigrants steadily augmented the group's ranks. Their level of exposure to the movement varied tremendously. Guido Baldoni, a barber born in 1859, immigrated in 1906 and had been among the circle of friends around Enrico Travaglini, Fano's most noted anarchist. Besides "taking part in all the demonstrations called by the movement," Baldoni had also played a role in the management of Fano's *In Marcia!* Most seem to have cut their teeth in the movement by way of Fano's constant mobilizations and clashes with the police and military from the 1890s. Luigi Ferri, a stonemason who arrived somewhat later in 1913, belonged to a Fanese group called "Neither God nor Master," and had first been arrested at the age of fourteen. In 1911 he took part in a clash of anarchists with a clerical procession in 1912 that led to another arrest along with twenty-six others. Nazzareno Falcioni, before immigrating in 1904 to play a role in New London's organizational wing, had also been arrested at fourteen. Italian authorities considered him "one of the most bold and fanatic supporters," "taking part in all the demonstrations of his and the other subversive parties." Arrested for selling anarchist journals as well as for carrying a pistol without a license, he became involved in one of the clashes of 1898, the "year of strong tensions," in which a group of anarchist youths tangled with police. "Falcioni tried to resist, throwing kicks and punches and was brought to arrest with much force." If a number of Gruppo L'Avvenire's supporters came to American shores having had significant exposure to anarchist doctrine and activity, others, such as Vittorio Federici, Efisio Bartolucci, and Paris Carnaroli, seem to have come without such experience. They proved open to the revolutionary currents extant in their new adopted country, and radicalized quickly.[19]

Whatever their politics, all Fanese immigrants headed to New London had to sail with the British-owned White Star Lines, one of the largest transatlantic passenger lines, and the only company that had representatives in Fano. White Star steamships sailed out of Naples and Genoa; New London–bound passengers used both ports. Even though the company had the reputation as one of the best passenger lines, two anarchists from Fano sent a note from Naples complaining of the service given to "fellow citizen immigrants." They labeled their treatment "dreadful" and especially denounced the quality of the food served. "In short in the steamship we are treated like actual beasts, and every complaint is refused."[20]

CHAPTER FIVE

TOWARD GALLEANISM

A chasm separated the struggles of immigrant workers from those of the craft unions in the United States between the 1880s and 1910s. The "respectable" efforts of native-born unionists of New London to enter into harmonious relations with their employers bore little resemblance to the unceasing and explosive rebellions of Italian workers in the city. These encounters continued into the new century. A contractor who defrauded both laborers building a reservoir and the City of New London in 1902 faced the threat of violence

> As soon as it became known that Potter was in the neighborhood the Italians started to interview him. They carried knives, axes, clubs and other weapons and, according to the story that comes from the wilds of Carr's Pont, they had him scared to death in a few minutes. Italians who have lost their wages are not inclined to waste time in talking and the chances of a murder being committed were very good.[1]

In May 1907, two hundred mostly Sicilian laborers laying double tracking for the Consolidated Railroad Company on Main Street struck for a raise from $1.50 to $1.75 for a day's work of nine hours. Padrones swallowed up 10 percent of the workers' pay. By the next day, strikebreakers, mostly Polish, were hired to replace them. Police noticed a few individuals who seemed to be acting like agitators among the strikers and ordered them to move on. A few days later strikers gathered at street corners on Main Street and led a two-pronged attack on police and scabs. After reaching a pile of upturned stones, they pummeled and drove their opponents from the field, injuring several policemen. But the next day, police brought reinforcements in to protect the strikebreakers and the strike ended. Gruppo L'Avvenire sent an outraged report to *La Questione Sociale* attacking a member of the local Italian middle-class for having "the shamelessness to call cowardly the two hundred strikers."[2]

Less than a week later, alarming news reached the authorities in New London of a thousand Italian laborers for the New York, New Haven, and Hartford railroad having struck, forming the "Italian General Labor Union of America" in the process. The strikers spread their insurgency southward and westward from Hartford, and threatened to halt all work on the new bridge over the Connecticut River at Saybrook. The movement dissipated as quickly as it had arisen, but not before murmurs of discontent began to surface in New London as union delegates appeared in the city to agitate among railroad laborers. The union issued a manifesto that breathed class-consciousness.

> Now we are able to answer with a complete strike which will make these (company) officers understand that under the skin of the workers, burned by the sun and hardened by callouses, there is a soul that feels, and a desire that raises us above their work of bare speculation . . . Workmen, now is the moment to make these people understand we alone are the bosses of the world, we who are the producers of all that comes from labor, have more than others the right to profit by it.[3]

Gruppo L'Avvenire's growth in the early years occurred during this period of upheaval. In Chicago in 1905, radical elements of the labor movement formed the IWW, or Wobblies, a group that would win the support of thousands of Italian workers across the country. Italians in western and central Connecticut came to provide the new revolutionary union with its most reliable base of support in the state. New London's anarchists aimed their vigorous propaganda efforts at an Italian community steadily receiving new exiles and potential recruits from Fano. Many articles and correspondence from New London exuded confidence; at a time when few others in the growing Sicilian and Napolitano communities had marshaled their forces, anarchists could hope to penetrate into non-Marchegian sections.

Efforts in this direction began not long after the Caroti-Galleani debate of 1905. In April 1906, a group member named Gino Cordiglia, probably boarding with the Donderos since he gave 108 Bank Street as his address, wrote an article stressing the need to reach the broad working-class with their propaganda. He first described the numerous obstacles to revolutionaries in the United States.

> The American environment is completely virgin with new doctrines and new social conceptions that tend to rise on the ruins of prejudices . . . the prejudice of authority has deep roots, the law has its over-pious worshippers, and the state from which the laws emanate, the country, has its savage and dangerous fanatics. It is difficult to destroy in the indigenous workers (the idea) that in the state, laws and authority were liberty and order; and the country is like a great common mother. The anarchist, even if more mild than the idealists, is an *outlaw*, a bandit, a worker who doesn't speak their Irish slang, is an enemy, and the wicked one who dares to tell them that the country, the league of harpies of trusts, stepmother to those humiliated from labor, should bend before the glorious dawn of a new humanity and brotherhood and liberty.

Corniglia felt these difficulties could be overcome with "assiduous, patient and determined propaganda." He recommended the production of leaflets and manifestos to be distributed freely in the streets, making available anarchist periodicals from New York and Chicago, as well as the writings of Emma Goldman and Haymarket martyr Albert Parsons. He referred to the local comrades who agreed with him as "a number of the exemplary who believe that . . . the methods we gather can permit us to show the light."[4] Mario Cardaci, the correspondence secretary of the group between 1908 and 1910, showed through his contributions to Cronaca that he had an interest in broadening the influence of Gruppo L'Avvenire whenever possible. But changes were on the way.

On one important occasion, the Group's outreach obtained what they called "unexpected and unusual results." On Sunday November 4, 1906, Galleani spoke in the Opera House and again filled it with Italian workers. The audience, according to an article in Cronaca signed by "I Coatti" (the Forced) was composed "not only of comrades and sympathizers, not only a public of Marchegian workers, broken more or less from prejudices and fears of anarchist ideas, but workers of the mezzagiorno resistant as far as here to our propaganda and colonial prominenti who have not as far as here . . . stooped to come to our meetings." A large number of comrades, on the other hand, were absent "for reasons of work."

Galleani, in usual form, lashed into "religious prejudices and patriotic prejudices as well as political fraud and the electoral market." Some of the audience left angrily, but most stayed, "those workers of the south," when Galleani defended the assassin Gaetano Bresci, of Paterson, comparing his act "with the relentless and necessary revolt of our Russian comrades." The entire audience "rose and applauded in a frenzied manner." If accurate, this article explains why the next few years would see the New London *prominenti* respond with an urgent drive to secure the loyalty of the Napolitano and Sicilian workers apparently reached by Galleani that Sunday night. A plethora of clubs and societies emerged in the non-Marchegian Italian community during this time. Another way to read this article is its unstated depiction of the limits of anarchist propaganda in New London: audiences of southern Italian workers at the group's events were a rarity.[5]

Gruppo L'Avvenire became involved in several unity efforts in defense of reactionary attacks on the anarchist movement, including a public meeting condemning the execution of Francisco Ferrer by the Spanish government in 1909, as well as trying to initiate a statewide movement of radical Italian workers against the recently proposed Penrose law that sought to gag the anarchist press, as well as perceived threats from the Roosevelt administration to the right of assembly. Correspondence secretary Mario Cardaci called for a "miracle of force and liberty" and for New London comrades to combine "in unison in one act with the diverse energy of the innumerable Italian workers of Connecticut!"[6]

In December 1908, the New London group's approach to spreading its propaganda came under attack from an unlikely source in nearby Westerly. In a report on fund-raising for Cronaca, Peter Berardinelli, then a farmer and the correspondence secretary of the Westerly group, attached a criticism of members of Gruppo L'Avvenire for having attended a party for a mutual benefit society in Norwich. Berardinelli had initially boarded with a retired Italian stonecutter in Waterford in 1897, and lived there until at least 1904, probably working in the quarries himself. A founding member of the New London group, Berardinelli had been born in the village of Cagli, in the province of Pesaro. To Berardinelli, the New London group had no business being in this arena of "lousy narrow-mindedness," where a flag was baptized, "a symbol of division and oppression."[7]

Gruppo L'Avvenire responded with a measured and comradely article that defended their attendance at the function. Only a few members, all younger men, went to the party, "and all to enjoy an hour of making ways to agitate in an environment hostile to our ideas." Flags and baptism were beside the point. They asked whether Berardinelli was "convinced that the anarchists should stay shut in their cocoons and never go out, never be with strangers, without contact . . . ," and if so, this might reveal a lack of faith in the anarchist idea on his part. We must make our propaganda "among people who don't want to know."

> We work for the emancipation of the proletariat, for the coming of a free society, in accordance with our weak forces but without weakness and without compromise, today as with tomorrow . . . and with equal if not better activity and ardor—and we have no other ambitions.

The group's response to Berardinelli did not lead to a rupture with either him or the Westerly anarchists. Relations between New London and Westerly remained close, with Berardinelli often attending Gruppo L'Avvenire's events and inviting them in turn to Westerly. It also must have helped that he had a longstanding friendship with Gaetano Lombardozzi. Differences in the anarchist camp did not always end so amiably—to say the least—as will be shown by the turn of events in New London.[8]

An example of the potential for widening anarchist influence in New London came with the founding in 1907 of the Circolo Filodrammatico di New London. This group relied on its own fund-raising efforts, supplied local talent, and put on at least two performances of the play *L'Idea Camina*. It may have been founded to a large degree by sympathizers rather than members of the anarchist movement, but it represented an avenue through which the Italian working-class public could be drawn to hear anarchist ideas. In 1908 the drama group hosted Ludovico Caminita of *Questione Sociale* to speak at one of its performances. The appearance of this exponent of organizational anarchism at the group's event no doubt raised the ire of the growing Galleanist tendency in New London, and payback was not long in coming. Also, as luck would have it, and only two weeks after Caminita spoke in New London, the federal government denied mailing privileges to *La Questione Sociale* at the urging of President Theodore Roosevelt and effectively suppressed it. Caminita was then arrested for "inciting to riot" charges based on his articles, and to make matters worse, he then ran off to Philadelphia with a married woman. Organizational anarchism suffered the loss of its mouthpiece at a precipitous time. By this time as well, two founding members of the New London group—Nazzareno Falcioni and Gustavo Dionisi—had left the city. Both had been anarchists back in Fano and had supported the Malatesta wing: Falcioni, a stonecutter, moved to Quincy, Massachusetts, and Dionisi eventually back to Italy.[9]

As the strength of the organizationists seemed to melt away, the Galleanists received reinforcements. The anarchist movement attempted to minimize the corrupting influence of authoritarian leader-types who could dominate revolutionary groups. Nevertheless, anarchist "influentials" assumed the role of leaders in all but name. The appearance of one such individual, one of the most defining figures in the history of Fort Trumbull anarchism, must be considered at this time.

Raffaele Petrini was born in Fano on November 4, 1883, to Giuseppe and Teresa Marcucci. The Italian government did not have him under surveillance before he came to the United States, but after that they kept their eyes on him until the fall of Mussolini. While the Casselario Politico Centrale puts him in New London as early as 1901, he had not actually immigrated until 1903 or later.

He lived a year in Stonington, Maine, working in a community of about 150 mostly Marchegian immigrants. Now a scenic coastal town popular with tourists and artists, Stonington at the beginning of the twentieth century had a number of active granite quarries located on small, scattered islands off the larger Deer Island. Some of the workers faced brutal and exploitative conditions, according to a column in *Cronaca Sovversiva* in 1907. At one quarry owned by "some Italian parasites" on nearby Green Island, an employer beat a worker with a stick after he demanded his back pay, and another's wife was nearly raped by the same "parasites." The majority of Marchegiani left Stonington, most settling in the small towns of eastern Massachusetts. For a brief period, however, Stonington hosted an active anarchist contingent, with donations and reports coming in to both the *Cronaca* and *In Marcia!* Galleani's speaking at the Stonington Opera House in September 1906 may have been Petrini's introduction to the anarchist movement, since his name begins to appear in *In Marcia!* soon after. At least two other future New London anarchists, Arturo Ghiandoni and Enrico Ciavaglia, were among the quarry workers of Stonington. By March 1908, Petrini moved from Maine and his name began to appear in *Cronaca Sovversiva* from southeastern Connecticut, first from the town of Montville to the immediate north of New London.[10]

Described in 1917 as short in stature, of medium build, and with light-colored hair, Petrini was carpenter by trade. He contributed his first article to *Cronaca Sovversiva* in 1908 about a notorious Fort Trumbull murder committed by a soldier unable to pay a debt to a neighborhood merchant. Talk on the street, Petrini wrote, had blamed "the dagoes" for the murder. Petrini blamed the US military as the true perpetrator of the vicious crime. The US Army had committed massacres of its own, so crimes such as the Fort Trumbull murder should have surprised no one. It was the last opinion piece he would submit for a number of years, but within a short time it became clear that he was a force on the local scene.[11]

By this time, a noticeable shift had taken place in the relationship of Gruppo L'Avvenire with the labor movement. As Fanese immigrants steadily poured into Fort Trumbull, the group grew more estranged from efforts to organize within the city's working class, in spite of a continuing wave of strikes during this period. This does not mean they ceased support for strike agitation and workers' rebellions against harsh working conditions. A different tone crept into the group's commentaries on the labor movement. Cynicism had often been present in the articles from New London comrades who described the "unconscious" workers around them, but that mood became predominant.

It would show up even from a member with a solid background in the organizational wing of the movement. In an article from 1905, Charles Coduri could not hide the disgust he felt toward the unions in the Waterford quarries where he worked. He attacked the union for returning to work after a two-day strike, "to the chains and, crowded together under the conditions of before." He denounced "the native worker element directed under the education and the tutelage of unionism more cynical and disgusting, of indifferent sheep, of a religion devoted to property, the law, and the boss. The strike meetings "give me the impression of dumb dogs with the usual habit of the collar and the chain . . . as if they missed the dog's bed and the kick."[12] Coduri seems to have drifted away from the movement when he moved to Westerly in around 1910, by which time work-related health issues led to his leaving the trade of stonecutting.[13]

Anarchists continued to work in local shipyards in significant numbers but we hear nothing from them. Nor is anything reported from the numerous area silk mills. The difference between 1900 and 1903 and 1908 and beyond is the lack of a direct connection with the trade union-oriented anarchists of Paterson, now publishing a new journal—*L'Era Nuova*—after the suppression of *La Questione Sociale*. From its inception *L'Era Nuova* became absorbed in the struggles of Paterson silk workers, identifying itself as an organ of the IWW. It functioned as a strike bulletin during the famous Paterson silk strike of 1913.[14] The flow of reportage and commentary that linked New London to Paterson ceased. The lack of skilled speakers and organizers from Paterson capable of providing direction to outlying groups like New London undoubtedly contributed to the political shift of Gruppo L'Avvenire. The personal difficulties of Ludovico Caminita and Gennaro Foschini would have prevented their serving as a counterweight to the enormous influence of Luigi Galleani.

The best evidence that Gruppo L'Avvenire had decisively shifted direction came decades later in obituaries in the Galleanist press of New London comrades. Two of these militants did not arrive in the city for several years after its founding in 1899, but the Galleanist press described them as having been founding members of the group. In this manner the entire organizational phase under the leadership of Cravello and Foschini of the New London anarchist movement was obliterated. Another obituary from the same time period expressed the developments more accurately, that during this time "the seed of the *Cronaca Sovversiva* took deep and vigorous root" in New London.[15]

CHAPTER SIX

BREAKDOWN

The year 1912 offered American radicalism unprecedented opportunities for growth. Socialist presidential candidate Eugene Debs polled 6 percent of the vote in an election where most of the candidates claimed to stand for substantial change. Historian Theodore Draper called the period "the Age of Unrest." The Socialist Party had grown to 118,000 members, elected 1,200 public officials across the country, and published over three hundred journals.[1]

Eugene O'Neill, living in New London and close to embarking on a theatrical calling, felt these rising sentiments of dissent. In 1912, O'Neill first read the writings of Marx, an experience that affected his political thought for the rest of his life. That year O'Neill and his cronies frequented the watering holes of downtown New London and met in Doc Ganey's second-floor office to discuss the pressing issues of the day. His group represented the coming together of strands of bohemianism and social rebellion. O'Neill would vote for Debs, and some leading intellectuals began to question the efficacy of the capitalist system and to align themselves with the rising radical labor movement, best represented by the IWW.[2]

The IWW had managed to break through in the eastern part of the country with a victory in the Lawrence, Massachusetts textile strike in January, which saw thousands of immigrant workers overcome ethnic and national divisions and remain united on the picket lines. The strike also offered proof that US workers were capable of following radical leadership. The IWW-aligned FSI proved to be one of the chief beneficiaries of Lawrence, since it had played an important part in organizing the thousands of Italian millworkers in that city. For a time, the FSI assumed a prominent role in Italian working-class communities across the country. In Connecticut, the group showed renewed vitality and its sections stepped up activity everywhere in the state, from smaller manufacturing towns like Wallingford and Meriden to sprawling industrial metropolises of New Haven and Bridgeport.[3]

While Italian anarchist groups in Connecticut probably did not grow to the extent as did the syndicalists, Galleanists and others proved capable of holding well-attended mass meetings in a number of cities—sometimes conflicting with, sometimes working jointly with the FSI. Perhaps most importantly, the Galleanist circle in the manufacturing city of New Britain attained an important position in the anarchist movement of New England. It hosted several key militants in the Galleanist movement and developed a well-known theatrical group that made the rounds throughout the region.[4]

Gruppo L'Avvenire—with its size and homogeneity, its recognized importance within the anarchist movement, and the experience of its militants—should have been able to further solidify its position in southeastern Connecticut. Within a few months, however, the group effectively ceased to exist.

This chapter will attempt to show how this happened, a task made difficult due to the lack of records or documents. No clearly written accounts exist of the grueling infighting that certainly took place. Nowhere are the issue(s) that caused the destruction of one of the most deeply rooted Italian anarchist groups in the country coherently discussed. In spite of this, it is possible through a careful reading of *Cronaca Sovversiva*, to discern the basic causes of the crisis. Italian anarchist groups in the United States often seemed to be in perpetual states of crisis, splitting or disappearing frequently as if to mimic the development of the movement in Italy as ably recorded by Nunzio Pernicone. Anarchists, like others on the left and perhaps people in general, often do not seem to get along. Regardless, self-destruction did not seem in the cards for Gruppo L'Avvenire.

Several unsettling developments preceded the group's crisis in the fall of 1912 that may have contributed to destabilizing Gruppo L'Avvenire. The Circolo Filodrammatica di New London had appeared in early 1907, trying to harness the "attempts of amateurs" who up until then had composed the local theatrical efforts to put on anarchist plays, with the goal of the "healthy popularization of anarchist ideas." The group had existed for two years when an article appeared in *Cronaca* in January 1909 signed by the Circolo that bitterly attacked Gruppo L'Avvenire for nonsupport of their activities. Members of the group were accused of setting up the drama circle to fail, for promising support and then boycotting their fund-raiser, and of sarcastic remarks to the Circolo: "Finally! The Circolo Filodrammatica is going to finish an action . . . philanthropy in the direction of social propaganda! Bravo, Circolo Filodammatica . . ."[5]

Gruppo L'Avvenire's response came quickly. The Circolo had done basically nothing for two years, they said, except run up a two hundred dollar deficit. The purpose of an anarchist drama group should be to raise funds for the group as whole, not themselves, and even in this they had failed. Anarchist comrades in the nearby towns of Waterford, Mystic, and Westerly agreed with Gruppo L'Avvenire's assessment of the problem. Comrade Luigi Camillucci had been scheduled to recite the monologue *Il Pezzente* (The Beggar) by Cordifero, but had not been allowed to because he had insisted that the funds should go to the group, not the theatrical circle. In the article, finally, and perhaps most damaging, the group claimed the Circolo had fallen under the influence of one Reverend Padre Mario Librino. They did not explain who this individual was, or why he had participated in anarchist activities. The reverend's name shows up in the February 13 issue as a donor, perhaps the only time a clergyman gave money to this group that had declared war on organized religion. No more is heard from either side in the matter, and Circolo Filodrammatica di New London probably dissolved soon after.[6]

We have seen that the theater group had a connection with *La Questione Sociale*, and had actually raised money for that paper. These transgressions may have been at the center of the Galleanists' hostility to them. Since at least part of Gruppo L'Avvenire's membership supported in some way the *Circolo*, they would have been left nursing grievances against the way the "influentials" handled it. The majority of the group probably agreed with Efisio Bartolucci, who included with his donation in the February 13, 1909 *Cronaca* the statement, "down with the chatterers." His statement is significant because no evidence exists that Bartolucci, or Camillucci for that matter, evolved into hardline sectarians during the next few years. The quarrel with the theatrical group must have deprived the group of a layer of radicals in the area who would have remained sympathizers, even if they were not committed revolutionaries.[7]

The second development would prove far more serious. In September 1911, Prime Minister Giolitti's government declared war on Turkey, the prime objective being the annexation of Libya. The Italian government promised economic benefits for all citizens of the country, including an end of the need to immigrate to the American continents. Libya could absorb large numbers of poor Italian workers and peasants, especially from the south. The war unleashed a wave of nationalism in both Italy and the United States, and would prove a harbinger of things to come during World War I and the rise of fascism. The Italian left opposed the invasion of Libya as an imperialist war that served only the interest of the ruling class—workers would become further impoverished and be forced to die in a war of plunder and chauvinism.

Anarchists and syndicalists across Connecticut organized mass meetings to get their antiwar message to the Italian working-class public. While they met strong opposition, especially from the *prominenti*, they successfully carried off the events, claiming to have at least blunted the rising tide of nationalist sentiment. In New London, Gruppo L'Avvenire faced a far more serious situation. They reported an "Italian proletariat fanatically for the Tripoli conquest." Attempting unsuccessfully to rent a hall to have Galleani speak on the war, they were forced to drop their idea for a public event. "With courageous pride and all our sympathy, and our unalterable solidarity" they had to "oppose the sectarian attacks." The anarchists settled for a "small family party" for "the sane and intelligent part of our workers."[8]

It is unclear what prevented the use of a hall for a meeting. The *New London Day* newspaper gave prominent coverage to the Italian invasion of Libya, with front-page headlines such as "Terrible Atrocities in Tripoli Charged to the Italian Troops," and "Cruelty of Italians Is Confirmed Again."[9] Italian nationalists who felt that Italy had the right, along with the other imperialist nations, to mercilessly pillage Africa, would certainly have taken offense to this. Incitement was a distinct possibility. When viewed together with the mention of "sectarian attacks," Gruppo L'Avvenire might have feared physical attacks from elements in the Sicilian and Napolitano communities. This development would undoubtedly have been seen as a setback in the face of more conservative leadership that had emerged outside of Fort Trumbull. Regionalism had become a factor that could not be avoided in the future.

By the end of 1912, conservative figures succeeded in mobilizing a large segment of the Sicilian community for a parade celebrating Italy's victory over Turkey. Two hundred and fifty men marched through New London's downtown to applaud "a death blow to the barbarism of the

Mohammedans." Shopkeepers, especially barbers, predominated in the leadership of the event that included not one Marchegian name. The political distance between Shaw Street and the Fort had irreversibly widened.[10]

Two other complications arose just before the crisis of 1912, and may or may not have had an influence because of their unsettling nature. Both were internal to the neighborhood but showed the impact of outside forces well beyond the control of anarchist circles.

New London, though a physically small city, lived with a massive presence of the US military with the Coast Guard installation in Fort Trumbull, the US naval base on the Thames River, the Groton shipbuilding facilities—soon to be combined into the Electric Boat submarine building company—and the continuous construction of offshore fortifications in Long Island Sound. This dominating network of bases, forts and military-based industry, on top of the constant infusion of public funds to build schools, roads, sewers, reservoirs, water projects, and so on, had an enormous influence on the local construction industry. A great deal of money could be had by contractors who knew what they were doing and perhaps with the right connections. The New London newspapers are full of stories of contractor bids for these jobs, and from an early date a number of the firms were Italian-owned.

In 1900, just weeks after the founding of Gruppo L'Avvenire, the correspondent who signed his name "the Wandering Pigeon" contributed an insightful article to La Questione Sociale. After a little rhapsodizing about "the snowfall that covered the streets with white, the houses and the countryside asleep . . . ," he got down to business.

> In my brief visit to New London, I was able to understand how in this republic . . . profiteering infiltrates everywhere, every administrative and governmental management.
>
> Near the city, in the middle of a bay, there are quite a few islands, in which the military government is constructing forts. Well, the rackets are exploiting this in the same shameful manner as the countries of old Europe.
>
> For example, I spoke with a comrade, working there in the forts, there were officials managing them that took advantage of everything. The government pays them 15 cents for every hour of work, asking only eight hours; but those striped ones (officers—RL) make you work ten hours for $1.35 a day.

> These representatives of military honor speculate on all: cheating the contracts of work, using in construction worse materials and skimping wherever possible.
>
> What does it matter if tomorrow the forts waste away? Isn't it easier than being demolished by an enemy?
>
> They pocket the money . . . and the American people made drunk daily with the imperialist spirit, pay for all.

The climate of corruption left the correspondent "sad and melancholic from the journey," even though he greatly enjoyed the company of the New London comrades. But at this early time, did he see the potential of this corruption affecting more than government officials, military officers and speculators?

Within a few years, several of the contractors who placed bids on these military contracts were anarchists, in particular the firm of Nazzareno Benvenuti, Fano-born and by then having moved from Smith to Goshen Street by 1910. A 1931 article in the *New London Day* outlined his endeavors.

> He came to America in 1885 after serving in the Italian army and was among the first of the local Italians to settle here. His early occupation here was varied but mostly with contractors. In 1895 he started in for himself and specialized on water, gas and sewer mains, also grading and excavating. Many of the first gas mains here were installed by Mr. Benvenuti; also water systems in Hartford, Norwich, Willimantic and Uxbridge, Mass.[11]

As we have seen, Benvenuti and his brothers Augusto and Enrico had been important allies and friends, though not actual members, of Gruppo L'Avvenire from its inception. In August 1906 a most extraordinary piece appeared in *La Questione Sociale*. It is titled "Open Letter to Augusto Benvenuti, Inspector of 'Water Pipe' in Uxbridge, Mass." The letter began, "In the labyrinth of business you perhaps have forgotten those who are not disposed to become skinned like slaughtered sheep." Benvenuti's workers asked for a lessening of the nine hours they currently worked because they had, they sarcastically observed, a "delightful one hour's trip, and another to return." They also complained that the board he charged the workers was more than they would have paid elsewhere.

On revealing his "parasitic soul," they threatened a strike. Augusto Benvenuti responded like a tight-fisted bourgeois—that he would rather lose the work contract than give in to his workers' demands. The workers left his employment, since "they knew more than you to leave work before you could sack them that the world is wide and has a job for all."[12]

Readers of the militant anarchist paper from Paterson must have raised their eyebrows at the piece, since the editors offered no explanation. Anarchists do not often address their employers to explain why they pursued a particular course. But these were anarchist workers addressing an anarchist boss. The letter had been signed by Augusto Peroni, a longtime member of Gruppo L'Avvenire, and Ariodante Ambrosini, who probably also was active in New London. An anarchist boss abusing his workers creates a dilemma for other anarchist comrades. This situation had happened once before, when the irascible Gennaro Foschini took to task an anarchist foreman at Eastern Shipbuilding for summarily firing a socialist worker. Actions such as this would "weaken and vex us," since how could other workers identify the group as defenders of proletarian interests with such individuals in their ranks?[13]

The rift with Augusto Benvenuti somehow healed, and he remained within the movement's orbit until at least 1940. Several years later, however, the crisis could not be contained. On September 19, 1910, an article appeared in the *New London Day* titled "Warrant Issued to Nab Barnezi." "Barnezi" was actually Ruggero Bargnesi, a subcontractor and foreman for Nazzarene Benvenuti on a section of state road. While Benvenuti was out of town, Bargnesi solicited his wife for money to pay bills and his workers, and apparently had been fronted funds previously without a problem. With $1,675 in hand, Bargnesi absconded, later sending a postcard to Benvenuti from Chicago, saying—probably only to taunt the latter—that he was on his way to San Francisco by train.[14]

Benvenuti went to the police to see that Bargnesi be apprehended, and placed a $150 reward on his head. Buenos Aires was a possible destination of Bargnesi, a police lieutenant reported. Then came the bombshell: "It is claimed," continued the *Day* article, "he is accompanied by Enrico Broccoli, an anarchist who has a brother there." This public charge brought Gruppo L'Avvenire into the somewhat sordid affair, since Broccoli had been a comrade from the early days in New London. The response a month later in *Cronaca Sovversiva* is worth quoting at length not only because of the implications the incident would have for Fort Trumbull anarchism, but of how it reflects on the moral belief system of the Galleanists:

A Trickster . . . Honest

That in America, how everywhere are vampires and scoundrels who live on the blood of others, is a thing by now so old that it's not worth repeating. But it happens sometimes that these good people have also the cheek of conceit to be a moralist, not just whoever does the slightest share he always did with others.

One of these types is a certain Benvenuti of New London, a construction contractor with a middleman, one certain Bargnesi and that because Benvenuti being known for his bankruptcy/failure and thievery, is no more able to present himself as an enemy of bourgeois commerce. And we don't tell not even the whole history of his sponging on the backs of poor immigrants; in this despicable exploitation of his workers is more or less the way he made his money.

Stuff of the sewer! Now, that Bargnesi has escaped from New London with a few hundred dollars, he has not only denounced the thief to the police; he has organized a real manhunt, putting on his head a price of $150! We do not want to defend the certain Bargnesi, but are asking simply of Benvenuti: if the first is worth a ransom of $150, what ransom merits the second? [referring to Broccoli]

The question should be able to be ended here, between the small thief who escaped and the big thief who makes honest; and we perhaps would not be worried if Benvenuti, having come to know a certain Broccoli has left New London, at other times who declared himself our comrade, should not be so hasty to denounce of complicity in the theft, because he has minimal proof; but he aims to incite the police for the capture of the two fugitives.

The honest thief in fact ensured that the newspapers have published that Broccoli is an anarchist, and that he had wanted to go to Argentina.

This is the true action of a spy and we propose with the intention two questions very embarrassing to Benvenuti: 1) if also he and Bargnesi are not avowed "anarchists," which time should we believe you 2) if you didn't know Broccoli had anarchist ideas when he served you as an employee to do your interests.

But Benvenuti has exposed his own[,] only now anarchy is served as a meal and he goes dancing like a scarecrow in the eyes of this hypocritical and imbecilic world, to achieve the arrest also of one who could be innocent. And therefore, after always being a thief, and wanting now to be honest, it won't be found another way in the transformation of making oneself a spy!
—the Anarchists of New London and Waterford[15]

The article raises several questions. The group mentions that Benvenuti had been one of their own, something probably deeply embarrassing. As recently as April 1910 Nazzarene Benvenuti had been identified in *Cronaca* as "friend" in an article sending condolences on the death of his ten-year-old son. But if Benvenuti was a trickster, thief, and exploiter of poor immigrants, why wait until now to expose him? The conflict had been brewing for several years between Benvenuti as successful contractor and Benvenuti as revolutionary anarchist, but he obviously controlled the purse strings that affected the livelihoods and employment of many Fort Trumbull building tradesmen. Working on public projects in the construction industry of New London necessarily meant compromises because so much of the work was military-oriented and monies came from public coffers. Gaetano Lombardozzi rushed into print a short article to assure Nazzarene's brothers Augusto and Enrico that the group regarded them as "two of our best friends," even though Augusto had just placed a bid for a water and sewer extension project at Fort Terry on Plum Island (later charged to be a US Army biological warfare research center).[16]

Benvenuti, despite being labeled a spy in the midst of an anarchist stronghold, continued to operate his business, and hire anarchists, from Goshen Street before moving around 1917. His defection—a significant one at that—revealed for the first time a fault line in Fort Trumbull. Up until that time, alternate power bases did not exist in the neighborhood, and Gruppo L'Avvenire could hold unrivaled ideological sway. This does not mean all residents were anarchists—a number of families evinced no interest in politics and only contributed to *Cronaca* on one or two occasions. The Benvenuti affair only showed the possibility of future splits in the community. It must be noted that local building contractors Efisio and Alfredo Bartolucci, and others as well, remained in the anarchist movement for decades. They built private homes, for the most part, and perhaps had not been seduced by the "labyrinth of business" in public infrastructure projects.

A fracture of a different kind came rather quickly. Twenty-seven-year-old Attilio Pierfederici, a millwright in a silk mill living on nearby Howard Street, had been a member of the group for several years, signing his name to two articles in *Cronaca*. In November 1911, the Italian Mutual Benefit Society, formed a number of years before, elected Pierfederici as its president. Several other Marchegian names appear on the officers' roster, the most notable of these being Antone Menghi. Antone, a stonemason, was on his way toward establishing his own contracting business. While *Cronaca* did not comment on the matter, Pierfederici's name did not appear in the paper for another seven years, and Menghi probably abandoned any sympathy from the early days. The rift with Pierfederici did not become a complete split, and he remained in the group's periphery; far more serious trouble with him would come.[17]

At the legal level, nothing seems to have developed further on the Benvenuti affair. Bargnesi remained at large, and Nazzarene Benvenuti never returned to the anarchist fold. He only continued to grow more prosperous. And in December 1912 Enrico Broccoli, under the pseudonym "Palombaro" was back in town, and along with his nephew Viscardo sent a donation to *Cronaca* "saluting R. Bargnesi," who, of course, was not back in town.

Across the state, the labor battles of 1912 allowed the Italian left to go on the offensive. In the midst of the Lawrence strike, which involved thousands of Italian workers, Massachusetts authorities attempted to frame two Italian IWW organizers—Joseph Ettor and Arturo Giovanitti—on a murder charge. The ensuing successful defense campaign brought a massive wave of support from Italian communities across the country. The IWW, FSI and other radicals found vastly wider audiences for agitation and propaganda than ever. In Bridgeport, Galleani spoke from the same platform as William D. Haywood, prominent IWW organizer, in one of a number of support activities in the state. Large demonstrations in both Bridgeport and New Haven drew in Italian businesspeople, social clubs, benefit societies, marching bands, and colony newspapers, with a joint committee comprised of anarchists, socialists and syndicalists formed in New Haven for Ettor-Giovanitti. In Middletown the IWW organized a strike of 1,200 Italian and Polish textile workers at Russell Manufacturing in June in a struggle directly inspired by Lawrence. Some of this strike sentiment reached New London in May 1913 during the IWW's attempt to organize the silk workers of Paterson in a months-long, ultimately unsuccessful struggle. Two hundred weavers of the Brainerd & Armstrong Company staged several walkouts for higher pay and union recognition over a period of a month. Led by the AFL's United Textile Workers, the picket lines consisted of Italian and Arab American ("Syrian") women; their strike met similar defeat.[18]

In nearby Westerly, the anarchist circle held a large, successful meeting for Galleani in June 1912 on the Ettor-Giovanitti case, in which the speaker further blasted the Libya invasion. All New London could seem to manage in this period of working-class upheaval were two private collections for Ettor-Giovanitti. That something was amiss with Gruppo L'Avvenire became clear in the donations column of September 14, 1912. With a contribution came the following salutation: "R. Giustini, R. Petrini, wishing this shameless spy of New London a good dose of blows with a stick."[19]

Renato Giustini, about twenty years old, had immigrated to the United States in 1907 from Senigallia. By the age of eighteen he had found work as an apprentice molder and had become active in Gruppo L'Avvenire, boarding with his uncle, Attilio Pasqualini at 85 Smith Street. Pasqualini, Giustini, and Petrini comprised an important part of the Galleanist hard core in New London.

A month later the group brought Umberto Postiglione as a speaker to the city. Based in Chicago and the editor of an anarchist newspaper there, Nunzio Pernicone described Postiglione as "one of Galleani's most militant acolytes," who had clashed over IWW strategy with Carlo Tresca a month before during a demonstration in Lawrence for Ettor-Giovanitti. Postiglione spoke to a successful public meeting in New London on "Peace and War," perhaps showing that Gruppo L'Avvenire had decided to confront rising local pro-nationalist sentiment. But he also apparently addressed a closed meeting for some of the members, because one comrade used the donations columns to raise an objection: "G. Arace, very sorry not having been able to hear the rebel Postiglione: What happened?"[20]

None of these charges and insinuations found their way to a discussion article. Then came another threatening remark in the back pages of *Cronaca* in early November: "V. Federici shouting down with spies." Vittorio Federici, twenty-one years old and born in Monteporzio in Pesaro province, had been active in the group for about three years and remained on the Italian government's watch list for thirty years. He also fit the bill as a recently radicalized Galleanist militant. Not content with his "down with spies" message to *Cronaca*, he sent the same angry outburst to Fano's *In Marcia!*[21]

The obfuscations did not end here but got even worse, when a few weeks later the following donation list from New London appeared in *Cronaca*:

G. *Arace* for the formation of a secret society in New London, what's the point to be secret?

R. *Giustini* why reveal a secret and make the allegation that to keep it jealously is for semi-serious people?

A. *Lombardozzi* is thinking that the new society will give some big surprises

A. *Peroni* if the cook had not changed the idea of his boiler to be able to slaughter the innocuous chickens

A. *Pasqualini* in expectation of tasting the soup

L. *Camillucci* the soup prepared by a society without credo, will be of bad blood

A. *Urbani* I do not believe in the soup and the theatre of San Carlino and will not speak after the first performance

Albani then we will see the fruit

U. *Carboni* there will be roses flowering

G. *Baldoni* the secret awakening will be to laugh, to remember the nice shape of the little chick

The list must be read together with an article appearing in the next issue signed by "A.G.," undoubtedly Giuseppe Arace, who is the main target of the Galleanist hard core. Arace, a native of Avellino province in Campania, had been active in the group since the end of 1910 and previously had been a member of an anarchist circle in Lynn, Massachusetts. On one occasion in 1909, while in Lynn he rose to question

Galleani at a public event, along with several others in the circle, on issues such as cooperatives, the IWW and the future postcapitalist society. He may have had some differences on questions of doctrine, and while he had not been in New London very long, he had friends among anarchists in the area, to judge from his numerous greetings to and from local comrades, and from the list above.[22]

Much time had elapsed since the days of New London anarchist involvement in the labor movement during the Cravello-Foschini period of 1898 to 1903. At the national level political differences between the two main wings of Italian American anarchism had if anything widened. In 1911, Galleani lashed out at Pedro Esteve, calling him "a Jesuit and dishonest." The organizationists responded by calling Galleani the "great cardinal" of the movement. "The wolf loses its coat but not its bad habits . . . and Galleani has more obstinate and stupid bad habits than one can imagine."[23] *Cronaca Sovversiva* took political differences beyond the level of invective and insult. Besides their hostility to carrying out work in trade unions on a sustained basis the New London group apparently had absorbed another trait from Galleani, the tendency to equate political differences with treason and spying for the police. For an anti-authoritarian, Galleani proved remarkably intolerant of those who differed from his version of revolutionary anarchism. This attitude penetrated the ranks of those he influenced, and became a staple of the Galleanist movement. Within Gruppo L'Avvenire, it surfaced and seems to have caused the disaster of 1912. It must be said that a haze envelops the whole matter and it becomes difficult to precisely understand how the group's worst crisis in its history came about.[24]

In his article, Arace admitted to spreading some of the gossip around "as to secret groups and open groups, and if it pains me today of the gossip spread, it is valid to speak with much anger of the allusions without validity in some of the arguments . . ." If he misunderstood some of the discussion, the fault was not his. It would have been different, "if in our meetings the discussion was held with a little calm, order and serious and persuasive reason." He clearly defended the idea of an open circle as one that will "give support and increase all the initiatives and all the manifestations of solidarity," but would be able to accept "the other," or secret circle, "that which no one wants."[25]

From the list, salutations, and article by Arace, it is clear that important members of Gruppo L'Avvenire became embroiled in a serious dispute involving the formation of a "secret group," that the grave accusation of spies had been leveled, presumably against other members of the group, and that the individuals on the list had lined up on different sides. None of those involved in New London denied the "secret group" issue, nor did the editorial staff of *Cronaca* weigh in as they had in the Foschini dispute of 1905. Those on the list supporting a secret group were Galleanist hard core. At least three of those who seemed to oppose it—Anselmo Lombardozzi, Luigi Camillucci, and Augusto Peroni—were longtime members. Lombardozzi, about twenty-three years old and born in Fano, had been active in the group since 1909. His occupation at this time is not known but he later worked as a molder in a shipyard. Anselmo was a younger cousin of Gaetano, and like the latter, had extensive personal connections in Westerly. Luigi Camillucci, previously discussed, was a stonemason and longtime member of Gruppo L'Avvenire. Augusto Peroni, about thirty-one and a gardener, was also a longtime member and had been a supporter of Foschini's efforts in 1905.

What of the "secret society"? The legacy of Bakunin may have come into play; from his activity in Italy in the 1860s to his death, the Russian revolutionary had stood for the creation of a secret revolutionary elite that would stand separate from the masses and plan the insurrection ushering in the future society. Anarchists who supported the anti-organizational perspective often supported the contradictory position of a select elite preparing the way forward. Carlo Cafiero, one of the most important figures in nineteenth-century Italian anarchism, and who came to support both an anti-organization perspective and clandestine activity, cited the need for security in supporting the secret group idea: "Why must we display all our forces to the public, i.e., to the police, so that they can know how and where to strike us?" He called for "establishing secret and firm bonds between all of us . . . Only this is renewal; only this is progress."[26] It is unclear whether Galleanists in other locales encouraged the formation of secret groups. Did Umberto Postiglione's presence in the city mean anything? And what purpose could a secret group serve? Did security concerns from nationalist forces and the *prominenti* over Libya play a role? Several years later, core sections of the Galleanist movement, partly in response to repression and partly stemming from their insurrectionary doctrine, would launch an armed, underground wing. Was New London's botched attempt in 1912 a harbinger of things to come?

Fred Dondero played no discernable role in the fratricidal battle. Marta had died in 1911 at the age of forty-six from a lifetime of respiratory problems. Her death elicited a very appreciative obituary in *Cronaca*. In 1905 she had contributed the only rank-and-file piece to the anti-Foschini discussion, and would probably have intervened in the new dispute. Fred continued to donate to *Cronaca* until 1915, but had probably dropped his position as correspondence secretary years before. He found himself not only with four teenage children and several businesses to run, but serious health issues as well. He retired by 1920, having turned the management of his businesses over to his daughter. Before dying in 1928 he joined the Catholic Church.[27] His position as secretary was filled for about a year by Mario Cardaci; not himself a hard-core Galleanist, Cardaci did not remain long in the city, moving first to Mystic and then out of the region.[28]

The vicious infighting left wreckage in its wake. Before discussing this, however, attention must be given to the departure of three more members from New London. Giuseppe Arace, the target of the spy innuendos, moved to New Haven by December 1912, sending a letter that the New London group characterized as "indecipherable" (a term that would describe almost all of what was written in this miserable affair), in which he claimed not to be embittered over "divergences that don't have a foundation." His next letter the following July, also from New Haven and signed "Joe Arace," voiced charges of corruption in the group, all "in the company of beer." After this, Arace is heard from no more.[29]

During the latter half of 1912, the venerable Gaetano Lombardozzi removed himself from the scene. Lombardozzi's companion Elvira Bartolini, mother of his four children, had died in Italy in 1907. He was about fifty-two at the time of the New London group's crisis and may have been incapacitated in some manner, since he began receiving a stipend from the group. Gaetano, unlike Anselmo Lombardozzi, took no apparent role in the dispute. He held no position marking him as a Galleanist sectarian, but nevertheless maintained strong anarchist convictions. He wrote to *Cronaca* blasting participation in the electoral process, calling for "tearing the ballot box and scattering the votes—our scorn for the fraud of suffrage. It is a stupidity . . ."[30] His role in Gruppo L'Avvenire was that of a dedicated stalwart doing what the radical movement termed "Jimmy Higgins" work. He staffed the ticket tables at functions, thanked after one for "the self-sacrifice of our watchful and restless Lombardozzi" and the "very good financial result." Judging from the numerous greetings he exchanged with friends and comrades during his years in New London, he placed good food, good discussion, and good company at the top of his list. "I cannot come because I am eating everything in sight," he wrote in excusing himself from a gathering. He shed light on his personality with some wry humor when he wrote in 1913: "Gaetano Lombardozzi in the hope of being first but following many others." Lombardozzi represented what the movement's journals described as a "classic anarchist type." "He was simple but with a big heart, as full of hate as with love, hatred of reigning privilege, and love for the deprived and suffering multitudes."[31]

Lombardozzi moved to New Haven, where a sizable Marchigian community existed. No evidence suggests Gruppo L'Avvenire's crisis was the reason for the move, but Gaetano would have been disturbed by the affair. He became active in the industrial regions of southern Connecticut to where the main battles for Italian anarchism and syndicalism had shifted. A *Cronaca* correspondent from Waterbury thanked Lombardozzi for his help at benefit picnic for Minnesota Iron Range strikers in 1916:

> And to the tireless work and tenacity of the old and untiring comrade of ours, Gaetano Lombardozzi, who is always present at our activities, always first for our initiatives, while many youth—while they show off fervent sympathy and anarchist idealism—they love to kill the time playing cards, deserting our meetings, neglecting educational lectures, fertile discussions and the work of education and revolutionary preparation.[32]

Despite his declining health, Lombardozzi moved back to Fano in 1919, expecting to take part in a proletarian revolution rising from the upheavals in Europe after World War I. He instead became "laden with pain," and a prisoner under Mussolini. His death in 1936 at the age of nearly eighty "comes like a liberation." Red flowers strewn by his comrades adorned his tomb.[33]

The person who may have helped initiate the entire affair in the first place, with his wishing "blows with a stick" comment, left the New London area. Rafaelle Petrini, with his wife Giovanna, was gone by November 1912, and saluted "E. Bartolucci and comrades of New London" from Revere, Massachusetts. Why the Petrinis left is unknown. There are two possibilities: Rafaelle may have gone in search of work as a carpenter, and he evidently settled in with fellow Pesaro-area anarchists in the North Shore area. Petrini reestablished connection with Arturo Ghiandoni, a hard-core Galleanist who had worked with him in Stonington, Maine, and presently lived in South Framingham, and became well known to the anarchist Circolo in Lynn, where *Cronaca* was published, and to the important Gruppo Autonomo of East Boston. The second reason he left could have been because of the turmoil in Gruppo L'Avvenire. He signed a salutation in March 1913, "R. Petrini rimanendo di stucco"—"of stucco" or "consisting of stucco"—to either identify with the building trades or advertise his toughness.[34]

Back in New London, Gruppo L'Avvenire ceased to exist. From October 1912 to November 1914, no mention exists of a single public anarchist function having been organized. A "G.B." wrote in January 1913, probably in response to Arace, "You need to thank us and insult us? Well it's the same, rancid gossip, and it didn't help us." The paralysis lasted into 1915.[35]

Anarchism in Fort Trumbull was down but not out, however. Anarchists continued to abound in the neighborhood, and supporter lists for the anarchist press were never greater. Private gatherings raised money for *Cronaca*, friends met in each other's houses, and comrades attended functions organized by anarchist groups in neighboring localities. Large collections were taken up in November 1912 and in August 1913 to send funds to *In Marcia!*, Fano's own anarchist journal. Anselmo Lombardozzi continued his activism in all the above, and served as a distribution agent for *Volontà* of Ancona as well. New London anarchists joined their comrades across the United States in providing essential financial support for this paper. (After the onset of World War I, donations from the United States comprised about two-thirds of the total received by *Volontà*.)[36]

Even if their group disappeared, anarchism in the neighborhood showed itself to be resilient. New recruits could even be won during this time of crisis. Anita and Lorenzo Montali made a dramatic appearance with a donation from Anita to *Cronaca* in November 1912, accompanied by a salutation: "Anita Montali, baker, hoping to convince her Lorenzo of the communist anarchist idea." The Montali's had married around 1898 in Senigallia and immigrated in 1904 or 1906. Raising six sons, they owned a bakery on East Street. Lorenzo had first dabbled in the saloon and fruit business and seem to have done well financially. Anita succeeded in a rare instance of a woman bringing her husband into this male-dominated movement. The couple remained firm supporters of the Fort Trumbull movement until the onset of severe health problems.[37]

What Gruppo L'Avvenire had called a "climate of solidarity and fraternity" had helped ensure the survival of anarchism in Fort Trumbull.

Rank-and-file anarchists in the neighborhood remained loyal to their ideal, in an environment that had been shaped to meet the needs of the working-class families that lived there. The existence of this neighborhood's radical subculture could and did transcend even the group's vicious infighting.

CHAPTER SEVEN

REBUILDING

On June 28, 1914, a Serb nationalist shot dead the heir-apparent Archduke Franz Ferdinand of Austria-Hungary in the streets of Sarajevo. One month later, steamship ticket agent Louis Dondero—son of Marta and Fred—reported that his Bank Street business had received "numerous inquiries" from local Italians who were ready to go fight against Austria should Italy enter the looming war.[1] At a time when nationalist sentiments steadily rose among Sicilians and Napolitanos in New London, the only political force that could have mounted a challenge to the war fever lay dormant in Fort Trumbull. The seriousness of the situation became apparent when a small group of local militants tried to reunite the membership of Gruppo L'Avvenire by calling an event in January 1915. It would feature an appearance by Galleani, who would speak on "Unemployment and War," with a party featuring dancing and a raffle to follow his speech. Almost all money raised, significantly, would go to *Volontà*, "our proud anarchist journal *anconetano*" (of Ancona).[2]

Galleani delivered a strong speech in which "his rage against turncoat wage earners remains a severe example of dignity, of coherence, of courage." He received "thundering applause," and the meeting was a financial success, with $55 (about $1,350 in 2018) raised for *Volontà* and five for *Cronaca Sovversiva*. It was not enough, however, and the initiators of the event knew it. (Even the address of the meeting, "Fastidi hall on East Street," did not bode well for the future, as *fastidi* can be translated as *troubles*.) "There are not four cats left in New London," commented the organizers, an expression meaning that few active anarchists remained in the city. If the comrades without energy and persistence would do something and give the "four cats" a hand, they continued, "we will not be such a vineyard for the imposters, scoundrels, hypocrites and turncoats." Perhaps this was not the tone called for at such a moment. The most significant development to come out of the event did not even elicit a comment—the article is signed Gruppo I Liberi ("the Free"), signaling that the process of rebuilding might have begun.[3]

While Fort Trumbull's anarchist movement struggled to gain footing, the non-Marchegian Italian community became engulfed by a wave of patriotic, prowar fervor after Italy's declaration of war on Austria-Hungary on May 23, 1915. A significant number of area Italians returned to the homeland to fight (with more than a few losing their lives). On July 30, the patriotic element turned out for a parade to escort reservists sailing from the New London pier; the *New London Day* described it as "a demonstration unique in the city's history." Participants were brought to "a high pitch of enthusiasm" in an event "remarkable for its fervor." Local Sicilians, with Antonio Caracausa playing a leading role, comprised most of both prowar marchers and military volunteers as well.[4]

Meanwhile, by October of that year efforts by New London anarchists began to bear fruit. A virtual refoundation manifesto gave the most honest description of what had transpired since 1912, the problems the group faced, and the tasks ahead.

> Should we want to come out in earnest from the state of sleepiness and impotence in which we have been during a long debate, *emulating the beautiful days in which we were at the vanguard of the subversive proletariat of New England* and we saw the vigorous awakening and were militantly victorious in every good initiative?
>
> We are almost authorized to hope this, looking at the enthusiasm that the festival on Sunday and the meeting with our good Galleani have awakened in all the comrades of the old guard and among the numerous young recruits.
>
> *But it is not useful to deceive oneself. The enormity of the task that now tragically imposes on all revolutionaries will not be confronted or resolved without mature preparation and without conscious, decisive pertinacity.* Comrades of good will abound. There are also more numerous youths who, if they catch a glimpse of the noble majesty of the ideal, will be able to

carry out the promise, to speed up the bright spring, and *they lingered only because until today they wasted in barren and malicious gossip, in envious, disgraceful competitions*, treasured energy that should have been dedicated to make stronger every moral fragility to a serious work of agitation, education and revolutionary preparation.

We are joining to break the ice, to call back enthusiasm to our family meetings and interest them also in problems more bloody and arduous than of the present. It is the good part of the task.

We don't give up now that the enthusiasm can be re-absorbed and, when the iron is hot, forge it on the anvil with a pair of arms, beginning with assiduous methods of work in propaganda, preparing the exploited of this neighborhood for the responsibility and the audacity of tomorrow for us to gather in *regular and serene discussions, inserting periodic conferences between the parties*, our taking an interest in the big battles of work crossed with that mature experience of the combatants of the great social war.

The encouraging result of the last party was the presence of numerous women and children at our family evening, the contribution of all, in spite of the crises, bringing concord.

We will put ourselves in rank with comrades of all America and we will study with generous emulation to achieve and to keep our place in the vanguard, if we have the thirst for liberty, the noble longing for more favorable and less sad tomorrows in the future of their children. To work! Without requiems, until the yearned-for battle, until the victory that will be the reward for the energy and tenacity, the self-sacrifice, baptism of denied rights. To work! [emphases added]

"Nick"[5]

A week before the manifesto appeared, *Cronaca* carried a New London donors' list of five names, without salutations. Two are Galleanist hard-core, uncle and nephew Attilio Pasqualini and Renato Giustini. Another is the experienced but probably less-sectarian Anselmo Lombardozzi. A fourth person, Ulderico Bini, had moved to the area in 1913. Bini was twenty-four years old and a baker by profession. Born in Senigallia, he had an Italian government *schede* for the past five years.[6]

The last name on the list is that of Rafaelle Petrini, absent from New London for almost three years. In Revere, Petrini seemed to have maintained his signature militancy when he cosigned a donation, "teaching a lesson to weak ones." Tragedy then struck him and his wife Giovanna. In 1910, while still living in New London, Giovanna had given birth to their first son, who they named Spartaco. Not long after moving to Massachusetts, the Petrinis had a daughter, Libera Theresa, who survived less than three years. An obituary in *Cronaca* mourns the loss of the little girl, "a flower scarcely blooming in the camp of the subversives, a proud hope of her parents, treated with infinite love." The staff of the paper, as well as two local groups (including Gruppo Autonomo of East Boston) sent their condolences. After Libera's death, the names of the Petrinis disappear from *Cronaca* for an entire year. It can be assumed that the couple had been left devastated by their loss and incapable of political activity, an occurrence that does not seem uncommon in the Italian-American radical movement. Catastrophes in the family could spiritually cripple surviving family members.[7]

For the first time since 1903 the group began to list a street address for a rented room at 20 East Street. (Their first address, the rear of 6 Maple Avenue, would have put their headquarters just outside of Fort Trumbull's boundary.) No further mention is made of the address. The need for rented space became apparent as regional strife and conflict with the *prominenti* escalated. The 1916 address was also that of the Petrinis. Twenty East Street had been the address of the merchant murdered in 1908. At some time after the murder, Augusto Ballestrini purchased the property, tore down the barn where the murder had occurred, and put up a hall with an attached apartment. Gruppo I Liberi rented at least some of this space, as it became the location for their functions. Within a short period, however, the group invested money in property at 75 Smith Street for space that could more adequately meet their needs for public functions.

Anarchist activity in the Fort slowly returned to its pre-1913 level, with Postiglione and Galleani speaking to large, enthusiastic audiences. In May 1916, Gruppo I Liberi formed its own theater group, another mark of renewed strength. The public functions of the group had one crucial difference from those of the past: all were conducted safely within the limits of their neighborhood. No more is heard of mortified *prominenti* at meetings, probably because they no longer came. The themes of the activities shifted as well; Postiglione spoke on "The Reaction and the

Anarchists" at a meeting/benefit dance to raise money for Alexander Berkman's financially strapped the *Blast* of San Francisco, which took a militantly antiwar stance on the European war. Another function helped with funds for "the arrested of Boston" in January 1917 for a group of Galleanists taking part in an antidraft protest in the north end of that city.[8]

During this period the Galleanists became consumed with the war in Europe that slowly but inevitably drew in the United States. Their paper devoted a large amount of space to antiwar propaganda, including a series of letters from soldiers at the front to comrades in the United States. One letter from a friend of Augusto Peroni described the horrors of trench warfare—the dead piled everywhere, incessant artillery fire, and dazed soldiers reduced to tears. Raffaele Petrini's mother wrote to him from Fano of the "slaughter of poor things that broke the hearts of the mothers."[9] The conflict both confirmed their prognoses of crises within the capitalist system that could lead to social revolution and sealed the fate of *Cronaca Sovversiva*. In contrast to *Cronaca*, the newspaper of the Connecticut *prominenti*, the New Haven–based *Il Corriere di Connecticut* had welcomed not only Italy's invasion of Libya in 1911, but also their homeland's intervention in World War I. To Galleani and his supporters, nothing displayed more the utter corruption of the leading elements of the Italian American community than their surrender to the howling national chauvinisms unleashed by the European conflict. Workers, they counseled, had no reason to support "that country of millionaires that spends to kill thousands of young lives, and has never given assistance to the hungry and ragged people."[10]

In October 1915, Connecticut Galleanists called a statewide meeting in New Haven to plan a joint action against the war, inviting various anarchist circles and groups as well as FSI sections. But Galleani had already issued what amounted to a forewarning in 1914 as to the movement's tasks during the fierce battles that lie ahead: "Continue the good war, the war that knows neither fear nor scruples, neither pity nor truce." It constitutes one of his first appeals to his supporters to ready themselves for armed struggle.[11]

In the midst of this approaching storm, New London awoke to its first and only general strike. The only advance warning came with a short walkout of Italian laborers in early March 1916. Then on May 1, a tiny announcement appeared in the *New London Day* titled "Notice to Contractors." It read, "Notice is hereby given by the Labor Shovelers, No. 1, International Protective of America, that on and after May 15,

1916, the standard wage will be $2.25 for an eight hour day." Signed by two names, President Angelo D'Elia and Secretary Nicolo Brucato (and appearing above a public health notice promoting the elimination of "indigestible waste" and "sour bile" from the digestive system), the laborers' innocuous declaration could not possibly have prepared the city for what was coming. By May 9 at least a thousand Italian laborers in New London and nearby towns—virtually the entire Italian workforce—had walked off the job in what the *Day* called the city's "Most Wide-Spread Labor Controversy in its History."[12]

The strike burst onto the streets of New London as hundreds of laborers marched in a disciplined procession up Bank Street and wound their way toward the city's waterfront, from there crossing the Thames River to Groton. Along the way they pulled laborers off the job, greatly swelling their ranks. While the strike's demands focused on the private building contractors, the city's highway and water and sewer departments were emptied of Italian laborers. The strike spread to workers building the state steamship terminal in East New London, laborers on a railroad bridge across the Thames, and state road builders and New Haven railroad road crews in Groton. Eventually, laborers unloading marble at Eastern Point, Groton borough laborers, Italian gardeners in the Pequot colony, laborers on a private estate on Ocean Avenue, railroad laborers in Noank, and the only rubbish collector at Ocean Beach Park all walked out. By May 19, the *Day* observed that, "construction work involving the employment of laborers is pretty much at a standstill throughout the city." The only violence occurred when an Italian woman strike supporter confronted the only Italian ash collector still on the job. Described as a "militant suffragette of his race," the woman "emphasized her appeal with a stone which struck the laborer in the head." The strikebreaker promptly quit his job.[13]

The contractors and the city authorities had their hands tied, stunned as they were by the effectiveness of the walkout. Employers had grown accustomed to the numerous but short-lived rebellions of Italian workers in the area. This one proved different, showing obvious evidence of planning. The May Day notification could not have been accidental. The strike also occurred when the Galleanist militant Umberto Postiglione was in town to speak on the European war; *Cronaca Sovversiva* reported that he "had a vibrant discussion last evening with the strikers, leaving a good impression." The police arrested Raffaele Petrini and several others as they moved through the city agitating for workers to leave their jobs. A number of anarchists may have recently returned to New London as the 1914 depression ended and taken jobs as laborers. The influence of the anarchists in the strike remains an unknown; its execution seems to have been the work of a combination of different forces in the local Italian community. The strikers chose as spokesmen two men not part of the local *prominenti* whom they could trust. John Turello was a local saloonkeeper and soon to be building contractor. About twenty-five years old and born in Tusa, Sicily, Turello was married to an Irish woman. Frank J. Philopena, a foreman for one of the contractors, served in the Connecticut National Guard. He had been born in Fano in 1889, coming to the United States at the age of four. He would become one of New London's first Italian policemen in 1919, reaching the rank of sergeant by the time of his death at age sixty-three. Both men's pronouncements during the strike reflected the uncompromising attitude of the workers' ranks; they served not as mediators between the two sides but as mouthpieces of the workers. The contractors and city representatives could only fume.[14]

The Italian general strike in New London found its greatest weapon in the serious shortage of labor available to area employers. Local factories and other businesses were crammed with work brought in as a result of the war raging in Europe. Workers who only a short time ago faced prolonged unemployment now found an abundance of job opportunities. The Italian strike came on the heels of a successful strike of one hundred and seventy-five Russian and Polish longshoremen in February, on the Central Vermont wharf. Using "clubs, stones, hammers, crowbars," the strikers attacked a train car full of scabs and drove more of them from the docks. Over forty strikebreakers were injured, some severely, to the extent that they had to be evacuated from New London. City authorities forbade the introduction of Pinkerton Agency operatives by the company, having had enough of the conflict, and the workers won their demand for a 10 percent wage increase.

To defeat the Italian general strike, contractors brought in a group of strikebreakers of Cape Verdean descent from Fall River, Massachusetts, only to have them go over to the strikers en masse. City police, reinforced by special deputies, state police, and carrying riot shotguns for the first time in history, patrolled demonstratively in the streets to no effect. Evidence began to appear that the strike had begun to spread to non-Italian laborers. On May 24, contractors caved in to the strikers' main demand for an eight-hour day at nine hours' pay, and a day later the strike was over. Raffaele Petrini and the other agitators had their charges dropped, leaving the courtroom with "their faces wreathed in smiles" and surrounded by crowds that had gathered since their arrests.[15]

What did the New London Italian general strike of 1916 represent? In 1910, Italian construction laborers in Providence staged a similarly well-organized strike that ended in victory. The walkout was described as having "combined secular and socialist" character with "Italian and American references."[16] In New London, the vast majority of the strikers had undoubtedly been Sicilians, and many had probably paraded for the Italian war effort only a year before. Yet they struck without the help of the several Sicilian societies they had built in the city since the turn of the century. Anarchists, not the *prominenti*, were present in the strike. No further mention is made of the independent shovelers' local that waged the strike—it may have been absorbed into the Laborers' union, which had sent organizers soliciting the workers' support, or it may have disappeared. But the Italian workers' mobilization of May 1916 showed that large sections of the Italian American working-class retained a combative relationship with the dominant forces of industrial America, as did other immigrant workers in Connecticut. Strikes involving Poles, Russians, Lithuanians, and Italians in Ansonia and New Britain exploded into violence that spring as workers battled police in the streets, resulting in the death of a striker in Ansonia. These conflicts only heightened the growing anxiety felt by employers and authorities as the labor movement boldly flexed its muscles. As if to drive the point home, seven hundred trolleymen struck within days of the culmination of the Italian strike in New London. The strike won "the almost unanimous sympathy of the public," as scab-driven cars remained empty of passengers and We Walk for Justice tags could be seen all over the city. Three thousand people attended a strike benefit at the Empire Theater. A week later, the strikers won almost all of their demands.[17]

The period just up until World War I comprises the classic years of the Italian revolutionary movement in the United States; developments both domestic and foreign gave hope for the continued rise of anticapitalist sentiment in broad sections of the working class. Raffaele Schiavina later called these years "dynamic times . . . (of) the worldwide awakening of the toiling masses to the consciousness of their place in society . . ."[18] How radical doctrines penetrated sections of the Italian working-class public in Connecticut can be examined by viewing who read which newspapers. The number of *Cronaca Sovversiva*'s nationwide subscribers stood at around 5,000 in 1917; of these, 330 lived in Connecticut. Actual readership was much greater, as a large number of copies were passed from hand to hand, left in places such as taverns, and sold individually. The figures offer an opportunity to partially gage New London's anarchist reading public compared with other Connecticut cities. Each of the larger cities, excepting Hartford, with populations of more than 40,000 in 1910 (compared with New London's 17,000) had more *Cronaca* subscribers: 36 in Bridgeport, 40 in Waterbury and New Haven, and 62 in New Britain, with 20 in New London. Hartford had less with 18. In readership density among Italians, New London's exceeded all of the major cities except New Britain. New Haven had twenty-eight times as many Italians as New London (21,919 to 783), but only twice as many readers; Bridgeport had almost ten times as many, but again only twice as many readers. More New London Italians subscribed than Hartford's 4,521. Only New Britain, with 2,005 Italians, slightly exceeded New London in readership density. In these other cities, readers were spread out over several areas of Italian habitation, while New London's were concentrated in one neighborhood. Only two of these readers lived outside of the immediate Fort Trumbull area, one being Fred Dondero on Bank Street.[19]

This picture of the anarchist reading public in New London and Connecticut is only complete when compared with that of *Cronaca*'s ideological rivals. *L'Era Nuova* of Paterson had a considerable readership in western and central Connecticut, especially in the cities of Bridgeport, New Haven, and Derby. In contrast, between 1913 and 1917, when the government suppressed *L'Era Nuova*, only two individuals in New London subscribed to the paper. (Gruppo I Liberi had a subscription as well.)[20]

Similarly, Errico Malatesta's Milan-based *Umanita Novà* in the post–World War I period gained a significant subscription base in western Connecticut, where syndicalism had predominated in the movement, with almost fifty in Waterbury alone. By contrast, the paper had no New London readers. And thanks to a raid by Naval Intelligence on the offices of the syndicalist *Il Proletario* on Hanover Street in Boston, we know that neither did this important journal possess even one New London subscriber among its hundreds of readers in Connecticut. The single-minded devotion of the Galleanist core in New London to their beloved *Cronaca* (and later *La Frusta* and *L'Adunata dei Refrattari*) goes a long way in explaining the longevity of the movement there.[21]

Developing world events bore down on the New London anarchists, creating both perils and opportunities for the newly conceived

Gruppo I Liberi. Their effects concretely illustrate the relationship of transnationalism to the migration process of Italian radicals. Italian radicals, as Carlo Tresca put it, had "always remained with our heads in Italy and our feet in America."[22] The war crisis revealed beyond doubt that Italian anarchists in the United States felt themselves tied strongly to the social conflicts raging in their homeland. We have the surviving correspondence of a New London anarchist from Senigallia thanks to Bureau of Investigation raids on the office of *Cronaca Sovversiva* in 1917. Aldo Candolfi, living on Walbach Street, had migrated in 1914 with his wife and daughter (named Libertaria), and probably served as newly formed Gruppo I Liberi's correspondence secretary for a time. Two of his friends and comrades from back home, obviously missing him a great deal, wrote two letters in 1916 that arrived in the same envelope. The first, from Achille (with an unreadable last name), described the recent "ferocious months" in the years since the insurrectionary Red Week in Italy that started in nearby Ancona in June 1914. After troops fired on demonstrators, killing three, a general strike was proclaimed in the city that spread throughout the northern part of the country. While the national strike called by the General Confederation of Labor lasted only two and a half days, it continued in the Marches and Romagna, with Errico Malatesta playing an important leading and agitational role. When it ended, repression ensued, forcing Malatesta to flee to London. Achille told Candolfi of the anarchist papers being shut down and comrades scattering. Only he and his friend Ottorino remained "at their posts." Comrades were being drafted and sent to the front. One, A. Angelini, had just recovered from a wound to his left arm from "Austrian lead" and was being forced to return to combat. Both friends mention the surviving anarchist papers without distinguishing on which side of the Atlantic they were published. Ottorino, his second friend, gives affectionate greetings to Aldo's family—especially Libertaria—and asks him to find out whether *Cronaca Sovversiva* plans to publish the article he sent to them. If not, he would submit it elsewhere. Candolfi did not return to his comrades, but moved on to Philadelphia by 1920, where he worked at the Baldwin Locomotive Works as a mechanic. He continued to contribute articles to the anarchist press.[23]

Monteporzio-born Paris Carnaroli, with an established carpentry business in New London, subscribed to at least two Italian anarchist papers—*In Marcia!* and *Libertario*. Police files report that he had not been active in the anarchist movement prior to immigration, but on returning to Italy for an extended visit in 1915, he took part in a demonstration organized by "a group of local subversives" against the rise in the cost of grain because of the war. As a US citizen since 1906, he may have felt safe in intervening in Italian politics.[24]

Luigi Ferri, mentioned in a previous chapter, arrived in the United States in early 1913. While his occupation is listed in the CPC as tailor, he briefly worked in the produce business in New York and Norwich, Connecticut, before moving to the New London area. He apparently went into business with his brother-in-law and lived on Fishers Island, receiving *In Marcia!* by coming into New London every Saturday for mail. His stay in the United States was relatively brief, returning to Italy at the end of 1914. In October 1915 the Italian military called him into service, eventually with the 212th battalion, which went to the front in August 1916. Ferri fell in combat a few days later.[25]

Gustavo Dionisi had left New London by 1906, after playing an important role in Gruppo L'Avvenire's founding years. He resumed his activity back in Fano without missing a beat and took a prominent role in antimilitarist agitation during the war. When he passed away in poor health in 1919, Fanese comrades described him as "unforgettable," a man who left his footprint behind in his dedication to the war against the "internal enemy, the exploiters of the masses," while at the same time keeping a smile on his face in confronting adversaries. Neither did the New London comrades forget him; a collection was taken up by Gruppo I Liberi for his wife and children.[26]

The activity of a significant number of New Londoners who made trips back and forth across the Atlantic continued for decades. They supported anarchist papers on both continents, found their ranks constantly replenished with new migrants, and even attempted to influence events in their region of origin. But New London was not a "nodal" city in the sense of London and Paris for the anarchist movement. It did not represent a link on a chain or a bead on a string, but retained its character as a city of destination for Fanese anarchists, despite the relentlessly moving chain of Italian radicals passing through. While New London anarchism certainly benefited from the transatlantic movement and communication, constant movement of experienced militants has its drawbacks. As Tomchuk observes, moving targets were hard for state repression to zero in on. But unless a substantial grouping remains "sedentary," and stays behind, the chances of building a revolutionary movement rooted in a particular community are next to nil.

As the United States prepared to enter the war, New London as a port city with a heavy military presence, war industries, and immigrants felt the effects of mounting social tensions. Events around the state brought the war to the city's doorstep. In February 1917, Connecticut Governor Holcomb initiated a Military Census to appraise the state's preparedness in the event of war, but with the less visible purpose of ferreting out potential opponents of US intervention through the creation of a "bad list." State government and business leaders in charge of the census assumed immigrant aliens to be the principal source of such "disloyalty." Little excitement followed from reports that immigrants in urban areas were not cooperating with the census, until the events of February 22, when massive fires broke out in downtown New Britain. After crowds of immigrants left their tenements and pushed into the streets, the authorities called in bayonet-wielding state guard troops to keep order throughout the city. Hysteria swept the state as many newspapers hinted that the fires had been caused by a criminal plot or anarchist conspiracy to impede the war effort, even though no factories were damaged. In the following weeks charges were hurled by the press about spies and traitors poised to burn down the cities, and of disloyal alien mobs ready to revolt; the *New London Day* asked, "How many bad eggs do you suppose we have here in New London who for a hundred dollars would set a bomb under city hall?" The city formed a "Committee for Military Preparedness and Defense" to protect "against dangers which might arise."[27]

The political climate in New London shifted drastically with the US declaration of war on Germany in April 1917. The *New London Day*, owned by German-born Theodore Bodenwein, had previously taken a neutralist position on the war; by July the paper urged the suppression of the "pro-German" IWW. On June 5, when all men of eligible age were required to register for the military draft, 2,580 registrants lined the streets to sign up in New London. Almost three months later, young Eugene O'Neill, spending the summer in Provincetown and having three plays in production in New York for the fall, returned to New London to claim exemption, stating his opposition to war and conscription. "He came here, he said today, simply to obey the mandate of the government," the *Day* reported.[28]

In the May 26, 1917 issue of *Cronaca*, Galleani published his "Matricolati!" ("Registrants!"), which urged Italian workers not to register for the draft. Although the law did not require aliens to serve in the military even after registering, Galleani reasoned that by giving the government one's name, the next step could be registrants being forced to carry out a service for the war effort, and this would be collaboration with the state. Galleani's manifesto, issued in a period when the government had begun to suppress antiwar and radical publications, caught the attention of authorities, and on June 15, federal agents arrested him at his home in Wrentham, Massachusetts. While the defiant anarchist was released, the government searched for measures and legislation with which to permanently silence *Cronaca Sovversiva*.[29]

The same day of Galleani's arrest, Bureau of Investigation agents unsuccessfully searched for Carlo Valdinoci, the paper's publisher. They had no better luck in staking out either his home in Lynn, Massachusetts, or anarchist meeting places, for Valdinoci had fled to New Britain. There, Irma and Giobbe Sanchini, a couple from the Marche active in the inner circles of the Galleanist movement, harbored him. The arrest of Galleani and the attempted suppression of their paper put into motion plans that the anarchists had discussed, but until then, rarely carried out. As early as 1905, Galleani had issued *La Salute e in voi!* (Health is in you!), a bomb-making manual. In 1914, Gruppo Autonomo of East Boston put out a collection of Galleani's articles titled *Faccia a faccia col nemico* (Face to face with the enemy), a large book that defended individual terrorist attacks against heads of state and tyrants. Between June and September 1917, according to Paul Avrich, the Galleanists launched plans for armed retaliation against the government for its attacks on their movement. At the same time, a group of about sixty Galleanisti went to Mexico for two alleged purposes: to avoid the military draft and to be able to escape to Europe when the waves unleashed by the Russian revolution began to engulf the continent.[30]

In September 1917, a bloody confrontation took place in Milwaukee between the police and local Galleanists; by the end of the year, eleven anarchists faced prison sentences of from eleven to twenty-five years. In retaliation, the Galleanists prepared their first nationally coordinated military response. Next to nothing is known of the actual planners, or how many anarchists were involved in the Galleanist bombing network. The aforementioned Schiavina most likely was part of the network, as well as Valdinoci and others in Massachusetts, Pennsylvania, Ohio, and Illinois. Both Nicola Sacco and Barthelomeo Vanzetti, who had also gone to Mexico, were also probably part of the dynamite group.[31]

Cronaca Sovversiva reported a January meeting for those jailed in Boston as the last New London activity to receive a full article.

Subsequently, the paper cursorily listed events, and on December 17, the use of full names in the paper donations section came to an end, since the federal government found the listings quite helpful in their pursuit of radicals. On March 9, 1918, the paper reported the results of a fund drive for "the incarcerated of Milwaukee." New London's amount was the largest by far, and public functions continued at least until the end of the month. But the time had arrived in which aboveground political activity became nearly impossible for revolutionary Italian anarchists around the country. Flight or lying low seemed a better option for many.[32]

FIGURE 1. Photo from the late nineteenth or early twentieth century of the Arch of Augustus, dating from 9 CE, at the entrance to the city of Fano on the Flaminia Way. Photograph courtesy of the Archivio-Biblioteca Enrico Travaglini, http://www.bibliotecaliberopensiero.it/index.php?option=com_content&view=article&id=133.

FIGURE 2. Close-up of arch shows anticlerical graffiti, "Down with Priests." Photograph courtesy of the Archivio-Biblioteca Enrico Travaglini, http://www.bibliotecaliberopensiero.it/index.php?option=com_content&view=article&id=133.

FIGURE 3. Home of Antone Menghi and Fortunato Renzoni at 90–92 Smith Street, from which the Bureau of Investigation alleged that *Cronaca Sovversiva* was distributed in New London. Photograph from 1980, courtesy of the Archives and Special Collections, University of Connecticut Library.

FIGURE 4. The Italian Mutual Aid Society hall at 68 Smith Street was built by nonanarchist elements in Fort Trumbull in 1922. Photograph from 1980, courtesy of the Archives and Special Collections, University of Connecticut Library.

FIGURE 5. Home of Anita and Lorenzo Montali, and original site of Montalis' Bakery at 26–28 East Street. Photograph from 1980, courtesy of the Archives and Special Collections, University of Connecticut Library.

FIGURE 6. Charles and Dusolina Coduri from the 1910s: Charles, born in the Lake Como region of Italy, was an important early member of Gruppo L'Avvenire in New London. Photograph courtesy of John B. Coduri.

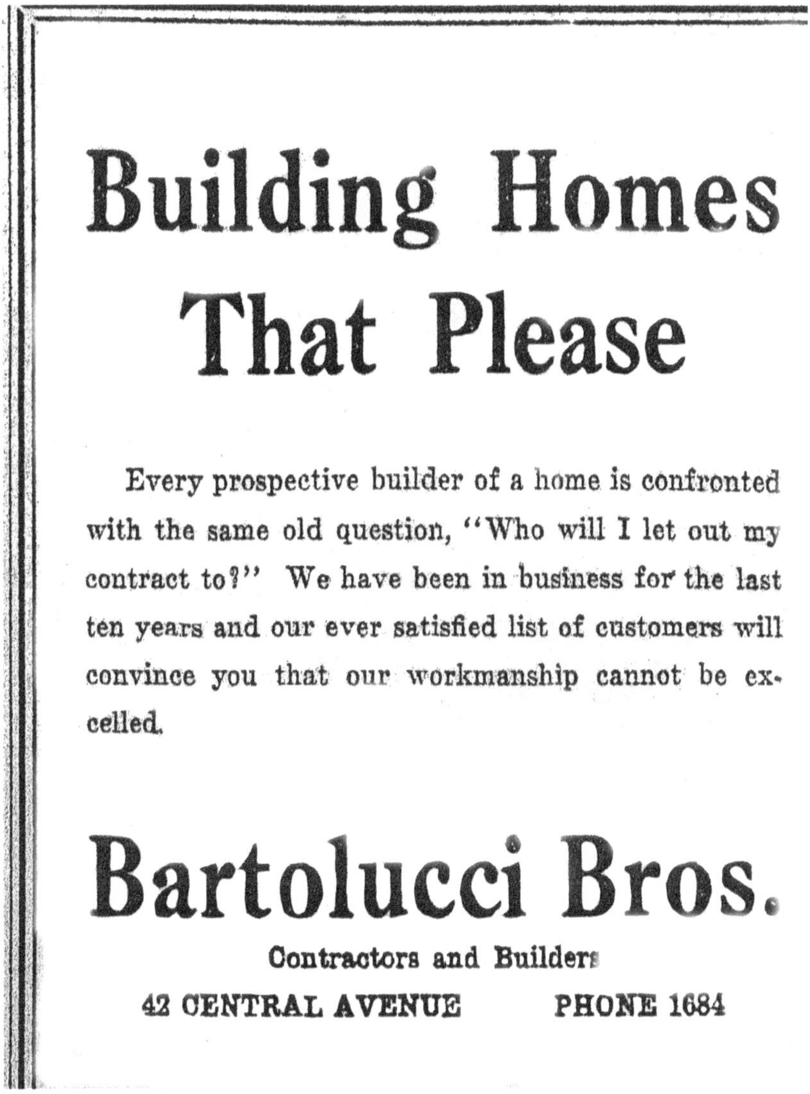

Building Homes That Please

Every prospective builder of a home is confronted with the same old question, "Who will I let out my contract to?" We have been in business for the last ten years and our ever satisfied list of customers will convince you that our workmanship cannot be excelled.

Bartolucci Bros.
Contractors and Builders
42 CENTRAL AVENUE   PHONE 1684

FIGURE 7. Advertisement for the building firm of anarchists Efisio and Alfredo Bartolucci. *New London Day*, July 17, 1922.

Veteran club members

Leo Camillucci, seated, and Victor Frederick, center, both long-time members of the Italian Dramatic Club, were honored Saturday for their years of service. Presenting the plaques are Louis Esposito, left, and Tello Frederick, right, club president and Victor's son. The club is isolated at 79 Goshen St., New London

FIGURE 8. 1975 photo of Leo Camilucci, son of Luigi, a founder of Gruppo L'Avvenire; Victor Frederick (Vittorio Federici), longtime anarchist militant and bootlegger; Louis Esposito (Espositi) one of the last members standing of Gruppo I Liberi. *New London Day*, March 3, 1975.

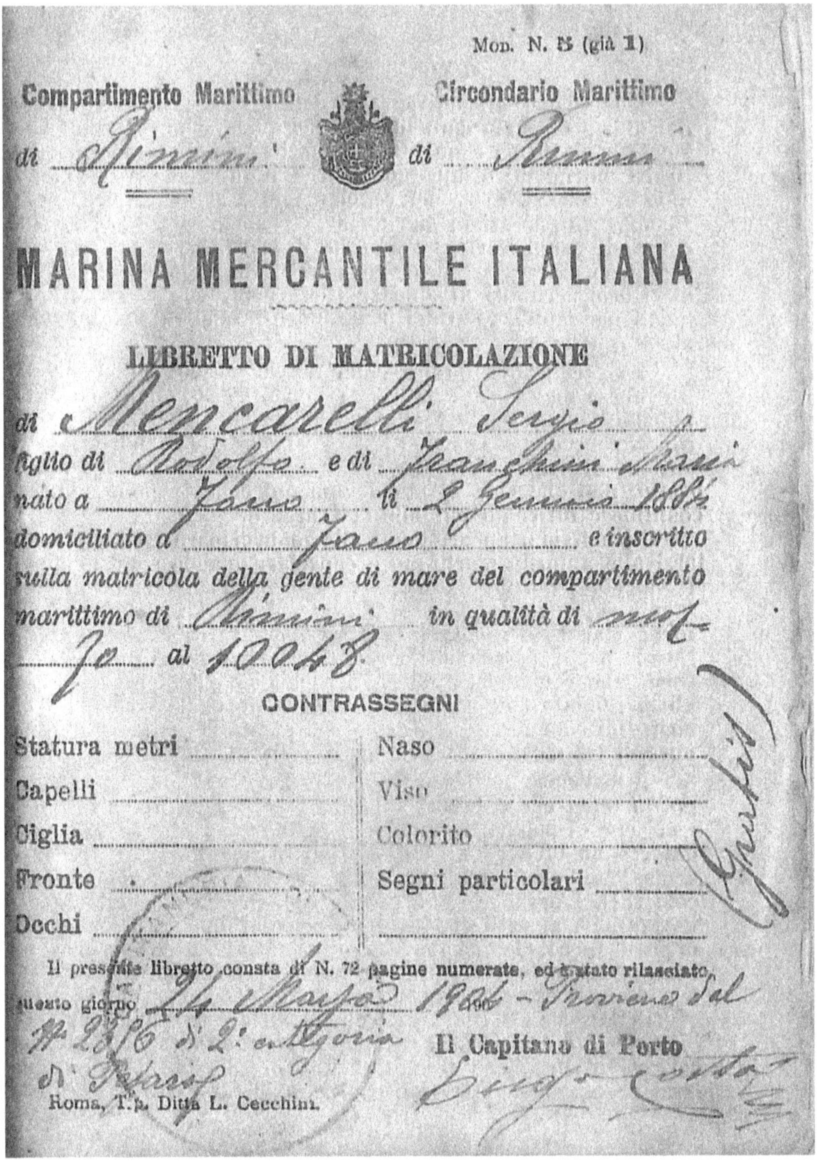

Mod. N. 5 (già 1)

Compartimento Marittimo di Rimini

Circondario Marittimo di Rimini

MARINA MERCANTILE ITALIANA

LIBRETTO DI MATRICOLAZIONE

di Mencarelli Sergio

figlio di Rodolfo e di

nato a Fano li

domiciliato a Fano e inscritto

sulla matricola della gente di mare del compartimento

marittimo di Rimini in qualità di

al

CONTRASSEGNI

Statura metri		Naso	
Capelli		Viso	
Ciglia		Colorito	
Fronte		Segni particolari	
Occhi			

Il presente libretto consta di N. 72 pagine numerate, ed è stato rilasciato questo giorno 24 Marzo 1906

Il Capitano di Porto

Roma, Tip. Ditta L. Cecchini.

FIGURE 9. Cover page of anarchist fisherman Sergio Mencarelli's maritime registration book in Fano, Italy, for his seafaring activity in 1906. Photograph courtesy of Shirley Mencarelli.

FIGURE 10. Sergio Mencarelli at his home on Dennison Street, New London, circa late 1940s, shortly before his death. Photograph courtesy of Shirley Mencarelli.

FIGURE 11. Sergio and Anna Mencarelli, third and fourth from left, with friends at Ocean Beach Park, New London, in the 1920s. Is the man in the middle saluting the warmth of the sun or the coming social revolution? Photograph courtesy of Shirley Mencarelli.

FIGURE 12. Sergio Mencarelli as a young man, probably before immigrating to the United States. Photograph courtesy of Shirley Mencarelli.

FIGURE 13. Gravestone of Guerino Menghi in St. Mary's Cemetery, New London. Whereas he was probably an anarchist sympathizer, he was killed in a nonpolitical shootout at 90 Smith Street in 1904; his marker reads, "Born in Fano, Italy, March 30, 1874, Assassinated by false friends February 28, 1904." Photograph by the author.

FIGURE 14. Italian Dramatic Club at 79 Goshen Street as it stands today. Photograph by the author.

FIGURE 15. View of the former Fort Trumbull neighborhood facing north, with the IDC hall in the background center; part of Smith Street ran diagonally from the left, the Italian Mutual Aid Society hall lay slightly below the IDC building; downtown New London is on the horizon toward the right of the photo. Photograph by the author.

FIGURE 16. View of former Fort Trumbull neighborhood facing south; Fort Trumbull State Park can be glimpsed in the left background, behind East Street (which is not visible). Photograph by the author.

FIGURE 17. Important exposition of Errico Malatesta's views published by Gruppo L'Avvenire of New London in 1903. Photograph by the author.

FIGURE 18. One of three plaques in the clubroom basement of the Italian Dramatic Club, the names composing a virtual roll call of militant members and sympathizers of the anarchist movement of New London. Photograph by the author.

CHAPTER EIGHT

SOLIDARITY NEIGHBORHOOD

The Italian immigrants comprising the anarchist movement of Fort Trumbull looked to the coming social revolution to sweep away all oppressive institutions and inaugurate an anarcho-communist society. Their heralded anarchist ideal rested on a shared faith in the ultimate victory of the workers and oppressed in the unceasing class war that they saw raging around them. Their ardor would cause them to name not a few of their children Libero, Alba, Spartaco, and Darwin, as if to help usher in the coming reign of freedom and reason. In the process of building a base of support for this struggle they created a subculture based on both an alternative living model and a means of resistance to capitalist society. As the fortunes of labor radicalism declined, the alternative aspect of their subculture came to the fore. They tried to live as close as possible to their cherished ideal, perhaps observing the precept that Malatesta urged on anarchists: "before thinking of establishing anarchy in the world they must think of making themselves able to live anarchistically."[1] The realities of Fort Trumbull in the early twentieth century brings to mind what Marx and Engels, two revolutionaries much at odds with the anarchists, wrote about human efforts to change the world: "we do not set out from what men say, imagine, conceive, nor from men as narrated, thought of, imagined, conceived, in order to arrive at men in the flesh."[2] The realities of the world of construction labor framed the political capabilities of the group and helped shape the members' individual characters. It kept many of them on the road much of the year and away from meaningful political activity, but also created a camaraderie among them that often lasted a lifetime. This established the framework on which Fort Trumbull anarchism rested.

Very soon after 1900, Fanese anarchists and nonanarchists alike established small firms that mostly specialized in home building. In an interview in 1998, Aldo Valentini, president of the Fort Trumbull–based Italian Dramatic Club emphasized the predominance of the building trades, running down a list of names that epitomized for him what the neighborhood stood for.[3] A third-generation Fort Trumbull descendant who wrote a paper on the neighborhood's history in the early 1990s captured this aspect of life.

> After the turn of the century, the Italian immigrants built homes and settled into their new neighborhood starting businesses to support their needs . . . They came from the Marche Province and all spoke the regional dialect. To them, after the arduous ordeal of their upbringing, living at the Fort was like being among family. Before they moved in they knew each other. They helped each other get established in the community. They would all pitch in and build a house. Money wasn't exchanged, they just helped each other. The second generation has carried on this tradition with building, plumbing, and electrical work. Those with a trade gladly donate their free time and skills to help their friends.
>
> The buildings they created lent an Italian character to this neighborhood. But this is only a skeleton of a close-knit community of hard-working immigrants. The story of their daily life can only be told by those who lived it.[4]

The Connecticut Historical Preservation Commission in its survey of Fort Trumbull architecture confirmed this last observation: "Many of these (Marchegian) immigrants were skilled in the building trades of masonry and carpentry. A number of homes and businesses were constructed using Italian building techniques and design, lending a distinctive flavor to the Fort Trumbull area."[5]

At least two sets of brothers previously mentioned, the Bartoluccis and the Benvenutis, supported Gruppo L'Avvenire activities and established substantial firms that took on major construction projects. They hired fellow anarchist craftsmen and laborers and provided financial support for activities. Efisio Bartolucci played an important role in the group for decades, as did his brother Alfredo. The role of these builders resembled that of Augusto Rossi, "a building contractor in Newton (Massachusetts) . . . (who) was an 'angel' of the Galleani movement." Born in Pesaro, Rossi provided funds and hid the *Cronaca Sovversiva* mailing list from the feds. (The Bureau of Investigation would find it in a barn Rossi had started remodeling on his property.) His house was a "haven for militants on the run."[6]

Some Fort Trumbull building tradesmen joined craft unions such as the Masons and Bricklayers and the Carpenters, while more worked for independent contractors like Paris Carnaroli. Born in 1884 and under Italian government watch, Carnaroli remained active in New London's anarchist movement from 1909 until his death fifty years later. Houses he built, along with those of his brother-in-law and others he teamed up with, are considered architecturally significant because they use "traditional American building designs, with certain building techniques reflecting their Italian heritage."[7] One of the techniques that caught the eye of architects was the beaded "macaroni" mortar joint. They also could not have missed the use of stucco throughout the Fort.[8] Anselmo Severini, under surveillance since 1910, had been active for the same period of time as Carnaroli. Born in Ancona province in 1884, he had apparently left Italy as a cobbler but by the time he registered for the military draft in 1917 he worked for himself as a builder, living on Goshen Street in the Fort.[9]

In 1914, a number of these Marchegian builders joined forces to form a cooperative of sorts to weather the devastating economic depression that hit the nation's economy hard. The *New London Day* noted the development in an article titled "Italians Have Building Scheme."

> Industrious Italian masons and carpenters in New London have combined in a novel plan which involved an investment of labor and capital to more than ordinary profit. These builders have been for several months engaged in the scheme and have placed their first products on the market for sale. The promoters of the plan have been employed by different contractors up to the time of the recent dullness. They then started by purchasing lots and building houses on them. In this way they were able to guarantee employment for themselves and two houses nearly finished will be sold at a price which will ensure them a return on the labor and money which they have put into the buildings and lots.

Additional land is being purchased with the idea of continuing this work through the winter. The houses are ordinary dwellings and will sell for approximately $2,500 each. Real estate men say the places are saleable.[10]

In January 1906, a large list of subscribers to *La Questione Sociale* appeared in the paper from Uxbridge, Massachusetts. The list included a number of comrades from New London, including Efisio Bartolucci and Paris Carnaroli. The group spent the better part of a year on a water pipe project in that town under the direction of anarchists Augusto and Nazzarene Benvenuti. This labor contract no doubt explains the Galleani event at the New London Opera House in 1906 that *Cronaca Sovversiva* described as having a large audience of southern Italian workers and few Marchegiani.[11]

Those Fanese construction workers on the road could return by train on weekends to Fort Trumbull but only with the completion of the job could they remain for longer periods. Fort Trumbull became their "home port," as a second-generation descendant put it at a 2000 reunion of two hundred former and present residents.[12] Only a rough estimate is possible, based on census data, obituaries, and draft cards, but of about seventy-five anarchist supporters whose occupations can be identified, 50 percent worked in construction. Of these, about a quarter owned contracting businesses of varying sizes. Others had migrated to industrial occupations, but most remained in the building trades for their entire work lives.

Roughly 20 percent of the anarchists owned their own businesses, though this figure may be slightly inflated since city directories and population censuses keep better track of these usually more sedentary occupations. The anarchist shopkeepers of New London included bakers, tavern owners, cobblers, a barber, a tailor, an ice dealer, and a confectionary store owner. These businesses provided a modest financial anchor for the group. Ten percent of the anarchist supporters worked in each category of maritime trades, shipyards, and various factories, including silk mills. Several of those who worked in the maritime sector worked as fishermen until their retirement.

Since a substantial number of Fort Trumbull anarchists worked in the building trades for fellow anarchists or for themselves as subcontractors, they would have been somewhat insulated from the tremendous obstacles facing the US labor movement during the early years of the twentieth century, even from issues facing the building trades such as jurisdictional disputes. Establishing work arrangements based on radical politics and regionalism put them at liberty to condemn the often-unsuccessful attempts by American trade unions to cope with employers.

While the anarchist movement anchored itself in the neighborhood, its members continued to display considerable mobility for decades. Some moved back to Italy and remained there, never to return. Others made the return trip, such as Augusto Peroni, who moved back to Italy between November 1912 and April 1913, again, "to receive medical aid," in 1920 (or possibly to avoid the postwar political repression). He later returned to New London and remained there for the rest of his life. The contractor brothers Efisio and Alfredo Bartolucci visited Fano in 1913, and used the columns of a local paper, *La Lotta Elletoralle*, for "returning the salutations of the comrades living in America."[13]

Histories of Italian American anarchism have given little attention to a vital component of the movement: those described as "sympathizers and friends" whose attendance at public functions was always considered so vital by those sending in communications to the anarchist press. This grouping is far less quantifiable than the actual membership of the groups and circles—they are usually nameless and undefined. Yet they provided a fairly broad base, certainly for Gruppo L'Avvenire and Gruppo I Liberi, than mere membership numbers suggested. Sympathizers might be described as those being in fundamental agreement with the Galleanists but not committed to day-to-day involvement. Friends would have been more on the periphery of the movement; perhaps they subscribed to *Cronaca Sovversiva*, gave occasional donations, or were workmates of the Galleanists. Fort Trumbull anarchist rolls are replete with names that appear and disappear at will, being replaced by steady stream of others who would come under the groups' influence. Some may have only tipped their hat to the revolutionary movement, while others remained supporters until their dying day. Without this layer, the hegemony of Galleanism in the neighborhood would have been inconceivable.

Anarchists in Fort Trumbull were quite conscious of the enormous obstacles facing them in building a revolutionary movement in less than ideal circumstances. The anarchists had to deal with the contradiction involving a heavy military presence; after all, Fort Trumbull's cannon overlooked the neighborhood. Anarchists interacted on a day-to-day basis with military personnel from the installation that did business in the neighborhood stores and rented apartments. They worked in the shipyards building warships for the US Navy and continued to help build island fortifications in the Long Island Sound for several years. Anarchist reporters also continued to visit Fishers Island, the antithesis of all they stood for, as if drawn by its very menace,. A writer who penned his article under the name "Souvarine" (the Russian anarchist in Émile Zola's novel *Germinal*) described the scene in almost Lovecraftian terms.

> Yesterday I visited a few comrades who work on that island. The sky was dreary, the air heavy, the life dying. The island still had vestiges of formless nature, in spite of their having torn its green canvas, cut into a mess with good taste, like an alcove sitting without love. In contrast with the carefree life of nature, indulgent with speculative attention of human thought, there was the figure of the monstrosity of modern/ancient feudalism.
>
> Exactly true—the monstrosity of ancient feudalism modernized. On its irregular edges as they stand described—joltingly—of the low angularity that they built with arrogance—as fortresses are defined—this surrounding the island like a crown of death.
>
> There the artillery of the government tests their cannons—some fail and millions of dollars are dispersed in the smoke of the shot—others promise well and dream of death.
>
> There the builders of this mess of good taste (casine del buon gusto) sleep in their huts like nomads, make their own sacred ground . . .
>
> In my visit how much hate was breeding in my heart against the criminal speculations of the bourgeois conservatives, how much pity and disgust for those unconscious workers, as primitive as the savages, indifferent to justice, effort, bravery, life of tyranny.
>
> And that ghastly exploitation by the hand of the subcontractors. They need to see how and where they live. The huts are filthy and poorly built where they sleep, eat, cook, wash . . .
>
> The degradation is of a high degree, and you see them passive and resigned as in regular life, I say the truth, because the pity is mixed up with nausea and scorn. Every new word of justice and freedom is mocked, denied. The psyche is dead.

> . . . In the blessed coils of the dead it is to sweep away at one time the vile despots and their vile slaves' faiths.[14]

Fishers Island embodied elements of the capitalist system they detested—militarism, workers reduced to barbarism, nature defaced, and a corrosive corruption that threatened to spread. Three years later a New London anarchist who signed his articles "Kitnis" and was out of work visited the island with a friend in the dead of winter.

> A northeast almost freezing wind blew that impeded even talking. My astonished look when it rested on the marvelous and fertile mansions intended for the delight of the bourgeoisie in the summer. After a certain amount of walking we found ahead the soldiers' quarters. We saw waving from a pole the American flag and saw the sentry like an automatic dummy walking back and forth to combat the cold, the only enemy at that moment. The gloomy aspect of that area, that showed before me a painful impression; and I stayed daydreaming of the coming of an era of peace here; we arrived beneath the fort that on its bastion was an enormous cannon that seemed to wait impatiently for the moment it could test its terrible power . . . And we continued silently, hills, plains, scattered mansions and elegant and exclusive lodges . . . Finally we arrived at our destination. And here was a painful sight of human misery making an enormous contrast to the delightful sight that had been presented before us.
> A group of huts . . . served maybe 150 of our co-nationals, divided into small groups, intended for the work of leveling. But now, for the coldness of the season, they were constricted to laze around. They were without any amusement, nothing to kill time. They abandoned to game, discussing most banal, and most stupid, degraded mostly, things. Unfortunately the major part of them is also immersed in ignorance and superstition; not a glimmer of healthy awakening, no hope of a better future enlivened their hearts. Their one and only goal, to scrape together whatever hundreds of dollars and return to Italy.
> Our ideas amongst them are almost unknown although a few comrades are found here. Facing a soil so arid, rare

comrades are found daring even to attempt to sew our ideas . . . if we dedicate ourselves seriously with love and faith to propaganda of our principles penetrating wherever, we will be redeemed, we won't have to complain of our little progress.[15]

The primitive living conditions and unreceptiveness to radical politics of the Fishers Island laborers greatly disturbed both writers. Another barrier that separated them from Gruppo L'Avvenire but left unspoken was that of regionalism, for assuredly these workers were not Marchegiani. Laborers from peasant backgrounds, not exposed to radicalism, may have been more susceptible to remaining under the dominion of padrones and other future *papas* of the Italian community. The Fanese, with a high proportion of skilled artisans, many of whom had been active in revolutionary movements in the homeland, stood a far better chance of establishing themselves in the American environment with the capability of taking at least some control of their community from the outset. The Fort Trumbull neighborhood provided the key, since the Fanese construction workers would have an increasingly secure haven to which they could return after their extended periods of time on the road. Fort Trumbull served as the ground on which they would shape a warm and fraternal environment, so unlike the solitary desolation represented by Fishers Island.

Many of Fort Trumbull's carpenter artisans would have equally rejected toil in nearby Groton's shipyards, the working conditions of which were the subject of a 1904 article in *Cronaca* titled "An Industrial Prison." The piece described conditions in the shipyard in terms reminiscent of the dawn of the era of the "satanic mills" of England: "In winter (the workers) suffer from intense cold, and in the summer the sun's rays exhaust all." Young boys work despite child labor laws, in "such barbarity . . . You need to see the place where we work, dirty, subject to all the suffering that a human creature could imagine, and working without rest, working in dangerous places putting our lives at risk."[16] Carpenters accustomed to work in the small workshops of a town like Fano would undoubtedly have been repelled by such an oppressive environment.

A few features of Fort Trumbull seem to embody the doctrine of Pierre-Joseph Proudhon, who in the mid-nineteenth century urged a future society based on small producers living in self-sustained communities outside the control of authority. While he was not a revolutionary,

Proudhon's thought continued to influence the anarchist movement (including Galleanists) as it grew and strengthened. Work skills and traditions rather than purposeful design, however, played the far greater role in shaping the neighborhood's employment structure. Even more important, regardless of a deep-set culture of mutual aid, Fort Trumbull remained at the mercy of the business cycle that afflicted the building trades with periodic unemployment.[17]

Local manufacturers who held city government in their tight grip (with Republican factory owners at times serving in municipal political positions) bragged of New London as a progressive, forward-looking metropolis; a pamphlet put out by the Chamber of Congress during the 1920s carried the unlikely title *New London Connecticut: Utopia of the North Atlantic, The Ideal City Winter and Summer*. A publication of the New London Shipyard and Engine Company even touted its safe and clean working environment when it opened its doors in 1916. (For a firm that required much of its work to be done out of doors even in winter, this was quite a stretch.) Fort Trumbull's anarchist value system could not have been more opposed to that adhered to by those who held the levers of power in local politics and industry.[18]

The anarchist militants who composed Gruppo L'Avvenire were under no illusions about their surroundings, and their fellow inhabitants of New London. Popular displays of jingoism, boosterism, and revelries appalled them. They mocked the celebrations that greeted the launching of a massive warship at Eastern Shipbuilding in 1901: "Splendid, magnificent, astonishing! . . . New London was in *festa*. The factories closed, the people eager and merry contemplating the spectacle," everyone ignoring "the hard toil, the sweat, the sacrifices of those poor workers that for two years exhausted their lives to construct the ship."[19] They poured sarcasm on another spectacle, that of a local election.

> Nothing extraordinary—the usual fanaticism, the usual corruption, the usual disgusting cynicism on the part of the canvassers selling the candidates. The taverns were closed that day. 'The voters should put in their ballot with a clear mind,' say the Americans, and then seeing them wander the streets drunk . . . As such were the plastered, the punches and those arrested, finished the election with a Republican victory. It's useless to tell you what measures were used by the politicians: prisoners were released to vote.[20]

The anarchists confronted a myriad of challenges that affected their congealing community. Incidents of violent crime in the streets of Fort Trumbull occurred only on rare occasions, compared to some downtown or "skid row" areas near the waterfront. When a violent incident did break out, it usually became a headline in the daily press. On September 29, 1904, four Sicilians, two of them from New York, entered Fort Trumbull to confront Guerino Menghi, a stonemason who lived among a number of family members on Chelsea Street. The Menghi name was an early one in the Fort, and several of its members often subscribed and donated to the early anarchist press. Guerino had been unsuccessfully courting a young Sicilian woman even after being warned by her brother to stop. After an initial argument, a gun battle erupted in Guerino's house that resulted in his death, and he was described as being "riddled with bullets." The streets of the neighborhood filled with people, with cries for revenge being heard from the crowd. Guerino's sister-in-law burst into a house on Smith Street allegedly shouting, "Come, they have killed Guerino!" Three of the first neighbors to reach the scene were anarchists, including Napoleone Zandri, a militant whose activism dated at least to 1895 back in Fano.[21]

Regionalism does not seem to have been the source of the conflict, since Guerino's brother was already married to the sister of the woman he had pursued. But a group of armed Sicilians having "invaded" the neighborhood had the potential of developing into a dangerous clash. The anarchists recognized this and immediately sought to calm tempers. They observed that the culprits had "fallen into the clutches of the law," but to what avail? "The law and the prisons have existed for centuries, but the wickedness has not disappeared, it will only be destroyed when the people have understood the sublime ideal of anarchy." They mourned the useless loss of workers' blood, and blamed the brutality of "this putrid and accursed society" for "the lack of affection and respect in the working class," causing them to despair of their efforts. Anarchists had to "defend our idea of love, of peace, of equality, we make them penetrate and conquer every environment."[22] Years later, in 1923, a "stabbing and shooting melee in the Fort Neck section" involved two brothers with the last name of Bartolucci. Alfredo and Efisio Bartolucci lost no time in reporting that they, "contractors residing at 42 Central Avenue, are not the Bartolucci brothers involved in the Fort Neck street fight Monday night. The resemblance of names has led to many inquiries and offers of aid to the contractors which they appreciated while regretting that their names were connected even by error with any such occurrence." As anarchists they sought to distance themselves from such needless violence.[23]

Did the anarchists "conquer" the environment of Fort Trumbull? Their effectiveness as a political and social movement is shown by the decades-long lack of rival clubs or societies in the neighborhood. Their anarchist subculture rested on a foundation of skilled artisans and the indispensible economic activities of neighborhood women. A common origin in the Fano area gave homogeneity, and the geographical isolation of Fort Trumbull kept the Italian revolutionaries out of the direct line of sight of prodding authorities. Unlike their comrades in Paterson and other cities, the Fort Trumbull anarchists did not attempt to form mutual benefit societies under their control. The distant workplaces of so many anarchists probably forbade this at first, but later the prevalence of Galleanism placed an ideological barrier in the path as well. Many benefit events took place to assist sick or disabled comrades and their families, but the financial assistance offered would have depended on the economic straits of the neighborhood at any given time.

In the 1905 debate with Galleani, Arturo Caroti criticized the anarchist movement as doing nothing but talk. With New London's group he could have added that they socialized, ate, acted in plays, sang, and danced. Nothing so motivated the comrades, sympathizers, and friends of the Fort Trumbull anarchists than a good party. Social occasions—from picnics to small gatherings in friends' houses—were enthusiastically related in the pages of their papers to a greater extent than lectures, rallies, or debates. Often these festive events combined with speeches from a noted anarchist figure or a business meeting of the group, blending the line between politics and entertainment. Musical and theatrical presentations throughout the decades of the anarchist presence in the Fort were many, and usually had themes of social protest.

These social events have come down to us not only in the pages of their newspapers but in the recollections of the second-, and sometimes third-generation, descendants of the Fort Trumbull anarchists. Memories of the early days of the Italian Dramatic Club (to be discussed in chapter 10) were strong: "In the first days of the new hall, there were plush chairs lined up along the outside walls, the children slept there while the parents danced and partied." They remember the Club for its picnics, Italian plays, concerts, holiday parties, and bocce games; a place for the men to go to talk, and for both parents to dress up for the many special occasions. "I remember as a kid on Sundays that there would be family gatherings at the club," one woman said. "My mother would fill a clothes basket with food, with a traditional Sunday dinner of macaroni, chicken, potatos [sic] and salad, and we'd all go to the club and have a good time." The *festa*, or communal feast, followed by a dance, was by far the most popular group social event in Fort Trumbull from the turn of the century well into the 1960s. Sometimes the *festa* would be accompanied by musical entertainment, and at other times would follow an out-of-town speaker.[24]

Extended families of the anarchists entailed further *festas*, as out-of-town visitors joined the get-togethers. One account describes the "grand outdoor Sunday feasts" hosted by the Camilluccis. Boys would spend the morning catching blue crabs, eels, and flounder and sometimes striped bass from boats in Fishers Island Sound; later, "the men separated and cleaned the catch while the women stuffed blue crabs, grilled and breaded filet of flounder, grilled fresh lobster, eels in tomato sauce . . ." "Endless varieties of fresh vegetables and salads" emerged from Luigi's garden, as Emilia, in the basement kitchen, "captained" the women in "baking and chopping, roasting and peeling, preparing everything they brought."[25]

The Fort never suffered from a lack of talent, whether "comrade Gino playing opera pieces on his clarinet," or Signora Gugliema Paoloni singing in "a beautiful soprano voice," promised the group in an announcement for the affair in *L'Adunata dei Refrattari*. Second-generation Victor Frausini, a bricklayer born in the Fort in 1929, remembered (Leo) "Camillucci" singing at social occasions in the old days, a tradition passed on by Leo's parents Luigi and Emilia Camillucci, who had been active since the early days of Gruppo L'Avvenire. Comrade A. Ghiandoni, a member since 1915 who previously had been active in eastern Massachusetts, performed a comedy routine.[26]

From their earliest days, New London anarchists sponsored theatrical performances. The earliest mention of a drama grouping came in September 1900 as the preparations were made for Gori's *Primo Maggio*. Most of the performances appear to have been ad hoc, with members and sympathizers of the group filling in when needed. But they also formed amateur theatrical companies such as the semi-independent Circolo Filodrammatica di New London, which, as discussed, ended on a sour note. The groups relied on their own efforts to put on plays and skits. Only in 1916 did they get around to organizing a theatrical company of their own, when the group announced the formation of the

Filodrammatica I Liberi. The names of nearly a score of plays performed in New London between 1903 and 1936 have been preserved. Of these, two, *La Canaglia* by Mario Gino and *Il Viandante e L'eroe* by F. Vezzani were anarchist plays performed by other groups around the country. Two others, one written in 1846, appear to be historical protest plays, and I have not been able to identify several others. According to Marcella Bencivenni, many of the plays that emanated from these radical circles have been lost. During the 1930s, two of the plays performed in New London focused on the effect of fascism on Italian society.[27]

Radical theater comprised an important part of the subculture built by the *sovversivi* across the United States. While they performed classic theater as well, most of the plays had positive, uplifting messages about the struggles of the working class and the dawn of a new society. Throughout the history of New London's anarchist movement, audiences seem to have been genuinely affected by the performances, since they were usually done in company with poetry, song, and speeches. Sometimes the messages of the plays were connected to the swirl of events in the world, such as the powerful and politically charged play performed by I Liberi's group, *Militarismo e Miseria* (Militarism and Poverty), in April 1917, and only days before the United States declaration of war on Germany. The antiwar play drew a large, enthusiastic audience composed of "every political color" to experience "apostolic education, with libertarian pride." Comrade Atillio Pierfederici played the part of Liberio with "exquisite touch," while "comrades [Fortunato] Renzoni in the part of the peasant, [Atillio] Pasqualini in that of the lawyer, [possibly Antonio] Centoscudi in the part of the revolutionary soldier and *signora* Ferro as Angelica interpreted well as they were assigned."[28]

The picnic became the most important out-of-doors event for New London anarchist groups, as well as for Italian radical circles across the United States. Most were held at Leverone's Grove in Waterford, about a mile down Boston Post Road from Fort Trumbull. Antone Leverone, its owner, had briefly been active in the anarchist movement in New London, and his Grove would become a familiar destination for working-class New Londoners, its landmark being known as "Station Seven" on the Shore Line Electric Railway, and later renamed Woodland Grove, where local professional baseball teams played (currently the site of the Woodland Trailer Park).

Dozens of anarchist picnics, or as the groups sometimes called them *feste rural*, were held here from 1909, when the park opened, until at least the end of the 1930s—the vast majority of these events being held on the July 4 and Labor Day holidays. Their preference for these two decidedly nonradical holidays could only have stemmed from being able to allow full participation from the many building trades comrades who often worked out of town, and others who needed time off for the holiday to make it to the events. The picnics at Leverone's Grove offered a gamut of activities to attract members and sympathizers, including music, such as the Colonial Orchestra of Hartford, as well as games, races, food, and drinks. A pavilion in the middle of a large field provided protection from inclement weather, while the surrounding woods shielded children from the prying eyes of parents. Anarchists from Westerly, Mystic, Old Saybrook, and other nearby towns usually attended; numbers were never given, but attendance probably reached into the hundreds. The first picnic at Leverone's was "challenged by rain (but) we stayed until nine at night in the best of company—talking, how to develop our propaganda." The next year, "It was pleasing to see reunited so many old and new comrades (they came in good numbers from Westerly) and to enjoy a day of pure joy." They reciprocated by attending a joint Westerly/Mystic picnic, where "a comrade from New London . . . read rebel poetry."[29]

The "Italians of New London Oral History Collection" at the Dodd Research Center at UCONN, contains a video titled "Interview of Italian Dramatic Club Dinner's Male Cooks & Interview of Individuals Present & Old Photos on Bulletin Board." Much of the tape is taken up with panoramic shots of a pasta dinner in the hall in the late 1990s, with the pasta being cooked, served, and consumed.[30] It is clear that this is a well-preserved tradition and one that is open to those of non-Fanese descent who are lucky enough to receive an invitation. They are indeed proud of the reputation of their pasta. These monthly dinners, and perhaps even the pasta recipe, have their origin in the Fort Trumbull anarchist movement of the early twentieth century. Their *festas*, or communal feasts, took place all year round for decades. The group held one in March 1927, for which they promised in *L'Adunata dei Refrattari* "refreshments with spaghetti—the sauce of 2 or 3 cooks from Chicago: Sussur, Merlotto and Palombaro." These are pseudonyms, and in giving their appreciation after the affair, the group gave "thanks to all, especially cooks Merlotto and Palombaro." Spaghetti was again promised, along with the Colonial Orchestra, at the July 4 celebration at Leverone's, and also at that year's New Year's festivities, "with the usual spaghetti cooked by the two special cooks."[31]

The name "Palombaro," which translates as "deep sea diver," had shown up in a New London subscription list to *La Questione Sociale* in 1903, and resurfaced again in 1912 in the Nazzarene Benvenuti embezzlement affair of 1910, which resulted in the split of Benvenuti with Gruppo L'Avvenire and longtime member Enrico Broccoli leaving town for a while. Viscardo Broccoli and "Palombaro" had given salutations to Bargnesi the embezzler in 1912. Now, fifteen years later, Palombaro/Enrico Broccoli was again tweaking the nose of Benvenuti—the identification as "Chicago cooks" is probably linked to Bargnesi's having announced that city as his flight destination.

What actual role Enrico had in the Benvenuti-Bargnesi affair is uncertain, but he clearly had a sense of humor. Born in Fano in April 1868, Broccoli had immigrated in 1896, worked on Fishers Island in the very early days and later aligned himself with the iconoclastic Foschini in 1905. Broccoli never married and worked as a construction laborer throughout his life, rooming with fellow laborer and anarchist Riccardo Lombardozzi at 6 Chelsea Street. (Lombardozzi, the brother of Anselmo, had an Italian government dossier on him from 1929 to 1939.) Broccoli's legacy is literally carved in stone—his tombstone in Waterford's Jordan Cemetery reading "Enrico Broccoli, 'Palombaro,' April 29, 1868–February 9, 1950." The origin and meaning of his nickname, however, will probably remain a mystery.[32]

At times the groups tried to target specific sectors of the community. To encourage an anarchist youth group, several militants hired the Armstrong Hall on Bank Street and an orchestra: "The suffocating heat that is proper for July reigned exactly the night of last Sunday . . . without a murmur of wind or fresh air introduced, for the hall full of dancing couples, perspiring like doing heavy and tiring work."[33]

"In the house of Camillucci among comrades" described an event from 1923 that the group felt deserved mention in the pages of their papers—that of simply socializing and relaxing with friends. Sometimes parties held in each other's houses had themes that reflected their views on the need for a social revolution in the family. One house party held for the Batellis focused on that family's decision to baptize their baby without the interference of the church. It became a celebration with music, where "we were entertained until a late hour, ten at night, lying around the house of friend Battelli and surrounded by the most beautiful vegetable plot where this scorching heat was better than in paradise."[34]

The group performed its own wedding ceremonies: "Celebrating the union without the black pig [priest] of comrades A. Paci and Irene Tarini. The comrades of New London recommending the healing anarchist propaganda of the Cronaca." Some of the anticlerical attitudes of the group have been preserved in the memories of the second generation: "People don't recall ever seeing a priest in the neighborhood, not even for a wake . . . There were those who had more extreme feelings against religion. They were anti-clerical and they rejected the church completely, even for special family occasions." They remembered "the existence of a few long-term common law relationships at the Fort." A story of the Fort's hostility to religion that has been passed down among New London Italians concerns a father of the bride refusing to enter St. Joseph's Church for the ceremony.[35]

Excepting the baptisms and weddings, none of these social occasions neglected a primary aim for the group: fund-raising. From the earliest days the anarchist press received the vast majority of monies raised in these efforts. All anarchist papers depended on the small donations of their working-class subscribers, and since very few of them accepted advertisements they carried heavy and relentless deficits. "The Deficit" raised its head from the pages as if it were enemy number one of the anarchist movement, and many a meeting focused on this never-solved problem. While *La Questione Sociale*, *Cronaca*, and *L'Adunata* received the overwhelming majority of donations from the collections, the anarchists spread the funding out as wide as possible. At least twenty-five anarchist papers, two of them English-language American anarchist papers, and about half of them published in Italy or France, received financial support.

The next most important destinations for New London's funding were militants who came under attack by the state, and for workers on strike. The largest single collection took place when eighty-one names of people giving donations to aid the striking cigar workers of Tampa, Florida, appeared in *Cronaca* in December 1910. The list includes comrades and friends, including some nonpolitical neighbors in Fort Trumbull. The New London movement always considered itself tied directly to events in Italy, and in the Marche particularly. It made no difference whether the jailed comrade lived in New York or Ancona. They raised money for "the arrested of Boston," for "the incarcerated of Milwaukee," for "the victims of fascism," for "the Colorado strikers," for "the political victims in Italy," and for "the action groups in France."[36]

Fort Trumbull anarchists succeeded in creating a climate of solidarity and mutual aid in the neighborhood, with practices spilling over into their nonanarchist neighbors. This does not, of course, mean that personal and social crises were nonexistent in the neighborhood. Conflicts between residents occurred in Fort Trumbull as they did elsewhere, sometimes resulting in violence. Money was always short in the Fort, regardless of how effective their innovative work relationships were in alleviating some of the harsher effects of periods of unemployment. Historians of Italian American radicalism, notably Marcella Bencevenni, have recently stressed the centrality of culture to the movement, especially its anarchist wing, "beyond the narrow confines of the workplace." Without Fort Trumbull's artisan-based employment structure, however, it is unlikely that the neighborhood's rebel stance could have endured as long as it did. Carpenters and stonemasons made possible, or constructed, literally, the base on which shared traditions from Fano flourished. The subculture created by the neighborhood's anarchists rested on preexisting familial and regional networks: families providing a safety net for migrating members, family members stepping in to sustain household income during hard times, and local shop owners consistently offering credit when economic conditions did not permit neighbors to pay with cash.[37]

The reigning social and political climate severely tested the subculture of the anarchists. They would not go unchallenged—including from forces that originated within the neighborhood. The opposition the anarchists faced in the 1920s developed for several reasons. First, the vision of social revolution faded as the left was forced on the defensive at close of World War I. Second, Galleanist practices often did not help matters, and put the beleaguered anarchists at odds with a growing number of people in the community. Finally, those who challenged Gruppo I Liberi for leadership of the neighborhood were a part of the shift within American society throughout the decade that doomed any attempt to sustain radical ethnic enclaves. As will be seen, however, when the Italian Mutual Aid Society was formed in 1921, this "opponent" group remained—at least in the beginning—within the orbit of the Italian left. This was a reflection of the durability of the Fort Trumbull anarchist movement that did not fade away, but remained a strong force with a large core of dedicated militants, even at the end of the decade.

In *The Visit of Malatesta*, O'Neill placed a passage in his notes for the character loosely based on the real Malatesta after he viewed the scene in fictional New London. Utopia was unattainable until humans outgrew their "base greed," he wrote. Only the lust for power could arise from movements unless men and women gained control of their own natures.[38] This pessimistic outlook reflects the cynicism that O'Neill felt toward social movements and those active within them. Is it an accurate observation concerning the values of Fort Trumbull anarchism into the 1920s? Even with the manifold trials facing the anarchists—members who had become wealthy contractors and let their radicalism slip, personal fights within the neighborhood, a workforce that traveled for a considerable part of the year, a damaging internal battle that paralyzed the group—it is possible to say that a subculture based on solidarity and fraternity had been built in Fort Trumbull, one that both fended off and absorbed these challenges to the anarchist ideal. It was not a simple creation, but rather like a Hegelian unity of opposites. It reflected the complicated personalities and motives of the Marta Dondero's, Rafaelle Petrini's, Vittorio Federici's, and Luigi Camillucci's that constructed it. Anarchists forged it with the "men (and women) in the flesh" on hand, and under enormous pressure. Like the quintessential anarchist rebel, the neighborhood embodied the values of opposed culture systems. It rejected but lived within and alongside of the greater society beyond the boundaries of the Fort.

CHAPTER NINE

ANARCHISTS AT WAR

Although *Cronaca Sovversiva* had not officially been outlawed until July 18, 1918, postal authorities denied its publishers the use of mailing privileges a year earlier. The authorities found that the paper continued to be distributed in bundles to groups of supporters across the country by American Express. Subscription lists and information on the paper's distribution network fell into government hands during the raids by local police and the Bureau of Investigation. In Connecticut, the Bureau reported to its agents that the paper had three distribution points. In Hartford, Girolamo Grasso, a longtime Galleanist and a machinist by trade, picked up the bundles. In New Haven, Circolo Pietro Gori received the papers. In New London, two individuals—Fortunato Renzoni and Ernesto Perella—had the responsibility of seeing that the paper reached its readers. On investigation, agents found the paper bundles being signed for by Renzoni and members of the Menghi family. Renzoni also had taken charge of collections for "our persecuted," those Galleanists and others who faced prison or deportation.[1]

The Renzoni connection has a dramatic character of its own. Renzoni, twenty-seven years old, had been around the group since 1910, and had previously caught the attention of the authorities, but not for his anarchist activities. Stocky and standing five feet tall, Renzoni had worked for the Hopson & Chase Manufacturing Company as a molder before plant closed. He tried to find work in Waterbury but had to move back to New London, where he was given a job by Antone Menghi, a masonry contractor and brother of Querino, who had been killed in a Fort Trumbull shootout in 1904 (discussed in chapters 8 and 13). In

1915, though broke and in debt, Renzoni relentlessly courted Antone's seventeen-year-old daughter Rose. Antone would have none of it, and after a violent altercation on Smith Street, Renzoni fired three shots from his pistol at Antone at point-blank range. He missed. Despite fleeing the city, no charges seem to have been pressed against Renzoni. Even more implausibly, within a short period of time Fortunato and Rose were married and living at the Menghi house at 90 Smith Street. The Bureau investigating agent mistakenly reported that the local anarchist "circle" met at this address. The relationship of the Menghi's—a somewhat large family with connections to the wider Italian community of New London—to Gruppo I Liberi is unclear, but the family included a number of anarchist friends and sympathizers.[2]

Ernesto Perella, born in Caserta province in the Campania region, had apparently served as correspondence secretary for an Italian anarchist group in Frankfort, Maine, that gravitated toward *Cronaca Sovversiva*. Frankfort was an isolated granite quarry town in the midcoastal region of the state, not far from Stonington, where Petrini had lived. Perella had most likely worked in one of the quarries on Mount Waldo and not been very impressed by the stark beauty of the local landscape, referring to it in an article as "desolate northern moors." He moved to southeastern Connecticut in 1911, first to Mystic and then Waterford, before living at 8 Hamilton Street in New London, most likely as a boarder. He was twenty-five years old, single and had also worked as a stonecutter for Booth Brothers Granite Company in Waterford. His name appears in Cronaca in 1914, for having helped organize a conference in Worcester, Massachusetts, between Galleanist groups in that state on the subject of the war and the anarchist press, and he traveled to Barre, Vermont, to play a role in anarchist disputes there. A hard-core Galleanist, judging from two analytical articles he contributed to *Cronaca*, Perella had been important enough to be included by the US government with the dozen or so key militants to be deported with Galleani in May 1919. He may initially have attracted the attention of the federal government when he registered as a conscientious objector to the draft in 1917, but it is more likely that his key role in both Gruppo I Liberi and the Galleanist movement in New England placed a target on his back. His correspondence with Raffaele Schiavina, publisher of *Cronaca*, became the property of the Bureau of Investigation after the 1917 raids on the paper's office in Lynn. In one letter Perella remarked, "You can comprehend how I had to work like four people."[3]

The war came home for New London anarchists on the morning and afternoon of May 15, 1918, when local police, on orders of Acting United States Commissioner Stockwell in Boston, took into custody Renzoni and Perella. Their arrests were part of a New England roundup of anarchists, eighty in all, described by Paul Avrich as "dedicated Galleanists." The arrests aimed at finally suppressing *Cronaca Sovversiva*.[4] Both New London militants posted bond, with Renzoni being "paroled." It was a different matter for Perella, who found his name on the initial deportation list that included Galleani, the Sanchini's of New Britain and others of the movement's hard core. The government failed to issue a final writ of deportation for Perella, resulting in not a little confusion among government agencies; Perella, however, was taking no chances. He jumped bail and disappeared. The Bureau began a manhunt that took them to a quarry town in Maine, but to no avail. In December 1920 he remained at large.

On May 15, 1918, in nearby Providence, Rhode Island, the Bureau raided the premises of the clubhouse of the Karl Marx Circle, a group formed at the turn of the century as a branch of the SLP. By 1908 the Circle had evolved into a base for the IWW, with a cooperative, bookstore and periodical, *Ragione Nuova*, closely aligned with it. The Circle provided a visible target for the authorities, with four members arrested and a large quantity of literature seized, including papers destined for the anarchist quarry workers in Westerly.[5] Things quickly heated up in New England. The bloody confrontation that took place in September 1917 in Milwaukee between police and local anarchists moved the Galleanists toward their bombing campaigns of 1919. It began in New Britain, Connecticut. Seventeen-year-old Gabriella Antolini, known simply as Ella, and her husband Augusto Segata, boarded a train in that city and eventually reached their destination of Youngstown, Ohio on the following day. On January 15, 1918, they met two men, one of them being Carlo Valdinoci. The other, probably Mario Buda, handed Ella a black valise containing thirty-six sticks of dynamite. She was to take it to Chicago, from where it would be delivered for use in Milwaukee. The next day, Valdinoci boarded the Chicago-bound train with Ella, but got off. Somehow a train porter became suspicious and searched the valise, and Ella was arrested when she disembarked from the train. While she eventually received a sentence of eighteen months on transportation charges, her arrest alerted the federal government to the existence of the "dynamite conspiracy" of Galleanist anarchists.[6]

Events in New London occurred in a mounting cycle of war, revolution, and repression that followed each other in rapid succession. Connecticut, with its numerous industrial cities and towns with working-class populations of Russians, Poles, Hungarians, Lithuanians, Italians, and others of the "new immigrant" wave became well represented on the map of American radicalism. The state's vibrant, contentious Italian radical movement appeared on the stage as thousands of Italian workers engaged in tumultuous mass strikes in the Naugatuck valley brass industry in 1919 and 1920. Of seventeen thousand strikers in the 1920 struggle, four thousand were Italians. Although led by a previously nonpolitical worker and fairly recent immigrant named Luigi Scalmana, the strike had clear syndicalist overtones. The New England Workers Association decisively rejected leadership from the AFL. While they remained independent of the IWW as well, they contributed to a fund for Italian political prisoners in America and proved receptive to radical speakers.[7]

Italian workers in the Naugatuck Valley joined thousands of Lithuanian, Polish, Russian, and Ukrainian immigrants who had been radicalized by industrial conditions in the brass mills and the rising wave of revolution in Europe that the coming to power of the Bolshevik Party in Russia had inspired. Connecticut became the base of large, sprawling revolutionary (left) socialist and anarcho-syndicalist movements that experienced an explosive growth. Cities like Ansonia rocked with strikes and mass meetings of immigrant workers carrying red flags. In the fall of 1919, an agent of the Bureau of Investigation sat in on an Italian anarchist meeting in that town held in the "Russian hall." He reported an enthusiastic reception for the Paterson-based speaker who he identified as Giuseppe Ciancabilla who, as it was, had been dead for fifteen years. The agent had apparently taken Ciancabilla's name from the titles of pamphlets for sale on the literature table.[8]

These industrial conflicts of immigrant workers in Connecticut also took place during a period of revolutionary uprisings in Italy, which culminated in the occupation of factories under the leadership of left socialists, syndicalists, and anarchists. A nascent Red Guard formation appeared to defend the workers against attacks from police and the rising fascist movement. Many Italian workers in Connecticut welcomed these developments enthusiastically. Italians in Wallingford gathered to send off comrade D. Gatti, who planned to return to his town of "Red Mirandola" in the Emilia-Romagna region, an area heavily represented by local Italian immigrants, and one at the forefront of the revolutionary wave known as the *biennio rosso*—two red years. "We say farewell to our beloved comrade, wish him a good voyage and good stay in the new, redeemed Italy. Fervent greetings to the red Mirandolese, hoping that they remember the American movement and the many political and industrial victims in jail, that they be conscious of this among the strong houses of labor of the Modenese. Make a good agitation for them." New Haven syndicalists of the Circolo Francesco Ferrer responded to local meetings of the nationalist *prominenti* by citing their admiration for the occupation of the factories in the north, and the land occupations in Sicily and Calabria, and saluted "red Puglia, extremist Tuscany and communist Romagna."[9]

Immigrants from Fano, Pesaro and Castelvecchio, a town about ten miles south of Fano, composed the membership of the Circolo Ferrer. In 1921–1922, they contributed to papers such as *Bandiera Rossa* and *Progresso Comunista*, both published in Fano by the local branch of the newly formed Communist Party of Italy. They hailed the Bolshevik Revolution in Russia, supported the IWW, and urged on Italian workers' groups such as the *Arditi del Popolo* and the *squadre d'azione comuniste* in the fight against the gangsterism of the fascists, who had been "scraped together from the shallows of the social puddles."[10] To the authorities, the Circolo Ferrer represented their worst nightmare: the coming together of previously fractured radical trends as the postwar revolutionary wave crested.

Just prior to their deportation, Galleani and Schiavina made final speaking tours, the former through Connecticut and Rhode Island, and the latter through Connecticut, Massachusetts, New York, and New Jersey. Both spoke in New London, a final farewell for Galleani (Schiavina would reenter the country illegally). *Cronaca Sovversiva*, still being circulated by the underground distribution network, observed that the tour found "new interest more vast" among "proletarian immigrants," a hopeful sign they felt, as the trapdoor of political repression slammed shut on them. This issue of the paper would be its last.[11]

Back in Italy, Galleani and his closest followers threw themselves into the country's raging struggles; Galleani restarted *Cronaca Sovversiva* in Turin, while Giobbe Sanchini, returning to his native Pesaro province, began publishing *La Frusta* (The Whip). Beginning with its May 1, 1920 issue, *La Frusta* came out of Fano; when Italian authorities suppressed *Cronaca Sovversiva* in October, the Fanese paper took on added importance as one of the few anti-organizational organs of Italian anarchism in the world. It reached thirty US cities and received contributions of "fundamental importance" from Galleanists there. The paper grew steadily until September 1922, reaching a circulation of four thousand. In November 1921, Ella Antolini, the former friend and comrade of the Giobbe and Irma Sanchini in New Britain, wrote for the Galleanists in Detroit after her release from prison to urge that *La Frusta* be adopted by anarchists in the United States as the "only voice of us anti-organizationals," and be financially strengthened and converted to a weekly.[12]

In November 1920, the wave of troop mutinies and uprisings that started in Ancona reached Fano, described by *La Frusta* as "the reddest city in the province," with hundreds of *sovversivi* and the majority of the population anticlerical. In the same month, Fanese living in New Haven sent a 500 lira donation to the paper, and anarchists in New Britain sent salutations to Gaetano Lombardozzi, who had moved back to the Pesaro province.[13]

Connecticut radicals became major targets of federal, state, and local authorities in their war on leftists of every stripe in 1919 and 1920. The press, along with government at both local and state levels, proved incapable of distinguishing between these radical trends. After the police picked up Perella and Renzoni in New London, the press described the two as "anarchists with German tendencies and of the bitterest type." Because they worked in the shipyard and lived in Fort Neck "adjacent to Fort Trumbull, the coast guard quarters and not far from the naval experiment station," they allegedly presented "a menace to the government and would have done damage to ship or yard, where employed, or some other points, at the first opportunity." The press warned that, "There are said to be several more anarchists in this neighborhood," and "they would be rounded up in short order."[14]

New London did not experience as tumultuous a strike wave as did other cities in Connecticut such as Waterbury, Ansonia, Bridgeport, and Hartford, but transportation nearly ground to a halt in the area when trolleymen and railroad shop workers struck. Trades such as local barbers and tailors went out in an effort to improve their wages and a host of factories along the southeastern Connecticut coast saw strike activity as well. Under the heading "Radical Activities—Connecticut District," the Bureau of Investigation noted the spread of strikes in New London to freight handlers on the Central Vermont Railroad and the state pier. Employer nervousness increased through the summer of 1919, as the planned, normally ritualistic New London Labor Day parade threatened to become a massive demonstration of support for striking workers.[15]

In an atmosphere of growing backlash toward the militant labor movement—with immigrants from Southern and Eastern Europe often at the forefront—the anarchists of Fort Trumbull came under increasing scrutiny from the authorities. This occurred during the period between the suppression of *Cronaca Sovversiva* and before the advent of that paper's successor, *L'Adunata dei Refrattari*. During normal times, anarchist groups supplied details of their activities in the pages of their press; now, however, police agency reports and daily newspaper reports must fill the information gap.

In late January 1919, the first of three inflammatory flyers issued by the Galleanist movement titled "Go-Head!" appeared throughout New England, and was a response to the initial deportation orders issued against Galleani and his closest circle.

GO-HEAD!

The senile fossils ruling the United States see red!
Smelling their destruction, they have decided to check
the storm by passing the Deportation law affecting all
foreign radicals.

We, the American anarchists, do not protest, for it is
Futile to waste any energy on feeble minded creatures led
By His Majesty Phonograph Wilson.

Do not think that only foreigners are anarchists, we
Are a great number right here at home.

Deportation will not stop the storm from reaching
These shores. The storm is within and very soon will leap
And crash and annihilate you in blood and fire.

You have shown no pity to us! We will do likewise.

And deport us! We will dynamite you!

Either deport us or free all!

The American Anarchists[16]

New London displayed the leaflets conspicuously, the Bureau of Investigation reporting that on the night of January 27, they were "pasted upon the public buildings and the trolley poles and electric light poles throughout the city." The "Go-Head" warning consisted of a sticker with glue on the back that could easily be affixed to surfaces by wetting them. The wide area of distribution throughout the city convinced the police and press that an out-of-town gang had been responsible: "That there is any camp & meeting place for Anarchists in this city is doubted." A month later, Naval Intelligence operatives searched the house of Raffaele Arace, a barber at 342 Bank Street, confiscating anarchist literature in English and Italian. Whether Arace had any connection with Gruppo I Liberi is not clear, but the coordinated nature of the "Go-Head" flyer activity should have indicated to authorities that they were not dealing with isolated individuals in New London.[17]

The *New London Day* reported on June 5 that the paper had received a "Bolshevik threat" through the mail. "Is there a Bolshevik organization in New London?" the paper asked. If the editors had been following national news developments, they might not have confused anarchists for Bolsheviks. The warning read,

> Do justice to all sides when you publish anything about controversy or something terribile happen to you be WISE.

A clue as to who was responsible for the flyer could be found in the Italian spelling of the word *terrible*. The threat came sandwiched between a mail bomb campaign in May and national coordinated bombing action on June 2—both by Galleanists—who targeted US government officials and political figures connected with the suppression of *Cronaca Sovversiva* and the deportation of Luigi Galleani and his closest supporters, which took place on June 24. Enclosed with the New London threat, the writing of which was "scrawly and in lead pencil," was a clipping from the *New York Evening Journal* that drew attention to the leaflet found at scene of the bombings titled "Plain Words." This flyer became the centerpiece of the Federal government's campaign to capture the bombers, who the Bureau of Investigation came to believe were Italian anarchists. Their successful penetration of anarchist circles in the northeast and subsequent arrest of two members of the New York Galleanist movement led to what some observers feel was the seven-year-long Sacco-Vanzetti ordeal.

The plain envelope that the *Day* received had been mailed at the local post office. "Plain Words" was a militant call-to-arms couched in extreme language similar to that of "Go-Head!" and the *Day* published it in full. The following excerpt captures its warlike tone:

> The jails, the dungeons you reared to bury all protesting voices are now replenished with languishing conscientious workers and, never satisfied, you increase their number every day . . . There will have to be bloodshed: we will not dodge; there will have to be murder; we will kill because it is necessary . . . We are ready to do anything to suppress the capitalist class, just as you are doing to suppress the proletarian revolution.[18]

The next day the paper carried a small article affirming that "Ernesto R. Penella," on the list for deportation with the unnamed Galleani, could not be found in the city directory, "and there is no record of the arrest of any such person at the police department."[19]

Galleanists spread their message across the small towns of New England where they had supporters, including nearby Westerly. A number of granite firms in that Rhode Island town owned by Italians had grown to importance, including one owned by Joseph Coduri, a former subscriber to the Italian radical press and father of Charles Coduri, a pioneer anarchist in the New London area. In 1919 the Bureau of Investigation paid Coduri a visit after a flyer titled "To the Working People of America" appeared in area quarries. The flyer saluted the revolutionary wave sweeping Europe and called on workers to arm themselves: "You alone do not budge. Are you afraid to follow their example? Are you afraid to take by force what rightly belongs to you?" Signed "A Group of Working Men," it appeared several days after a failed attempt by Galleanists to dynamite a struck textile mill in Franklin, Massachusetts. Four Italian anarchists died in a premature explosion. This broadside has not been discussed by historians, though it certainly was a product of the same authors of "Go-Head" and "Plain Words." It differs from the latter two in that "To the Working People of America" addresses workers directly, but displays a complete disconnect between the strategy of the Galleanists and the prevailing mind-set of the US labor movement.[20]

If the police and press still remained unaware of the strong Galleanist cohort existing one or two trolley stops from downtown New London, they could be excused for missing another clue a bit later. Shortly after midnight on July 21, Special Railroad Officers Roach and Greene noticed activity around a freight car in the New Haven road yard in Fort Trumbull. For the past few months, freight cars of the New Haven and Central Vermont Railroad had been robbed by a gang of thieves. Peering inside, they discovered three men moving boxes to the door. The three tried to flee but an altercation developed. One of the robbers struck Greene with an object, causing him to call out to Roach, who was tangling with the other two. As a result, the two officers ganged up on the robber who had struck Greene, subduing him and allowing the other two to escape. At the police station, the thief was identified as Victor Frederick, who lived on Smith Street, where he operated a grocery/confectionary store. Frederick, the officers noted, had called out to his fellow robbers in Italian. The object with which he struck the officer was a special army type .38 caliber Colt revolver, and he also had carried a knife with an eight-inch blade. Frederick refused to identify his companions, so the two officers returned to the neighborhood to search for them. In Frederick's store and house they found what they tentatively identified as some of the items missing from the freight cars. The police were sure that in capturing Frederick they had caught the head of the gang, but his cohorts successfully slipped away.

They may have caught the gang's leader, but they had also apprehended a militant member of Gruppo I Liberi, Vittorio Federici, under the Americanized name he would use for the rest of his life. The gang robbery of the local yard represented part of a growing and expensive national trend for the railroads. Robberies of goods in transit that had cost railroads under two million dollars in 1914 rose to thirty million dollars in 1917. Freight cars in urban railyards presented a vulnerable target to a diverse collection of thieves: urban youths, ethnic gangs, and railroad employees. The organized gangs, called "land pirates and vandals" by one private security figure, presented the greatest threat.[21] The question, though, is why an Italian anarchist would be involved in such a matter.

The Galleanists, as has been shown, belonged to a wing of the anarchist movement that justified individual acts of terror or violence that were aimed at the oppressors: kings, capitalists, and others. Galleani also defended robberies, or individual expropriations, carried out by revolutionaries. He held that "besides the material advantages for the movement, it (expropriation) initiates, enables, and encourages the multitude to proceed to the final expropriation of the ruling class for the benefit of everyone. This has been our desire and our aim."[22] More obscure for historians has been the actual relationship of Galleanists with armed expropriations, such as bank robberies and thefts like the one for which Federici was nabbed. "The most distinguishing aspect of expropriationism among Italian anarchists in the United States," wrote Nunzio Pernicone, "was its almost complete absence. The only Italian-American *espropriatore* about whom anarchist literature has anything to say is Cesare Stami, a wild individualist anarchist (not a Galleanista)." According to Paul Avrich, "Stami and his gang of expropriators carried out holdups in Pennsylvania, Ohio and West Virginia, as well as of a bank in Detroit."

Stami may have been a wild man, but he had extensive connections with the wider Italian anarchist movement. He spoke publicly in New York and contributed a number of articles to *Cronaca*, especially in the paper's final years, and was listed among "Gli Ostaggi" (The Hostages) in 1918, as one sought by the government as a distributor of the paper. He also spoke in western Connecticut in 1916 to both Galleanists and syndicalist-oriented groups. According to Bureau of Investigation informer Eugenio Ravarini, Stami had been involved in insurance scams in New York, apparently with criminal elements. In 1924, Stami and several of his men were killed in a train holdup gone bad in Pennsylvania.[23] The only other account that connects Italian American anarchists with robberies, I believe, is an interview by Paul Avrich with the son of a Pesaro-province-born anarchist who was a member of the important Gruppo Libertà of Needham, Massachusetts: "Some anarchists . . . robbed freight cars in Framingham and other towns. I knew the guys who did it. They're all dead now."[24]

Many anarchists, especially those in the tradition of Malatesta and Merlino, strongly opposed individual expropriations carried out by the anti-organizationists, especially those in Europe, where several mostly Paris-based groups were active. They argued that these acts inevitably corrupted revolutionaries who often personally benefited from the robberies. The most famous of these groups, the Bonnot gang, operated between 1911 and 1912 in Paris, and pulled off a number of heists (using an automobile for the first time) before being killed in clashes with the police, executed by guillotine, or sent to prison. The gang seemed motivated as much by the egoistic philosophy of Max Stirner and the will to power ideas of Friedrich Nietzsche as by revolutionary anarchism. An Italian group called L'Anonimato operated out of London and Paris during the 1890s; champions of individualist anarchism, they vilified Malatesta and Merlino.[25]

The "personal benefit" aspect initially seemed to be the case with the New London freight car break-in of July 19, 1919. The two railroad detectives that night found "a large wooden box containing a large amount of candy and a 75 pound bag of coffee beside the railroad tracks," as well as similar merchandise in Frederick/Federici's home and store. Frederick went to trial in Norwich Superior Court in September 1919; it took a jury fifteen minutes to render a guilty verdict. A judge sentenced him to two to five years in the state prison in Wethersfield.[26]

In 1921, Detective Roach traveled to Worcester, Massachusetts, to identify one of the escaped thieves of the July 1919 New London robbery. Pietro Facendo and five other Italians were on trial in that city for being part of a gang robbing railroad cars of cotton, cloth, boots, and shoes in Connecticut, Rhode Island, and Massachusetts. The "Fort Neck," or Fort Trumbull robberies over a period of several months had targeted woolen goods, not candy or coffee. On the night of July 19 the latter may have been taken, but the principal target of the robberies appears to have been the products of New England factories, in line with the Massachusetts gang. Facendo and his confederates had also been involved in "liquor running." The scale of the operations, taken together with his future endeavors, makes it plausible that Frederick used some of the income to fund the anarchist movement. Freight car robbery required skill and preparation on the part of the gangs: "From the spotting of the shipments at the point of origination to the last step in making the delivery to the 'fence,' the operation required careful planning and the assignment of every active member to his post."[27]

Several prominent Italian residents in New London became factors in the affair. Charles Satti, the nephew of one of the earliest Italian immigrants in New London by the same name who came to the United States in 1876 from Tuscany, worked as a railroad detective in Worcester. Satti infiltrated the jail where Facendo and company were being held and, posing as a prisoner, engaged the incarcerated rail thief and gained the above information. He found that Facendo had previously lived in New London and had tended bar in the saloon of Antone Leverone—owner of Leverone's Grove—on Golden Street. A "Pietro Facendi" living at 50 Winthrop Street is probably the same person. On his draft registration card, he superimposed the *i* and *o* in his signature of the last letter in *Facendo*. Thirty-four years old, his wife Letizia still lived in Pesaro province in the Marche, so Facendo/Facendi was probably from the same area. However, the name does not appear in the anarchist press connected with New London.[28]

Victor Frederick served fewer than three years of his five-year sentence, being released shortly before February 1922, and, a newspaper article claimed, he "is believed to have been an aid to the authorities in further cleaning up of the crime." It is questionable whether he served as an informer; he actively supported Gruppo I Liberi throughout the 1920s, with his name appearing in L'Adunata dei Refrattari at least five times. Within months of Frederick's release from prison, state police arrested him in Niantic for bootlegging. Freed after posting $2,000 in sureties, Victor Frederick was only getting started.[29]

It is extraordinary that at no time during Frederick's freight car robbing career did the daily press connect him to the Italian anarchist movement, and this in spite of an abundance of intelligence information on him. The Italian government had their eyes on him as early as 1910, when police files reported his patronage of the saloon of Fred Dondero, "a noted anarchist." Charles Satti—who must have been clued in to the politics of the Italian community in New London—could have raised a flag. But above all, the Bureau of Investigation was well aware of who Frederick was, and their information came from a local policeman named Hammond. In a report titled "Victor Frederick: Undesirable Alien," BI Agent J. W. R. Chamberlain said that according to Hammond, Frederick was "active with the radical Italian element in New London. He stated that this man has an automobile from which on various occasions he has used a red sweater as an improvised flag." "I shall endeavor," promised Chamberlain, "to procure further information relative to the activities of subject with a view to future deportation." Indeed, Chamberlain's report on Frederick landed his suspect on a rather exclusive list of Connecticut radicals "as subjects for prospective deportation." Russian anarcho-syndicalists and socialists composed the vast majority on the list of seventy names; the only Italians besides Frederick were Perella and Louis Antolini, brother of Ella, and who by then actually lived in Chicago.[30]

Frederick's audacious skirting of Connecticut's red flag laws by waving his sweater is entirely in character with his activities in the coming decades. His utter disregard for both the law and reigning bourgeois morality, combined with his Galleanist militancy and growing entrepreneurial abilities, would keep both him and law enforcement quite busy.

A question might be posed as to whether Gruppo I Liberi played a role in the bombing campaigns of the Galleanists between 1918 and 1920. Certainly not a few of the group's building trades members were familiar with dynamite. Nonetheless, no names of New London anarchists have been connected to the core of militants who waged the armed actions. The BI partially broke the bombing case through information supplied by two sources. The US government held Ludovico Caminita, former editor of *L'Era Nuova* and strong foe of anti-organizational anarchism, under threat of deportation on Ellis Island. J. Edgar Hoover interviewed him in February 1920, and Caminita offered up likely bombing suspects within the anarchist movement. Even more damaging were the reports of Eugenio Ravarini, a spy the BI had successfully infiltrated into the heart of the Galleanist movement. While they identified key militants in Massachusetts, neither Caminita nor Ravarini linked New London to the bombings.[31] Significantly, no evidence shows New Londoners traveling to Mexico with the group that was to comprise the bombing "conspiracy." One of the principal reasons given for the migration across the border was to avoid the military draft. A startling divergence with the rest of the *Galleanisti* nationwide is suggested by the large number of leading Gruppo I Liberi members having complied with the US government and registered for the draft. These included Angelo Asci, Efisio Bartolucci, Victor Frederick, Anselmo Lombardozzi, Arthur Paci, Attilio Pasqualini, Ernesto Perella, Raffaele Petrini, and Anselmo Severini. The majority must be considered dedicated Galleanists from articles they wrote and political activities in which they took part. The reason for their having registered cannot be from timidity in confronting the state power, since many had been or would be arrested in the course of their activism—unless their registration had a political motivation behind it. Most registered on June 5, 1917; slinking down to the draft board individually would have been out of the question, since hundreds of other registrants could have identified them, including a number of New London *prominenti* who served as interpreters that day. (A total of 2,580 men registered on that date in New London.)[32] That they made a collective decision to do so seems likely, but for what reason? Registering would offer the authorities one less reason to raid homes and meeting places; Galleanists who recrossed the border into the United States from Mexico did face prosecution. Did Gruppo I Liberi hope to better protect itself in the face of growing government persecution? It is possible that registration had become a necessity for work in defense plants and government construction jobs engaged in by most of the above members.

Given the heavy military presence in New London, it remains somewhat unclear why Gruppo I Liberi did not face stronger attacks than it did. Naval Intelligence certainly kept a watch on local radicals. Naval Intelligence operatives tended to come from New York blueblood backgrounds and old money, and certainly were prone to pursue alien radicals.[33] They had searched the apartment of Raffaele Arace, placed a spy in an IWW textile workers local in Mystic, and provided the Bureau with information on possible suspects. In 1918 they had taken in an anarchist in Derby who was found to have among his possessions a copy of Galleani's bomb-making manual *La Salute e in Voi!* Bureau operatives prepared to invade New London, as a Derby police lieutenant named Urbano had claimed that there "further anarchistic activities can be unearthed." But no raids or arrests resulted, and the Fort Trumbull anarchist movement continued to dance around overt political repression.[34]

A connection between the Galleanist group in Milford, Massachusetts and members of Gruppo I Liberi during this period is worth exploring. It involves two militants active in Milford, both of whom had been born in Fano. One may never have set foot in New London, while the other would live and be politically active there for the rest of his days. Both were most likely involved with expropriation activities.

In the fall of 1917, shortly after the arrest of Galleani for writing "Matricolati!," Bureau of Investigation agents appeared in Milford in an apparent fishing expedition for Italian anarchists in the wake of a strike at a textile machinery manufacturer. There they noted the names of several of the especially "bad ones," among them one "Saco," undoubtedly Ferdinando Sacco, who later went by Nicola Sacco (Sacco had left for Mexico sometime after the end of May. The BI must have relied on informants' testimony to get his name, but this clearly shows they had him in their files at an early date, however unfocused their reports initially were).[35] Agents returned a year later with a clearer mission, having received a phone call from Milford's chief of police about recent freight car robberies.

While Sacco had settled in a community of fellow immigrants from Foggia province, quite a few Milford Italians hailed from the Marche, two among these being Romolo Baldoni and Paolo Rinaldoni. Baldoni, it was believed, was "someway connected" to the robbery of US government property from freight cars in the area. Police raided his home on the first floor of 34 Cedar Street, finding several weapons, including revolvers and shotguns, and money—all of which they seized—but no Baldoni. Above his living quarters the cops discovered the meeting place of the local Galleanist group, the Circolo di Studi Sociali. Bureau agents joined in the search, and again they came up with Sacco's name on a list of "a few of the more rabid agitators" (and living at an address, 76 Hayward Street, where he hadn't been for at least a year). But the targets of the Bureau were Baldoni and Rinaldoni, who they learned was "a certain Italian who runs a cobbler shop in town."

Born in 1878, Baldoni had received his introduction to the anarchist movement in the streets of Fano during the tumultuous nineties, being arrested numerous times. Not one for book learning, Baldoni, a stonemason, was a quintessential anarchist man of action. During the events of 1898, according to the police, he stood before the barracks of the *carabinieri* with knife in hand and shouted, "Hurrah for Anarchy! Hurrah for Social Revolution! Down with the priests and bourgeoisie!" For this episode Baldoni found himself in court, testifying that he could not have been at the demonstration because he had gone to a bar that evening and didn't remember anything. The judge obliged by adding public drunkenness to his charges.

Between 1907 and 1913 he lived in the US in Barre, Vermont; Logansport, Indiana; Woonsocket, Rhode Island; and New Haven, where he became active in Circolo Pietro Gori. In 1910 he lived briefly in Willimantic, Connecticut. From Fano, to which he returned in March 1913, he saluted Gaetano Lombardozzi, along with other US comrades in the pages of *In Marcia!* He arrived back in Italy on June 7, 1914, to play a significant role in the events of Red Week. Red Week began in Ancona after troops fired into demonstrators, killing three. In Fano, Baldoni's prominence in the ensuing general strike resulted in his being called into the office of the high commissioner of the municipality to help calm events (without success).[36]

To avoid legal action Baldoni left for Paris, met Malatesta in London, and found himself back in the United States. By this time he had crossed international borders at least thirteen times in his transnational wanderings. He now he settled in Milford, but where he worked is unclear. He apparently served as correspondence secretary for "La Rivolta," another anarchist circle. Only days prior to the police raid of

1918, ironically, he registered for the military draft, his card describing him as a "metalworker, not now employed," and of medium height, medium build, with gray eyes and black hair.³⁷

During the late summer of 1918, a robber gang stole seven thousand dollars worth of government property from freight cars in central Massachusetts, leading to the arrest of four Italians in Springfield. Deliveries of the stolen goods by truck to the homes of Baldoni and Paolo Rinaldoni during various evenings had been reported to the police. The state police intercepted a telegram sent by one of those arrested to Rinaldoni stating, "Tell Augusto to get out now." Rinaldoni, thirty-eight years old, married with no children, owned a shoe repair business in town and had lived for four years in nearby Hopedale before moving to Milford. Agent Feri Weiss brought Rinaldoni to the Milford police station for a four-hour grilling. Weiss, an important operative in the Boston BI and himself an immigrant, would refer to foreign-born radicals as "vermin," and had a hardline position on the suppression of dissent. He later wrote what has been described as "a book length rant against immigration." The subject of anarchism dominated his interview with Rinaldoni.

Q: Do you believe in God?

A: I have never seen him.

Q: Do you believe in things only when you see them?

A: I believe in you because I see you.

୶

Q: Do you know [Raffaele] Schiavina?

A: I heard him speak.

Q: Where?

A: Here

Q: How often did you hear him speak?

A: Only once.

Q: When was that?

A: You were there yourself.

∽

Q: How was it in your library we found nothing but Anarchistic books, with the exception of [Camille] Flammarion?

A: I like to read.

Q: But you said before that you read all kinds of books, then why do you keep only Anarchistic books in your possession?

A: Because I like to read them.

The interview proceeded along these lines until Weiss's desire to know population demographics got the best of him, showing him to be clueless in his interrogation of a wiseguy:

Q: How many people from Fano are in America?

A: I am the only one.[38]

Rinaldoni denied any knowledge of the telegram or who could have sent it: "If that telegram is written by a crazy man do you think that I am responsible for it?" Finally, Rinaldoni seems to have tired of the whole thing. According to Weiss, he admitted, "Yes, I am an anarchist and all these anarchistic books are mine. What are you going to do about it?" Not much, apparently. The BI released Rinaldoni with a warning, since they had found no evidence of the stolen property at either anarchists' home.[39]

Baldoni had given the police the slip, having crawled out the back window during the first raid. He hid in the woods, according to a Bureau report, depending on food supplied by comrades. He returned from Providence to where he had fled and was taken into custody. After questioning, the police released him. In May 1919 he was again picked up in a raid in Milford as a suspect in the bombing campaign and released for lack of evidence. He moved to Woonsocket, where he apparently worked for a few days in the Social Mills, and then dropped from sight. Rumor later reached the Bureau of Investigation that he had absconded to Philadelphia. Their information seems to have been correct, since the Italian authorities reported his passage on a ship from Philadelphia to Genoa in June 1921, where he was arrested, but later amnestied, for desertion from the military. He returned to Fano, then moved to Genoa in 1926, took a job as a waiter on a trans-Atlantic steamship, and may have lived in the United States clandestinely. By the 1930s, his revolutionary activity probably ended. The police ceased their surveillance of him and reported his membership in a fascist building trades union in Genoa in 1935.[40]

Rinaldoni and his wife Annunciata soon moved to New London, a logical choice to avoid the constant police and Bureau dragnets conducted in eastern Massachusetts. The Bureau did note that Rinaldoni continued to visit Milford where he "presided" over meetings of the local group, perhaps assisting them to rebuild in the wake of the raids, and that he continued to have family ties there, with his sister married to a local anarchist.[41] The activities of Baldoni and Rinaldoni offer a glimpse into the shattered state of the Galleanist movement in their Massachusetts stronghold. Many others besides them had scattered or gone to ground. New London starts to emerge as a destination for anarchists fleeing hostile territory.

Anarchist-led gangs clearly operated during these years in the central region of Massachusetts, where Galleanists clustered in small textile and quarry towns. In 1920 the Bureau of Investigation claimed to have uncovered another one in the Uxbridge area, about six miles from Milford. Amedeo Parecchini, of whom little information exists, apparently worked for a section gang for the New York, New Haven and Hartford Railroad. "Radical in his talk," according to the Feds, he disappeared after railroad detectives discovered that "the whole gang were looting cars." While stolen goods were found in his home, he also succeeded in "getting away in the dark."[42]

The Galleanist movement throughout New England engaged in armed expropriations on a scale perhaps more than historians have been aware. No evidence, at least that I have come across, links either Nicola Sacco or Bartholomeo Vanzetti to the crime for which they were accused. In their search for Galleanist bombers, the Bureau of Investigation stumbled across Italian anarchists who robbed freight cars. Their reports contain the names of Sacco and Vanzetti as supporters of the Galleanist movement and subscribers to *Cronaca Sovversiva*, but contain nothing connecting them to robberies. Their trial, by most accounts, contained enough discrepancies to warrant a retrial. This does not mean the defendants were not capable of carrying out the South Braintree robbery; they were members of one of the most militant local anarchist groups affiliated with a movement that supported the tactic of armed expropriation. The jury is still out, in my opinion.

By the end of 1919, the US government had clearly turned its attention toward the fledgling communist parties that had emerged from an internal struggle within the Socialist Party, and the anarcho-syndicalist Union of Russian Workers. Both of these movements had a substantial presence in Connecticut, at times holding massive public meetings; the government saw them as the principal revolutionary threat to the established order. At the same time, the Bureau of Investigation continued its intensive manhunts for the Galleanist perpetrators of the bombing campaign. These efforts escalated with the terror bombing of Wall Street on September 16, 1920, that killed thirty-nine people and wounded hundreds more. Historians writing about the event seem to agree with Paul Avrich that Mario Buda, a Galleanist militant living in the Boston area, had carried out the bombing. Buda was a member of Gruppo Autonomo of East Boston (and also rumored to have been involved in the fencing of stolen goods from freight car robberies).[43] Nicola Sacco and Bartholomeo Vanzetti as well belonged to Gruppo Autonomo, as did Carlo Valdinoci and others involved in the use of dynamite. (The former were behind bars for their alleged role in the South Braintree, Massachusetts robbery of April 1920, and the latter had blown himself to bits with an improperly fused bomb on the steps of A. Mitchell Palmer's house in June 1919.)

Even before the Wall Street bombing, the authorities had their finger on the individual suspected of being Galleani's principal bomb maker: Nicola Recchi. "A real man that one!" an unsuspecting anarchist in New York told a BI informant. "He was a Marchigiano. He just left for Italy. He had a hand in the explosions that occurred in Boston two years ago at the courthouse and at the police station. He was just handling a cap that exploded while he was holding it. Alone he went to a comrade doctor, a Frenchman, and got his wound dressed. Nobody knew anything about that act." Recchi had left the Boston area and vanished, but the BI did not believe he had returned to Italy. Their nationwide manhunt for an Italian anarchist with a disfigured left hand brought them to New London. Agents searched employment rolls of area shipbuilders, the New Haven railroad, docks, and the maritime industry for Recchi, to no avail. They approached Albert Caracausa, son of Antonio, an important Sicilian-born member of the local Italian *prominenti*, to gain information. Caracausa had been cleared as "reliable" by local authorities. Nothing could be learned of Recchi's whereabouts.

A short time later, an unfortunate Italian worker living in Naugatuck with a missing left hand and a first name similar to Recchi's fell under suspicion of the Bureau of Investigation. They cleared him of wrongdoing after it was found that he worked for the Connecticut Fireworks Company. (Recchi died in Buenos Aires in 1975.)[44]

The string of run-ins with authority on the part of anarchists in Fort Trumbull—Petrini's arrest in 1916, Renzoni and Perella's in 1918, Frederick's identification as anarchist by the Bureau of Investigation during his arrest, and the coordinated posting of "Go-Head"—might plausibly have directed the attention of the government toward New London more than actually occurred. In the Justice Department's scramble to solve the 1919 Galleanist bombing conspiracies, their energies focused on eastern Massachusetts, the true center of the movement. In Connecticut, the BI, state police, and private detective agencies devoted most of their resources in destabilizing and suppressing the mass-based "Bolshevik" strikes of the Naugatuck Valley. In comparison with their comrades in these areas, Fort Trumbull anarchists were quite lucky indeed.

CHAPTER TEN

FACING THE 1920S

Italian radicals in Connecticut viewed their struggles and those of workers in Italy as part of the same worldwide fight against capitalism and the state. As the political winds shifted, new challenges arose; defense campaigns against jailings, deportations, police raids and the rising tide of fascism came to absorb nearly all of the energy of the Italian American left. This continued through the 1920s. A harbinger of these developments occurred during the 1919 and 1920 strikes in the Naugatuck Valley, as ethnic workers saw their leaders arrested, one striker killed, meetings raided, street parades forbidden, and laws passed to forbid the display of red flags. In 1920, two Waterbury strikers, a Russian and an Italian and both alleged anarchists, were arrested for planning to bomb the police superintendent's house. They received stiff sentences in an affair that smelled strongly of entrapment. Martial law removed most civil liberties for the thousands of immigrant workers exercising their right to strike, and slowly strangled their struggles. Ethnic divisions between "American" and foreign-born workers also played a strong role in the strike's defeat.[1]

The Bureau of Investigation amassed hundreds of pages of reports detailing the influence of the left on the Naugatuck Valley strikes, the most important of these written by operatives of the Burns Detective Agency. In 1919, these industrial spies engaged strike leaders in conversation, attended strike meetings, and went to Polish socialist dances and Italian syndicalist parties. The Bureau suggested that political power in the industrial town of Ansonia had partially passed to the workers' strike headquarters at the hall on Maple Street that housed the Union of Russian Workers and the Russian Socialist Federation, complaining that the manufacturers had lost control.

> The peculiar condition with regard to the manufacturers is that Ansonia is purely a plant town and that few or none of the manufacturers themselves either live there or are actually in touch with conditions. They seldom if ever see their men except their subordinate officials on whom they rely . . .[2]

For a critical moment the left did play a key role in providing organizational backbone for the Brass Valley strikes. The misgivings the Department of Justice had over the lack of employer and local police resolve in dealing with the radicals became a moot point with the Palmer raids of November 1919 and January 1920 that heavily targeted the Naugatuck Valley. Hundreds faced deportation and prison, with the revolutionary left being driven partially underground in the aftermath.[3]

The outcome of the brass industry strikes fell far short of the expectations of Italian revolutionaries. *Il Proletario* attacked the Italian leader Scalmana for negotiating with priests and manufacturers above the heads of the workers, which led to a split developing in the strikers' ranks. FSI and IWW supporters in Waterbury expressed frustration at the failure of Italian workers in developing alternative working class institutions, as had the more-politicized Lithuanian and Russian workers. An IWW writer on the scene unfortunately (but somewhat typically) used racially charged language to take the strikers to task: "These workers in the Naugatuck Valley, less than two hours from New York City, might as well be in the heart of Africa, so far as intelligent leadership and education along working class lines is concerned . . . What is to be done with them—for them?"[4] The FSI did not fare any better, even as it attempted to regain its leading role in Italian communities. Repression and poor leadership resulted in the Connecticut FSI being reduced to a "haggard minority" as branches disappeared.[5]

Groups like the Ferrer Circle in New Haven held large, enthusiastic meetings during the postwar upsurge with which they greeted the dawn of a new revolutionary era, but found themselves outmatched by the power of the *prominenti*. The syndicalists complained of the prowar, promonarchist "speechifying" of various Italian public figures that resulted in two hundred thousand dollars worth of war bonds being bought by local Italians. In 1918, General Emilio Guglielmotti, a military attaché to the Italian embassy in Washington, spoke to a crowd of five thousand in Yale's Woolsey Hall. Nationalist fervor had caught up in its grasp the Italians of New Haven, and would hold them for the rest of the decade.[6]

In New London, the first Palmer raids of November 1919 targeted, as they did across Connecticut, the Union of Russian Workers. The Department of Justice arrested about half a dozen members and transported them to Hartford for deportation proceedings. Authorities also seized a large amount of radical literature. In January a similar raid netted members of the newly formed Communist Party. Local authorities continued the pattern of political repression when the police broke up an attempted street meeting of the Socialist Labor Party in downtown New London, leading to the Socialist Party threatening to launch "free speech meetings."[7]

In Italy the revolutionary wave subsided in the face of growing attacks by forces of the state that cooperated with fascist gangs in using widespread violence against the left. The leadership of the labor movement fatally drew back from the question of the seizure of power and allowed the initiative to be seized by the right. Fascism stepped into the breach, and *L'Adunata dei Refrattari* would lament over "the agitation of 1919 and 1920 that closed an epoch and opened a farce."[8]

Fascism, meanwhile, had arrived late in Fano. While the workers' movement in other regions such as Emilia-Romagna to the north had been devastated by fascist *squadrista* attacks, the Marche remained relatively immune from Mussolini's hordes. What sporadic attacks that occurred depended on outside fascist reinforcements from Umbria and Emilia. Balsamini and Sora have credited this anomaly to the "strength of the Pesarese movement deeply rooted in the social fabric." In 1921, fascist squads entered Fano to hold an electoral rally, after which they sacked the socialist hall. The few local fascists approached the socialists in the aftermath and paid for the damages, saying they didn't want reprisals and promised not to invite outside fascists in the future. Nevertheless the fascist tide continued to advance nationally. *La Frusta* warned in June 1922, a very late date.

> Raise the dikes, comrades, revolutionaries, free men! Raise the dikes of defense, if we are not to be swept away by the torrent of fascist reaction. If we don't intend to suffer the club, we need to think well. No need for exasperated chatter. We want actions that inspire fear and respect. At least the Marche is one of the few regions saved from fascist reaction, maintains its independent position.[9]

The reversal of fortunes for the American left proved a jarring experience for many. "1919 seems to have happened ages ago," wrote J. B. S. Hardman, editor of the monthly paper of the then-radical Amalgamated Clothing Workers.[10] Cynicism abounded. In 1923, after the police in Waterbury twice forbade Carlo Tresca from speaking, well-known IWW leader Elizabeth Gurley Flynn told a May Day rally in Bridgeport, "Not far from Bridgeport they still believe that one man can start a revolution, but the workers of America are more interested in Babe Ruth and Charlie Chaplin then in starting a revolution . . ."[11] "All members care, is how they look in a hat," commented a delegate to a Connecticut Federation of Labor convention. In the late 1920s, delegates to that body's annual meeting met in a plush, nonunion hotel in New London. The Communist *Daily Worker*'s commentary on the meeting had the bite of H. L. Mencken.

> And bootleg whiskey in rivers ran. And real beer found a ready market, and cigars, both union and non-union made, were freely passed, and hours merrily chased, and wise-cracks cracked, and daddy, mammy songs lustily sung, and speeches lengthy by fat and pompous gentlemen, glorifying our 'institushuns' held, and all was well and everyone was happy. It was Connecticut labor holding its 43rd state convention.[12]

Gruppo I Liberi confronted the realities of this new era. Much of the Galleanist movement of New England had scattered, and would only slowly begin to partially rebuild itself. Damage inflicted by the spy Eugenio Ravarini had been enormous and had led to many arrests. He had infiltrated the anarchist movement as close as Providence, Rhode Island, where he attempted to gain names of anarchist supporters in the area before falling under suspicion and disappearing. New London appears to have escaped his attention, and the group did not suffer devastating police raids, as did Providence's Karl Marx Circle.[13]

Valerio Isca, an anarchist not affiliated with any particular trend, commented that the Galleanists during this period, "never went out into the streets after the Palmer raids and the dissolution of the Bresci group" (an important formation in the Galleanist armed wing) and that they "isolated themselves from potential recruits."[14] Events in New London would both confirm and contradict this observation.

The onset of this decade saw a turn of events that shaped the neighborhood for decades to come. For the first time since Fort Trumbull had become predominantly Italian, a new group appeared that posed an alternative to the anarchist movement. By the end of 1922, two new meeting halls would stand within a block of each other on Smith and Goshen Streets, respectively. Construction on the first began in November 1921 by a group chartered, in January 1922, as the Italian Society for the Mutual Aid of Men and Women of New London, Inc. This group, known more commonly as the Italian Mutual Aid Society, immediately began holding social functions in the new hall.[15]

The birth of the Italian Mutual Aid Society came as a result of developments both within the neighborhood and American society during this complex period. First, the group formed as a benefit society, providing sick benefits and life insurance to its members, functions frowned on by the Galleanists. Across the country, Italian anarchists, socialists, and syndicalists had built benefit societies, cooperative stores, and other alternate institutions that helped sustain their radical subculture. Supporters of *Cronaca Sovversiva* and its successor, *L'Adunata dei Refrattari*, had not taken up this practice. Such activity entailed the possibility of creating a bureaucracy, in their view, which would deflect from the goal of social revolution. But these societies assisted Italian immigrants adrift in the vortex of American capitalism; if radicals did not build these societies, other forces would. The Mutual Aid Society in Fort Trumbull simply stepped into a vacuum left by the Galleanists' indifference.

Second, coming in the aftermath of intense political repression directed against Italian anarchists, the Aid Society's birth occurred during a time of decline and regroupment for the radical movement. Many Italian workers in the United States who had previously given some support to the movement felt that the time to lie low was at hand. Political repression dovetailed with an intensive Americanization drive across Connecticut and throughout the country directed against "foreigners" prone to radical ideas. New London saw the birth of an especially aggressive campaign to teach immigrants how to be "100% Americans." Americanization efforts in the city, described by sociologist Bessie Bloom Wessel as "all that was finest and all that was crudest" in bringing immigrants into the fold, placed much attention on the Italian community.[16]

New London's Americanization campaign fell under the control of the same forces that had sought, since the beginning of the century, to "morally" uplift the mass of immigrants who populated the city. Groups such as the Daughters of the American Revolution, Women's Christian Temperance Union, and the Women's Relief Corps especially devoted their energies to the public school system. One idea floated was to have foreign-born workers be required to give a "report card" to their employers, as was done in Torrington, to ensure their attendance at night school for English.[17]

Nativism surfaced in more malevolent form with the growth of the local Ku Klux Klan. Only months after the chartering of the Mutual Aid Society, a *New London Day* article announced, "Ku Klux Klan Has Several Hundred Members Here." The KKK gained a base of support among the officers and sailors at the naval base and held several rallies nearby, developments surely not missed by local Italians.[18]

A number of Fort Trumbull residents held politics that did not differ from those of non-Marchegian Italians in New London. Guerrino Pierpaoli, a twenty-five-year-old stonemason living at 93 Smith Street who had immigrated in 1915, won a prize in a 1921 essay contest sponsored by the Daughters of the American Revolution. Pierpaoli praised American freedoms, and promised, "if some day she is in danger or peril again I shall fight for her rights and for her justice. I am proud and glad to live under the flag which has the stars and stripes."[19]

Residents of Fort Trumbull who had either been on the periphery of Gruppo I Liberi as friends or sympathizers, or had never been connected with anarchism, composed the founding core of the Mutual Aid Society. At some point, probably in 1921, this grouping held a meeting in the clubroom (or speakeasy) of Michael Giri, a contractor, located in the back of a building he owned at 75 Smith Street. (He also apparently rented space at the same address to Gruppo I Liberi.) Those at the meeting voted to form a separate organization, a move seen as a "break away" from the anarchists.[20] Stephano Tonucci was probably the individual closest to I Liberi who played a role in the new group's formation. A donor to the anarchist press between 1907 and 1915, Tonucci was skilled as both a mason and carpenter and later described in the Historic Resources Inventory that surveyed New London neighborhoods in the 1990s as "one of the most important builders in the area." A number of charter members had donated to collections taken up by the anarchists for strikes or their press, but few seem to have been active members of the group. Others had family members who were anarchists. Many held religious beliefs and church weddings became more common in the Fort. The occupations of the members did not differ from those of their anarchist neighbors—carpenters, laborers, silk mill weavers, and small business owners.

Gruppo I Liberi saw the erection of the Mutual Aid Society hall as a direct attack and, lacking a domestic journal, registered their anger in the pages of *La Frusta*. Calling the rival group "troublemakers from Fano and Senigallia," and signed by "a Fanese," their article accused the Mutual Aid Society of trying to sabotage activities of the local workers' movement. "Those who do so are disgusting to all that is anarchistic and are in league with our enemies." They held that the anarchist meeting place at 75 Smith Street, directly across from the Aid Society hall, existed for the entire community, and now some of these families stood in opposition to the anarchists. A rival social hall was superfluous—to Gruppo I Liberi the neighborhood's values were embodied in social environment they had painstakingly built. They charged the head of the society of being both a fascist and an "anarchophobe," and renewed the Galleanist movement's criticisms of benefit societies, that in Italy had been "wretched palliatives" and in America "a trap to bleed those penniless in poverty."[21]

If the Italian Mutual Aid Society demonstrated that the neighborhood's anarchist movement did not speak for all Fort Trumbull residents, neither did the new group join with the myriad of clubs and societies formed by non-Marchegian Italians in New London. Another name used by the Mutual Aid Society for decades was the "Italian Labor Society," or a variation of this. Founders of the new organization did not view themselves as splitting from the traditions of the Italian left. A. Matt Orsini, born in Mondolfo in the Marche in 1913, operated and owned a grocery store on Goshen Street until the early 1960s. He described both clubs as "radicals": "I was against Mussolini, so was my father (Massimiliano). He was anti-government, like the Chelsea Street club (IDC), but he belonged to the Mutual Aid Society."[22] From its inception the group remained aloof from other Italian organizations. It did not join in festivities that praised nationalism and remained uninvolved in the affairs of the status quo. It kept separate from political currents that would provide a base for fascism in New London, especially among Sicilians. Regardless, the Mutual Aid Society represented a break from the Galleanist politics for which their militant neighbors stood.

The article in *La Frusta* was a warning shot fired across the bow. After a dance on a Saturday night in April 1922 that disbanded at about three in the morning, a fire broke out that totally destroyed the Mutual Aid Society's wooden building. Damages were estimated at $7,000. Although no arson investigation followed, suspicions arose in the neighborhood as to the fire's origins. In "The Fort," a paper written in the 1990s, Elissa Giommi recorded that these suspicions centered on unnamed "extremists": "They figure it was due to jealousy." To Matt Orsini, who was there when the fire broke out, and who later served at least two terms as president of the Aid Society, it was "definitely" the anarchists. People in the neighborhood allegedly had recognized a man on the roof pouring gasoline, and that soon after the fire, some from the "other club" had left the city and moved to the Boston area. In view of future incidents in the neighborhood, as well as in the trajectory of the group itself, it is not a stretch to say that elements of Gruppo I Liberi had torched the rival hall. Such an act would have been viewed as preventing the rise of a nonrevolutionary force in their midst. Nevertheless, the Mutual Aid Society completed construction on a new hall at 68 Smith Street, this one of masonry (and probably more fireproof), and one that served them until the dissolution of the club in the 1970s.[23]

Gruppo I Liberi had another response to the Mutual Aid Society. Buying land at the corner of Goshen and Chelsea Streets, with a street address of 79 Goshen, the anarchists built a hall considerably larger than that of their rivals. The style of the building was described as "20th century Italian vernacular," which "relates to other stuccoed buildings on Smith and Goshen Streets." As with the Mutual Aid Society, Gruppo I Liberi built their hall with the communal labor of the members, there certainly being no shortage of carpentry and masonry skills. They erected their hall under the auspices of the Italian Dramatic Club, and the building has remained so until the present. No public celebrations with ribbon cutting fanfare boasted of their accomplishment; only one article in the *Norwich Bulletin* announced the opening of the hall with a ball and concert on the night of July 1, 1922 (with music provided by the son of Anita and Lorenzo Montali). The Italian Dramatic Club might as well not have existed for the public at large, since I believe that not until 1947 would the club's name next appear in the press, and then only because a member had a fatal attack inside the building. The Italian Dramatic Club may have been rented to members for social occasions such as weddings and showers in the earliest days, but Gruppo I Liberi built the hall primarily as a place for holding their anarchist political and social events. In *L'Adunata dei Refrattari*, the group for decades referred to the Club as "our hall" or "our headquarters." The names of three individuals, all supporters of Gruppo I Liberi, appear on the deed: Efisio Bartolucci the building contractor, Lorenzo Montali, the bakery owner challenged by his wife Anita in 1912, and Nostralio Facchini, who worked as both a machinist and truck driver. Other Italian radical groups across the country erected halls during the 1920s to continue activities more safely behind closed doors, with similar innocuous-sounding names gracing the entrance door.[24]

Gruppo I Liberi built their hall during the same year as the Galleanists reestablished their press in the United States with the paper *L'Adunata dei Refrattari*. Under varied editors, but primarily Raffaele Schiavina, now returned from the deportation to Italy that he had shared with Galleani, *L'Adunata* continued the militant, anti-organizational stance of *Cronaca Sovversiva*. The existence of *L'Adunata* allowed for a degree of regroupment of the Galleanist movement, stemming from the critical role newspapers and journals played among the anarchists. With their revived press and their new hall—and perhaps because of the competition they now faced from the Mutual Aid Society—Gruppo I Liberi's functions increased to a scale that rivaled the pioneer days of Italian anarchism in New London. Much, but not all, of this activity took place behind the closed doors of their impressive hall.

All Italian radicals active in cities like New Britain, Waterbury, New Haven, Hartford, and Bridgeport fought strenuously for influence in their communities; New London anarchists faced a challenge of building cross-regional political activity. While regionalism in other cities created neighborhoods with a majority of settlers from Emilia-Romagna, Sicily, Tuscany, Campania or the Marches, few other Italian communities faced such a sharply defined separation by geography and politics as did New London. The semi-isolation of the peninsular neighborhood of Fort Trumbull that allowed a strong radical movement to take root also separated it from developments in the other Italian neighborhood of Shaw Street. These differences grew more pronounced during the important, transitional decade of the 1920s.

Only one Sicilian, Melili-born Giuseppe Camillo, can be identified as a contributor to the anarchist press from New London during its entire history.[25] How did Sicilians in New London view their Marchegian neighbors and the uncommon path they had taken? Angelina Moscarella, born in Caltavuturo and who lived on Shaw Street, said in an undated interview, "The old Marchegiani families from Fano lived in

Fort Trumbull. They used to think that Sicilians were below them." Did Sicilians see the radical politics of Marchegian anarchists as a veneer for regional prejudice? (A southern Italian who grew up in New Haven made a similar remark about Marchegiani in his city: ". . . they always felt they were better-educated, trade people and they considered themselves a little better than the people from the Wooster Square area.") The Italian anarchists often engaged in name-calling and insults with little intention of persuading their opponents; it would have been easy for tradition-oriented Sicilians and others to see the anarchists as typically prejudiced northerners. It also would not have been very difficult for leaders of the Sicilian community to play this against the Fort Trumbull *sovversivi*. And northern contempt for southerners undoubtedly did creep into the attitudes of some Fanese. Alberto Mencarelli, son of anarchist Sergio, told his children, "The Italians are a really good people, but watch out for the Sicilians." Regionalism began for Matt Orsini before he even touched American shores at the age of seven in 1920. After departing with his mother from the port of Genoa, his ship docked in Naples and Palermo to pick up more passengers. "Keep away from those kids," he was warned.[26]

Anarchism, despite the rise of opposing forces both within and outside of the neighborhood, remained a strong force in Fort Trumbull during this period. Gruppo I Liberi probably had about fifty to sixty members throughout the decade, plus an even greater number of sympathizers. Perhaps a dozen or so moved from other locales, including a number from Italy. Among the newcomers were Pasquale and Jennie Paglia, who moved to New London from Milford, Massachusetts in 1919, remaining there until 1922. Jennie recounted the presence of Gemma Mello in New London to Paul Avrich in a 1988 interview. Mello, about thirty years old when she lived in the city, had been a member of the Galleanist group Gli Insorti in New Jersey. The Bureau of Investigation suspected that she and her companion Filipo Caci had planted the bomb that blew up the home of a textile mill owner in Paterson during the June 1919 bombing wave. She had also seen to the distribution of *Cronaca* in Paterson. She withstood a fierce interrogation; after questioning her all night, the Bureau could not break her down. Mello was moved to Ellis Island for deportation but later released. In 1920 she worked in a New London silk mill before moving to Brooklyn; her status in Gruppo I Liberi is uncertain.[27]

Gruppo I Liberi maintained if not strengthened its important position in the national Galleanist movement during the decade. The group's political and social activities provided a steady stream of financial support to anarchist political prisoners and press both domestically and internationally. They deepened their adherence to Galleanist ideological positions; in 1925, in response to a debate from within the movement, they wrote that they "do not intend to make an organized anarchist society with a lot of dictators and commanders, and with this we are in agreement with the comrades of Needham, Massachusetts and of other localities . . ." The Boston suburbs—Needham, Milford, Newton and others—contained a number of anarchist circles. Many of their members, such as Riccardo Orcciani, Adelfo and Renato Sanchioni, Augusto Rossi, Evaristo Ricciardelli, and Fernando Tarabelli, were of Marchegian origin, as were Nicola Recchi and Ferruccio Coacci, who had fled and been deported, respectively.[28] The Needham/Milford and New London groups especially developed close ties. The members exchanged social visits and correspondence of both political and personal nature.

Gruppo I Liberi benefited from having both a relatively young group of militants still in their thirties, like Raffaele Petrini, Renato Giustini, and Anselmo Lombardozzi, as well as veterans Luigi Camillucci and Enrico Broccoli, who had been around since the birth of New London's anarchist movement. The continuing adherence to the group of a significant number of building contractors also gave it a degree of stability probably not offered to most anarchist circles around the country. These factors, added to the neighborhood's regional composition and semi-isolation from the rest of the city, allowed the breathing room for Galleanist anarchism to remain the predominant influence in Fort Trumbull in the 1920s.

At the onset of the decade, in May 1920, two members of Gruppo Autonomo of East Boston, Nicola Sacco and Bartholomeo Vanzetti, were arrested and charged in connection with a robbery of a shoe factory payroll in South Braintree, Massachusetts, in April. A paymaster and security guard died in a hail of gunfire during the robbery. Police apprehended the two on a night while they were attempting to hide either anarchist literature or dynamite.

The campaign in their defense that lasted until the pair's execution in 1927 proved pivotal for the Italian radical movement. Members of Gruppo I Liberi, along with a gamut of Italian syndicalists, communists, socialists, unaffiliated radicals, and labor union members, threw themselves into the fight to save their imprisoned comrades. Nonradical sectors of the Italian community saw the arrests as a nativist attack on

Italian immigrants, and a substantial number of intellectuals and liberals across the country rallied to their defense. Italian radicals formed numerous Sacco-Vanzetti campaign committees across Connecticut in all the industrial cities. New Britain seems to have built the most effective movement, having been the seat of an important Galleanist group since around 1910, as well as hosting a substantial radical community among ethnic workers.

Gruppo I Liberi organized defense functions from 1921 to 1927 that included rallies, lectures, dances, picnics, and a festival to publicize the case. One of these, a protest meeting in February 1925 at the Brainerd Building on Main Street, featured Joseph Ettor, longtime labor activist and former IWW organizer during the Lawrence textile strike of 1912, who was touring the northeast for the Sacco-Vanzetti Defense Committee of Boston. Announcements ran in both *L'Adunata* and the *New London Day*, but no follow-up articles reported the results, and neither is a sponsoring organization named.[29]

The Sacco-Vanzetti campaign came to symbolize the defensive struggle waged by both the Italian American radicals and the US left during the 1920s. The years from their arrest in 1920 and execution in 1927 contained significant lapses of political activity, between appeals, court appearances, and the like. It was a decade of distraction for most people, including members of the labor movement, in which a long bitter fight came to a tragic conclusion. New London had a direct connection with the case in Riccardo Orciani, a Fanese anarchist living in Massachusetts, who had been with Sacco and Vanzetti the night they were picked up. Orciani had an "airtight" alibi for the day of the robbery in South Braintree that the prosecution believed was bogus. Orciani, who traveled by motorcycle throughout New England, was seen in New London on at least one occasion, and probably was a frequent visitor because of social connections. He returned to Fano in 1923 after playing a role on the Defense Committee and never returned to the United States.[30]

In the final weeks before the August executions, a "deathwatch" bus of supporters from New York passed through New London on its way to join the demonstrations held on Boston Common. R. Frank Waugh, a former member of the jury that had rendered the guilty verdict for the pair of anarchists had moved from Quincy, Massachusetts to New London shortly after the trial; he declined to comment on the case. New London police announced that they were keeping an eye on "the few persons of radical tendencies known to reside here." On August 11 the *New London Day* received a crudely printed but threatening note.

Beware.

Take Heed.

The Day Office, Post Office & (Union) Depot

is due to be bomed [sic] Wed—midnight

Police regarded the note to be the work of a practical joker rather than supporters of Sacco and Vanzetti.[31]

While members of Gruppo I Liberi fortified their position, Italians in the Shaw Street neighborhood steadily built organizations based on nationalism, religion, and regional ties. Events like the Feast of the Assumption and Columbus Day celebrations became occasions to showcase the growing presence of the Italians in New London, each of these being chaired by lists of the local *prominenti*. Clubs emerged based on loyalty to the Democratic and Republican parties. In 1927, the Italian American Citizens Club added "Republican" to its name, though its efforts were soon dwarfed by the formation of the "Democratic juggernaut" in the Italian community led by Doctor C. John Satti. While the Democratic-led coalition only came into its own in the Great Depression of the next decade, its origins lie with the patient base-building work of Satti during the 1920s. Satti was the son of Tuscan-born Charles Satti, Bank Street grocer and saloonkeeper and one of the few practicing Italian family doctors in New London. Republican hostility to immigration and support for Prohibition gave the Democrats an opening that they exploited well in the presidential campaign of Al Smith in 1928.[32]

Still divided politically, the coalescing of the Italian community during the 1920s led to the formation of an umbrella group in 1931, the Italian American Citizens Association, and still later, the Central Council of Italian Societies. Sicilians both led and comprised the membership of these bodies. Residents of Fort Trumbull—anarchists or not—did not participate in them and remained apart from their fellow countrymen of Shaw Street. Paradoxically, as Italians living in the United States began to view themselves on national rather than regional lines, partially as a reaction to the pressure of rising nativist prejudices from the American public, New London Italians divided even further.

Organizing efforts by the radical movement in New London offered the possibility of counteracting this growing split and ironically gave Fort Trumbull Italians a chance to blend with the American "mainstream."

A small nucleus of the Communist Party (CP) existed in New London, probably composed of Slavic and Jewish immigrants, beginning in 1919, but had been smashed by the Palmer raids and its members arrested or driven underground. By the early 1920s a small unit of the Workers Party (the name the CP adopted after emerging from illegality) formed in New London and began to carry out activities directed toward the labor movement, ethnic communities, and of a general propaganda nature.[33]

Efforts by the WP/CP to gain a foothold in the local trade unions proved unsuccessful until May 1926, when a strike erupted of one hundred weavers at the Bloom silk mill in New London after management slashed their wages by 25 percent. The walkout challenged management's treatment of workers by "straw bosses" on the mill floor, demanding recognition of a union that would allow workers to be treated "like men and women and not like lugs." While the strike appears to have been spontaneously organized, it soon earned the support of labor and ethnic groups in the city, including the local labor council, the plumbers' union, a Finnish society, the Sicilian Tusana Society, and the Workmen's Circle, as well as a city councilman named May. The strikers and their supporters, including a number of very young women, staged parades through downtown New London and confronted strikebreakers entering the mill not on foot but by way of the still-new consumer convenience of the time, the automobile.[34]

Throughout the strike, two WP-led organizations, the International Labor Defense (ILD) and the United Front Committee, played important roles. The former provided legal assistance to arrested strikers while the latter was a labor center independent of the American Federation of Labor. It arose in New Jersey during the WP-led silk strike in Passaic, New Jersey. Left-wing speakers including Ella Reeve Bloor, a former Connecticut socialist leader, appeared in New London. A delegation of Passaic strikers also arrived in New London as part of a joint relief effort in July. The WP's *Daily Worker* devoted several articles to the strike.[35]

Italians appear to have been the principal ethnic group involved in the strike. One of the first strike support meetings took place on Chelsea Street. The strikers elected Philip Cavoli, a Tusa-born former-cobbler, as president of their ad hoc committee. As with most textile strikes of the decade, the workers could not reverse the cutbacks imposed by the employers; the strike ended when the Bloom Company moved the mill's machinery northward to the Quinnebaug river textile town of Putnam.[36]

From these organizing efforts and from earlier attempts to conduct party activities—and possibly from their involvement in Sacco-Vanzetti defense efforts in the area—the CP gained a toehold in the Fort. Two donations reached the International Labor Defense from New London, the first within month of the strike's end and consisting of a collection for *Labor Defender* taken up by Arturo Pettinari, a laborer at the Electric Boat shipyard who lived at 48 East Street. Pettinari had been born in Fano around 1900, and had migrated to the United States in 1914. He would eventually join the ranks of the Fort's "reputable" carpenters (and will be heard about again in chapter 12). Pettinari's name never appeared in the pages of *L'Adunata dei Refrattari*; he was later affiliated, however, with the Italian Mutual Aid Society. Another Mutual Aid Society member, Giuseppe Giulletti, sent donations in early 1928. The ILD had succeeded in winning the support of rank-and-file anarchists across the country, and this may have been the case with Pettinari. The CP and the Galleanists became implacable foes during the decade over issues related to the Sacco-Vanzetti campaign, the Communists charging the Galleanists with sectarianism and the latter responding with accusations of the CP acting in its narrow self-interest. The Mutual Aid Society sent a donation to the *Labor Defender* a year later. The clearest evidence of a least some degree of CP influence came in 1931, after the deportation proceedings against Guido Serio, an Italian-born Communist and national organizer of the Seamen's Union in Italy who had entered the United States illegally. Facing deportation to fascist Italy where probable death awaited him, Serio, with the help of the ILD, succeeded in changing his destination to the Soviet Union. Farewell parties took place in several cities in the northeast, among them in New London on November 31 at the Mutual Aid Society hall.[37]

Communist events in New London regularly had Italian speakers, and several members of the Italian community joined or moved close to the party. The tactics employed by the Workers Party in the 1920s served as dress rehearsals for the left coalitions built during the next decade. The CP would utilize its strength in various ethnic communities, as it did in the 1920s, to organize workers into the Congress of Industrial Organizations (CIO) that arose during the early and mid-thirties. With varying degrees of success, the Communists attempted to overcome their base in the ethnic clubs of Hungarians, Lithuanians, Russians, and Jews in Connecticut where the party had a presence, and push their members toward labor's mainstream. By contrast, the ability of the Italian anarchist movement to influence events in the workers' movement lessened drastically as the pre–World War I years faded into the past. Even if they maintained strongpoints like Fort Trumbull, they faced extinction without the recruitment of new supporters. These would have to come from the second generation—their children—born into the rapidly changing capitalist society of the United States. And here was the rub.

CHAPTER ELEVEN

THEY FOUGHT THE LAW

On September 4, 1924, a motorcade of police cars, a patrol wagon, and a motorcycle sped into the Fort Trumbull neighborhood and proceeded to addresses on Smith and Chelsea Streets. It took only minutes to draw a crowd of hundreds that watched as the enforcers of the law hauled large quantities of contraband liquor and the equipment with which to manufacture it onto the streets. At 50 Smith Street they found cellars divided into locked compartments, each "loaded with kegs and barrels of wine. In a closet upstairs the officers found full cases of beer. In other places, the cellars were found to be stacked with kegs of wine, ranging from raisin liquor to stuff which it seemed was nearly pure alcohol." Police found bags of hops and cans of malt syrup stuffed into a huge wooden box "filled to its capacity."[1]

Police raids such as this one, which netted three suspects besides the contraband materials, became a regular occurrence in the Fort from 1919 to 1933. A distinguishing feature of this particular operation was its having been initiated by the US Coast Guard. Three chief petty officers from the destroyer *Jouett*, moored at the New London state pier, had applied for the search warrant and led the police in the search for illegal booze, an unprecedented land invasion by a branch of the armed services meant to protect the nation's shoreline. But it revealed the central role played by the residents of this relatively small piece of land jutting into the mouth of the Thames River during what has come to be known as the Prohibition Era.

Fort Trumbull had early on attracted the attention of the guardians of moral order just as it drew those who wished for the neighborhood to be leveled with a wrecking ball. The Board of Trade in New London had opposed the sale of liquor in the neighborhood as far back as 1891, "due the several manufacturers and ship builders located on Fort Neck, where fully 500 men are employed," and "opposed the locating of a liquor saloon there." By the end of World War One, the antiliquor forces in New London, after losing a referendum in 1915 that would have banned saloons in the city, put their hopes on national political scene.[2] Recently, historians such as Lisa McGirr have shown the class and ethnic factors behind the enforcement of the 18th Amendment and the Volstead Act that made illegal the use, manufacture and distribution of alcohol from 1920 to 1933. Police and federal attention "rarely strayed," in her view, from the ethnic working-class. Working-class saloon drinking as well as "kitchen table drinkeries" remained targets of choice for the forces behind the temperance movement and antiliquor crusades.[3]

Ethnic working-class kitchen bars and unlicensed saloons (of which seventy supposedly existed in the city in 1917) received the blame for New London's crime and disorder, with the Shaw Street and Fort Trumbull neighborhoods holding center stage. The *Bridgeport Herald* claimed that the illegal sale of liquor, "has been the cause of New London's gaining the reputation all over the state as the most wide open burg in Connecticut . . ." Police raids of the Fort Trumbull neighborhood were not uncommon even before Prohibition. In 1914 an Italian highway-robber-turned-informer named Ferraci "guided (the state police) about Smith and Shaw streets where Italian kitchen bars are numerous," eventually leading them to the home of Louis Petrini at 11 Smith Street. Petrini, a barber, kept a one-chair barbershop and a kitchen barroom in his house. During World War I, the navy threatened to patrol the neighborhood with armed troops because of the number of drunken servicemen about in the streets.[4]

Fort Neck offered those in search of drink at any hour, "clubrooms where the main business is done on Sundays, and where anyone who is able to climb the flights of stairs, push the button, will be admitted into a bar room where any amount of booze can be purchased." The cost for the alcohol was slightly higher than in licensed establishments. Business boomed for the kitchen bars "to such an extent that now real dance halls, with bar attachments are the rule rather than the exception . . . Dances are held from Saturday night, well into Monday morning and beer is on tap sale as long as there are customers to serve."[5] (For some reason, reporters could describe in fine detail the operations of these clubrooms.)

As great a problem as hordes of drunken sailors and soldiers on the streets presented, to the horrified middle-class elements the greater threat centered on the "detriment to the morals of the rising generation." The state police stood ready to intervene since the local police often had their hands tied: "Special references were made to places in Fort Neck and Shaw Street districts. State Attorney Hull has decided that there must be moral reform in New London."[6]

Bootlegging operations in Fort Trumbull during Prohibition represented the culmination of decades of social and cultural conflict between the predominantly Yankee forces of order and the Italian working-class immigrants from Fano and other regions of Italy. Campaigns undertaken to "clean up" the heavily immigrant cities of the United States invariably took on the appearance of being drives aimed at the lifestyles of the working class. In New London they became connected to efforts to root out pervasive corruption in the city's political circles. Saloons, kitchen bars and houses of prostitution became linked together, as in this account from 1908: "Chief among the low dives of New London is that of the Hebrew meat dealer Joe Soltz, whose saloon on Bradley Street is one of the lowest and most notorious places in the state." The establishment, claimed the *Bridgeport Herald*, operated with police protection, under "the complete and peaceful sway of the god of vice and corruption which has ruled the city since Mayor (Benny) Armstrong went into office . . ." Police allegedly served as bouncers in the fifteen "houses of ill-repute" in New London, "the worst governed city in the state of Connecticut."[7]

From its inception, the city's temperance movement consisted of a cross-section of Protestant New London's upper and middle classes who took aim squarely at both immigrant neighborhoods and downtown dives. The Women's Christian Temperance Union, Daughters of the American Revolution, and YMCA combined with crusading political figures and clergymen in an attempt to ban saloons in a referendum vote in 1915, and lost heavily. They decided not repeat the effort the next year because businesses that had supported the referendum had been boycotted.[8]

In 1915, the Civic League of New London formed, with a membership also representative of the city's respectable citizens. The "Clean Up Campaign" of 1916, a part of the nationwide Clean City Movement, became a major endeavor that the League hoped would improve living conditions for the city's population. They set the month of May for their war on dirt and garbage, with Fort Neck as a prime target: "A section of the city that could not be authentically described as picturesque or endowed with that degree of cleanliness which is denominated as next of kin to a high state of spiritual welfare is Fort Neck, in the vicinity of the Coast Guard Academy." The group intended to start with dirt but finish with the "moral conditions" of the city.[9]

The campaign in New London never got off the ground. On May 1 Italian laborers launched their general strike, depriving the Civic League of the only local workforce available for scrubbing clean the neighborhoods. At first, hopeful articles appeared in the *New London Day*, itself a sponsor of the Clean Up Campaign, that all was well, and that the Highway Department functioned normally. By May 9, however, they were forced to bow to the inevitable, that the campaign "had met a serious setback." Soon their plans for a celebratory parade were canceled, and then the whole effort had to be abandoned. Civic League boosters bemoaned that New London could not compete for the winning trophy from a group in Boston that apparently functioned as the national center.

The strike revealed the complete indifference of the Italian working-class to the moral reform efforts of the city. Italians (and Poles, Russians, Germans, and others) simply ignored their grand designs to beautify the city's streets. None of the middle-class reformers had bothered to include either immigrants or trade unions in their quest. The Clean Up Campaign went the way of local temperance efforts, and was not revived the coming year.

New London—as a port city only a short distance from Rum Row where offshore cargo ships unloaded their goods to smaller craft—developed the reputation as one of the "wettest" cities in Connecticut during Prohibition. In 1924 the Coast Guard based at least four destroyers there as part of a "dry fleet" to intercept liquor shipments.[10] Every neighborhood, from East New London to Shaw Street, had their speakeasies, distilleries, and breweries that ran continuously through the 1920s, but none compared to the scale of these activities engaged in by the residents of Fort Neck/Trumbull. Despite its being wedged against the principal Coast Guard base between New York and Boston, Fort Trumbull became an important unloading point for bootleggers in southeastern Connecticut. One shipment successfully landed "under the very noses of the Coast Guard" in 1931 at Bentley's Creek at the end of Trumbull Street. The authorities noted the "many fishing vessels that moor in the creek" that may have been used. Indeed, the maritime and fishing skills of the Marchegiani came into constant use throughout the decade. Neighborhood residents had grown up accustomed to integrating swimming, fishing, and the use of beaches into their daily routines, in a neighborhood with the ever-present tidal waters of the Thames River lapping the shore only a few feet from many of the homes.[11]

As significant as smuggling was to the region's trade in bootleg liquor, however, Fort Trumbull gained an unequaled reputation as a center for the manufacture, distribution and sale of these substances. By the end of the decade the neighborhood had become commonly known as "New London Oasis."[12] The police staged repeated—and at times nightly—raids in Fort Trumbull, seizing large quantities of liquor and their means of production and arresting numerous suspects. Announcements that the neighborhood had been "cleaned up," would inevitably be followed by another series of raids. The very audacity of Fort Trumbull's bootleggers became a defense attorney's line of argument in court, when in 1921 he sought to refute the testimony of a Coast Guard sailor/spy in the neighborhood. How could a speakeasy have operated on East Street, right across from the Coast Guard Academy, since "the very fumes of the liquor ought to have reached them. Yet they are not here with a single complaint against the man."[13]

The man in question was Lorenzo Montali, husband of Anita, and an important member of Gruppo I Liberi. He would be far from the last Fort Trumbull anarchist to run afoul of the existing liquor laws. A roster of anarchist militants composes a large part of the list of targets of police, federal prohibition, and Coast Guard raids in the neighborhood. Among those anarchists either arrested or raided were Nostralio Facchini, Alfredo Muratori, Fortunato Renzoni, Louis Vescovi, Alberto Servadio, and Luigi Camillucci. A number of other violators had been sympathizers of the anarchist movement or worked as bartenders, brewers, and so on, for still-active anarchists.

The extent of their involvement varied. Nostralio Facchini of 72 Goshen Street faced charges in 1924 for the illegal transportation of liquor, after having served a year in the Franklin Street jail on the same charge. Alberto Servadio ran a speakeasy at his house at 50 Goshen Street, at which he was raided twice. He served twenty days in jail, but mostly for having severely beaten two drunken sailors he accused of having started a fight in his establishment. Most of those convicted, however, faced fines of several hundred dollars. Anarchists backed up their comrades by providing bond money. When an anarchist was arrested in 1921, Lorenzo Montali, and Sarah Menghi, sister-in-law of Fortunato Renzoni—and both tied to bootlegging—bailed him out.[14]

A number of nonanarchists participated in Fort Trumbull bootlegging as well; their primary motivation, as with their revolutionary neighbors, was economic. The liquor trade provided supplementary income in a neighborhood dependent on the cyclical (and seasonal) building trades industry. Bootleggers had the public's sympathy in New London, as they did in industrial centers across the country. When a New London–based Coast Guard vessel opened fire on a rumrunner in Narragansett Bay, killing three crew members, riots started in Boston. In New London, a gang badly beat up two Coast Guard sailors in the Central Vermont Railroad yard as a response. Another group stoned a houseboat owned by the officer in charge of the Coast Guard vessel.[15]

Women played an important part in the substantial activities of the liquor trade in the Fort during the 1920s. One woman ran a walk-in cellar speakeasy, while others served in a variety of duties from accountants to bottlers. Another woman, her husband in jail for running illegal liquor, put the alcohol in canning jars and delivered it throughout the neighborhood in a baby carriage.[16] The survival of families depended on the income earned by these women. When the police arrested Clotilda Frausini of 99 Smith Street on the charge of selling beer in 1922, the *New London Day* carried an expansive article on her case and that of several others appearing in court.

> She told one of the frankest stories ever revealed on the liquor question in local court and was let off easy. She stated that since the death of her husband she had worked for five years in a mill to raise her children and then last year she got sick and had to quit work and then started making home beer to sell. Eighteen cases of this beer were found in her home. She stated that she sold the beer at ten cents a bottle—iced and all—and she did nothing to rob the public as was being done. She said she had to make her living this way 'to keep the family going.' She claimed to have been in business for the past four months.[17]

The need to feed her children led another woman, Anna Marie Montesi, to run a speakeasy in her home after losing her husband to the Spanish influenza epidemic after World War I. Perhaps her reputation as the producer of the best bathtub gin in the Fort brought in as a customer Sergio Mencarelli, an anarchist fisherman and a member of Gruppo I Liberi, whom she would marry. Women's involvement in Fort Trumbull bootlegging had begun the neighborhood's pre-Prohibition period. In 1918, Mrs. Giustina Giri, whose family seems to have been in the orbit of the anarchists, was sentenced to three months in jail and a two hundred dollar fine for the illegal sale of beer. Her lawyer unsuccessfully pleaded that the defendant had recently moved from "the discouraging environments of the Fort Neck section." She had two prior convictions.[18]

Residents of Fort Trumbull have accurately recounted in interviews the absence of street crime in the neighborhood in which they grew up. The Prohibition period offers an exception, as violent actions in the streets—fights, stabbings, and a shooting or two—seemed to escalate. Bootlegging may have required extensive cooperation among participants to keep the production facilities operating, but it apparently led to some frictions and jealousies as well.[19]

Members and sympathizers of Gruppo I Liberi were not out of step with either Fanese or non-Fanese Italians, but their heavy involvement in bootlegging seems to have involved more than the earning of personal income. The continuing exploits of Victor Frederick/Vittorio Federici, who spent the first years of Prohibition behind bars in the state prison in Wethersfield for his freight car robbery caper are revealing. On his release he lost no time in entering the front ranks of illicit liquor traders of New London. If the city became one of the pivot points of the Connecticut's rum traffic, with Fort Neck as the nerve center, Frederick served as chief supply master in the neighborhood's bootlegging industry. Frederick eclipsed all others in the scale of his operations and in the attention given him by the federal and local enforcers of the liquor laws.

From the outset, Frederick showed audacity in his activities. His first arrest after being released from state prison in 1922 emanated from an operation he had set up in the Pine Grove Camp in nearby Niantic, a spiritualist retreat. Still in existence today, the Camp is run under the belief that God and the spirits are the same thing: "Spirits are everywhere. It is not unusual for visitors to say they have seen, heard or felt spirits." Apparently they didn't appreciate Frederick's spirits, so they turned him in. Neither did military officers next door at the National Guard's Camp Niantic—the soldiers of which were assuredly Frederick's principal customers.[20]

During Prohibition, Frederick would face not only fines as punishment, but would have his properties attached at 29 and 33 Walbach Street for the sum of $7,173. He owed the federal government from his revenues as the result of a suit in federal district court by US Attorney George H. Cohen: "The action is the aftermath of raids upon Federicci's [sic] home in Walbach Street on June 19, 1926 and August 19, 1926." This approach of the federal government against Frederick resembled that used against gangster Al Capone in Chicago, and speaks to how seriously they viewed Frederick's operations.[21]

By 1930, Frederick had emerged with his properties untouched, probably from having made a deal with the federal court, but he only increased his activity. In January even the *New London Day* seemed taken aback by the level of Frederick's operations: "Fort Neck Beer Garden Raided; Liquor and Apparatus Seized; Owner and Employees Held."

> The tenth anniversary of national prohibition which was recently observed was marked by Victor Frederick, bootlegger, according to the police, by the erection of an up-to-date beer garden in the rear of his home at 33 Walbach Street. The garden, which was completed only a short time ago, is a one story frame structure completely furnished with tables, chairs, small bar, and with attractive curtains and rugs.
>
> It was raided today by a squad of police and more than 50 cases of beer, together with considerable malt, hops, sugar and other articles used in its manufacture; up to date bottling and capping apparatus and much alcohol, wine and whiskey were seized.

Police also raided Frederick's house and garage, and in the former found some contraband wine and discovered the house outfitted like a small brewery. John Bartolucci was arrested and charged with manufacturing. Eugene Gianetti was charged as bartender in the beer garden and he was taken into custody on a charge of illegal possession. While the police officers removed the contraband they had seized, Frederick put in an appearance; police charged him with selling, possessing, and manufacturing liquor.[22]

The Day observed that, "Frederick has an unsavory record as a bootlegger and has been convicted in both the local and federal courts." The next day the authorities announced that the raids were a "complete success," that Fort Neck speakeasies had closed while their owners "scurried for shelter." Their elation proved short-lived; the following day the police raided another beer garden on Smith Street.[23]

Frederick's use of two names may have confused the authorities as to who they were dealing with, and it seems likely that he better concealed whatever anarchist literature he must have possessed than he did his liquor. (He may have been shielded from overzealous scrutiny since the local police seem to have been some of the bootleggers' best customers throughout the decade.) City authorities never publicly connected Frederick with the anarchist movement. By contrast, the Italian government had a dossier on him since 1910, three years after he emigrated from Pesaro province. His name first appears as a donor to *Cronaca Sovversiva* in 1909, a year before the Italian authorities noted his subscription to the Fanese anarchist paper *In Marcia!* Federici apparently did nothing to attract the attention of the Italian government while in his homeland; his frequenting of the saloon of the "noted anarchist" Federico Dondero—as it did with a number of other Fanese living in New London—put him on their list as a subversive. Tall, of medium build, and with brown eyes and black hair, Federici became a militant Galleanist. He had sent his 1912 salutation "Shouting Down with the Spies" to both *Cronaca* and *In Marcia!* in Fano.[24]

Except for being listed as "shirtmaker" while an inmate at the Wethersfield state prison in 1920, his occupations from the time of his arrival in the United States are nonskilled: "carter" on his CPC dossier, laborer in a shipyard, coal truck driver in censuses, and "truckman" on his draft registration card. From at least 1919 until well into the 1930s, Frederick sought to earn his primary income outside of the law. His prior arrest for freight car robbery tied him with a gang that operated in localities in Massachusetts, where Italian anarchists were similarly active. Italian police records indicated an arrest of his in 1929, probably for bootlegging, and noted that his application for US citizenship had been rejected. Keeping in mind that hearsay and exaggeration from police agents entered the files of the CPC, the Italian fascist government later reported Frederick as having traveled to Europe to meet with exiled anarchist groups in France and Switzerland. While it cannot be corroborated, the trip would have further confirmed Frederick's central role in Gruppo I Liberi for decades to come. This much is certain: Frederick deftly combined revolution, criminality, and entrepreneurialism throughout his career, a triad from which he seldom wavered. A

1905 photo of him taken in Italy still hangs on the basement wall of the Italian Dramatic Club. I was unable to reproduce the photo; the reader must try to envision the image of a young man poised jauntily, as if challenging the world.[25]

Several other members or sympathizers of Gruppo I Liberi engaged in illegal activities, though information is scanty. Victor Frederick apparently hired the hard-swinging, former speakeasy operator Alberto Servadio as a bartender when he maintained his unlicensed operations after the demise of Prohibition. A single man, Servadio worked in restaurants and taverns in New London throughout his life. Another anarchist, Alfredo Muratori, had been involved in a possible theft ring in northern Connecticut and southern Massachusetts in 1920 and later apparently bootlegged in Fort Trumbull. A longtime member of Gruppo I Liberi, his obituary in *L'Adunata dei Refrattari* somewhat cryptically described him as having been "very well known in Connecticut," where they called him "Piracion."[26]

Luigi Camillucci may well represent the typical Fort Trumbull anarchist in his involvement in bootlegging activity. Police raided his home on Nameaug Street in March 1921, finding twelve cases of home brewed beer, two forty gallon barrels of "mash and liquid," and a bottle-capping machine. The authorities considered his operation to have been fairly substantial, but it came at a time of high unemployment in the construction trades; Camillucci, a stonemason, was most likely out of work. He seems not to have been arrested a second time. By 1922, he was an active member of the local bricklayers' union. As if to juxtapose the complex makeup of the Fort Trumbull anarchists, on the same day the police raided Camilucci, the Salvation Army dedicated its new building on Main Street—built by the anarchist Bartolucci brothers, themselves on hand for the ceremony.[27]

It is difficult to determine whether Fort Trumbull anarchists' involvement in bootlegging represents an aberration within the national movement. In 1907, Italian anarchists had been drawn into a local battle over kitchen bars that proliferated in Barre, Vermont. Barre provided the base for *Cronaca Sovversiva* and Luigi Galleani until 1912; anarchism's strength in the town rested on stonecutters from the Carrara region of Tuscany. Temperance forces attempted to defeat a referendum that would have allowed the licensing of saloons; anarchists seemingly took the side of the Christian crusaders in supporting a "no license" vote. Emma Goldman and Galleani took the platform at a special meeting of between five hundred to nine hundred townspeople. Both opposed licensing because it would have forbade an economic activity vital to many working-class Italians, especially women. *Cronaca* described the situation as an "equivocal dilemma: whether to support privileged license or the hypocritical Temperance, showing how it can only lay bare the betrayal, the lies, the corruption." Goldman told the audience to "vote against granting licenses to a few 'spies,' and to give the right of selling liquor to everybody." The anarchists opposed giving government authorities more power than necessary in economic activities vital to sections of the working class. The licensing law passed, but the kitchen bars of Barre went on, subject to relentless police raids. Even though Italian bootlegging provides a backdrop in *Like Lesser Gods*, Mari Tomasi's 1949 novel about Barre's stonecutters, the extent of the town's anarchist involvement in the trade is unknown.[28]

Fort Trumbull's unique coastal position undoubtedly made bootlegging an irresistible proposition for anarchists and nonanarchists alike. While the extent of Gruppo I Liberi's engagement with related "underground" activities cannot be precisely determined, an interview conducted by Paul Avrich in 1989 with anarchist John Vattuone contains a passage placing the New London group firmly in the Galleanist camp in this arena. Vattuone was a Sardinian-born maritime worker who jumped ship in New York in 1922 and remained in the United States for the remainder of his life. He joined an anarchist group in the Williamsburg section of Brooklyn, and had close relations with the Galleanists. Among his recollections of the Italian movement of the period is a brief account of the New London group:

> Clemente Duval lived in Bruno's house for a while. When Duval's *Memorie autobiografiche* came out, the comrades in New London held a symposium about it and brought Duval there. Bruno was also there—I think it was 1929. They had a big group. There was lots of wine, a lot of talk, and of course a collection.[29]

This passage contains several key bits of information. Clemente Duval was a French anarchist expropriator and a jewel thief who had escaped from imprisonment in French Guyana. Galleani enthusiastically approved of Duval's methods; he translated Duval's memoirs and serialized them in *Cronaca Sovversiva*, beginning in 1907. Part of the memoirs were published in 1917, and the entire book, with a lengthy introduction by Galleani, in 1929. Galleanists had smuggled Duval into the United States and supported him in New York City until he died in 1935. The "Bruno" mentioned was Raffaele Schiavina, previously deported in 1919 and editor of *L'Adunata dei Refrattari*, and also brought into the country by Galleanists.[30]

The symposium did not receive mention in *L'Adunata*, possibly so as not to call attention to an event with two participants illegally in the country. It also placed Gruppo I Liberi, or perhaps a faction of it, squarely in the camp of supporting armed actions, expropriations, and involvement in the "underground" economy. This position had been extremely controversial within the anarchist movement since the rise of the illegalists, as they were called, in Europe in the 1880s. As the 1920s proceeded, more light is shed on Gruppo I Liberi's involvement in these activities.

CHAPTER TWELVE

"THE 12TH OF OCTOBER IN NEW LONDON"

The general alarm fire that broke out in the Odd Fellows hall at 205 Bank Street on June 1, 1924, may have had an accidental origin. Arson, though, was more likely its cause. Stores and businesses above street level suffered heavy water and smoke damage, while rooms in the basement were swallowed by flames. A number of fraternal and lodge groups rented space there, among these the Societá Siciliana. The Sicilian group held their meetings here, but more importantly they stored their bejeweled flag of Italy, with the monarchist emblem of the House of Savoy. As with tradition, the flag had been christened by the Catholic Church and the group carried it in parades and festivities. Oral tradition in the Fort has maintained that Marchegiani carried out the arson attack because of differences with the Sicilians over these matters. A more likely reason would have been the rise of profascist sentiment in the New London Sicilian community. The appearance of fascism was not isolated to New London, as it spread throughout the area where migrants from Tusa had settled, in Pawcatuck, Stonington, and Westerly. If anarchism's face in the New London region was primarily Marchegian, fascism's was at least partially Sicilian.[1]

Westerly became a city with a heavy Italian presence, mostly Calabrese and Sicilian. As late as 1984, 40 percent of the population had single Italian ancestry and 25 percent more mixed Italian parentage. Strong extended families and business and social networks were the rule. Pawcatuck, crammed into the southeast corner of Connecticut, became an Italian center from a spillover effect from Westerly. A textile mill town,

Pawcatuck's St. Michael's Catholic Church played an enormous role in the life of the Italian population. Sicilians in New London embraced the Feast of the Assumption, celebrated first in Pawcatuck in 1920. The procession originated over three hundred years ago in Tusa, and commemorates the ascent of the body of the Virgin Mary into Heaven. "A strong belief in the Roman Catholic faith is a natural manifestation of many of the members' upbringing," observed the historian of the Maria Assunta Society of Pawtucket in 1998.[2]

Just as the traditional American values of hard work and duty seemed to dovetail with Mussolini's programs in Italy, the conservative and religious traditions of the Sicilian communities in Westerly, Pawcatuck, Stonington, and New London allowed for the introduction of profascist, or at least pro-Mussolini sentiment, during the 1920s. Criticizing "Il Duce" in Pawcatuck could be hazardous; a 1936 stabbing in a bar had seriously injured a twenty-seven-year old non-Italian man after he had spoken ill of Mussolini. The newspaper account mentioned the remark had been "resented by a number of people of Italian extraction who were in the place at the time."[3]

It is possible that the spoon-fed Americanism doled out to the Italians in New London after World War I created a backlash in the community. Americanization's "melting pot" presumptions tended to denigrate the social and cultural behavior of Italians; in reaction, even while their integration into American society continued apace, the need for the community to cling to their homeland grew. When a particularly offensive article appeared in the *New London Day* in 1922 (discussed in chapter 1) the Sons of Italy requested and received a meeting with the reporter who had written the piece, in which they defended the Shaw Street community.[4] The intensely patriotic processions of Sicilians down Bank Street at Italy's entrance in war had already revealed the growing appeal of nationalism to New London Italians, a sentiment that would reach a fever pitch with the coming to power of Mussolini and fascism. The fascist government met a largely positive response from Italian Americans, who saw in Mussolini a dynamic figure who could rescue their homeland from its status as a much-maligned, second-rate power. As did the American public at large, and especially business and political circles, Italian Americans looked favorably on the promises of social transformation in the homeland.

Historians have discussed the reasons for fascism's appeal to Italian Americans during the 1920s and 1930s. John P. Diggins wrote in his classic work *Mussolini and Fascism: The View from America*, "In telling the Italians they were something less than 'American,' nativists created enclaves of emotional estrangement within the country, thereby leaving the alienated Italian American nowhere to turn." Philip Cannistraro noted the "new-found nationalism in the face of the hostility and scorn heaped upon them by American society," and asserted that Italians' support for Mussolini, "was not a result of ideological fervor, or even understanding, but of wounded pride." Further, Cannistraro observed that under the immense pressures exerted by their American environment, Italians abandoned their regionalism and he quoted an Italian historian: "In Italy they had never been Italians, but in America they became Italian nationalists . . ."[5]

Profascist—or at least pro-Mussolini—sentiment found a strong base in New Haven, Waterbury, Hartford, and Bridgeport. The Italian American left found itself on the defensive in resisting this tide that originated with the *prominenti*. The situation proved extremely difficult for antifascists in these cities at times, where sizable layers of Italian businesspeople and professionals leaned almost instinctively, as had their counterparts in Italy, toward fascism. Large numbers of Italians in these cities could be attracted to profascist mass events and pageants. New Haven, the center of the Italian community in Connecticut, also became the strongpoint for the state's fascist-leaning movement. New Haven was home to two powerful allies of Mussolini: the Italian consulate on Wooster Square, staffed by vice-consul Pasquale De Cicco, and the *Corriere del Connecticut*, a paper that moved further to the right as the decade proceeded. A barometer of the Connecticut *prominenti*'s fascist proclivities came with the publication in 1933 of *Il Progresso degl'Italiani nel Connecticut*, which featured a message from Mussolini and photos of various Italian community leaders striking bombastic Il Duce–like poses and proclaiming their fascist beliefs. (The book reads like a parody of this layer, and must have been embarrassing to them a decade later.)[6]

Pasquale De Cicco played an important role in the Italian communities in Connecticut, and is certainly a figure of interest regarding New London. During the 1920s, differences often arose between Italian diplomats in the United States and Italian American fascists over the nature of the fascist movement and its relationship with Italy's foreign policy needs. These antagonisms may not have existed between Pasquale De Cicco and the pro-Mussolini elements in Connecticut. About forty-nine years old in 1928, De Cicco had become an American citizen in

1909 and was appointed Consular Agent in New Haven in 1915. That year he enlisted in the Italian army and served for five months, before being sent on various missions to London by the Italian government. In 1919 he again took a position with the Italian consulate in New Haven, serving principally as vice-consul, and in 1925, during a trip to Italy, joined the fascist party. Although he retained his US citizenship and continued to vote in New Haven, he had reentered the United States as a citizen of Italy. This would become a matter of controversy during World War II.

His service to the political right predated his fascism, as he had unsuccessfully appealed to Italian brass mill strikers in Waterbury in 1920 to return to work. Throughout the decade he played took an interventionist role on the side of the fascist forces in Connecticut's Italian communities. He would later be denounced before the House Un-American Activities Committee as one of the most active Italian diplomats in this regard. In 1923, a flying chair hit De Cicco during a fracas in New Haven between fascists and antifascists. Liberal antifascist exile Gaetano Salvemini described De Cicco as a "wild fascist." An antifascist (and former Galleanist) from New Britain claimed in 1942 that the consul agent "has poisoned the minds of many Italians." (De Cicco would be interned by the US government during World War II as part of a group of 257 allegedly profascist Italian Americans. His claims of simple patriotism for the United States and Italy were less than truthful.)[7]

Prefascist organizations appeared in New Haven and Bridgeport in the early 1920s. In Bridgeport, former Italian war veterans formed the Italian Legion in December 1922 "strictly in accord with the principles and motives of the Fascists."[8] Street battles and confrontations raged across Connecticut, as they did throughout the country, between fascists and antifascists in the Italian neighborhoods and at public events. Antifascists, usually outnumbered, continually mobilized to bring their message to the Italian public, and refused to give ground to the fascists. The Italian American left succeeded in drawing large audiences to their events. In New Britain, rather than being swamped by fascist numbers, they were able to neutralize the enemy by forming united fronts between anarchists, socialists, syndicalists, and communists. Antifascists in that city probably controlled most Italian organizations because of their historic strength in the Italian working-class and the relative weakness of the *prominenti*. Other towns, usually smaller in size and possessing radical groupings of northern Italians such as Wallingford, Stafford Springs, Hamden, and Stony Creek, might have held their own.

A unique situation presented itself in New London, where the two Italian communities pursued seemingly parallel tracks. Events in 1928 made for a collision. The annual Columbus Day celebration—until then entirely noncontroversial and undertaken in a somewhat perfunctory, ritualistic manner by the Italian groups and clubs—proved to be different that year.

Preparations began two years before and included nearly every non-Marchegian Italian club in the city. The elaborate planning far exceeded past efforts for Columbus Day. Besides mobilizing large numbers for the celebration, at the close of the ceremonies a sixteen-foot statue of Columbus would be unveiled at Tyler Square, at the corner of Bank and Howard Streets. A local barber, Nicholas Salegna, headed the Columbus Statue Fund. The statue itself would be sculpted in Pietrasanta, Italy, and shipped to the United States. Forty units would march in the enormous parade that would wind through the principal streets of the city, headed by military units, and followed by the various Italian societies, including at least a dozen lodges of the Sons of Italy. Non-Italian groups included the Veterans of Foreign Wars, American Legion and Daughters of the American Revolution. Political figures, both Italian and non-Italian, would abound in the celebration and dinner and dance to follow the festivities. Fireworks would cap the evening.[9]

The critical difference between past celebrations and that of 1928 was the participation of the local branch of the Fascist League of North America (FLNA). This organization had been founded in New York in July 1925, in coordination with the Mussolini regime to both propagate fascism in the Italian communities of the United States and to act as an agent to strengthen ties between the fascist government and the United States. The FLNA grew to about seven thousand members by 1926; while it was only one of a gallery of profascist Italian groups in the country, it obviously attracted the most hard-core and extreme elements, and was a prime target of the antifascist left.[10] To include the fascists in the New London parade preparations showed the degree to which Italian-American communities had warmed to most aspects of the Mussolini regime. Not only did the FLNA sit on the planning committee, they were to be among the contingents—blackshirts and all—marching in the parade.[11]

The New London FLNA rented storefront space on the first floor of a three-story building at 72 Shaw Street. Formerly a spaghetti factory, the building contained apartments above and was located roughly in the middle of the Shaw Street community. The membership numbered in the dozens in 1928 and rested in the hands of two brothers, Antonio and Salvatore Ficarra, barbers who lived on Truman Street. Salvatore, in his early thirties, was slightly older than the young men who composed the membership. (He later became president of the Italian Republican club in New London.) More typical was his twenty-four-year-old brother; they were born in Trapani, Sicily, while most of the others came from Tusa. Their occupations, based on limited information available, appear to have been principally small shopkeepers or employees of these small businesses; no *prominenti* names appear as members. Little research has been done on the social base of Italian-American fascism, but New London's FLNA branch clearly had a plebeian character. Nationally, Mussolini's hardcore supporters mistrusted the *prominenti*, viewing them as grasping, untrustworthy opportunists.[12]

The New London fascist branch included members from Norwich and other surrounding towns; among these was Giuseppe Tudisca, who played a prominent role in the group. Tudisca owed a shoe repair business on Mechanic Street in Pawcatuck and boarded with another Italian at 19 Downer Street. By 1928 he had lived in Pawcatuck for about three years. Born in Tusa in 1890, he had migrated in 1913 and had left a wife and daughter behind in Sicily. His brother Gaspare, a stonemason and war veteran of the Italian army, was his only family living in the United States.[13]

The FLNA clearly made some inroads into the Shaw Street community, in the view of both neighborhood residents and the anarchists of the Fort. People who grew up in the neighborhood can recollect blackshirts on the street, marching proudly; after decades, a residue of respect for the fascists remained. One man, born on Shaw Street and interviewed in 1998 remembered seeing a fascist flag on their building, with the words, "A Noi!," perhaps referring to a fascist journal by the same name. The fascists emphasized "education" of the community in their political activities in New London.[14]

The fascist presence on Shaw Street represented a threatening beachhead to Gruppo I Liberi. The anarchist movement, along with the entire Italian American left, regarded fascists as their mortal enemy; indeed, they drew a line of blood between them. To Gruppo I Liberi, the fascists in New London were an extension of the same enemy that had terrorized, beat, and murdered their comrades in Italy. Fascism's entry into Fano may have been tardy, compared to other Italian labor centers, but it arrived to crush a workers' movement that had taken five decades to build. Fascist squads murdered Fanese leftists and shuttered all the workers' papers, including *La Frusta*. Fascist attacks scattered radicals in the area; the last issue of the paper remarked that, "We don't know therefore if the papers we send to arrive at old addresses are read or burnt."[15] Fascist actions in Fano may as well have taken place in the Fort Trumbull neighborhood. On the night of August 5, 1922, a fascist squad returning from attacking radicals in Ancona stopped in Fano and murdered Amilcare Biancheria and Giuseppe Morrelli, both antifascists. Biancheria, a twenty-three-year-old stonemason and a Communist supporter, came from an anarchist family. His uncle Adimero Biancheria was an anarchist textile worker living in Stafford Springs, Connecticut. Fascists on Shaw Street represented a threat that they felt compelled to act against; the Columbus Day celebrations provided the conjuncture for their response, and the anarchists would write about the events circumspectly thirty-five years later. Fascism had attempted to "pitch its tent" in New London in 1928, and aimed at becoming the "driver of the Italian community." The Columbus Day parade would provide publicity for their group, and they observed that fascists had been using the day for the same purpose around the country. In Detroit that very day a confrontation between fascists and antifascists resulted in an anarchist being fatally shot. In New London, nothing seemed out of the ordinary leading up to the day's festivities. Two longtime supporters of Gruppo I Liberi—Lorenzo Montali and Alfredo Bartolucci—both well-known local businesspeople, had even contributed to the Columbus statue fund.[16]

The parade plans called for marchers to assemble in the vicinity of Jefferson Avenue and Bank Street, and at 2 o'clock to proceed down Bank Street and wind through roughly twenty-five blocks before proceeding to Tyler Square, where they would be received by politicians, Italian community leaders, and Pasquale De Cicco. The fascists would assemble at the upper end of Ocean Avenue, several blocks northwest of their headquarters; the New London *fascisti*'s place in the line of march put them between Prince Post of the American Legion and the Ladies' Catholic Benevolent Society.[17]

Friday, October 12 dawned with exquisite weather for a parade, a warm day that brought back memories of summer, the sky cloudless and blue. Across the city, the different sections of the parade began to congeal, the marching bands taking their places between the numerous floats. Shortly before 2 o'clock, several cars filled with at least two dozen men left Fort Trumbull and proceeded to converge on the intersection of Steward and Shaw Streets. The men carried an assortment of weapons—clubs, canes, pipes, and blackjacks. One car approached from the north on Shaw, another down Steward, perhaps two up Shaw from the direction of the Fort. The cars arrived in time to catch part of the fascist contingent as they left their clubroom door at the back of the building. Forced to run a gauntlet, the blackshirts were pummeled from all sides. "They would wait for them as the fascists emerged," recalled Matt Orsini. "One guy came out, hit him, another, bang—as they came out they got banged." Some of the fascists—Paots Lo Verde, Giuseppe Tudisca, Longo Sabbatini, Maloroma Pietri, and Jennuru Parreta—attempted to run but were swiftly caught. Blows continued to reign down on the blackshirts. If their testimony is to be believed, Lorenzo Montali struck Tudisca in the face with a blackjack, Angelo Giano and Augusto Peroni beat Parreta, while Renato Giustini and Vincenzo Gaudenzi pummeled Lo Verde. The street fight ended within minutes; by the time six patrolmen arrived, the fascists lie wounded and bleeding on the pavement and the assailants had piled back into their cars and left.[18]

Renato Giustini apparently had been an important initiator or organizer of this antifascist action; his obituary in *L'Adunata dei Refrattari* almost forty years later would be the only one from New London linking an individual to this engagement. He played a vital role in the local movement for a number of years, having immigrated to the United States in 1907. Recognized as one of the most fiercely dedicated anarchists in New London, Giustini had cosigned the salutation with Rafaelle Petrini in 1912 (chapter 6), urging violence against the unnamed "spies" in New London. Unlike most other male anarchists in the neighborhood, Giustini seems to have worked in factories from his arrival, first as an apprentice molder, and then settling into his lifetime career in the skilled occupation of loom fixer in the Brainerd & Armstrong Silk Mill, living at 56 Smith Street. Whatever his exposure to anarchism in the Marche, he undoubtedly became an unrelenting Galleanist in New London.[19]

The attack on the blackshirts represented a combined operation, a united front between Gruppo I Liberi and antifascists of the Mutual Aid Society influenced by the Workers Party, although most of the attackers came from the IDC. On the face of it, a joint effort between the two factions constituted a remarkable development. Only two years before, Galleanists and Communists had nearly come to blows in New London at a public lecture by Enea Sormenti, head of the Italian section of the Workers Party and editor of their publication *Il Lavoratore*. The meeting may have taken place at the Smith Street hall, and the topic of Sormenti's talk was "Fascism and the Class Struggle." Sormenti, born in Trieste as Vittorio Vidali, had been smuggled out of Italy in 1923, after engaging in more than a few street fights with the fascists. In New York he teamed up with Carlo Tresca to continue physically confronting fascists wherever they showed their faces, and played a major role in forming the *Alleanza Anti-fascista del Nord America* (AFANA). The Galleanists, typically, shunned the alliance.

A large portion of Gruppo I Liberi's membership turned out for Sormenti's talk, and as he began to speak they rose and issued a physical challenge to the "red fascist" to clarify a dispute that originated in New York. The audience contained a number of unaffiliated Italian workers, *astanti*. According to an article signed by the group, Sormenti began to "tremble" and "mumble," and the Communist speaker was further called a "chicken." This scenario seems unlikely in view of Sormenti/Vidali's future career as a Comintern operative and allegedly as part of an enforcement unit during the Spanish Civil War. His character has been described as anything but meek. The incident illustrates the enormous gulf between the two competing groups. Despite collisions such as this one—and there surely must have been more—and in spite of the arson attack of 1922, their hatred of fascism forced them together in 1928. Again, Orsini commented, "In the Fort there was wind of a Mussolini group marching in the parade . . . that was a big day for the Mussolini gang . . . They decided 'we gotta do something' . . . the clubs got together and had (weapons). They were armed. They would bang the hell out of them."[20]

The fascists, nursing their wounds, at first would not reveal the identities of their attackers. The parade began as scheduled, with the remaining fascist contingent marching under heavy police protection. When the parade finished its route around the city's downtown area it met an enormous crowd at Tyler Square. They heard speeches for the statue dedication exercise from Mayor Malcolm Scott, Congressman Richard Freeman, State Secretary Ernest Rogers, Michelangelo Russo, a high official in the Connecticut Sons of Italy, and Pasquale De Cicco. A banquet at the Mohican Hotel on State Street followed the festivities, with a hundred prominent guests attending, including political and military officials, as well as local Italian *prominenti*. De Cicco addressed the gathering, apparently in English, and praised Mussolini's policy of encouraging Italians not to emigrate. Fireworks ended the evening, and as luck would have it, an errant aerial bomb injured nine people, one seriously, to further dampen the euphoria of the celebration.[21]

While the festivities drew to a close, the beaten fascists had a change of mind and began to identify their attackers. That evening a police sergeant and two patrolmen escorting several of the fascists entered Fort Trumbull and arrested three alleged attackers: Arturo Pettinari, twenty-eight, of 48 East Street; Augusto Peroni, forty-seven, of 26 Nameaug Street; and Lorenzo Montali, fifty-nine, of 28 East Street. When the police and fascists reached the vicinity of Smith Street, the New London Day described the hostile reception they received, as "they were booed and hooted at by Italians who flocked to doors and windows of their houses." The cry "Down with the fascisti!" came from the enraged neighborhood. Apparently at least one of the arrested was nabbed on the street, allowing for the greater intensity of the reaction from the community.[22]

Saturday morning brought three more arrests: Angelo Giano, twenty-eight, of 25 Fourth Street; Vincenzo Gaudenzi, twenty-eight, of 54 Goshen Street; and Renato (identified as Raymond) Giustini, thirty-six of 54 Smith Street. The police, apparently acting on information from a fascist coworker, arrested Gaudenzi at his job at the Corticelli Silk Mill. This prompted an immediate walkout by the entire workforce of the mill. The police charged all those arrested with breach of peace and inciting to riot; they were arraigned in police court and each posted $500 bond and were released. A policeman found a heavy club near Steward Street, and a fascist identified it as one of the weapons used in the attack.[23]

Arturo Pettinari and Renato Giustini have been discussed, and we know Lorenzo Montali, at fifty-nine the oldest of the alleged attackers. As coowner of a bakery that had moved from East Street to 230 Shaw Street, where it became the "Italian Bakery," Lorenzo was a "figure" around New London. The address of the bakery placed it at the lower end of the street and very close to Fort Trumbull (since leveled with a traffic rotary occupying its approximate position). Several others from the Fort, including Raffaele Petrini (in 1922) moved into this section, as if staking claim to it for the Marchegiani.[24]

Augusto Peroni entered New London's anarchist movement in its infancy, having played a quite visible role in major events that shaped the course of the groups' history. He had been attacked by Galleani as an ally of Gennaro Foschini in 1905, and had cryptically criticized plans for a "secret group" in New London. It is possible that Peroni never became a Galleanist.

Listed as a member of the anarchist fishermen's union in Fano, Vincenzo Gaudenzi may have immigrated in 1921. His name appeared only once in the Italian American anarchist press, in 1925, and soon after he moved into the ranks of the local Communist movement. A textile worker during the 1920s, he later became a stonemason contractor. Little is known of Angelo Giano. He earned a CPC file after the Steward Street attack, which lists him as having been born in Fano.[25]

One might have expected the organizers of the Columbus Day festivities to denounce an attack on one of the participating contingents in their parade. Instead, their reaction was one of a total silence that seemed to suggest a curious neutrality. The image of parading blackshirts in the streets of the United States had, in fact, become a matter of controversy in leading American circles. The State Department did not warm to the idea of foreign-controlled, uniformed militants, even if antiradical, marching in the streets of the United States. Perhaps this development urged the improvised hands-off approach of the New London *prominenti*. In any case, they did not intervene in support of their injured fascist compatriots. However sympathetic the aspiring Italian politicians and business leaders of the city were to Mussolini's regime, they were mindful of what would affect their future agendas.

The *New London Day* uttered not an editorial peep. Two Connecticut newspapers, the *New Haven Register* and *Norwich Bulletin*, referred to the attack as a battle between the fascisti and the mafia. This confusion may have originated with the widespread awareness of Fort Trumbull as the center of bootlegging; given the times, the public might understandably have believed that any organized Italian group engaged in illegal activities in that neighborhood had to have been a "racket." But the fascists and their allies of the *Corriere del Connecticut* knew who was behind the attack: sovversivi, the reds and anarchists at the core of Italian American opposition to fascism.

Reports of planned demonstrations, threats, and "rumblings of trouble" could be heard in the street, but due to heavy police presence both sides seemed to have avoided open confrontations. The calm broke when, in the late afternoon of Friday, October 19—one week after the street battle—two Mystic fishermen, William La Blanc and Antone Carmeau, found a body floating in the Mystic River and dragged it to shore. After being identified by his brother Gaspare, the body turned out to be that of the fascist Giuseppe Tudisca.[26]

Tudisca, described as "one of the most important witnesses for the state" in the Steward Street attack, had not been in the water long. A notebook in his coat pocket was still dry; Tudisca had several other items on his person as well, including his fascist membership card. The absence of water in the lungs suggested that he was dead when he entered the river. The initial medical examiner, Doctor E. L. Douglas of Groton, oddly found no bruises on his body, considering that Tudisca had been clubbed and blackjacked a week ago. Two newspapers, the *Hartford Courant* and the *Norwich Bulletin*, reported the finding of a "severe bruise" on his head and either dilated or bulging eyes, indicating prior violence. The medical examiner in any case refused to list a cause for Tudisca's death.

Suicide emerged as a possible cause of death; the vital organs were removed and sent to the state chemist's lab in Hartford to examine for the presence of poison. Relatives and the local fascists disputed this possibility immediately, since they revealed that Tudisca had planned a return trip to Italy to rejoin his wife and daughter only two weeks after his death.[27]

The location of where the body had been found in the Mystic River, between West Mystic and Mason's Island, would indicate that Tudisca had fallen or been thrown from West Mystic or the Mystic River railroad bridge and drifted at ebb tide to a location across from Mason's Island. All who knew Tudisca testified that he had no business to conduct whatsoever in Mystic. A discrepancy existed as to Tudisca's last whereabouts: he had not returned to his boarding house on Thursday the 18th, but police had reports that he had been seen at 10 o'clock in the morning on Friday in New London, at about the time he visited a doctor for an undisclosed stomach ailment. Efforts were being made to trace Tudisca's movements, as numerous rumors and last sightings poured in.[28]

As the mystery of Tudisca's death deepened, trial began in police court on November 23, for the antifascists accused of the Steward Street attack. Charged with breach of peace and inciting to riot, all parties concerned knew that the real issue that loomed over the courtroom scene was the Tudisca death—with his relatives, the police and the fascists convinced he had been murdered by the antifascists of New London, possibly the defendants themselves. Among those present in the crowded courtroom were Pasquale De Cicco and his legal counsel, a lawyer named Paterno. The anarchists and communists charged that De Cicco played a role on the prosecution's side, not implausible in view of his record of support for fascist forces in Italian Connecticut. De Cicco and the

Italian consul in New Haven would at least have furnished prosecution with the intelligence that the Italian government had collected on the New London anarchists.[29]

The trial—which would determine whether enough evidence existed to proceed to Superior Court—lasted a day. The prosecution took the entire morning building their case, based on the testimony of the four remaining fascists who had been beaten; the afternoon was given over to the defense side, which consisted of at least eight witnesses who swore that the various defendants had been nowhere near the scene of the street fight. Six of the eight lived in the Fort; one of them, Gruppo L'Avvenire founder Luigi Camillucci, said he had no connection with the antifascists, when he testified that Augusto Peroni was at his house on Nameaug Street during the fracas. Peroni added that he too was not involved with either side.[30]

Judge John J. McGarry, only filling in for the trial, had heard enough by the end of the day. A newspaper article written over twenty years later captured the courtroom scene.

> (Judge McGarry) decided to bind over all the accused to Superior Court after he was overwhelmed by the perjured testimony of many of the witnesses. Practically everyone in the courtroom who heard the attempt made by friends of the accused to place them at various points far from the scene of the fight could tell that the alibis were manufactured to confuse the court and effect the discharge of the prisoners. The judge called most of the stories "palpable lies."[31]

Trial in Superior Court was set for January 2. The fascists, meanwhile, had been busy organizing public events for their dead member, who they considered a martyr for the cause. After services in Tudisca's brother's house in Pawcatuck, Tudisca's body lie in state in the fascist hall on Shaw Street, before being put aboard a ship to be sent back to Sicily. The Mayor of Tusa and a crowd of thousands greeted the corpse in Palermo, with a blackshirt honor guard providing an escort back to his home village. Fascist dignitaries and Tusa's population turned out as the funeral procession entered the town. As Tudisca's body was placed in the family tomb, brief speeches by fascist leaders highlighted his "supreme sacrifice," with fascist militia banners waving throughout.[32]

The New London case received two articles in *Labor Defender*, the organ of International Labor Defense, and Carlo Tresca's *Il Martello* solicited defense funds. Gruppo I Liberi responded to the fascist publicity onslaught with a blunt and dismissive article in *L'Adunata dei Refrattari* titled, "The 12th of October in New London." It is true, they said, some fascists had been "chased down and beaten a little with sticks," but not enough to have sent them to the hospital. The six comrades hauled into court had sufficiently proved their nonpresence at the scene of the "scuffle." After finding the body of "Tudisca pescato" (fished out), some attempted to link the "blows struck on Columbus Day" with the death. "Still the authorities have not been able to establish the cause of the death of Tudisca that all here believe was that it was suicide caused by an incurable disease he had: syphilis." The fascist consul and the "vulgar, envious" local fascists had been "stirred up" by the press coverage and now sought to settle old grudges: "It is to be, we hope, a bubble of soap, that comes and leaves nothing when it leaves, just if it puts a light on the suspicious maneuvers of the consul in New Haven and the wicked interests of the . . . fascists here."[33]

While the anarchists and fascists sparred, the state chemist reported that no traces of poison had been found in the body. An autopsy revealed that Tudisca was dead when his body entered the water. No further evidence emerged, however, and no witnesses came forward to break the wall of silence in Fort Trumbull. The trial in Norwich Superior Court was almost an afterthought by January; the defendants were all fined twenty-five dollars and their cases nolled.[34]

Matters were not settled, however. Throughout February and early March, unidentified parties made numerous attempts to burn down the fascist headquarters. The nearest to success came early in the morning of March 3, when the fire department barely extinguished a blaze ignited by gasoline and alcohol on the hall's floor. Two men had been seen emerging from an alley and fleeing down Shaw Street. No arrests followed, and just as in the Tudisca killing, the case remained open.[35]

The anarchists of Fort Trumbull decades later maintained that the tide of fascism in New London had been turned by the events sparked on Columbus Day, 1928. The local fascists certainly remained on the defensive. No retaliatory moves seem to have been made against Gruppo I Liberi or the neighborhood that sustained it. Militarily, the anarchists had the initiative in New London; a balance of forces existed because of their exceptionally strong position in Fort Trumbull. The local Sicilian community, whatever their feelings of sympathy toward Mussolini, did not rally en masse to the cause of the FLNA. No indignant outbursts came from the prominenti against their Marchegian neighbors, who they undoubtedly knew were the source of the violent measures taken against fellow Sicilians who supported fascism. The attention of many community leaders in the Shaw Street neighborhood had turned to the presidential election that fall, in which most supported the candidacy of Al Smith, who ran on an antiprohibition plank. Bruised or even dead fascists may have been an inconvenient distraction. And by December 1929, the Fascist League of North America was no more, disbanded on orders of Mussolini. The ever-present violence surrounding the FLNA proved embarrassing to his government, and serious investigations by the US government loomed over domestic Italian fascist activities.[36]

The Columbus Day events had found Gruppo I Liberi in top form. Two months prior, a large list of fifty-four names appeared in *L'Adunata dei Refrattari* as a voluntary fund drive for the paper. Articles on successful fundraisers for the anarchist press and political prisoners and striking miners, a grand ball in the IDC, and a well-attended picnic all exuded confidence in the future.[37]

The three (alleged) arson attacks (in 1921, 1924, and 1929), the Steward Street operation, and the killing of Tudisca seem to hint at the existence within Gruppo I Liberi of a clandestine unit. Such a network for conducting illegal activities existed throughout New England Galleanist groups dating from at least World War I. The Galleanists were known to have funded several assassination attempts on Mussolini. The antifascist actions in New London bore marks of both careful planning and decisiveness, carried out by committed and experienced individuals. Gruppo I Liberi contained members with personal involvement in conducting political activities outside of the law. The Fanese possessed both the maritime skills and seafaring craft to have made a body simply disappear, but Tudica's attackers decided on a land-based operation. Was the Mystic River immersion—in which a body was sure to turn up—a way to send a stronger message? As far back as 1912, the group had had some kind of debate over a "secret group" within their ranks. These actions may provide some proof that those plans came to fruition.

One consequence of Columbus Day would be another of the endless, destructive squabbles within the Italian radical movement, in this case involving the differences between the Galleanisti and Carlo Tresca. Tresca, a nonsectarian anarcho-syndicalist with a long history agitation in the labor movement, edited *Il Martello* and had a devoted following among Italian American workers. Personal jealousy on the part of Galleani probably constituted the source of his relentless attacks on Tresca, which escalated in the 1920s. Nunzio Pernicone characterized the Galleanist attacks as "sheer malevolence and mindless fanaticism" that "had no equal among the fratricidal conflicts of the sovversivi."[38]

Perhaps the most infamous attack on Tresca by the Galleanists during the 1920s occurred in Hartford in May 1928, only months before the Columbus Day events. At the home of Girolamo Grasso, the Galleanists conducted a "jury of honor," which tried Tresca (in his absence) and condemned him as a police spy. Six Galleanists signed the verdict, while Felice Guadagni, a syndicalist, refused. This incident, as historians have noted, caused further harm to the Italian anarchist movement and a number of non-Italian figures denounced the Galleanists. In a personal letter from Grasso to a Galleanist in Newark, the original list of "jurors" included four New London names—Rafaelle Petrini, Artimio Angeloni, Giordano Cesarini, and Luigi Facchini—with a pencil line through them. Their role or nonrole in the proceedings is uncertain.[39]

Regardless of the differences between him and the Galleanists, Tresca usually took up all defense cases involving antifascists or radicals threatened with deportation. Two hundred dollars had been raised for legal funds for the New London defendants, with the social democratic antifascist paper *Il Nuovo Mondo* maintaining that the money had been sent to Tresca. Tresca claimed not to have received it, and charges and countercharges ensued in the Italian radical press. In the end the money could not be located and five members of Gruppo I Liberi, including Petrini, Giustini and A. Ghiandoni, signed an article in *L'Adunata* that referred to Tresca as a demagogue and called him by the nickname given him by the Galleanists, "Pagnacca," or spy. The sordid affair illustrated the level that the diatribes had reached, causing great harm to the antifascist cause.[40]

An unusual legacy of the Columbus Day battles may have been a sandlot football game. At some time during the late 1920s, players from Fort Trumbull and Shaw Street—the "Forts" versus the "Shaws"—began to meet on Thanksgiving Day to play no-rules, no-officials, no-equipment football. The games became a tradition as charity fundraisers, lasted in to the 1950s and were viewed by several thousand spectators. I have not traced their source, but it is possible that elements in the Italian community, from both Shaw Street and Fort Trumbull, could have come up with the pick-up games as an alternative to street clashes. Fights between youths from the neighborhood, according to several accounts, had become frequent at dances and other social activities in New London. Some of these must have had politics as their cause. Were the decades-long Forts-Shaws rivalries on the gridiron invoked at least in part to cool political tensions?[41]

A particularly memorable game occurred in 1950; while every meeting of the teams proved fierce, this one sent four players to the hospital. After organizers announced plans to stage a second game to benefit the injured four, more players stepped forward to reveal that they too had been hurt. The lack of healthy players forced cancelation of the planned game. The violence of a 1950s football field had perhaps been a vague reenactment of an ancient, dimly remembered political street fight.[42]

One more significant event took place in the wake of the Columbus Day battle that probably bore no direct connection with the fracas, but symbolized possible shifts within the local Italian community. In October 1930, Alba Camillucci made her debut opera performance at the Lyceum Theatre in New London to the accompaniment of great fanfare reserved for talented locals. Alba was the daughter of longtime anarchists Luigi and Emilia, and had studied during the 1920s in a conservatory in Pesaro in the Marche. Numerous advertisements from members of the community announced her coming appearance that breached the neighborhood divide, including Nicolas Salegna, Charles Satti, and the contracting firm of the Turello Brothers, as well as the Italian Ladies' Aid Society ("to our friend and neighbor"). Politics still separated the two neighborhoods, since the 1930s brought even more world developments over which to fight, but the Camillucci performance may have been the first time leading elements of the community sat under the same roof and applauded the same thing, greeting what Lorenzo Montali, in an ad for the Italian Bakery referred to as "welcoming a native daughter."[43]

Another factor may have come into play and opened the door to a softening of attitudes. Luigi and Emilia Camillucci drifted away from the anarchist movement during the 1920s; Luigi's connection may have ended around the time he testified as a witness in the trial of the antifascist defendants. Their donations to the anarchist press ceased in 1924, although Luigi donated to the cause of Basque refugee children during the Spanish Civil War as part of a group of left-wing New London Italians. Luigi continued to work as a stonemason until at least the age of seventy-three in a Works Progress Administration project in 1940. The couple's exit remained unremarked on by their comrades, and a break, if it occurred, probably came gradually. They retired from politics in their sixties, perhaps worn out from too many meetings and too many internal quarrels.[44]

CHAPTER THIRTEEN

ALLIES AND ENEMIES

LE DONNE

The 8th of September 1908 probably dawned the same as usual for thirty-four-year-old Anita Montali. She walked from her home in Fort Trumbull, likely somewhat groggy, since she and her husband often stayed up half the night tending ovens for their bakery. She headed south to 20 East Street, the home of Dyer Copeland, from whom she bought grain for the horse used to pull a delivery wagon for their business, which was located at their home address at 28 East Street. Copeland was a neighborhood merchant of sorts who supplied, besides feed, corn, chickens, and eggs "whenever he found a customer." After knocking on the door and getting no answer, Anita walked to the back and noticed the barn door open. Inside, she found Copeland lying dead on the floor next to his horse, his skull bashed in.

Her yells to neighbors alerted an officer from Fort Trumbull's garrison, and before long the police arrived. The press, after misspelling her name as "Montari" (common during that period), described Anita briefly as a woman who "speaks but little English" and who "acted hysterical."[1]

The reporter warned the public of the "human fiend" who was capable of committing such a crime and still at large, but the police announced they had a suspect. The culprit turned out to be a private from an artillery unit stationed in the fort, unable to pay a debt to Copeland. Trying and finding him guilty, the court sentenced Copeland to years in the state prison, while Anita returned to her previous anonymity. She did not fare any better in the US population Census two years later in which, despite her bakery chores and the additional "minor" responsibility of raising six sons, her occupation is listed as "none."[2]

In 1912 her name again appeared in a newspaper, in her brief appeal to Lorenzo that appeared in the November 12 issue of *Cronaca Sovversiva*.[3] Anita's missive also boldly rejects the Census's zeroing of her multifaceted contributions. She identified herself first as a *baker*: she worked in a bakery, saw to the delivery wagon's operation, and stayed up to make sure the bread was baked, all in addition to her domestic household chores. Her voice, as with other anarchist women in Fort Trumbull, has been lost to history to a far greater degree than that of the neighborhood as a whole. This in spite of Fanese women's having played a central role in the evolution of the neighborhood; men may have built the houses, but women constructed the world in which they, their spouses and children, lived.

Women played a substantial role in sustaining New London anarchism because of their economic and social activities in the local community, which had allowed the development of a spirit of self-reliance and communal solidarity. These activities proved vital in families' weathering the periodic devastating economic downturns—not to mention seasonal factors—that put the Fort Trumbull building tradespeople out of work. Marchegian women made decisions regarding the crucial issues of food supply and conservation; they started and tended gardens and bartered, relying on the neighborhood social network. If a family had farm animals such as chickens, this fell to the women. They opened businesses, as in the case of a widow with a large family who became a successful grocer and later a meat cutter. Women played a strong role in the Fort's bootlegging industry during Prohibition, staffing the speakeasies, keeping the books, manufacturing and distributing liquor, and taking busts along with their husbands and companions.[4]

A woman whose ironworker husband had been killed from a fall off a bridge in New York moved to the New London area around 1920 with three small children. The family was "very poor" and lived in a "miserable place" in Uncasville. Necessity dictated her entrance into the manufacture of beer during Prohibition on moving to the Fort. These harsh conditions often did not produce meek, submissive women; as to family life "Mother ruled the roost," commented a woman born in the midst of the 1930s depression.[5]

Reports from New London to *Cronaca Sovversiva* that consistently showed women's presence at New London anarchist events also reveal that the anarchists found this a necessity in their building of an oppositional subculture. They were very aware that the church targeted these same women, hence the practice of holding secular birth celebrations and civil weddings. Women's names appear throughout the years in donor salutations and subscriptions to the paper, sending messages or greetings to friends or in honor of prominent anarchists: "Gilda Bartolucci saluting Rina Stranesi," or "Emilia Pasqualini saluting the rebel Postiglione hoping to have him here for a lecture."

In 1925, *L'Adunata dei Reffratari* carried a separate list of ten women donors who sent the paper a money order for $7.30 to help with its deficit. The women did not mention whether they pooled their money at a meeting of their own. The list is headed by Giovanna Petrini, the wife of Rafaelle. Giovanna on several occasions sent her salutations to the anarchist press separately from her husband; her comments indicate that she was a committed Galleanist. These women averaged thirty years of age and were mostly the wives of anarchists. The only one with an occupation listed in the Population Census, Orvidia Cesarini, ran a grocery store with her husband. Born in Senigallia in the Marche, she had immigrated in 1911, and then met and married her husband Giordano, an anarchist textile worker, in 1914. (They would later buy a chicken farm in Waterford.)

The "woman question" raised its head at the inception of New London's anarchist movement, even before the formation of Gruppo L'Avvenire. Pedro Esteve gave a series of lectures for a weekend conference in July 1898 that laid out the basic postulates of anarchism for the new recruits. On the third day he spoke on "Women and Children in the Future Family," emphasizing the obstacles to women joining the Italian anarchist movement, "that today woman is the servant of man." The doors of the locales frequented by the anarchist men—clubs, meeting rooms, cafés, and barrooms—were closed to women, while the doors of the church were open to them,

> where they teach submission, where is inculcated the spirit of religion, where the fixations, the lies take root of the future world, where is fed the prejudices. It is needed to assert to all anarchists, with every power, to win the complete emancipation of women, it is needed to be kind, full of generous affection, of delicate sentiments, of sublime leaps, in order to have the woman comrade in the struggle against this vile society.[6]

Esteve's bringing attention to the role of women in the anarchist movement was far from incidental; his lifelong companion, Maria Roda, was a highly respected revolutionary active since a teenager in anarchist circles in her native Como, Italy. They would have eight children together. Roda formed Gruppo Emancipazione della Donna (Women's Emancipation Group) in Paterson in 1897, and would work closely with Ernestina Cravello. According to Jennifer Guglielmo, after Esteve became editor of *La Questione Sociale* from 1899 to 1906, "women's writing was most voluminous" in the paper.[7]

Two other early interventions—both by men—raised the woman question within the ranks of New London's anarchists. Galleani spoke, probably his first time, in the city in June 1902 on the theme of "The Emancipation of the Workers and the Anarchist Ideal," Galleani was introduced by Gennaro Foschini, who called for agitation against militarism, for the general strike and, "above all, for the emancipation of women." During his speech, Galleani emphasized "the urgency of the revolutionary education of the women." "Last evening," the report of the event continued, "(Galleani) said to the women comrades, to a dense feminine audience brief words congratulating them that in spite of the systematic and habitual anathema with which anarchy and anarchists are slandered, the women dare to enter and approach . . ."[8]

On May 30, 1903, at the *festa* held to celebrate the publication of Malatesta's *Il Nostro Programma* by Gruppo L'Avvenire, a party that went on until five the next morning, Foschini took the opportunity to again raise the woman issue in an oddly timed, offhand manner.

> In the middle of the dance later, with all exhausted from much dancing, Foschini turned to the women for a few words—inciting the anarchist movement to take an active part because as he said, as he foresaw in the coming social revolution as the workers' emancipation, but women, the men deny them every right of emancipation in the house until they don't know how to win them."[9]

A month before this, Gruppo L'Avvenire sponsored another successful and well-attended event at the Opera House. A theatrical group from New York presented Gori's *Senza Patria* in the afternoon, to be followed, according to the issue of *La Questione Sociale* the week before, by a "lecture on the woman" by Maria Raffuzzi, a close collaborator of Roda and

Cravello's, and a woman active in the anarchist women's network in the New York area. When the day arrived, however, Maria's comrade Luigi spoke in her place; Maria was absent for "an indisposition."[10] Her speaking engagement, as far as can be determined, was never rescheduled. In fact, from the earliest days until the 1930s, announcements and articles in their newspapers did not list a single woman speaker—except Emma Goldman—for an event in New London.

The results of a fund-raising celebration in October 1903 to benefit anarchist propaganda efforts pleased Gruppo L'Avvenire. It revealed "a symptom of good omen."

> The participation always more spontaneous, always more intense, always more conscious, of the feminine element of our celebration, of our meeting, of our struggle.
>
> In preceding years at our propaganda events the women would not come or only on rare occasions: their attendance in every case weak in showing courageous adhesion to our principles but were only timid expressions of personal sympathy or sentiments of innate courtesy. Now they come instead to our meetings not to ask in quivering, fleeting (voices) for a festive life but to affirm strongly their rebel faith, their highest ideal of emancipation, their ineffable treasure of sentiment and goodness.[11]

The commentary is double-edged: the women attending the function are commended for their serious commitment but also reminded of their previous "sentiments of innate courtesy" and desires for a "festive life." The opinion expressed by the writer, which was repeated throughout the history of the Italian anarchists in New London and many other locales as well, shows an understanding that women's full participation in their revolutionary movement was of critical importance—but a goal that could never be brought to fruition.

Like the rest of the Italian anarchist movement, New London's groups and circles were male dominated. Part of the anarchist subculture in New London rested on the "clubs, meeting rooms, barrooms and cafes" mentioned by Esteve, which were exclusively male. To hang out at Dondero's Bank Street saloon marked one as a suspected anarchist in the eyes of the Italian police. Almost half of the New London anarchists with police files on them in Italy were listed as "frequenters of the saloon of the known anarchist Dondero." Anarchists in the city and its environs working predominantly as carpenters, masons, construction laborers, factory workers, and fishermen gathered in Fred's establishment, and certainly others, to play dominos and cards, discuss politics over beer, and generally carry on conversations as an extension of their common experiences on the job. What became "serious" spilled over from their work situations—where they interacted with non-Italians, craft unionists, bosses, and nonanarchist radicals. They would have to balance their shared world of work with their family situations, and there is no doubt that the vast majority of radical Italian American workers were devoted to their families. Their political outlooks would have been shaped largely on the job and among fellow male coworkers, a world at odds with the setting of family-based anarchism in the Fort. When the group began to rent space on East Street, Smith Street and Maple Avenue, these practices invariably carried over to these locations. One needs look no further than the plaques that hang today in the basement room of the Italian Dramatic Club; nearly all early names of deceased members, starting with Luigi Camillucci, were anarchists, but all are male. From its first day, the IDC's membership was limited to men. Anarchist activity as a male retreat had become a norm, arising in the early days before wives and fiancés arrived.

But families did arrive during the first decade, and quickly. Fort Trumbull anarchism, while male dominated, based itself on the stable and cohesive character imparted by the family structure. Despite many obstacles, women became members of the movement in Fort Trumbull, and they seem to have been mostly wives or sisters of male members. From their earliest days, Fort Trumbull anarchists organized what they called "family evenings" at their public events. (Italian, Russian, and Jewish anarchists in early-twentieth-century America, as advanced were their views on marriage and women's equality, devoted much effort to construct their activities around family-oriented events.) Women, with children in tow, were encouraged to attend in most announcements for events, with free admission offered and a mention of the group's family orientation. They created a barrier that fended off opponents across the spectrum from socialists to *prominenti*.

Some male anarchists in the Fort might have shared the sentiments of Aldo Candolfi, who lived on Walbach Street. Candolfi and his wife Edvigia had immigrated from Senigallia (see chapter 7). He took a prominent, but brief, role in the group, and had contributed articles to the anarchist press for nearly a decade. In a preimmigration article in Fano's *In Marcia!* in 1906 titled "To the Women of the People," he attacked women for their role in damaging the anarchist movement and held them as "the cause of much misfortune that afflicts humanity, because too much darkness is in your minds in connection with the necessity of knowing of social struggles. You know nothing but to serve, ignoring even the right of existence, for the pleasure to submit." "Your consciousness is in a deplorable state of corruption and degradation," thanks to the women letting in the priests, who "instill prejudices and superstitions that weigh on your brain oppressively." As "protecting angels of the family," women needed to instill the love of freedom and separate from the religious pest.[12] Other New London commentaries do not approach the level of hostility held by Candolfi for women. Candolfi probably aimed his criticism at women married to anarchists who he viewed as slowing the movement's progress. At the same time he urged on their maternal instincts as protectors and nurturers of the family. One of the aspects of the anarchists' heritage remembered by descendants in the neighborhood is their fervent hostility to religion, and gave religious participation as one of the reasons for the forming of the Mutual Aid Society. Undoubtedly, the all-or-nothing stance on religion of the Galleanists kept some women from joining.

Women sang and recited revolutionary poetry at countless New London anarchist functions but seldom spoke on political topics. Only in 1931 did a woman address a New London meeting. Virgilia D'Andrea, an exiled anarchist poet, spoke on "Ours and Other Peoples' Violence" as part of a national tour to help revive the flagging movement. She addressed a "modest public meeting." Another well-known woman militant, Aurora Alleva, spoke a year later at a Leverone's Grove picnic on the topic of political victims.[13]

Jennifer Guglielmo observes that in the Italian anarchist movement, women participated in public functions such as debates, plays, picnics, and dances but were not invited to internal meetings where decisions were made. How can this be reconciled with the obviously strong roles played by Marta Dondero and Anita Montali? Marta contributed a *Cronaca* article, while her husband Fred did not, on a highly political, controversial topic in 1906. She took a hard-line Galleanist position against several local anarchists. Her 1910 obituary described her as a fierce anarchist, and Malatesta had her address, not Fred's, in his address book when he left New London in 1899. Anita had publicly invited her husband to become an anarcho-communist. Both women contributed money to the anarchist press in their own names. Would they have allowed the men to exclude them from meetings? Unfortunately only scattered mention is made of the meetings themselves, so nothing is certain. A fair guess would be that they attended and participated in meetings. Recently arrived from Milford, Jennie Paglia offered a somewhat ambiguous remark concerning the "not pretty, but intelligent" hard-core militant Gemma Mello's role in New London. "She went to the group, to the men, crossed her legs and smoked—not my type." If she "went to the group," she obviously took part in activities, but does the passage suggest that Mello's behavior was irregular because she functioned in Gruppo I Liberi as an unattached woman rather than as the female half of a married couple?[14]

During the late 1930s and early 1940s, women initiated several activities in Fort Trumbull, one as Il Gruppo di Donne. As usual, noted Giustini and Petrini, the women knew how to take the "lead" in organizing events to benefit the movement. While the articles are short on details, women apparently stepped up efforts to defend the movement through "family recreation" at a time when political isolation of the Galleanists had increased.[15]

Male dominance of Fort Trumbull's anarchist subculture put strong women militants at a decided disadvantage; they would have faced a fight in the groups to be heard. Many Italian anarchist women probably shared the perception of the movement that feminism represented a bourgeois, middle-class ideology, one that meant little to Italian immigrant women. They would not have become involved in the suffrage movement, since they viewed voting in elections as a waste of time. New London women might have benefited from the presence of Paterson's Ernestina Cravello from 1898 to 1900, but no evidence exists of her taking a role in the early group.

In other localities in Connecticut, the voice of Italian radical women had been heard to a greater degree. In nearby Mystic, a hotbed of anarcho-syndicalism and socialism for at least a decade, and a locality with a close relationship with the anarchists of both New London and Westerly, a women's group emerged early (see below). It is possible that the intersecting of radical political tendencies in Mystic, both Italian and non-Italian, served to encourage a wider understanding of women's role in the revolutionary movements. That the Italian women in Mystic came from the Val di Zoldo, a region that benefited from Austrian rule by having progressive legislation for women on the books, might also have contributed.

Two strong women emerged from the Galleanist circles of New Britain: Ella Antolini and Irma Sanchini, both of the same intransigent mold as Gemma Mello. None could doubt the bravery and dedication of Ella "Dynamite Girl" Antolini, who had done eighteen months in federal prison for transporting explosives for a planned bombing in Milwaukee (see chapter 9). Antolini became an important figure in the New England movement, and took part in discussions of critical political issues. Irma Sanchini's husband Giobbe would be the future editor of La Frusta in Fano. When Bureau of Investigation agents raided the headquarters of New Britain's Gruppo Coltura Moderna at 85 Mill Street, also the home of the Sanchinis, Irma nearly offered physical resistance to the intruders, harassing them with a baby in her arms. In arresting the couple, agents viewed Irma as the real prize: "Although an anarchist, (Giobbe) is not a capable one and does not seem as rabid as his wife." US Attorney Spellacy allegedly felt the same: "Upon her arrival, she astounded him by her resourcefulness and her disregard for consequences." She died in 1925, in the Marche after deportation; her obituary in L'Adunata notes her important role in the New England movement.[16]

One notable revolutionary woman from the Italian radical movement in Connecticut arose not from an anarchist but from socialist and syndicalist background. Helen Manfreda, a neglected figure in Connecticut women's history, was born in Wallingford in 1893; her father had been a former supporter of Garibaldi who successfully pushed his ten children to pursue white-collar careers. He forbade the speaking of Italian in the home. Helen became a stenographer and served in a number of roles in the state headquarters of the Socialist Party of Connecticut, as well as running for office on the Socialist Party's ticket. After World War I she gravitated toward the FSI, which had an active branch in her hometown. Wallingford resembled Mystic as a crossroads of syndicalist, socialist, and anarchist currents. In 1920, Helen appeared at a mass meeting in New Haven for political prisoners, one of the few Italian American women to do so in the state; in her talk, given in English, she "made some correct reproaches against subversives who make a preconceived error of not bringing women to meetings, to educate them in our principles and those of the working masses . . ." A week after this meeting, Helen's mother's death led to her father having a mental breakdown.

Forced into the position of sole support for her siblings, she dropped out of the radical movement, never to return. In 1954, as the owner of an insurance business, she was honored at a testimonial dinner as "one of Wallingford's most popular businesswomen." She died in 1966 as a result of Parkinson's disease.[17]

I DINTORNI

New London's Fort Trumbull neighborhood did not stand alone as a focal point for Italian radicals in southeastern Connecticut. Along the Long Island coast, from Westerly across the border in Rhode Island, to Branford next to New Haven, Italian revolutionaries formed circles and groups to propagate their Ideal. These towns and hamlets included Mystic, Groton, Stonington, Norwich, Gales Ferry, Waterford, Old Saybrook, Stony Creek, Leete's Island, and Ivoryton. The groups ranged in size from a few individuals to several dozen, and most had a lifespan of several years at most. They originated in the regional migration patterns of particular industries such as quarrying and construction. Each had its distinctive history with its attendant triumphs and crises.

In Stony Creek, Italian socialist and anarchist stone cutters and quarry workers helped build strong trade unions in the granite quarries, as well as construct, along with fellow English, Scottish, and Finnish workers, an extraordinary labor subculture. Anarchists in Norwich, many of them Marchegiani, created an amateur drama group to accompany their propaganda efforts. In Ivoryton, Italian socialists and anarchists working at the Comstock-Cheney Company, a manufacturer of piano keys, formed a mandolin orchestra that toured in the area, and possibly helped lay the cultural foundation for the Ivoryton Playhouse (the product of the paternal owner of Comstock-Cheney).[18]

Few announcements for anarchist events in New London passed without an invitation to comrades and sympathizers from neighboring towns—*i dintorni*—to attend. For Gruppo L'Avvenire, and later I Liberi, the most important and long-standing bonds were those with the anarchist circles in Mystic and Westerly. Decades of joint activities such as fund-raisers, picnics, and dances, as well as numerous greetings exchanged between the comrades of each locale, attest to the close political and social relationships that existed between these coastal towns. It needs to be emphasized that one of the first links in the transnational chain for New London anarchists could be found next door, composed of comrades with whom they exchanged information, planned strategy, and partied fiercely.

Only a few miles east of New London, Mystic could be easily reached by shoreline train or steamboat. Composed of several rural villages ideal for outdoor gatherings and festivals, it was also the location of substantial silk and shipbuilding industries. Along with its present-day stature as a site for penguin exhibits, early 1800s seafaring New England, and famous pizza (Mystic Aquarium, Mystic Seaport, and Mystic Pizza), the town also possesses a radical past.

German immigrant weavers at the Rossie Velvet Company on Greenmanville Avenue, which opened its doors in 1898 (across from present day Mystic Seaport), planted the first seeds of socialism in Mystic, building the Frohsinn Society Hall on the same street. By the first decade of the twentieth century, locals of both the Socialist Party (SP) and Socialist Labor Party (SLP) existed in the town. In 1909 the Mystic SP, which had been organized in July 1903, had sixty-eight members, including seventeen Germans, forty-three "Americans," and eight of other nationalities, and consisted of both workers and small businesspeople. Mystic became a hotbed of socialist agitation during this period, possessing a socialist library open to the public, distributing five hundred copies of the socialist weekly *Appeal to Reason*, and conducting well-attended "Socialist Sunday School."[19]

The Mystic SP came under the leadership of Edward Perkins Clarke, a descendant of John Fish, one of the original white settlers of the town. Born in 1872, Clarke became a principal of a school for the deaf in New York State before returning to his hometown as a strong advocate of socialism. While not attracting more than 6 percent of the vote in local elections, the Mystic Socialists could rally hundreds at meetings, lectures, and picnics. These events were often held in the German weavers' hall. Under Clarke's watch, Mystic for a brief time became the state headquarters of the SP, with latter being elected state secretary.[20]

Mystic's textile mills as well became constant flashpoints in trade union struggles in the early decades of the twentieth century. Strikes against the running of multiple looms and for better pay were common, and both craft and industrial union locals appeared with regularity in the town. The Palmer shipyard in Noank also saw efforts by carpenters, blacksmiths, iron workers, electricians, steamfitters, and painters to organize by craft. Even though Clarke was a socialist of the mild reformist variety, elements in Mystic remained sympathetic to the SLP's version of industrial unionism. A local of the SLP-led IWW, known as the "Detroit IWW," formed around 1911 and existed for at least eight years.[21]

Into this mix of radicalized German, Syrian, Armenian, French, and Polish workers came immigrants from the Valle di Zoldo in the Dolomites region of northern Italy. Most left the mountainous area because of drastic changes in the iron-making and textile industries, but also to escape from Austrian domination. Large numbers of Zoldani workers migrated to neighboring European countries, such as Russia, France and Switzerland, where they were exposed to radical political currents. Socialism, not anarchism, influenced the vast majority. Migrants working in Zurich brought socialism back to the Zoldo, where a branch composed of laborers and building tradesmen formed in 1895. The towns of Forno and Campo became strongpoints of socialism, and would provide large numbers of immigrants to Mystic. The Italian Socialist Party in Zoldo provided aid to migrants to the United States, even on employment matters. On arriving in the US, Mystic-bound Roberto Cercena received a pamphlet published by *Il Proletario* that urged immigrants to become US citizens, learn English, and join a trade union. Regionalism may have played the determining element in migration for the Zoldani, but it was heavily mediated by politics.[22]

Employment patterns of the Mystic Italians were similar to those of the Fort Trumbull Marchegiani, in that skills learned in the homeland aided their placement in local industries. Men experienced in metal-working and blacksmithing found jobs in the machinery maintenance department of the Rossie Mill, as well as in the blacksmith shops of local quarries and other manufacturers. Ernesto Cini, who subscribed to anarchist papers for over a decade, immigrated in 1896 and lived first in Stafford Springs before moving to Mystic a few years later. He began as a laborer in a woolen mill in Stafford Springs, then became a foreman in a velvet mill (probably Rossie) in Mystic, and still later a grinder in a machine shop. Angelo Panciera, another longtime anarchist supporter, migrated in 1902 and worked for most of his career as a laborer in the Noank shipyard. Women worked as weavers and finishers in significant numbers, at least until marriage.[23]

A number of Mystic Italians followed the path of the New London Fanese and other recent Italian immigrants in the United States by moving from the camp of socialism to that of anarchism. Mystic names began appearing in the columns of the anarchist press four months before those of New London, with one longtime militant, Raffaele Sommariva (chapter 3), playing a role in the foundation of Gruppo L'Avvenire. The speaking tours of prominent anarchists such as Malatesta, Esteve, and Raveggi coincided with the birth of the small Zoldani community in Mystic. As with Italian immigrant workers across the United States, the nonvoting status of these workers lessened their interest in the electoral tactics of the socialists.

Correspondence from Mystic reveals boundless confidence in the future struggles of the working class, as in an obituary written by Sommariva on the death of a fifteen-year-old anarchist named Angelo Campo, from blood poisoning following an accident. Campo had been fully committed to the "battles for justice that one day not distant the poor and outcast of all the world will unite to achieve their demands." According to Sommariva, the young militant's last words were "the hymn of social struggle, 'We Have to Struggle.'" Sommariva thanked "our stonecutter friends, Angelo Buciera and Pietro Berardinelli, who spontaneously and freely (made) a tombstone to remember our mourned friend."[24]

In 1901, after the management of the Rossie Velvet mill levied fines for weavers who damaged goods, the plant's entire workforce walked out. Anarchists in the mill immediately took an active role in the strike; the strike started in waves, with Italians from the finishing room leaving the mill and entering the strikers' hall to the cheers of the German and American weavers. A letter to *La Questione Sociale* saw great potential in the struggle: "Although the strikes like these are not made for emancipation because they won't destroy capital, it nevertheless is a very important weapon for the means of those workers who can impede the capitalist greed and exploitation. For the anarchists are ready for the task to develop, with our propaganda, the trend for a general strike." When the company recruited fifteen strikebreakers in Hoboken, New Jersey, an anarchist there alerted them to the existence of the strike, successfully dissuading them. "A dozen youths" were brought from Stafford Springs, Connecticut—where a number of Zoldani had settled—to replace the strikers, but on being told by their innkeeper of the strike they went as a group to a strikers' meeting before leaving the area in search of work.[25]

After three and a half months the strikers began to show signs of wear as scabs entered the mill. "Some comrades of ours, Italians, together with a few German socialists," suggested mass picketing to keep strikebreakers out. The resolution passed at a strike meeting, "but when the moment came to go to their posts, instead of a hundred men only fifteen moved." The strike collapsed in defeat, with the fines in place and active strikers fired. The anarchists drew two lessons from the loss, that "the workers will learn that without a strong and potent class organization conscious and strong, and until they start using force," the capitalists would continue to win.[26]

Their strike activity seems to place the Mystic group within the pro-organizational wing of Malatesta and the Paterson anarchists, but they defied this easy categorization. They hosted Galleani as a speaker, contributed to *Cronaca Sovversiva*, and maintained close relations with the Galleanists of New London and Westerly, and also held a number of joint activities with the active section of the FSI in Mystic. A similar nonsectarian orientation existed among Zoldani anarchists living in Meriden and Stafford Springs. Not possessing the numbers and the closed neighborhood environment of the New London Fanese, Mystic anarchists were forced into cooperation among themselves and with the socialists in the face of always-present opponents.

Galleani spoke in Mystic in 1906 to a gathering in the private home of a comrade, because "the numbers of our countrymen are thin." A significant portion of the Italian community turned out. The attendees include "quite a lot of comrades," as well as sympathizers, adversaries, and women, which gave Galleani the opportunity to "engage in conversation . . . for more than an hour, on our present conditions, on the cause on which we are determined, on the methods." Galleani addressed the "doubts of sincere and modest adversaries," a technique not associated with the hardline anarchist editor. The meeting became a community event, if even for an hour, "different from the solitary grey existence in the factory and the boarding house." The "calm discussion" for all involved left an impression that was "profound and pleasant." Differences, it seems, could be put aside when appropriate for the Italian radical movement. The temptation to have an enjoyable, nonconfrontational evening probably proved too difficult for all to resist.[27]

The Mystic anarchists and socialists took full advantage of the their town's surrounding ocean and river scenery for outings. One particular account from *Il Proletario* particularly highlights the importance that Italian radicals of this period placed on these gatherings of comrades.

> The members and sympathizers here were pleased to have a party with comrades from Westerly in the country in a very attractive spot. With a trip to the beach, with appropriate

boats, we went to a pleasant place on one of the many islands in the vicinity. After a frugal meal, the afternoon was spent . . . playing music, telling jokes of every kind until sunset. By various manners we returned to our towns, singing to the world, waking up the local population not used to the noisy vivacity of us Latins.

And worthy of note is that among the attendees there was the greatest cordiality not ruined by even a small incident, leaving us by evening the best of friends, and not wanting to make this party the last, to have many others, always beautiful and orderly.

Praise to the comrades from Westerly.

Our vow: like this party will be the others, to cheer our spirits up after an entire week of work, is worthwhile, to wake up fraternal feelings . . .

The membership of the radical Italians in Mystic probably never reached more than a few dozen, including sympathizers, with their members roughly equal between the anarchists and socialists. One distinctive feature of the Mystic anarchists was the existence of a women's group, Le Donne Libertarie di Old Mystic. They sponsored activities for the entire group in their name but no detailed reports of their efforts appear. Their names do—of about eighty names from Mystic in their papers between 1900 and 1930, over 10 per cent are of women, a far larger proportion than many locales. Many of these women, perhaps most, found employment in the local textile factories, such as Rachele Carocari, daughter of anarchist Dionisio, who worked as a weaver in a woolen mill, and Sofia Favretti, who worked in the Rossie Mill. This employment outside the home, at least as young women, added to the intersection of various currents of radical thought in Mystic, may have helped in the emergence of their women's group. The Mystic Socialist Party had successfully made efforts to recruit women members. Women spoke as Sunday street speakers and seem to have been integrated in meetings and discussions.[28]

By the 1920s the Mystic anarchists had adopted the name Gruppo Alpino di Mystic; 1924 saw the construction of the Alpine Club on a backstreet behind the Rossie Velvet Mill. Records of the club have apparently not survived, but in a 1927 issue of *L'Adunata dei Refrattari*, Gruppo Alpino referred to the building as their "locale." The group held at least two Sacco and Vanzetti protest meetings, one of them with heavy attendance from Westerly and New London, in the hall. Functions could be securely held behind the doors of the hall by the dwindling membership, as they were in similar clubhouses across the country. Group activities continued on a limited basis until the mid-1930s.[29] Anarchist proprietorship of the building probably did not survive beyond the decade, their membership melting away as a result of the slow drift of aging Italian radicals into the American mainstream. (The English-speaking Socialists of the town had experienced this defection from radicalism early on, when their principal organizer and agitator Charles Perkins Clarke abruptly resigned his position as state secretary of the Connecticut SP in 1911, and took a managerial position at a nursery in Norwich. He later became an associate editor of the *Hartford Courant*.) By 1948 the officer roll of the Alpine Club, while still listing names like Scussel, Fain, and Ballestracci, contained a large number of non-Italians. In 1953 the Mystic Grange took ownership of the building, dedicating it as their own.[30]

The granite quarries of Westerly gave birth to a very active if short-lived radical Italian community that included syndicalists as well as anarchists. The earliest Italian quarry workers and stonecutters came from the northern Lombardy region, followed by larger numbers from Calabria and Sicily. Historians have described the Westerly Italians as a "bastardized version" of radicalism, or as "exotic" for their Galleanist element, although it is unclear which tendency predominated in the town.[31] Early manifestations of radicalism among northern Italians may have been overwhelmed by southerners, including Tusanese, who, like their relatives in New London, held more conservative and traditional outlooks. Conflict between local *prominenti* and radicals proved fairly explosive, and nationalist politics eventually triumphed in the community. Galleanist Ernesto Perrella described the reception given an Italian academic in 1913, whom he described as a "charlatan mercenary." During an exchange between an anarchist and the professor, a *prominenti* shouted out "Viva l'italia!" after which "all the imbeciles clapped their hands of which the professor took advantage and was saved."[32] A group of Galleanists remained active in the city through World War I, but the *prominenti* dominated Westerly through the 1920s. The town ceased to have public anarchist functions.

Comparison of the anarchists of Mystic and Westerly with New London reveals a great difference in the level of stability attained by the groupings. In this sense the former two locales possessed features that made them more representative of the Italian American anarchist movement than Fort Trumbull. In Mystic's case, the town's small size allowed Italian radicalism to be submerged by mainstream forces by the late 1920s, whereas Westerly's character as a town built on the fortunes of the granite industry helped lead to an ephemeral, "hot house" variety of Galleanism that could not survive.

I PROMINENTI

No social grouping provided Italian American radicals with such a target for verbal attack and ridicule as did the *prominenti*, the often self-appointed leaders of the Italian community. These could be found in every Italian colony; usually they were doctors, lawyers, aspiring businesspeople, or shopkeepers who placed themselves in strategic positions to provide services to Italian immigrants, act as liaisons with local authorities, and enrich themselves and expand their influence in the process. The *prominenti* were an organic outgrowth of industrializing America in the late nineteenth century, a climate full of opportunities for those with the connections, ambition, and cash. In New London the future power brokers of the Italian colony could be found behind the growing number of fruit stands on Bank Street and vicinity, a modest beginning certainly, since anarchists could be found there as well. The two sides were never far from one another, a situation that ensured both clashes and cooperation.

One of the most prominent of the embryo class of powerbroker/fruit dealers was Genoa-born Antone Leverone. Leverone soon added a tavern to his properties on Bank Street and his picnic area in Waterford, and eventually opened an ice cream stand at Ocean Beach Park, a city-owned facility on Long Island Sound in New London. He had been a member of the anarchist *circolo* for a short time when it formed, reciting revolutionary poetry at its second meeting.[33] Flirtation with the revolutionary movement was not atypical among Italians of different social layers during the early period of settlement.

The Italian Mutual Benefit Society appeared around 1898, the same year as the city's first organized expression of anarchism. The *New London Day* wondered why the group reacted as it did after the assassination of King Umberto in 1900. "The Italian Benefit Society," the paper observed, "the only Italian organization in this city held its regular meeting yesterday, but did not pass resolutions of sympathy on the death of King Humbert, as so many Italian societies have done."³⁴ Most New London Italians may have held sympathies for deep social change at that time.

It did not take long before a shift began to occur within the growing numbers of newly arrived Sicilians and Napolitanos. By 1901 the Mutual Benefit Society had come under the leadership of President Gennaro DeLuca, a barber in his early forties from Naples who operated a shop on Bradley Street. Antonio Caracausa, born in Trapani, Sicily, also rose in status. Before immigrating to the United States and moving to New London in 1891, he had owned a merchant ship. In New London Caracausa opened a fruit business, then a steamship agency and finally a money exchange business.³⁵ The anarchists referred to the three as "the triumvirate" because of their control over functions of the Benefit Society.

In 1901, Gennaro Foschini took aim at DeLuca in the pages of *La Questione Sociale*. Through the Benefit Society, DeLuca had organized a "grand dance and *festa*" to raise money for the Lawrence Memorial Hospital in the city. The event became an elaborate affair, with no expense spared. Foschini accused his fellow barber of staging the event with "wild and crazy" costs, squandering the members' money, and not raising any money for the hospital which, he allowed, was a worthy cause because it "admits many times sick Italians." DeLuca acted out of a "show of ambition" to be "the *papa* of our colony." One of Foschini's charges in particular may have inflamed DeLuca most. The latter had invited a committee of "respectable American persons" to judge a dance contest, the winner getting an expensive gold medallion. Out of deference to *papa*, the committee awarded DeLuca first place. Hisses of disapproval could be heard from the audience, and many members questioned the acts of their president.³⁶

The outcry made it to the New London *Morning Telegraph*, where DeLuca blamed the anarchists for the uproar. Soon Foschini received a letter from DeLuca's attorney, threatening to sue him for defamation of character should his criticisms continue. Gruppo L'Avvenire entered the picture with a response to the threat of legal action with a letter to the *Morning Telegraph*. (The editions of the *Telegraph* from this period have unfortunately not survived; the discussion is translated from *La Questione Sociale*.) The letter answered DeLuca's charges, saying that the press was attempting to incite a campaign against the anarchists. Signed by six members, including Cravello, the letter also offered a short summary that compared anarchist beliefs with "the words of our forefathers of America, that all men are created equal, with a bold right to life, liberty and the right to happiness; and our main spirit is to propagate everywhere the resistance to tyranny . . ." The letter remarked that the members of the Benefit Society "neither read or write," an observation that might have been interpreted as a regionalist slur. While declaring their solidarity with Foschini, the six members of Gruppo L'Avvenire took pains to say that they did not concur with all of the former's criticisms of "members of the society," and revealed that Foschini had actually tried to join the Benefit Society but had been rejected.[37]

No more came of the affair, but it obviously had created a climate for future confrontations. Foschini left New London and moved to nearby Ivoryton, Connecticut for over a year, where he organized among Italian workers at the Cheney & Comstock Company. It is possible that his move was a consequence of the DeLuca episode, but Foschini relocated continuously during his years of activism in the anarchist movement.

An episode that revealed the growing gulf between the *prominenti* and the Fort Trumbull anarchists occurred in 1904, with the murder of Guerino Menghi (mentioned in chapter 8). Anarchism emerged as an issue during the trial of the four Sicilian assailants when one of them described on the stand how Guerino refused to cease his pursuit of the woman he loved: "No, I am an anarchist and if I can't have her no one shall." The prosecution would have none of it, with their attorney dismissing the accusation by claiming that Guerino had carried an American flag during processions of the Italian Mutual Benefit Society. The trial revealed that at this early stage a rising Italian middle-class had begun to assert itself. The principal assailant, Frank Shandeor, worked as a shipbuilder in nearby Noank, and was the nephew of Antone Caracausa. All of the assailants came from Trapani, Sicily, as did the Caracausas. Among the many character witnesses for Shandeor was the superintendent of the shipyard where he worked, who testified that "the shipyard officials had procured many of their Italian help through the Shandeors and Caracausas."

Days before the murder, Guerino's brother Antone had traveled to Noank with Gennaro De Luca to negotiate with Frank, who had claimed by custom the right of an older brother to choose his younger sister's spouse. While unsuccessful, the meeting showed clearly that the Italian community recognized DeLuca as a mediator in disputes. The legal assistance provided by the *prominenti* paid off: Shandeor, even though he obviously had organized the foray into Fort Trumbull, received a five-year sentence in state prison while two other codefendants were given life sentences.[38]

As the Foschini-DeLuca affair showed, anarchist opinion regarding the *prominenti* was far from unanimous. A number of Fort Trumbull anarchists continued to denounce members of the *prominenti* in their press, while others maintained social and business ties with some of the leading elements. Only three years after the Foschini-DeLuca episode, Federico Dondero's name appeared on the officers' list of the Italian Mutual Benefit Society. (Two Menghi's, as the prosecutor in the trial had revealed, were listed as standard bearers.) When Joseph Conti, a very early Italian immigrant to New London, died in 1911, Dondero served as a pallbearer along with Charles Satti, John and Antone Leverone, and Antone Menghi, despite the funeral and burial services being under Catholic auspices. Dondero's saloon on Bank Street may have been the favorite watering hole for local anarchists, but it also served as a meeting place for nonradical leaders in the Italian community. Negotiations over the Menghi/Shandeor squabble were initially held in Dondero's saloon. Marchegiani also appear to have frequented saloons on Bank Street owned by Sicilians and others. Ties such as these could be mutually beneficial, and may have helped ensure the availability of Leverone's grove to the anarchists for decades. Some clashes between anarchists and nonanarchists arose, as they did in other social circles, from personality differences.[39]

The Bank Street anarchists and nonanarchists who owned businesses often faced a common foe in city authorities that kept tabs on their practices. Both Dondero and Charles Satti, the Tuscan-born father of future Democratic Party wheel horse C. John Satti, faced charges of leaving doors open from their saloons to their rented rooms, which violated city ordinances. An open door to living quarters signaled a kitchen bar for off-hours serving of liquor. Police charged Satti both with selling liquor on Sundays and for selling it with no license at all. Fred Dondero, the revolutionary who had hosted Malatesta and Galleani, faced similar charges, won praise from the prosecutor who "had no knowledge of a disturbance ever taking place" in his saloon. Revolution, alliance-building, and earning a living mingled and crossed paths on the busy pavement of New London's commercial center.[40]

In 1904 stonecutter Nazzareno Falcioni wrote an article that contrasted the recently formed Italian Ladies' Mutual Aid Society with others in New London. Falcioni praised the women's group as a model that could serve for the rest, since it "never showed the flag, our tricolor, the badges in many men's societies to protect their usual patriotism, how as well they could give a damn about loud honorary titles." Falcioni gave "sincere wishes to this society that gives lessons of seriousness to people."[41]

In 1906, members of the group attended a function of the same society, with different results. Soon after the festivities commenced, an anarchist comrade shouted out a cheer for the recent Russian revolution. The *prominenti* were present in strength, and one of them, outraged, responded, "We are not Russians, and that being Italians we need to shout 'Viva l'italia!'" This started a ruckus, and ended with the anarchist mounting a platform, saying, "I'm the one who yelled and will also yell 'Viva la Revoluzione Russia and down with all the homeland assassins!'" The correspondent for *Cronaca Sovversiva* wrote, "I saw that the patriot was in a fall and that in the room, he felt the smell of *senza patria* (an allusion to Pietro Gori's play), (and) the future knight and brave thinker slipped through the door and left." While counting this confrontation a victory, the correspondent further observed that the local working-class had not yet been educated in what "elevates them above all the foolish and stupid prejudices that are concentrated in their patriotism."[42]

A little over a year later, Gruppo L'Avvenire complained of the difficulty of renting a room for their public functions. It is highly likely that the *prominenti* played a role in this. Few mass meetings of the anarchists would ever take place beyond the boundaries of Fort Trumbull. A wall of sorts now separated the group from potential recruits in the city outside of the Marchegian community.

Gennaro DeLuca continued his organizing activities with a vengeance. Although he changed his line of business from barbershop to Italian grocery store after twenty years, he relentlessly worked to consolidate and build the societies of his countrymen in New London. He succeeded in eventually converting the Mutual Benefit Society into the Christopher Columbus lodge of the Sons of Italy, of which he became president for about ten years. DeLuca played a major role in establishing what later became an umbrella group of most of the Italian clubs in the city, paving the way for Italians' later involvement in the Democratic and Republican Parties. His death in late December 1927 was followed only days later by that of Fred Dondero, anarchist pioneer and fellow Bank Street businessperson.[43]

CHAPTER FOURTEEN

FROM NEW DEAL TO WORLD WAR

Historical figures often have the opportunity to touch or influence a wide scope of political and social currents as they carry out simple daily activities over the course of their lives. In the unlikely person of Attilio Pierfederici, a number of trends that affected Italian Americans seemed to converge during the period that came to be known as the New Deal era: a waning commitment to radicalism, efforts to build community social organizations, the rise of industrial unionism, and a deepening turn toward the patriotic mainstream. Pierfederici was last heard from in 1911, shortly before the dissolution of Gruppo L'Avvenire, when this longtime supporter of Fort Trumbull anarchism had taken the non-Galleanist step of becoming president of the Italian Mutual Benefit Society. While he later resumed ties to Gruppo I Liberi, he probably did so as a sympathizer rather than as a member. Over the years, Pierfederici displayed great interest in the theater; he acted in and directed plays performed by local Italian theater groups, as well as played guitar at public events. It is quite possible that he had helped form the Filodrammatico di New London, the radical troupe that caused the Galleanists no few headaches between 1907 and 1909.

Pierfederici became a "figure" in the Italian community during the 1930s for his cultural activities well outside of the anarchist movement. Several local groups had formed during the decade, among them the Italian Cultural Club, which performed a play by the antifascist writer Roberto Bracco and the "Antognietti Dramatic Club," whose members put on a play called "Joan José," in which Pierfederici played the character Paco. Besides his cultural interests, Pierfederici also partnered with anarchist Lorenzo Montali in a sideline wholesale grocers' venture in the early 1920s.[1]

Along the way, his politics drifted from anarchism to socialism, and he may have supported the views of the Communists for a time. Pierfederici found employment at the Brainerd & Armstrong Company on Water Street shortly after migrating to the United States in 1904. He worked as a millwright, or loom fixer, a skilled trade occupation that carried great weight within the textile mills. On September 1, 1934, four hundred thousand textile workers from Georgia to Maine walked off the job seeking better wages and union recognition in one of the largest but lesser-known strikes in US history. As the strike spread through Connecticut and Rhode Island, workers at the Brainerd & Armstrong and Bloom mills in New London set up picket lines. They were joined two days later by twenty-one loom fixers at Brainerd, who walked out in support and issued a signed announcement in the press for a meeting with the union at the Workmen's Circle hall; half the names were Italian and several lived in Fort Trumbull. As a typical example of the role of radicals in labor battles such as these, the names of Pierfederici and Renato Giustini headed the list. Although the strike went down to defeat across the country, textile workers in New London stayed out longer. The loom fixers struck until the company rehired all those who had supported the strike.[2]

The insurgency of New London textile workers found Gruppo I Liberi at its center; it also brought to a head a clash between Italian radicals in the city that was long in the making. While Giustini played an important role, other members contributed heavily as well: Artimio Angeloni, an anarchist supporter born in Senigallia, had signed the loom fixers' list; Giuseppe Valentini, a construction laborer and father of longtime IDC president Aldo Valentini, had seven family members involved in the strike; Giordano Cesarini, a weaver and an anarchist until his death in 1962, "was one of the first to leave work when the strike was proclaimed"; Orvidia Cesarini, married to Giordano and who managed their grocery store, was arrested along with ten other women, many of them Fanese from the Fort, for setting upon a strikebreaker in a city park.[3]

The strike resulted in another round of conflict between local Communist Party supporters and Gruppo I Liberi. Anarchists accused the Communists, who were also involved in strike support, of attempting to build an independent union, the National Textile Workers Union, as opposed to the AFL-affiliated United Textile Workers. Two local organizers, one of them Italian, approached Giustini for support; Giustini responded to their invitation, "saying clearly and sharply what I thought of unions and of union organizers, concluding with a flat refusal." Soon the Communists began to charge the anarchists with lack of support for the strike; Giustini, they said, had remained on the job for two days after the strike began. He responded by saying that Local 1889 of the UTW had agreed with the company in keeping skilled maintenance personnel at work to ensure the functioning of equipment. Giustini blasted this pact, "Only conceivable," he charged, "in the unionism of this country." While on the job before their walkout, the loom fixers staged a work-to-rule slowdown to support the strikers.[4]

The clash between Gruppo I Liberi and the Communist Party of New London indicate the fault lines between classic, anti-organizational anarchism and Leninist party-building. The Galleanists rejected both trade unions and revolutionary political parties as weapons in the struggle, while the Communists sought to work within unions, unemployed organizations, and fraternal groups to construct a party that could lead workers in a socialist revolution. For the first time since the very early days of the 1900s, Fort Trumbull anarchists faced a significant opponent on the left that sought to organize on "their" turf; the issues involved resembled the debate points between Luigi Galleani and Arturo Caroti in the New London Opera House of decades past.

The Communists proved a more resilient opponent than Caroti's FSI. Forming the Circolo Cultura Operaia—Workers' Culture Circle—in early 1934, the CP gained a group of perhaps a dozen Italian members and sympathizers, including a number of textile workers, from both the Shaw Street and Fort Trumbull neighborhoods. Most were first-generation immigrants, and the CP's section organizer, L. Marra, may have been Sicilian.

The 1934 textile strike row in New London had been touched off by an article sent by an alleged CP sympathizer to the Party's Italian-language organ, *L'Unita Operaia* that attacked by name local anarchists for their role in the walkout. Soon after, a member of Gruppo I Liberi responded by rising at a strikers' mass meeting and, after identifying himself as an anarchist, denounced the presence of five or six Communist strikers in the hall. The incident, apparently, raised not a few eyebrows.[5]

An unbridgeable gulf separated the two radical factions, differences that originated with the Marx-Bakunin conflict in the 1860s and sharpened even further with differences over the Bolshevik Revolution. Both sides were capable of committing sectarian stupidities against the other, but in the end the doctrines espoused by the anarchists placed them in splendid, harmless isolation. Even though perfectly placed in a working-class Italian community at the advent of the 1934 textile strike, their hostility to trade unions left them back at the starting line. Communist organizing in the local labor movement as well as the unemployed struggle at least raised the possibility of recruiting in the Sicilian community, a task impossible for Gruppo I Liberi.

Vincenzo Gaudenzi, a textile worker and resident of Fort Trumbull who had been arrested for the 1928 Columbus Day attack, wrote a perceptive article in 1934 in *L'Unita Operaia* about Gruppo I Liberi, perhaps the only critique of the neighborhood's anarchist movement, and a fairly comprehensive one at that, written by another left-wing group. Gaudenzi appears to have been influenced by anarchism at an earlier time. The tone of his article, titled "We Give to the Youth a Proletarian Culture," has both a scolding and mournful tone, and it addressed vital issues confronting the remaining revolutionaries of New London. The vast majority of Marchegian *sovversivi* in the city, he conceded, were still anarchists. "It's already deplorable the fact," he charged, "that nearly all the youth—including children of subversives—are regularly attending church—and are soaking up the religious opiate." He accused the anarchists of using "insult and violence" against their left-wing opponents and of "leaving an open field for the priests to conquer the youth" by not conducting political education. Gaudenzi observed further that social occasions even in families with anarchist members were being conducted with church participation.[6]

Others on the left, including anarchists, could have made these criticisms. The faults of the Galleanists were certainly no secret to many in the movement. Gruppo I Liberi, at least in their press, did not respond to Gaudenzi. The CP would maintain a presence for at least a decade in the Italian community in New London, principally Fort Trumbull. Like the Italian Mutual Aid Society, they filled a gap left by the self-absorption of Galleanism.

1934 marked a turning point during this decade of decisive labor struggles that resulted in the union organization of America's basic industries. The textile strike occurred along with walkouts of longshoremen in San Francisco, teamsters in Minneapolis, and auto parts workers in Toledo; these latter three were led by radicals whose goals went well beyond bread and butter demands of the mainstream labor movement. In 1935, the left, especially the Communists, played an important role in forming the Congress of Industrial Organizations (CIO) and while influencing some of its policies, could not move the new federation in the direction of revolutionary industrial unionism as envisioned by the IWW.

Across Connecticut the labor movement came to life; a plethora of organizing efforts took place as small, often independent union locals emerged. Italian workers, many still remembering the old battles fought before World War I, took a strong role in these drives. Italians formed an important part of the CIO unions such as the United Electrical Workers and Mine, Mill and Smelter Workers in industrial centers like New Britain, Hartford, Waterbury, New Haven, and Torrington.

Most of the organizing campaigns waged by these unions focused on Connecticut's vital metalworking industries. In the New London area, the companies that rose on the Groton site to form the Electric Boat Company (EB) in 1928 heavily drew the attention of labor organizers since the early 1900s. By 1934, workers at EB attempted to replace a company union as well as a catchall AFL federal union with a rank-and-file industrial union, a formation that evolved into Local 6 of the Industrial Union of Marine and Shipbuilding Workers of America. Within a year the union suffered a disastrous reversal when its leadership deserted to the side of the company union, "making it impossible at present to recruit new members openly." In February 1937, shortly after the epochal Flint sit-down strike in Michigan, union supporters in the welding and molding departments of EB tried a similar tactic, but were ousted and arrested by Connecticut State Police dispatched by the Democratic governor Wilbur Cross. Despite strenuous organizing efforts, workers voted against the CIO in favor of an independent union in 1942; later the Metal Trades Council, a federation of craft unions, won a vote for recognition that it holds to the present day.[7]

The rise of the industrial union movement took place against the backdrop of the Democratic Party's ascendancy in Connecticut's urban centers, New London among them. Italians took part in the state's political transformation that occurred alongside the continued development and increased sophistication of Italian American fraternal organizations. Pierfederici's activities in this arena—which were not out of the ordinary for a politically involved Italian but fateful for a former anarchist—would invoke the wrath of his old comrades.

In April 1932 the New London Italian American Democratic Club formed—a propitious time on the eve of the Rooseveltian New Deal. The club quickly came under the leadership of Doctor C. John Satti, who had carefully laid the groundwork in the Shaw Street community by providing services to residents, teaching math and English courses out of his office, and helping with job connections. In return for these services, Satti built a strong political base cemented by personal loyalties. Satti also gathered around him a group of idealistic recent graduates from local colleges as a hardworking core of campaigners. As one historian of New London observed, Satti's popularity translated into power. He launched his political career on the election wave that propelled the Italian community of New London into the leadership of the Democratic Party—wresting it partially from the Irish—and forever changed the face of the city's politics. While unsuccessful in his quest for a seat on the state Democratic ticket, he obtained a minor local position. On election night 1932, Satti led a massive parade through the streets of New London and the Shaw Street neighborhood as the Republican political lords looked on nervously. The Democrats swept New London and carried the city into what became the New Deal era. The pro-Republican *Day* commented, "Dr. Satti is the undisputed Democratic Boss, like it or not. The doctor has proved himself an adroit politician and effective political manager." The local Italian Communists, while describing Satti as "a good little fellow quick and intelligent," warned Italian workers not to "vote for him and his friends, a group of hypocritical and false Irish politicians."[8]

Satti may have dominated political life in the city's Italian community by the early 1930s, but he by no means monopolized it; factions emerged that sometimes defied easy categorization. C. (or Faust) Tramontano, a non-Marchegian, published a small Italian-language paper, the *New London Tribune*, beginning in 1933 (of which no issues apparently have survived). The paper contained articles criticizing capitalism along with others praising fascists, Democratic Party candidates, and touting "the superiority of our stock." Tramontano came under heavy CP criticism but later formed a bloc with them after he organized the League of Small Home Owners to agitate for lower property taxes. He later devoted his energy to activity within the Democratic Party.[9]

These mobilizations, as well as the continued building of Italian societies in the city, initially included little involvement from the Fort Trumbull neighborhood. This began to change as the decade progressed.

In December 1935, Fort Trumbull names show up on a list of attendees at a Democratic women's activity. In January 1937 the newly formed Central Council of Italian Societies held a banquet to honor Satti at the Mohican Hotel in downtown New London. As usual, the event was hosted by a number of Sicilian clubs; this time, however, the sponsoring list included Joseph Filippetti, a grocer who lived at 31 Smith Street, for the "Società Operaia di M.S.," which may have been at least a faction of the Italian Mutual Aid Society. Filippetti had immigrated from Fano in 1907, had used his grocery store in a manner similar to Satti. He offered help to neighbors in procuring legal documents and sometimes provided financial assistance. According to his granddaughter, he "wore his patriotism proudly." This appears to have been the first open involvement of elements of the Marchegiani in local Italian politics traditionally dominated by Sicilians.[10]

The New London Italian community's move into the New Deal column came with complications. In October 1935, Mussolini invaded Ethiopia from Italian colonies in East Africa. The Ethiopian army put up stiff resistance against a modernized foe but were defeated by the following May. The fascists dropped large quantities of poison gas on the Ethiopians as part of a barbaric campaign. Italian Americans who enthusiastically welcomed Mussolini's invasion saw their support as a means of showing patriotism for their homeland. Support for the fascist government reached new heights; Pernicone calls it the "most shameful hour in the history of Italian Americans." Across the United States, Italian communities raised funds for the Italian Red Cross for use in Ethiopia; the collections, probably illegal, raised monies that went directly for the Italian war effort rather than wounded soldiers. The fund-raising efforts are best remembered for the thousands of Italian American women who donated their gold wedding rings to be melted down. Under the direction of Rocco De Biasi, president of the Central Council of Italian Societies, New London Italians raised over one thousand dollars by the time the war was nearly over. Vice Consul De Cicco issued invitations to about forty individuals from New London who had aided the collection to attend a mass rally in the New Haven Arena to celebrate the fascist victory; of the list, all were Sicilian or Napolitano save one—Attilio Pierfederici.[11]

Pierfederici may have had no sympathy for Mussolini or fascism. Nationally, the list of Italian American New Deal Democrats, labor organizers, socialists, and others who similarly supported the Italian Red Cross drive is long, and partially shows the pressure these individuals came under during the Ethiopian war, as well as the feeling that they still considered themselves "patriotic" Italians. Even liberal political figures like New York mayor Fiorello La Guardia had avoided criticism of Mussolini (while freely attacking Hitler).[12]

As a result of his efforts on behalf of Mussolini's war, in February 1936 Pierfederici found himself the target of a letter in *L'Adunata dei Refrattari* signed by "Una Senigallese" (almost certainly Giustini). The piece referred to Pierfederici as a "charlatan," a "tightrope walker," and a "comedian." Pierfederici's working in the same department at Brainerd & Armstrong as Giustini might have made for some explosive confrontations on the job. If Pierfederici's action demonstrated the corrosive effects of pronationalist or -fascist sentiment among Italian American workers, it also showed that very few in Fort Trumbull followed the same route. Pierfederici was the exception—an important one, for sure—but he was held up as an example not to be followed. The anarchists had similarly responded to others in the community who had crossed a line of some sort—Gennaro Foschini in 1904, Nazarene Benvenuti in 1910, and the Mutual Aid Society in 1922. By the 1950s, Pierfederici had become a "poet and radio personality," speaking at public events, active in the Italian American Civic Association, and reading his poetry at a Republican Party dinner. He had quit Brainerd & Armstrong to open the Subway Restaurant on Pequot Avenue, probably in the 1940s, running it for twenty-five years. He passed away in 1975.[13]

Another figure made a similar, protracted shuffle away from the anarchist movement during the same period as Pierfederici. Fortunato Renzoni, married to the daughter of Fort Trumbull building contractor Antone Menghi and once caught up in US government raids on the *Cronaca Sovversiva* distribution network, left work in the construction field to open the Brass Rail restaurant on Bank Street in the 1930s. Perhaps he learned from his enterprising activity during Prohibition, and his family ties certainly didn't hurt, as he came to at least partially embody the definition of his Latin name ("prosperous, blessed, happy"). In the summer of 1936, Fortunato was robbed at gunpoint outside his home on Smith Street after closing up his restaurant for the night. The gunman relieved him of thirty-five dollars in cash, an expensive wristwatch, and a three thousand dollar diamond ring. The police determined that a robber gang operating out of Mystic and Westerly had targeted Renzoni, showing that "expropriation" cut both ways. Renzoni continued to support the anarchist press until 1940. Father-in-law Antone Menghi would later become a Republican supporter while Fortunato became active in the Italian American Civic Association in the late 1940s. Fortunato resembles the O'Neill character Tony Daniello in *The Visit of Malatesta*, with his newfound affluence from the liquor business and a wife named Rose, but probably only by coincidence—or maybe not.[14]

Other defections might illustrate how some ex-radicals had found the exit door; in 1936, the name of Dulio Luzi, a longtime anarchist militant, appeared on the New London voting roll. Perhaps he had only wished to placate a relative or friend. Or perhaps he planned to vote for Roosevelt and his New Deal that year.[15]

Earlier in the decade, while labor and political struggles surged across the American landscape that were to permanently change greater society, the New London anarchists had chosen to look inward as a way of maintaining their cohesiveness and direction. In November 1933, Gruppo I Liberi published a special number, or *Numero Unico*, of the long-suppressed *Cronaca Sovversiva*. This would be the group's signal contribution to their weakening movement during the decade; anarchist groups had regularly issued special numbers of their journals to celebrate events like the Haymarket trial or May 1st. In this case, I Liberi's *Cronaca* consisted entirely of excerpts from the writings of Luigi Galleani from 1903 to the paper's suppression in 1919, with notes inserted to update the material for a new audience they hoped would gain from what this "ardent anarchist apostle" could offer.[16] Galleani had died two Novembers previous while under house arrest in the Tuscan mountain town of Caprigliola. He remained steadfast in his revolutionary anarchism even as Mussolini's press censorship had silenced his pen. Errico Malatesta died almost eight months later in Rome, also under house arrest and without a public organ to reach across continents with his formidable powers of agitation.[17]

To celebrate the publication of the special issue, the Galleanist movement in the northeastern United States mobilized for a weekend event in New London "in the vast room of the circle." The first speaker, A. Fabbri, emphasized the qualities of steadfastness and self-sacrifice in the movement built by Galleani; he "recalled episodes ignored or long forgotten, recalled the struggles and hopes of days long gone . . . the persecution of the enemy, recalled the agony of all the fallen in the sharp struggle that inevitably separates the enunciation from the triumph of every great ideal."

Raffaele Schiavina, the editor of *L'Adunata* using the name Max Sartin, focused on the ideological continuity of the anarchist movement, and recounted the slow process of building the revolutionary movement in Italy. "In the bosom of the anarchist movement Galleani emerged as a figure of the first order, who brought an original contribution as well as the undisputed force of his firm character and of adamant rectitude."

As important as was this reaffirmation of their core, insurrectionary anarchist beliefs, the weekend event also gave the comrades a chance to mingle "in all hours in a cordial atmosphere (in) hospitality where they could exchange ideas, opinions, with profit for all . . ."[18] Throughout the 1930s, Gruppo I Liberi held public events that combined revolutionary politics and their radical subculture; picnics, dances, and parties continued to raise money for anarchists persecuted in North and South America and in Europe. Revolutionary events in Spain from 1931 to 1939 drew much of their attention, as the last mass anarchist movement in that country battled alongside communists and socialists against the forces of Franco's fascism. Above all, Gruppo I Liberi raised money for *L'Adunata dei Refrattari*, the heart and soul of their beleaguered movement.

World War II converted New London into a center of military enterprise; the federal government took control of property in Groton to greatly expand facilities for the building of submarines. The new shipyard brought five thousand jobs—Fort Trumbull faced a massive increase in military presence in the neighborhood. The installation of Fort Trumbull "filled with naval activity"; a school to train merchant marine officers doubled in size; and scientists arrived to conduct research in antisubmarine warfare in a facility under the direction of Columbia University. These developments brought new employment opportunities and a potentially different job structure to the neighborhood, but constituted a double-edged sword for Fort Trumbull. The wrecking ball, invariably, accompanied the employment gains.[19] The economic and political forces that had earlier taken aim at Fort Trumbull had begun to bear down again in the 1940s. To expand their underwater warfare research center, the Navy in 1943 acquired and razed properties on the east side of Smith Street, the north side of Walbach Street and the west side of East Street. The loss of this significant amount of housing put pressure on the neighborhood, forcing a number of families to move, but a steady outward migration process would have taken place in any case.[20]

World War II found dozens of Fort Trumbull's young men of prime military age. Some found employment in Electric Boat (EB). Others, including sons of neighborhood anarchists, joined or were drafted into the service along with second generation Sicilians, Poles, Portuguese, and others in New London. Victor Frederick's son Otello saw duty in the

Army Air Corps. Dulio Luzi's son Ray served in the postwar occupation in Europe. Alfredo Bartolucci's son Ray served in the Army in Germany. Fortunato Renzoni's son Leo saw duty on a US Navy cargo ship. A son of Nostralio Facchini served as a medical corpsman on a hospital ship in the Pacific. At least two sons of Rafaelle and Giovanna Petrini served in the military: Arthur in naval construction as a See Bee, while Nevio, who had joined the US Army in 1940, received a battlefield citation for action in Western Europe, and would retire as a lieutenant colonel after twenty years of service. Renato Giustini's son Louis served with the 10th Mountain Division in Italy, seeing some of the hardest fighting on the western front. His father had fought fascism in the streets of New London, and while Louis had attended and contributed to at least one anarchist function in 1946, he had combatted fascism in uniform with a rifle issued by the US Army. As his unit faced the Kesselring Line in the Apennines and the fierce resistance of German troops and Italian fascist diehards, perhaps coming into contact with the Communist-led resistance fighters, what were Louis's thoughts for the future? What meaning could the classic revolutionary movements of the working class have had as violent and uncontrollable world events swirled around him? The young men and women of Fort Trumbull had grown up in a society in which the immigrants of the last wave had gradually found a place within the Roosevelt New Deal coalition. They did not abandon or shun their Italian heritage, since family connections with the Fort remained strong, but the revolutionary politics of their parents seemed not to provide answers in a society confronted by a myriad of challenges.[21]

When Nevio Petrini retired from the military in 1960 he worked at EB, eventually rising to the position as "Superintendent of Ships." When Louis Giustini returned from the military he also found a job at EB but soon went on to work in the fire department of the Naval Undersea Warfare Center, retiring as chief in 1977. His brother-in-law, a police captain, described Louis as "a kid from the old Fort section who was a good father and a hard-working man who put three children through college. Everyone liked and respected him." Louis was a lifelong member of the IDC, serving as president in the 1990s, but radical politics had nearly disappeared from the experience of the generation emerging from the war. Louis donated to a collection for "agitation in Ancona" in 1946, along with a considerable number of others from the Fort that included a few other second-generation members. But his name never appears again in *L'Adunata*. And neither do others of his generation.[22]

CHAPTER FIFTEEN

"TESTED BY ATTACKS OF TIME AND ILLNESS"

In April 1953, armistice talks to bring the Korean conflict to an end remained deadlocked. Groton's Electric Boat, in the midst of a hiring boom for all shipbuilding trades, placed ads in the local paper appealing for housing for their rapidly expanding workforce to build the Navy's nuclear submarines. Newspapers were satiated with advertisements for new refrigerators and clothes dryers, and a new Jerry Lewis/Dean Martin movie, *Scared Stiff*, was about to be released. And on Saturday, April 25, Italian anarchists from across New England and New York gathered at the Italian Dramatic Club in New London to confront the new realities they faced in the vortex of this Cold War, consumer-driven America.

The two-day conference allowed for a considerable exchange of ideas and opinions among the large number of attendees, most of whom had known each other for decades. "As usual the comrades gathered were numerous and the meeting was a *festa* without a sense of merrymaking but with a sense of joy when the comrades had common opinions, memories, proposals, and hopes." They were especially conscious that "they were in New London because there is a good group of men and women comrades of extreme importance . . ."

On Sunday they gathered in the "great hall," the large meeting room upstairs that could hold several hundred people, to summarize the weekend's discussions. The article, signed by an anonymous out-of-towner as "one who was there," attempted to summarize the remarks: "The fact that the ideas of freedom and justice find much coolness among the new generations is undeniable . . . it is part of the general reactionary tendency of the last forty years." A list of the factors contributing to this was the legacy of World War II, "Nazi-Fascism," "Bolshevik totalitarianism," the "restoration of Roman Catholicism," and the threat to human survival from atomic and biochemical war. The long view of human history was needed to see past the reactionary present, to understand that human aspirations for freedom would conquer in the end, that the oppressed and disinherited of the globe would triumph. "Although few, we, each of us, today is the bearer of that shining torch of light that is now impossible not to see and later not to ignore."[1]

It was also impossible not to see the irreversible decline of the Italian radical movement in the United States, a process underway since the 1920s. If Gruppo I Liberi held onto its base membership because of its strength in the Fort, the young—as the article pointed out—were staying away. A few exceptions stood out—two sons of Rafaelle and Giovanna Petrini, Spartaco and Bruno—came to anarchist functions, and one of them contributed to L'Adunata into the 1960s, but neither rose to take the place of their graying parents. (Bruno and another son, Libero, moved to Needham and started a construction business that survives to this day.) If the sons and daughters did not reject outright their parents' radicalism, they remained aloof from it, their "coolness" being Italian American anarchism's most unforgiving foe.[2]

The late 1940s witnessed the last major rally point for the left in New London, followed by a deepening Cold War reaction against radicals of all types. Throughout 1948, strong organizing efforts took place in the city by the Progressive Citizens of America (later the Progressive Party) to establish the campaign of Henry Wallace for president. The movement had significant involvement from the Communist Party, but represented a section of American liberalism that sought to blunt the threat of war between the United States and the Soviet Union. The New London group had a multiethnic composition, with heavy representation from Jewish professionals. As the year progressed, redbaiting of the group increased. A mass rally at Bulkley High School in March drew attacks from local veterans groups and politicians. Among the critics was Fred Benvenuti, son of Nazzarene, who had helped found Gruppo L'Avvenire in 1899. Fred had taken over his father's contracting business in 1934. During World War II he became involved in the Republican Party and rapidly rose in its ranks due to his connections. Local Republicans had long utilized anticommunism and anti–New Deal sentiments as a staple of their electoral efforts. Benvenuti did not have a base in Fort Trumbull but among non-Marchegian Italians. If Fort Trumbull did not rally to Benvenuti, neither did it mobilize for Henry Wallace; Italian speakers at New London Progressive Party events were invariably out-of-towners. Other local Italians, meanwhile, supported the antiradicalism of Benvenuti. A group called the Unity Club met at the Mohican Hotel "to have all members with relatives in Italy to advise them in writing not to vote for the Communist Party" in coming parliamentary elections in April 1948. The regaining of office, even if temporary, by the New London Republicans represented part of a conservative reaction across the country to "big labor" and New Deal politics. Benvenuti, as "a towering figure in city public works projects," fit the bill perfectly, and was chosen for three terms by the city council as the city's first mayor of Italian extraction. As mayor, though, he supported the closed shop for the conservative building trades unions.[3]

In the summer of 1948, eighteen organizations united to form the Italian American Civic Association (IACA), cochaired by Benvenuti and C. John Satti. A number of Marchegiani became active in the group, including Attilio Pierfederici, Matt Orsini, and Enzo Filippetti. Large Italian American public events that crossed partisan political lines became the order of the day. Sons of Italy picnics and Columbus Day parades, finally, as the 1950s commenced, became affairs of most segments of the New London Italian community.[4]

At a dinner dance sponsored by the IACA in November 1948, Benvenuti credited joint work by local Italian Americans' fund-raising for postwar relief efforts in Italy as providing the impetus for the formation of the group. The American Relief for Italy, Inc. came under the leadership of anticommunist forces in the Italian community, and the same forces sympathetic to Mussolini during the 1920s and 1930s initiated the letter writing to Italy in 1947–48.[5]

Luigi Rocco Camillucci died on November 14, 1948, a comrade whose affiliation with the group predated his actual residence in the city, when he sent in correspondence to the anarchist press from Fishers Island in 1899. No obituary appeared in *L'Adunata* for Luigi, an indication that he had left the movement. Camillucci and his wife Emilia, also an anarchist, had three sons and three daughters. Daughter Alba (see chapter 12), had married a member of her band (also named Camillucci but of no relation), and immediately became pregnant. This closed the door to her career as a professional opera singer. Luigi and Emilia had expected Alba to make it to the Metropolitan, not "marry a struggling musician . . ." After moving to New York, Alba reputedly kept the existence of her son secret from Luigi for three years. She taught voice lessons until her death at the age of forty-four. Her son, under the name "Dick Cami," married into the Genovese crime family, and in the early 1960s oversaw the evolution of the Peppermint Lounge in Manhattan from a mob-connected bar into a premier rock-and-roll joint known as the birthplace of the twist.[6] Emilia and Luigi's daughter Louise married Vivian J. Nossek, whose grandson Ronald became the Democratic mayor of New London in the 1990s. At least one son of Luigi, Leo, whose given name apparently was Libero and who followed his father's trade of stonemason, remained active in the IDC until his death.[7]

At the time of the 1953 anarchist conference, Fort Trumbull stood on the edge of another threat to its existence as a distinct northern Italian community: suburbanization. Throughout the 1950s and 1960s, a steady stream of first- and second-generation Marchegiani—anarchist and nonanarchist alike—moved to quieter, less-urbanized nearby towns, Waterford being the primary destination. They shared with their fellow Italians of Waterbury, New Haven, and Hartford, and other ethnic groups as well, the desire to "move on" with their lives a join the postwar surge into the suburbs. Redevelopment continued to chip away at the neighborhood. The next big hit came in 1975, when the city announced plans to build a waste treatment facility on the west side of Smith Street and to the south of Walbach Street. These amputations of street sections created a truncated residential district, a pinched urban grid that no longer cohered.

A particularly venerated site of the local anarchists—the wooded area in Waterford known as Leverone's Grove, where for decades they had gathered boisterously for picnics—met its end during this time of postwar social and economic development. The pavilion and baseball field are gone; the woods that nestled the Grove eventually eviscerated to make way for a trailer park. Rousing anarchist hymns from the depths of this one-time popular resort for New London's working class have been replaced by the drone of traffic from nearby strip mall–lined US Route 1.

Gruppo I Liberi survived this difficult environment, an accomplishment in itself. The Italian Dramatic Club remained firmly in the hands of its anarchist founders, at least until the 1960s; gradually *L'Adunata* began to refer to their meeting place as "our room" rather than "our locale. But for at least a quarter of a century after World War II, they continued to hold their events in the IDC. In the years immediately following the war, Gruppo I Liberi held special fund-raisers for purposes ranging from building maintenance to anarchist activities in Italy, with an occasional outside speaker who would give a talk on current events. For this entire period, the Fort Trumbull anarchists hosted spring and fall festivals that drew comrades from Connecticut, Rhode Island, and Massachusetts.[8]

As their movement shrank, the Galleanists throughout New England drew closer, attending each other's events when possible. Gruppo I Liberi continued its close relationship with the Needham, Massachusetts circle and its fellow Marchegiani. The larger Connecticut cities, once the site of boisterous and substantial Italian radical groups, now contained scattered individual holdouts. By the postwar period, only one other Italian anarchist group existed in the state, Gruppo Luigi Bertoni, named for an exiled anarchist who had fought in Spain and had died in 1947. This group consolidated the former circles in Wallingford, Bristol, New Britain, and Hartford, and used the Casa del Popolo on Maple Avenue in Wallingford for their public functions. The Casa had been founded prior to World War I by syndicalists active in the northern Italian community of that town. A substantial grouping of Spanish anarchist exiles in Wallingford and Meriden also met here.[9]

As the years passed, a column in *L'Adunata* appeared with increasing regularity, first called "Quelli che se ne vanno," and then "Quelli che ci lasciano"—those who have left us. The quantity of obituaries from New London show that Gruppo I Liberi retained the loyalty of many of its veteran members until the end. When Vincenzo Marcucci died at the age of sixty-five of an undisclosed illness, his obituary noted that "he came from Fano before the First World War and with the comrades of New London—strong, numerous and unshakeable in their convictions from the first hour—he was active with a sincere spirit from adolescence until his final days." Marcucci had settled first in Framingham, Massachusetts, before settling in New London, where he worked as a stonemason; he had been active in the local bricklayers' union and had served as a past president of the IDC. "To his tormented family, to the comrades of New London already tested by attacks of time and illness," the editors saluted their "faith unshakeable in the common ideal."[10]

Many of the obituaries spoke to the members' unrelenting hostility to organized religion; when Paris Carnaroli died in 1962, his ceremony was "contrary to religious superstitions a civil funeral." For Pia Zanghetti

Lombardozzi, the widow of stalwart Anselmo Lombardozzi, who had died a few months earlier, the comrades "carried the last farewell to her simple funeral, conforming to her character, strictly civil."[11]

Gruppo I Liberi's numbers continued to shrink. When a member passed away, their obituary often noted "the hole left in the ranks" that could not be filled. This would never be truer concerning the loss of two comrades who had epitomized the militant core of New London anarchism since before World War I. After suffering from a debilitating heart disease for ten years, Rafaelle Petrini died on July 8, 1956, at the age of seventy: "For the comrades of Connecticut and for the entire movement, his is a heavy loss. For many, like us, who were his comrades and friends for their entire adult life, the pain that connects us with that of his devoted companion and his entire family, finds comfort only within the consciousness and intention to continue the work of agitation and propaganda of our ideas of freedom and justice to which we have held together for so many years." It is unlikely that Petrini's views softened as he aged. He was a man who had fought a campaign within the group against "spies" that at least partially led to its self-destruction. The Mussolini regime had accused him of making a death threat against his fascist brother in Italy as well as attempting to establish contact with Italian political prisoners.[12]

For the last decade of his life, Petrini's attending physician had been C. John Satti, retired from politics after running afoul of Democratic Party factionalism. Did the pair discuss politics during visits—one who more than any single individual had kept alive the local anarchist movement, the other responsible for building an urban political machine? Rafaelle's companion Giovanna continued to attend anarchist events and donate to the press for several years but seems to have dropped from activity before her death in 1966. She would not be the only spouse to do so on the death of her anarchist husband.[13]

In 1963, Renato Giustini passed away while on a visit to his native Senigallia, which he had not seen for fifty-six years. "He was one of the convinced and the good ones. He came to our movement at a young age, a little after his arrival in New London . . . and where he spent the rest of his life laboring dedicatedly for all of what could be useful to the cause of the Idea which he embraced with so much love." Members and friends of the anarchist movement in Senigallia attended his civil funeral ceremony, indicating that Giustini had established prior contact with them.[14]

Giuseppe Busca had fished the local waters with his own boat since his arrival in New London from Fano around the time of World War I. He had docked his boat in the backyard of his house on Smith Street until losing his property to the government in the 1940s. When he died in 1971, the city lost a popular fish merchant, owner of the New London Public Fish Market on Bank Street, as well as an avid baseball fan. Described as a "Yankee worshipper," the *Bridgeport Sunday Herald* in 1959 had warned that Busca stood poised to jump off a nearby highway bridge because of the terrible season his beloved team was having. Busca had been as fervent in his support for anarchism as for baseball since his immigration, and his commitment seemed to increase during the final years, "especially in these times when the ranks are starting to thin out and the survivors feel the need to continue the work of the precursors." *L'Adunata* nostalgically invoked Busca's coming of age during the "times of (Giobbe) Sanchini and (Giralomo) Grasso," well-known Galleanists of New Britain and Hartford, respectively. New London knew well Busca's devotion to fishing and baseball; few knew of his commitment to anarchism.[15]

The March 27, 1971 issue of *L'Adunata* announced the inevitable folding of their paper after a fifty-year run. The editors cited age, health, and the rapidly declining readership for the demise of the last organ of militant Italian anarchism on the North American continent. Small groups hung together to the end, in Boston, Providence, Philadelphia, Los Angeles, New York, Detroit, Fresno, Miami, San Francisco, and Tampa, and continued to gather, as did Gruppo I Liberi, to reminisce of the hopes and battles that had animated their lives.[16]

The Fort Trumbull anarchists had been the last Connecticut group standing since the early 1960s. Gruppo Luigi Bertoni of Wallingford disappeared years earlier; the few remaining comrades were forced to sell their *vecchio edificio*, the Casa del Popolo in December 1962. They received eleven hundred dollars for the building, dividing the sum among anarchist papers and political victims, keeping three hundred dollars "for now."[17]

Comrades throughout Connecticut and New England, some with long connections with Gruppo I Liberi passed from the scene—Tony Santi of Revere, Massachusetts in 1959, Donato LaPenna of Hartford, who had been a member of Gruppo Autonomo in East Boston and for a while the editor of *L'Adunata*, in 1965, and Giuseppe Tomaselli of Providence and James Peretta of Kensington, Connecticut, in 1968.

In 1969, Camillo DiDomizio, a former member of the Galleanist circle in New Britain "in the time of Galleani" passed away in a hospital in Yonkers. While on his deathbed he received a visit from his nephew, a priest, who offered to give him absolution. DiDomizio responded that he needed a doctor, not a priest.[18]

The New London anarchists did not face the same dilemma as had their comrades in Wallingford; a successful transition had been made during the 1940s and 1950s, with the building remaining with its founders or their children. The second generation may not have sustained their parents' radicalism, but they kept the club alive as a leading social center of the neighborhood. By serving as caretakers they ensured the survival of this vital aspect of Fort Trumbull's heritage. A "blood tie to the area around Fano," including through marriage, remained the prerequisite for membership in the IDC.[19]

Radical politics, however, no longer entered the equation. A student from Connecticut College captured the IDC's ambience at the time of the eminent domain battle: "The manager of the club, an old Italian man, showed me around the inside of the pink Goshen Street structure, full of old pictures and pasta machines. Upstairs is a big hall with a stage, and I imagined the many Italian dances, meals and performances that were celebrated in that place over seventy years ago." On one occasion protesters from outside the Fort made an appearance. In 1984 the neighborhood became the site of an anti–nuclear weapons protest, with demonstrators coming from across New England to picket the Naval Underwater Systems Center. *L'Adunata dei Refrattari* had welcomed the "ban the bomb" movement of the early 1960s, but, of course, no longer existed to lend its voice to the current wave of dissenters. Fort Trumbull residents interviewed in the press, some of them descendants of anarchists, showed little hostility, but little interest as well, in the protest. Zenaide Luzi, wife of former anarchist Dulio, commented, "They can do whatever they want. They can holler as long as they don't come knocking at the door." She said that she and her husband "will keep an eye on activities up the street from their dining room window.[20]

The best evidence of Gruppo I Liberi's passing from the scene, I believe, consists of the group's final announcements in *L'Adunata* and surviving correspondence. In 1970, for the first time in decades, the group did not put on an autumn *festa* at their hall; the only news coming from New London in that last year consisted of obituaries and memorials. In the *L'Adunata* manuscript collection at the Boston Public Library are two surviving letters, written in 1965 and 1970, to Raffaele Schiavina from Luigi Espositi, a comrade in New London. Espositi had immigrated in his youth from Ancona province and worked as a stonemason for contractor Mike Giri until age sixty-five. Living on Summitt Avenue with his niece, Expositi never married. He may have been Gruppo I Liberi's final correspondence secretary. Both letters are wholly devoted to the topics of illnesses and deaths among comrades in New London, especially concerning a comrade who needs a "big operation" from which the doctor sees "little hope of recovery." In early March 1975, the *Day* carried a photo of awards being presented to founding members of the IDC, Victor Frederick and Leo (son of Luigi) Camillucci. Espositi, one of the presenters, would be dead by the end of the month at age seventy-nine.[21] A good number of Fort Trumbull's anarchists made their final trip several hundred yards down US Route 1 from Leverone's Grove to be buried in Waterford's Jordan Cemetery.

Considering the deaths of so many key supporters and the drifting away of others, the dénouement of Fort Trumbull's anarchist movement could have come no later than the mid-1970s. Its culmination nearly coincided with the last struggle of the intractable Victor Frederick.

Frederick continued to collide with the law across the decades. Even after the demise of Prohibition, he maintained an unlicensed bar in his garage on Walbach Street. When the police raided the establishment in 1937, he avoided arrest by posing as a patron at one of the tables. In 1941, his son Alexander applied for a wholesale beer permit with the liquor control commission, and Victor launched a career in wholesale liquor distribution—finally within the law. In 1939, Frederick faced breach of peace charges for allegedly calling trespassing children "vile names." The judge, of Sicilian descent, dismissed the charges after determining that Frederick had been having trouble with the youngsters for some time. In 1952, he was arrested for parking his car to block traffic, for an unexplained reason, across North Bank Street.[22]

In November 1976, Authority arrived in the form of directives from the city of New London; Victor Frederick became enmeshed in a fight he could not win. Bulldozers dispatched by the City Redevelopment Agency clanked onto Walbach, Trumbull and Nameaug Streets to begin the final leveling of buildings for the proposed waste treatment plant. Among the properties marked for demolition was Frederick's house at 33 Walbach.

> Victor Frederick, who's lived in the same house on Walbach Street, the north side of the block, for 56 years, is now bedridden and too old and sick to fully understand why he should be in the same rush to leave as his neighbors . . . All have been caught up by what one city official describes as a lack of communication—a failure that sent city-contracted bulldozers into their backyards just three days after they were abruptly given notice to leave their homes immediately . . . Frederick has lived in the same neighborhood for the seventy years since he came here from Italy. He owns his own home, plus three others with apartments, plus the building that houses Foley's Café on Walbach Street. He reacted angrily when asked about having to move. "I live here 55 years. I move when I good and ready."

His son Otello, who helped manage the IDC, explained that the city's plans were forcing stable families out of the Fort and that his father's properties had become "flophouses." "Who's going to move in when they know the place is scheduled to be torn down?" Unknown to all the actors involved, the stage was merely being set for the final reckoning of 1998–2005. Victor moved into an apartment three blocks away at 224 Shaw Street, not far from the last home of the Petrinis and Montali's Bakery. He passed away less than a year later.[23]

CONCLUSION

Fort Trumbull's decline had been underway for decades before the New London Development Corporation finished the job in the early twenty-first century. The Connecticut Trust for Historic Preservation's naming the neighborhood a "threatened historical area" in 2000 seems not to have slowed the razing plans for even a moment.[1] In reaction to the encroachment by postwar development, second-generation Marchegiani had taken the hint and left, whether agreeably or grudgingly. By the time they moved on, few among them could recall what someone named Malatesta or Galleani had written, or what all those heated political spats among their parents had been about.

The "bright shining torch" of radicalism in the Fort had not so much been lost, as in other Italian American communities, but quietly dropped. Fort Trumbull did not suffer a bruising political transformation during the 1920s; the need to challenge fascism within Fort Trumbull never arose because it had been denied entry from the start. The principal rival of the anarchists, the Italian Mutual Aid Society, initially had more in common with their radical neighbors than with the new political formations in the Shaw Street neighborhood. It did not overshadow the IDC in Fort Trumbull during a time of political reaction. The group ultimately symbolized a turn away from the left, but it did not mesh easily with the more conservative, nationalistic groups of Italian New Deal New London. The Fort had its isolated Republicans, patriotic flag-wavers, and churchgoers, but they proved unable to organize within the community. The experience of leading city Republican Fred Benvenuti provides an example. His base remained among Shaw Street Italians and he did not make his electoral runs until after World War II. Well into the 1930s, political leaders bemoaned the division in the

Italian community in New London—two parallel worlds that seldom met. Fort Trumbull residents simply had not joined the hoopla parade of mass society—yet.[2]

Fort Trumbull's first generation, including those who arrived through the 1920s, consisted of active anarchist militants deeply educated in the traditions of a revolutionary movement. The second generation, even if they had attended anarchist functions in their youth, did not enter that movement's ranks. They went to multiethnic high schools, often forming friendships with non-Italians; the young men entered the military during World War II, emerging with family, careers and postsecondary education as priorities. They never became part of their parents' unorthodox political culture. Complete lack of interest, rather than hostility, seemed predominant in their thinking from the 1940s.

In their immunity to anarchism's influence, the second generation of the Fort much resembled other ethnics in Connecticut whose parents had committed to radicalism. In the Finnish American community in small towns of the eastern part of the state, where a strong socialist, communist, and syndicalist element existed, the children strenuously avoided any connection with the left, or with their parents' occupations as poultry farmers for that matter. In Waterbury, a Russian club that oriented toward the Communist Party retained hundreds of members into the cold war period, but as a former CP organizer remarked, "None of these people brought their children to come into the communist movement, none of them did."[3]

It might be said that regardless of the separate paths taken by New London's two Italian neighborhoods, both ended up within the boundaries of mainstream America. This observation would be correct in its essentials. It would not be accurate to say that anarchism did not influence the future character of Fort Trumbull. Maintaining a solid front against fascism during the 1930s—when Mussolini's popularity reached its height in Little Italy's across the country—was no small accomplishment. While a few children of Shaw Street Italians still have a kind word for Mussolini in interviews, descendants of the anarchists in contrast have often remarked that their parents had no use for the blackshirts, were anti-Mussolini, and hated the fascists. They were aware that many differences between their parents and the local Sicilian *prominenti* had had political origins. That Gruppo I Liberi maintained its strength for a decade after World War I reflected the high level of respect in which a number of leading anarchists in the neighborhood were held, while adhering to the tenets of Galleanism, a belief system that projected a purist "us-against-the-world" outlook that rooted itself in this geographically isolated neighborhood. In 1908, the New London group responded to criticism of their reaching out to nonanarchist Italians by saying they had no intention of "living in a cocoon." They would come full circle on this, since from the 1930s their efforts revolved almost exclusively around keeping the group alive as an end in itself. In a recent article on Italian American anarchism, Gerald Meyer pointed to the "danger to the most important goals of anarchism lurking in this elaborate, highly satisfying culture."[4] Galleanism provided an ideological refuge in which lifelong comrades and friends could gather to face the outside enemy. It also proved irrelevant to the children of the anarchists, incapable of sustaining a fight during the social conflicts of the Depression era, and powerless in the post–World War II years.

As was mentioned in the Introduction, a number of descendants of Fort Trumbull anarchists have retained bits of historical memory of their ancestors' political leanings. Shirley Mencarelli, granddaughter of anarchist fisherman Sergio Mencarelli, remembers her father telling of Sergio having "read the old anarchist papers." In a 1998 interview, Victor Frausini, a second-generation stonemason, when asked about anarchism in the Fort, at first remarked that he had not previously heard of this, but then said, "The anarchy thing . . . happened when they first came over." Others had more vague recollections: in 1998, Aldo Valentini, the president of the IDC, said that their parents "were always against Mussolini," and "never bothered with the blackshirts." The men, he said, "didn't go to church." Those who are aware of the anarchist past sometimes offer the explanation that their parents faced harsh working and living conditions in Italy and during the first decades in America: "They were hurting," offered Frausini.[5]

Descendants of the Italian Mutual Aid Society tend to have slightly more jaded memories of the anarchists. The group at the "big hall," the IDC, remembered Inez Ciofi Frausini, born in Tuscany in 1911, "had different ideas—religion and everything." They did "a lot of talk, they didn't accomplish anything." Rita Ferri Frausini, born in the Fort in 1932, had been told the IDC members "were atheists," and "believed in the communist way of living, not the capitalist way." Others are noncommittal. Vilma Frausini, born in 1932 of a father from Fano and mother from nearby Mondolfo, said, "We went to church—they celebrated May Day. They were different. I didn't pay any attention to politics. We were all friendly."[6]

Across Connecticut the Italian left had fought a difficult battle during the 1920s, its supporters often reduced to circles of diehard veterans. By the 1940s the radicals retained only a shadow of the influence they once commanded. But they did not disappear without a trace. They undoubtedly helped seed future movements for social change, as a French-Canadian official in a textile workers' local in West Haven remarked in a 1930s interview for the Federal Writers' Project. He found in organizing Italian workers in his shops that he received "valuable assistance from some old Italian Union men, some of them old Socialists, who have a good deal of prestige in the shops." The president of the Musicians' union of New Haven, of second generation Russian Jewish descent, remarked to the same interviewer that, "the Italians and the Jew are the most progressive elements in the union."[7] Italian antifascist and internationalist propaganda during the 1920s made CIO organizing efforts easier. In the industrial center of Torrington, for instance, Italian syndicalists remained active throughout the 1920s, probably cooperating with the local Italian branch of the Workers Party. They formed the base for the local unit of the independent Mechanics' Educational Society of America (MESA), a group that became an important nucleus of the United Automobile Workers in the 1930s. In 1935, the Torrington MESA unit reconstituted itself as a local of the IWW's Metal and Machinery Workers' union, probably the last Wobbly local in the state.[8]

In the days before the rise of the CIO, Italian radicals formed part of a labor movement that had been reduced to a small nucleus of organizers, often those who questioned the values of the dominant society. In Connecticut they may have resembled what cultural historian Michael Denning called the "recurring figure of the Italian American anarchist" in John Dos Passos's *USA Trilogy*: "They are the repository of traditions of rebellion and solidarity, of the crafts of work and the arts of living, the keepers of red wine and accordions."[9] Two figures from New Britain might be mentioned in this regard (maybe minus the accordions). John Vaninetti began his labor activity as a socialist in the brickyards of Kensington in the early 1900s, ran for mayor as the Socialist Party's candidate in 1940, and become vice president of a CIO United Electrical Workers local. Aurelio Canzonetti, the owner of a shoe repair shop, had been a key figure in New Britain's important Galleanist group. In the 1930s, both went on to become leaders of the Italian Fraternal Society and helped keep the organization on an antifascist path.[10]

Memory erasure of past radicalism across Connecticut's Italian communities seems prevalent, however. During the 1930s, the late Rudolph J. Vecoli, pioneer scholar of Italian American radicalism, grew up Wallingford, a town with such a heavy left presence in the old days. His father a construction worker and his mother a garment worker, Vecoli was raised in what he called "not a politically radical family," that "among my earliest memories are the picnics, dances, and plays at the Italian hall. I have no recollection of speeches of an anti-clerical or radical nature."[11]

Some Italian radicals in Connecticut fell far short of the romantic image that Michael Denning portrayed. The title of Joanna Clapps Herman's memoir of growing up in an Italian family in Waterbury says much: in *The Anarchist Bastard* she describes her grandfather as a violent and abusive man who "ruled his fiefdom with all the tyranny of the minor feudal lord." He apparently held meetings of the Tresca group in his home, but would explode if his *Il Martello* were not placed near his plate at supper.[12] A number of Italian radicals proved incapable of passing on their politics to their children; their offspring could be indifferent or even repelled by the odd politics of the "old folks."

Sometimes, the remnants of the Italian left are nearly archeological. In 1911, Italian radicals in Stafford Springs formed the Italian Cooperative and Social Club to provide groceries at a discount. The Cooperative formed a part of a host of radical groups formed by Italians in the town: an IWW local, Amalgamated Textile Workers local, as well as syndicalist and anarchist circles. Renamed the Workers' Cooperative Union in the 1920s, the group remained an important institution for local working-class radicals and still later spawned the Workers' Federal Credit Union, which has survived to the present day.[13]

Cities and towns of Connecticut that contained Italian radical groups with a socialist and syndicalist lineage were more likely to feel the impact of these formations on their respective labor movements. The heritage of Italian radicalism in New London remained almost exclusively within the boundaries of one neighborhood, although it certainly did not go unnoticed by non-Marchegian Italians in the city. In many aspects, New London's anarchism has an ideological and geographical character that distinguishes it from other Italian radical groupings across Connecticut that have been considered here. But it is difficult to determine what comprises a "typical" left-wing Italian group, since each faced widely varied obstacles, from circles in New Haven and Waterbury swamped by rising nationalist sentiment in the community to smaller ones in towns like Mystic and Stafford Springs that interacted with cross-currents within the anticapitalist movement. Virtually all had disappeared by the 1930s, sometimes being absorbed into the progressive forces that pushed forward the New Deal.

In the crucial period between 1904 and 1908, the Galleanist trend of anarchism became dominant in New London, never to lose its grip. What might have happened, by contrast, if the "Paterson" idea, of building radical industrial unions, had triumphed? New London's large Italian anarchist base of supporters resting on important local industries such as construction, shipbuilding, textiles, and machine shops might have provided a foundation for a stronger IWW presence in Connecticut. Throughout the state, IWW agitators had tirelessly attempted, to little avail, to establish stable union locals. Building an industrial union movement would certainly have opened the door to the Sicilian working-class in New London, a grouping that showed no lack of militancy in defending their rights on the job. The long-term impact on the local labor movement from this alternate course might have been profound, even if open IWW organizing had brought with it the certainty of attacks by agencies of the state.

It is highly doubtful that Fort Trumbull's anarchist movement could have survived as long as it did had it taken this route, however much multiethnic organizing in local industries would have benefited the workers' movement as a whole. Fort Trumbull anarchism endured for decades *because* it was Galleanist; it rested on a cohesive, if extreme, doctrine perfectly crafted for a company of comrades and friends united by common origins and living habits. An old Italian American Communist from Rhode Island, certainly hostile to anarchism, told historian Paul Buhle in 1983, "Galleani told people how to live, and that was important." In the chapters, "Dago Red" and "Young America," of his novel *Boston* (a fictional account of the Sacco and Vanzetti ordeal based on years of research), Upton Sinclair captured the ability of Galleani to espouse revolutionary doctrine, making it not just meaningful but integral to the lives of working-class Italians in Plymouth and other towns of eastern Massachusetts.[14] Despite differences among the Fort Trumbull anarchists, the symbol of Galleani above all others remained as the yardstick against which to measure their dedication and self-sacrifice to the ideal.

CONCLUSION 241

New London anarchists in their majority stayed put. Their city became what is now called a "sedentary" hub in the transnational anarchist migration chain. New Londoners resolutely defended their place within the community, which ultimately rested on their longtime residency. In their anarchist papers in the early 1900s they spoke of their local circle's lack of stability caused by constant movement in search of work by the neighborhood's construction workers. Scores of militants raised their families and built their own homes in Fort Trumbull. One can compare a list of local *Cronaca Sovversiva* subscribers in 1912 with a *New London Day* article about the neighborhood from the late 1990s and find a substantial overlap of last names.

As much as Fort Trumbull's anarchists drew strength from their connections with comrades in their movement across the globe, their efforts partially broke down in the face of intense, insurmountable regionalism on the local scene between Marchegiani and Sicilians. It is as though their movement, which sought proletarian unity in the class war, could not overcome an enemy in the form of such mundane issues as regional dialect and cuisine. Even now, over a century after they established their separate communities, I have heard these differences expressed among Italian Americans in New London.

Many people in Fort Trumbull remained loyal to Gruppo I Liberi until the final moment, outlasting the partisans of nearly every ethnic-based radical group in the state. As with any cluster of humans, they contained diverse of personalities—from those who showed a penchant for clashing with all forms of authority and other anarchists as well—to an anarchist *prominenti* of sorts, who valued their reputations in the greater New London community as respectable, hardworking, and amiable individuals. The beloved ideal of a future society kept this disparate assembly together: fishermen, building tradesmen, textile workers, shipyard workers, small business owners, and, critically, the women who worked within and outside of the home whose labor ensured decades of successful anarchist functions.

If Galleanist politics threw their movement off course and led to isolation, the same might not be said for their efforts to live fraternally within the shell of the present society. Two aspects, at least, of their oppositional legacy remain for us to consider: the fight against irrational, antisocial ideologies like fascism and xenophobia, and the need to reject foreign wars based on mindless jingoism and plunder. The Fanese anarchists of Fort Trumbull viewed with disgust what they saw as the reigning climate of corruption and greed, and, were they around today, they would undoubtedly find much to criticize. As this is being written (2017–2018), truly retrograde political and social forces seem to be multiplying on a world scale—including within this country. A society based on solidarity and rid of exploitation seems as far from being realized as at any time in the past. But precisely for this reason, the only way to combat rising bigotry and racism might be to raise the banners of old, based on social unity and struggle. If a new dawn of humanity is a goal worth striving for, and I believe it is, then the anarchists of Fort Trumbull have something to teach future generations.

NOTES

PREFACE

1. Jeff Benedict, *Little Pink House: A True Story of Defiance and Courage* (New York: Grand Central Publishing, 2009); Juan Gonzalez and Amy Goodman, "Eminent Domain Outrage in Connecticut," transcript, November 13, 2009, Democracy Now, https://www.democracynow.org.

2. Paul Avrich, *Sacco and Vanzetti: The Anarchist Background* (Princeton: Princeton University Press, 1991). Avrich's valuable collection of interviews with aging anarchists, *Anarchist Voices: An Oral History of Anarchism in America*, contains almost three dozen interviews with Italian Americans. Since the book was published in 1995, historians of all sectors of the Italian radical movement in the United States have relied on this invaluable collection. New London is mentioned by three of those interviewed. Interviews with Jennie Paglia, Jenny Salemme, and John Vatuone, in Paul Avrich, *Anarchist Voices: An Oral History of Anarchism in America* (Princeton: Princeton University Press, 1995), 96, 97, 109–10, 152.

3. Elissa Giommi, "The Fort" (unpublished paper, n.d.); Italians of New London Oral History Project Collection. Archives & Special Collections at the Thomas J. Dodd Research Center, University of Connecticut Libraries; Ann Baldelli, "Where Everybody Knew Your Name: Decades Ago, Fort Trumbull Was a Close-Knit Ethnic Neighborhood," *New London Day*, February 20, 2005.

4. Sarah Elizabeth Hansen, "The Fort," A History of Italians in the Fort Trumbull Neighborhood, New London, Connecticut, 1900–1938," honors thesis, Connecticut College, May 2001, 51, 56.

5. Philip V. Cannistraro and Gerald Meyer, *The Lost World of Italian American Radicalism* (Westport, CT: Praeger Publishers, 2003); Jennifer Guglielmo, *Living the Revolution* (Chapel Hill, NC: University of North Carolina Press, 2010); Michael Miller Topp, *Those without a Country* (Minneapolis: University of Minnesota Press, 2001); Kenyon Zimmer, *Immigrants Against the State: Yiddish and Italian Anarchism in America* (Urbana, IL: University of Illinois Press, 2015); Travis Tomchuk, *Transnational Radicals: Italian Anarchists in Canada and*

the US 1915–1940 (Winnipeg, Manitoba: University of Manitoba Press, 2015); Nunzio Pernicone, *Carlo Tresca, Portrait of a Rebel* (Oakland, CA: AK Press, 2010); Marcella Bencevenni, *Italian Immigrant Radical Culture: The Idealism of the Sovversivi in the United States, 1890–1940*).

6. Davide Turcato, "Italian Anarchism as a Transnational Movement," *International Review of Social History* 52 (2007), 407–8.

7. Luigi Balsamini and Federico Sora, editors, *Periodici e Numeri Unici del Movimento Anarchico in Provincia di Pesaro e Urbino, Dall'Internazionale al fascismo (1873–1922)* (Fano, Italy: Edizioni dell'Archivio-Biblioteca Enrico Travaglini, 2013); Luigi Balsamini, "Libraries and Archives of the Anarchist Movement in Italy," *Progressive Historian* 40 (Fall/Winter 2012).

8. Quoted in Bruce Watson, *Sacco & Vanzetti: The Men, the Murders, and the Judgment of Mankind* (New York: Penguin Books, 2008), 305; Pietro Gori, "Inno del primo Maggio," in Italian: "Date fiori ai ribelli caduti/collo squardo rivolto all'aurora," https://www.antiwarsongs.org/canzone.

9. April 21, 1906, *Cronaca Sovversiva*.

10. Eugene O'Neill, *Eugene O'Neill at Work: Newly Released Ideas for Plays*, edited by Virginia Floyd (New York: Frederick Ungar Publishing Co., 1981), 314.

11. Eugene O'Neill, *The Unfinished Plays, Notes for The Visit of Malatesta, The Last Conquest, Blind Alley Guy*, edited by Virginia Floyd (New York: Continuum) 1988, 1–37; Eugene O'Neill, *Eugene O'Neill at Work*, 298–316; Robert M. Dowling, "On O'Neill's 'Philosophical Anarchism,'" in *Eugene O'Neill and His Early Contemporaries*, edited by Eileen J. Herrmann and Robert M. Dowling (Jefferson, NC: McFarland & Company, 2011), 270–91.

INTRODUCTION

1. Lucien van der Walt and Michael Schmidt, *Black Flame: The Revolutionary Class Politics of Anarchism and Syndicalism* (Oakland, CA: AK Press, 2009), 44–47, 56–60.

2. Daniel Guerin, *Anarchism* (New York: Monthly Review Press, 1970, 27–33; Guerin's *No Gods, No Masters: An Anthology of Anarchism* (Oakland, CA, 2005) contains a wide representation of essays and articles from the 1840s to the 1930s. Vernon Richards's *Malatesta: Life and Ideas* (Oakland, CA, 2015) is a collection of excerpts from Malatesta's writings (and relevant to New London's movement). Also recommended for its exposition of the goals of the anarchist movement is Peter Kropotkin's classic *The Conquest of Bread* (London: Penguin Books, 2015).

3. Bruce Watson, *Sacco & Vanzetti*, 27.

4. Kropotkin, *The Conquest of Bread*, 31, 34; See Luigi Fabbri's "Preventative Counter-Revolution," https://www.libcom.org/library.

5. Paul Buhle, "Black International," in Mari Jo Buhle, Paul Buhle, and Dan Georkakas, *Encyclopedia of the American Left* (Urbana, IL: University of Illinois Press, 1992), 93–94; van der Walt and Schmidt, *Black Flame*, 132.

6. John Merriman, *The Dynamite Club* (New Haven: Yale Press, 2016), 51–54; Chris Ealham, *Anarchism and the City: Revolution and Counter-Revolution in Barcelona, 1898–1937* (Oakland, CA: AK Press, 2010), 32–52.

7. Philip Cannistraro and Gerald Meyer, *The Lost World of Italian-American Radicalism*, 2003; Marcella Bencevenni, *Italian Immigrant Radical Culture*, 224.

8. Donna Gabaccia, *Italy's Many Diasporas* (Seattle: University of Washington Press, 2000), 11; Donna Gabaccia, *Militants and Migrants: Rural Sicilians Become American Workers* (New Brunswick, NJ: Rutgers University Press, 1988), 2.

9. Travis Tomchuk, *Transnational Radicals*, 6,7; Davide Turcato, "Italian Anarchism as a Transnational Movement, 1885–1915," *International Review of Social History* (52): 2007, quoted in Tomchuk, *Transnational Radicals*, 10; Constance Bantman and Bert Altena, *Reassessing the Transnational Turn: Scales of Analysis in Anarchist and Syndicalist Studies* (Oakland, CA: AK Press, 2017), introduction, 12; Davide Turcato, *Making Sense of Anarchism: Errico Malatesta's Experiment with Revolution* (Oakland, CA: AK Press, 2015), 246–49.

CHAPTER ONE

1. Nunzio Pernicone, *Italian Anarchism, 1864–1892* (Oakland, CA: AK Press, 2009), 231–32; L'Avanti cited in Paola Magnarelli, "Societá e politica dal 1860 a oggi," in Sergio Anselmi, editor, *Le Marche* (Torino: Giulio Einaudi, 1987), 151; Carl Levy, "Errico Malatesta and Charismatic Leadership," in Jan Willem Stutje (ed.), *Charismatic Leadership and Social Movements: The Revolutionary Power of Ordinary Men and Women* (Amsterdam: Berghahn Books, 2012), vol. 19, *International Studies in Social History*, 89; June 9, 1906, *The Speaker: The Liberal Review*; https://www.marchecountryhomes.com.

2. Federico Sora, "Nascita e sviluppo del movement sindicale e dei lavoratori a Fano: cronistoria e specificita," in Andrea Bianchini (ed.), *Lavoro, diritti, memoria, La Camera del Lavoro della provincial di Pesaro e Urbino dale origine ai primi anni '70* (Pesaro, Marche, Italy: Metauro Edizioni), 2007, 71–75; Alceo Pucci, "Socialismo Rivoluzionario Anarchico a Fano," Urbino, 1973–1974, tesi di laurea, Urbino: n.p., 203; https://www.sistemabiblioteca.riofano.it; Pernicone, *Italian Anarchism*, 124n67; Magnarelli, "Societá e politica," 150.

3. Dennis Mack Smith, *Modern Italy: A Political History* (Ann Arbor: University of Michigan Press, 1997), 135–42; Dante Piermattei, *L'Uomo del sidecar* (Fano, Italy: Grapho 5 Edizioni, 2015), 60; John A. Davis, "Italy 1796–1870: The Age of the Risorgimento," in George Holmes (ed.), *The Oxford History of Italy* (Oxford: Oxford University Press, 1997), 207–9; Michael L. Blim, *Made*

in Italy: Small-Scale Industrialization and Its Consequences (Westport, CT: Praeger, 1990), 25, 91.

4. Magnarelli, "Societá e politica," 143; Blim, *Made in Italy*, 67.

5. Magnarelli, "Societá e politica," 147; Michael L. Blim, *Made in Italy*, 91; 22 September 1921 *Bandiera Rossa*, cited in Franca Del Pozzo, *Alle Origini del PCI: Le organizzazioni marchigiane 1919–23* (Urbino, Italy: Argalia Editore Urbino, 1971), 167.

6. Sora, "Nascita e Sviluppa," 76–77; Luigi Balsamini, "Carta e anarchia: una collezione di giornali anarchici della provincia di Pesaro e Urbino (1873–1922), http://e-review.it/balsamini-carta-e-anarchia.

7. June 15, June 24, and July 13, 1890, *Che Siamo!* (Pesaro).

8. Federico Sora, "Storia degli organismi sindacali della marineria fanese," 1–17, https://www.bibliotecaliberopensiero.it; Libretto di Matricolazione, Sergio Mencarelli, Compartimento Marittimo, Marina Mercantile Italiana, Rimini, 1904.

9. May 5 and 12, and June 24, 1906, *In Marcia!*

10. Pernicone, *Italian Anarchism*, 244–56; Vernon Richards, *Malatesta*, 201.

11. Sora, "Nascita e Sviluppa," 78.

12. Pernicone, *Italian Anarchism*, 292.

13. June 15, 1890, *Chi Siamo!*

14. May 12, 1906, *In Marcia!*

15. Alexander Skirda, *Facing the Enemy: A History of Anarchist Organization from Proudhon to May 1968* (Oakland, CA: AK Press, 2002), 48, 50.

16. Errico Malatesta, "Anarchism and Organization," http://theanarchistlibrary.org; the debate is covered in Davide Turcato, *Making Sense of Anarchism, Errico Malatesta's Experiments with Revolution* (Oakland, CA: AK Press, 2015), 101–75. See also *A Long and Patient Work: The Anarchist Socialism of L'Agitazione 1897–1898*, edited by Davide Turcato (Chico, CA: AK Press, 2016).

17. March 18, 19, and 31, 1891, *New London Day*.

18. March 9, 1906, *New London Day*.

19. November 3, 1904, December 26, 1914, and January 7, 1927, *New London Day*.

20. Connecticut Historical Preservation Commission Records, New London Surveys, "East New London and Fort Trumbull," Introduction, Box 1, Archives and Special Collections, Thomas J. Dodd Research Center, University of Connecticut Libraries; Robert Owen Decker, *The Whaling City: A History of New London* (Chester, CT: Pequot Press, 1976), 130–35.

21. Robert A. Richter, *Eugene O'Neill and "Dat Ole Davil Sea": Maritime Influences in the Life and Works of Eugene O'Neill* (Mystic, CT: Mystic Seaport, 2004) 10, 11, 17–18.

22. Louis Sheaffer, *O'Neill, Son and Playwright*, vol. I (New York: Cooper Square Press, 2002), 110; Robert M. Dowling, *Eugene O'Neill, A Life in Four Acts* (New Haven, CT and London: Yale University Press), 2014, 430; Gregory N.

Stone, *The Day Paper: The Story of One of America's Last Independent Newspapers* (New London, CT: Day Publishing Company, 2000), 18, 78.

23. October 1890, *Granite Cutters Journal*.

24. May 10 and 11, 1886, *New London Day*.

25. April 1885, *Granite Cutters Journal*.

26. US Population Censuses, 1910, 1920, 1930; Hansen, "The Fort," 27–28.

27. April 29, 1892 and June 13, 1914, *New London Day*; 1880 US Population Census.

28. May 20, 1913, *New London Day*; Robert M. Nye, "Alessandro Secchiaroli: With Eleven Dollars in His Pocket," Alessandro Secchiaroli Barn Limited Conditions Assessment Study, Nelson Edwards Company, Architects, Branford, Connecticut, 2011; 1880 US Population Census.

29. Sarah Elizabeth Hansen, "The Fort," 27.

30. October 23 and November 10, 1890, *New London Day*.

31. May 7, 1900, *New London Day*.

32. July 31, 1943, *New London Day*; Elissa Giommi and Angelo Cacciatore, "The Italians," in Carmelina Como Kanzler *New London: A History of Its People*, edited by Carmelina Como Kanzler (New London, CT: City of New London 350th Anniversary Celebration, 1996), 56–57; Anthony Di Renzo, "St. Sebastian Day is the Anniversary of the Caltavatura Massacre," January 20, 2014, https://www.timesofsicily.com; Jennifer Guglielmo, *Living the Revolution*, 35.

33. August 7, 1922, *New London Day*.

34. November 22, 1912, April 7, 1915, March 4, 1916, January 22, 1917, *New London Day*.

CHAPTER TWO

1. Bartholomeo Vanzetti, *The Story of a Proletarian Life* (Boston: Sacco-Vanzetti Defense Committee, 1923), 10–13; Paul Avrich, *Sacco and Vanzetti: The Anarchist Background* (Princeton, NJ: Princeton University Press, 1991), 32–36.

2. Philip M. Rose, *The Italians in America* (New York: George H. Doran Company, 1922), 53; Samuel Koenig, Works *Immigrant Settlements in Connecticut: Their Growths and Characteristics* (Hartford: Connecticut State Department of Education, Works Progress Administration, Federal Writers' Project for the State of Connecticut, 1938), 19; A. Francini, *Italiani nel Connecticut* (New York: Tipografia Sociale de Lucia Jorio, 1908), 7; Nathan L. Whetten and Henry W. Riecken Jr., *The Foreign-Born Population of Connecticut*, Bulletin 246 (Storrs: University of Connecticut, 1943), 18.

3. Bruce Alan Clouette, "Getting their share: Irish and Italian immigrants in Hartford, Connecticut, 1850–1940, PhD diss. (Storrs, Connecticut: University of Connecticut), 1992, 217–21; Francini, *Italiani*, 6.

4. Michael J. Petriccone, "The Immigrant City of New Haven: A Study in Italian Social Mobility 1890–1930," senior honors thesis (New Haven, CT: University of New Haven, 1979), 43–53; Elisa Giommi and Angelo Cacciatore, "The Italians," 52–53.

5. Doris Matsen, "Italian Group," Federal Writers' Project, New Britain, Connecticut, Ethnic Group Studies, Box 128; Richard Lenzi, "Stout Proletarian Hearts: The Socialist Labor Party in New Britain, Connecticut 1895–1900," *Connecticut History* 37, no. 1 (Spring 1996): 2, 10; Rev. Arthur J. Benedict, "Kensington," *Connecticut Magazine* 6, no. 2 (September–October 1900): 408; September 13, 1992, *Hartford Courant*.

6. Gerald Farrel Jr., "Pane e Lavoro: The Emigration of Italians to Wallingford" (video) (Wallingford, Connecticut: Wallingford Historic Preservation Trust), April 4, 1995; *Wallingford Directories*, 1899–1915.

7. June 1888, September 1891 *Granite Cutters' Journal*; Salvatore J. LaGumina, et al., *The Italian American Experience: An Encyclopedia* (New York: Garland Publishing, 2000), 423–24.

8. Town of Stafford, *Stafford, Connecticut: 50th Anniversary* (n.p.: n.p., 1969), 118–19; Stafford Library Association, *The History of the Town of Stafford* (Stafford Springs, CT: n.p.: 1935), 28–31; William Young, ed. *Stafford Illustrated, A Descriptive and Historical Sketch of Stafford, Connecticut* (n.p.: Young & Cady Publishers, 1895), 76–92; September 18, 1930, *The Press* (Stafford Springs, CT).

9. Connecticut Bureau of Labor Statistics, *First Annual Report*, 1885 (Hartford: State of Connecticut, 1885), 62; April 9, 10, and 14, 1885, *New London Day*.

10. Connecticut Bureau of Labor Statistics, *Eighteenth Annual Report*, 1902 (Meriden, CT: Journal Publishing Company, 1902), 512–21; Connecticut Public Documents, *Labor Bulletin*, Bureau of Labor Statistics (Hartford: State of Connecticut), 1908, 88; April 24, 1902, *New London Day*; July 24, 1902, *Hartford Daily Courant*.

11. Jonathon H. Gillette, "Italian Workers in New Haven: Mutuality and Solidarity at the Turn of the Century," in *Support and Struggle: Italians and Italian Americans in a Comparative Perspective*, edited by Joseph L. Troper, James E. Miller, and Cheryl Beattie-Repetti (Staten Island, NY: American Italian Historical Association, 1986), 33–53.

12. Michael Miller Topp, "The Italian-American Left: Transnationalism and the Quest for Unity," in Paul Buhle and Dan Georgakas, editors, *The Immigrant Left in the United States* (n.p.: State University of New York Press, 1996), 123–33; Rudolph J. Vecoli, "Primo Maggio: Haymarket as Seen by Italian Anarchists in America," in Dave Roediger and Franklin Rosemont, *Haymarket Scrapbook* (Chicago: Charles H. Kerr Publishing Company, 1986), 229–31; Kenyon Zimmer, *Immigrants Against the State*, 58–59.

13. Bruno Cartosio, "Sicilian Radicals in two Worlds," in *In the Shadow of the Statue of Liberty: Immigrants, Workers and Citizens in the American Republic 1880–1920*, edited by Marianne Dibouzy (Paris: Presses Universitaires de Vincennes, 1988), 128.

14. Avrich, *Sacco and Vanzetti*, 45–57; Miller Topp, 119–23.

15. September 12, 1901, *Naugatuck Daily News*; October 17, 1885, November 30 June and 17, 1888, *The Alarm*; Johann Most, *The Beast of Property* (New Haven: International Working Peoples Association, 1887); Albert R. Parsons to William H. Brewer, January 26, 1886, cited in Paul Avrich, *The Haymarket Tragedy* (Princeton: Princeton University Press, 1984), 475n66; Chaim Leib Weinberg, *Forty Years in the Struggle: The Memoirs of a Jewish Anarchist* (Duluth, MN: Litwin Books, LLC, 2008), 91.

16. Edwin Fenton, *Immigrants and Unions, A Case Study: Italians and American Labor, 1870–1920* (New York: Arno Press, 1975), 159–63.

17. August 13 July and 24, 1901, December 12 July and 6, 1902, November 11 June and 12, 1905, and January 10, 1914, *Il Proletario*.

18. Zimmer, *Immigrants Against the State*, 77–78; Augusta Molonari, "Luigi Galleani: Un anarchico italiano negli Stati Uniti," *Miscellanea Storica Ligure* VI, no's. 1–2 (1974): 261–86.

19. Avrich, *Sacco and Vanzetti*, 48–49, 95; Travis Tomchuk, *Transnational Radicals: Italian Anarchists in Canada and the US 1915–1940* (Winnipeg, Manitoba: University of Manitoba Press, 2015), 130–36.

20. Paul Ghio, quoted in Avrich, *Sacco and Vanzetti*, 49.

21. May 1, 1921, *La Frusta*.

22. B. Cappelli, "L'Emigrazione anarchica italiana negli USA," *Volontà*, revista anarchica bimestrale, November–December 1971, 6.

23. Avrich, *Sacco and Vanzetti*, 51–57.

24. Paul LeBlanc, "Making Sense of Trotskyism in the United States: Two Memoirs," *Labor Standard*, no date, online at http://www.laborstandard.org/NewPostings/Camejo-Evans-Review.htm; Paul LeBlanc, *Left Americana: The Radical Heart of US History* (Chicago, IL: Haymarket Books, 2017), 42–43, 214.

25. March 1946, *Party Builder* (SWP).

26. See Cecelia Bucki, *Bridgeport's Socialist New Deal, 1915–1936* (Urbana: University of Illinois Press, 2001), 35–39, for a description of this radical subculture in the metalworking industry of Bridgeport around the time of World War I. Also see Steve Thornton, *A Shoeleather History of the Wobblies: Stories of the Industrial Workers of the World (IWW) in Connecticut* (n.p.: Shoeleather History Project, n.d., circa 2014) for the impact of the IWW in the state between 1905 and 1920. Reading of left papers such as *Appeal to Reason* and *Daily Worker*, as well as the daily press such *New London Day* during the early decades of the twentieth century leads to an appreciation of the radical subculture in New London.

CHAPTER THREE

1. Ministero dell'Interno, Direzione Generale Pubblica Sicurezza, Casellario Politico Centrale; lists of subversives from Federico Sora, Archivio-Biblioteca Enrico Travaglini, Fano, Italy; Italians to America Passenger Data File 1855–1900, The National Archives, http//aad.archives.gov/aad.

2. Certifica, Municipio di Fano, March 8, 1897.

3. May 8, 1900, *New London Day*.

4. January 6 and 13, 1900, *L'Aurora*; Pierce Rafferty and John Wilton, *Guardian of the Sound: A Pictorial History of Fort H. G. Wright, Fishers Island, N.Y.* (New York: Mount Mercier Press, 1998), xvi.

5. April 27, 1898, *New London Day*; August 31, 1901, *L'Aurora*; July 1, 1899, *La Questione Sociale*; United States Surgeon-General's Office, "Report of the Surgeon-General, United States Army, to the Secretary of War" (Washington, 1901), 50–52; Pierce Rafferty and John Wilton, *Guardian of the Sound*, xviii.

6. Jennifer Guglielmo, *Living the Revolution*, 158–59; July 10, 1898, *La Questione Sociale*.

7. July 10, 1898, *La Questione Sociale*; February 6, 1915, *Cronaca Sovversiva*; 1910 US Population Census.

8. Federico Sora, compiled dossier of Alberico Biagioni, in author's possession.

9. December 30, 1899, *La Questione Sociale*.

10. December 10, 1898 and July 14, 1900, *La Questione Sociale*.

11. Kenyon Zimmer, *Immigrants Against the State*, 75.

12. October 7 and December 9, 1899, *La Questione Sociale*; the six address book names are D. Levinson, 356 Bank Street; R. Sommariva, Box 2, Mystic; A. Rochetti, 128 Bank Street; Gennaro Strozza, 672 Bank Street, Gaetano Olivieri; 62 Smith Street; and Marta Dondero, 25 Golden Street. This information comes from Davide Turcato, in an email to Federico Sora, January 9, 2016.

13. December 30, 1899 and January 6, 1900, *La Questione Sociale*.

14. December 3, 1898, 2f1, and January 28, September 9, and December 30, 1899, *La Questione Sociale*; US Population Census 1900; New London and Waterford *Directory*, 1905.

15. Guglielmo, *Living the Revolution*, 160–62.

16. August 6, 1900, *Hartford Courant* (reprint of *Day* article, titled "Queer Talk from that Quiet Town"); August 14, 1900, *New London Day*.

17. September 3, 1900, *New London Day*; September 8, 1900, *La Questione Sociale*.

18. January 13, 1900, *L'Aurora*.

19. November 10, 1900, *L'Aurora*.

20. November 25 and December 16, 1899, *L'Aurora*.

21. July 1, 1899 and March 24, 1900, *La Questione Sociale*.

22. October 6, 1900, *New London Day*.

23. October 9, 11, and 12, 1900, *New London Day*; October 20, November 3 and 10, 1900, *La Questione Sociale*.

24. For full discussions of the organizational anarchists' role in the Paterson labor movement, see Salvatore Salerno, "No God, No Master: Italian Anarchism and the Industrial Workers of the World," in Philip Cannistraro and Gerald Meyer, ed., *The Lost World of Italian-American Radicalism*, 171–87, and Kenyon Zimmer, *Immigrants Against the State*, chapter titled "*I Senza Patria*: Italian Anarchists in Paterson, New Jersey."

25. August 18 and September 1, *La Questione Sociale*; CPC, busta 2134.

26. Paul Avrich and Karen Avrich, *Sasha and Emma: The Anarchist Odyssey of Alexander Berkman and Emma Goldman* (Cambridge, MA: Belknap Press of the Harvard University Press, 2012), 149; Candace Falk, ed., *Emma Goldman: A Documentary History of the American Years* (Berkeley: University of California Press, 2003), 510.

27. July 6, 1902, *Il Proletario*.

28. June 13, *La Questione Sociale*; http://www.bibliotecamarxista.org/malatesta/riv; S. A. Gruppo, "L'Avvenire di New London, Conn.," introduction to Errico Malatesta, *Il Nostro Programma*, printed in Paterson, New Jersey, 1903.

29. December 9, 1911, *Cronaca Sovversiva*; May 25 and July 10, 1898, *La Questione Sociale*; March 2 1906, *New London Day*.

30. Federico Sora, "Storia degli organismi sindicali della marineria fanese," unpublished paper, 2016, 3.

31. Federico Sora, "Nascita e sviluppo," 78.

32. January 1898 *La Questione Sociale*; January 6 and 13, 1900, *L'Aurora*; June 7, 1902 *Il Proletario*; September 19, 1903 *Cronaca Sovversiva*; November 15, 1948, *New London Day*.

33. Avrich, *Sasha and Emma*, 156; September 28, 1901, *La Questione Sociale*.

34. Zimmer, *Immigrants*, 75, 77, 125, and 127.

35. Guglielmo, *Living the Revolution*, 160–62.

36. June 23, 1900, *New London Day*; August 6, 1900, *Hartford Courant*.

37. Coverage of the strike/lockouts is contained in *New London Day* from May 27 to September 12, 1903.

38. June 6, 1903, *Cronaca Sovversiva*.

39. June 13 and 20, July 20 and 25, and August 1, 8, 15, and 29, 1903, *La Questione Sociale*.

40. November 21, 1903, *Cronaca Sovversiva*.

CHAPTER FOUR

1. *Il Proletario*, July 23, 1905.
2. June 4, 1904, *La Questione Sociale*.
3. August 13, 1904, *La Questione Sociale*; CPC schede.

4. September 17, 1904, *La Questione Sociale*.
5. September 24, 1904, *La Questione Sociale*; February 11, 1905 *Cronaca Sovversiva*.
6. Interview with John B. Coduri, July 23, 2015.
7. February 11, 1905, *Cronaca Sovversiva*.
8. April 14, 1903, January 9, 1904, and May 20, 1905 *La Questione Sociale*.
9. April 14, 1903; May 19, and January 9, 1904, *La Questione Sociale*; March 4, 1905, *Cronaca Sovversiva*.
10. March 4, 1905, *Cronaca Sovversiva*.
11. March 25, 1905, *Cronaca Sovversiva*.
12. May 27, 1905, *Cronaca Sovversiva*.
13. Richards, *Malatesta*, 81.
14. Nunzio Pernicone, *Carlo Tresca*, 22–23, 31; Elisabetta Vezzosi, "Radical Ethnic Brokers: Immigrant Socialist Leaders in the United States between Ethnic Community and the Larger Society," in Donna Gabaccia and Fraser M. Ottanelli, *Italian Workers of the World, Labor Migration and the Formation of Multiethnic States* (Urbana: University of Illinois Press, 2001), 126–27.
15. The fullest coverage of the debaters' remarks can be found in July 16 and 23, 1905 *Il Proletario*.
16. August 5, 1905, *Cronaca Sovversiva*.
17. Nunzio Pernicone, *Carlo Tresca*, 28, 92, Bencivenni, *Italian Immigrant*, 26; Guglielmo, *Living*, 180 and 187; Vezzosi, "Radical Ethnic Brokers," 126 and 127.
18. October 27, 1905 *Cronaca Sovversiva*; June 23, 1906, January 5, 1907, and May 25, 1907, *La Questione Sociale*.
19. Federico Sora, Enrico Travaglini Archivio/Biblioteca, compiled dossiers of Guido Baldoni, Enrico Ferri, and Nazzareno Falcioni, in author's possession.
20. April 14, 1906, *In Marcia!*

CHAPTER FIVE

1. April 24, 1902, *New London Day*.
2. June 8, 1907, *La Questione Sociale*.
3. May 23, 1907, *New London Day*.
4. April 21, 1906, *Cronaca Sovversiva*.
5. November 17, 1906, *Cronaca Sovversiva*.
6. August 8, 1908 and November 13, 1909, *Cronaca Sovversiva*.
7. March 16, 1897, *New London Day*; December 12, 1908, *Cronaca Sovversiva*; United States New England Naturalization Index, 1791–1906; Italy, Pesaro e Urbino, Civil Registration.

8. November 12, 1908 and January 2, 1909, *Cronaca Sovversiva*.
9. September 14, 1907 and March 7, 1908, *La Questione Sociale*; list of subscriptions to Marchegian anarchist press, from Archivio/Libreria Enrico Tavaglini, Fano.
10. June 9 and September 29, 1906, *In Marcia!*; September 22 and 29, 1906, January19, February 23, June 22 and August 10, 1907, and March 21, 1908, *Cronaca Sovversiva*.
11. September 19, 1908, *Cronaca Sovversiva*; Raffaele Petrini CPC schede, busta 3905; Petrini Draft Registration Card, 1917; July 9, 1956, *New London Day*.
12. March 18, 1905, *Cronaca Sovversiva*.
13. Coduri later became a farmer, married late in life, and died of tuberculosis in Norwich Sanatarium in 1926. State of Connecticut, Medical Certificate of Death, Charles Coduri; interview with John B. Coduri, July 23, 2015, by author.
14. Kenyon Zimmer, *Immigrants*, 83–87.
15. May 31, 1962, July 13, 1963, and February 5, 1966 *L'Adunata dei Refrattari*.

CHAPTER SIX

1. Theodore Draper, *The Roots of American Communism* (New York: Viking Press, 1957), 36–49; James Weinstein, *The Decline of Socialism in America, 1912–1925* (New York: Vintage Books, 1969), 27.
2. Doris Alexander, *The Tempering of Eugene O'Neill* (New York: Harcourt, Brace & World, 1962), 166; Louis Scheaffer, *O'Neill, Son and Playwright*, vol. I (New York: Cooper Square Press, 2002), 224.
3. Peter Cunningham Baldwin, "The Italians in Middletown, 1893–1932: The Formation of an Ethnic Community," BA honors thesis in American Studies, Wesleyan University, 1984; September 7 and November 16, 1912, *Cronaca Sovversiva*.
4. Paul Avrich, *Sacco and Vanzetti*, 96–97; February 15 and August 23, 1913, CS; September 8, 1917 and May 16, 1918, *New Britain Herald*.
5. January 9, 1909, *Cronaca Sovversiva*.
6. January 30, 1909, *Cronaca Sovversiva*.
7. February 13, 1909, *Cronaca Sovversiva*.
8. January 13, 1912, *Cronaca Sovversiva*.
9. November 4 and 13, 1911, *New London Day*.
10. December 14 and 16, 1912, *New London Day*.
11. July 4, 1931, *New London Day*.
12. August 11, 1906, *La Questione Sociale*.
13. November 28, 1903, *La Questione Sociale*.

14. August 3, 1940, *L'Adunata dei Refrattari*; September 19, 1910, *New London Day*.

15. October 22, 1910, *Cronaca Sovversiva*.

16. See Michael Christopher Carroll, *Lab 257: The Disturbing Story of the Government's Secret Germ Laboratory* (New York: William Morrow, 2005), and Ruth Ann Bramson, Geoffrey K. Fleming, and Amy Kasuga Folk, *A World Unto Itself: The Remarkable History of Plum Island, New York* (Southold, New York: Southold Historical Society, 2014).

17. November 29, 1911 *New London Day*; March 12 and April 23, 1910, *Cronaca Sovversiva*.

18. March 9, May 11, July 27, and August 31, 1912, *Cronaca Sovversiva*; June 8 and 15, 1912 *Solidarity*; May 21–June 15, 1913, *New London Telegraph*.

19. June 8, July 20, August 31, and September 14, 1914, *Cronaca Sovversiva*.

20. October 19 and 26, 1912, *Cronaca Sovversiva*; Nunzio Pernicone, *Carlo Tresca*, 54.

21. November 9, 1912, *Cronaca Sovversiva*; Centro Politico Castellario, in Federico Sora dossier of Vittorio Federici, busta 1987; November 23, 1912, *In Marcia!*

22. August 21 and September 11, 1909, *Cronaca Sovversiva*; list of subscribers to Italian anarchist press (from Archivio/Libreria Enrico Travaglini, Fano, Italy).

23. Italian page of August 19, 1911 *Regeneraçion* (Los Angeles).

24. Nunzio Pernicone described Galleanist methodology as "fanatical sectarianism and inflexibility in matters of thought and action." "War Among the Italian Anarchists: The Galleanisti's Campaign Against Carlo Tresca," in Cannistraro and Meyer, *The Lost World*, 78.

25. December 12, 1912, *Cronaca Sovversiva*.

26. Pernicone, *Italian Anarchism*, 169.

27. January 9, 1928, *New London Day*.

28. September 30, 1911, *Cronaca Sovversiva*.

29. December 7 and 14, 1912, and July 12, 1913, *Cronaca Sovversiva*.

30. September 26, 1908, *Cronaca Sovversiva*.

31. November 17, 1906, September 7, 1912, December 20, 1913, September 26, 1914, *Cronaca Sovversiva*; and August 8, 1936, *L'Adunata dei Refrattari*.

32. Letter from Lombardozzi to Galleani, April 11, 1915, BI Files, Old German Files 1909–21, Case #8000-89610, Suspect R. Lombardozzi; September 23, 1916, *Cronaca Sovversiva*.

33. August 8, 1936, *L'Adunata dei Refrattari*.

34. January 25, February 1, March 29, July 19, October 4, 11, and 25, November 8, 1913, January 17 and March 14, 1914, *Cronaca Sovversiva*.

35. January 18, 1913, *Cronaca Sovversiva*.

36. February 8, November 1, 1913, July 25, August 29, and September 26, 1914, *Cronaca Sovversiva*; Davide Turcato, "Italian Anarchism as a Transnational Movement 1885–1915," *IRSH* 52 (2007), 427.

37. November 9, 1912 and January 9, 1915, *Cronaca Sovversiva*; October 3, 1925, *L'Adunata dei Refrattari*; CPC schede, busta 3223, at https://www.liberopensiero.it; US Population Census 1910, 1920.

CHAPTER SEVEN

1. July 27, 1914, *New London Day*.
2. December 19, 1914, *Cronaca Sovversiva*.
3. January 9, 1915, *Cronaca Sovversiva*.
4. May 25, June 7, 12, and 24, July 17, 19, 22, 23, 30, and 31, 1915, *New London Day*.
5. October 2, 1915, *Cronaca Sovversiva*.
6. September 25, 1915, *Cronaca Sovversiva*; CPC busta 656.
7. November 8, 1913 and June 27, 1914, *Cronaca Sovversiva*.
8. Avrich, *Sacco and Vanzetti*, 101.
9. December 18, 1915 and January 22, 1916, *Cronaca Sovversiva*.
10. December 23, 1916, *Cronaca Sovversiva*.
11. Avrich, *Sacco and Vanzetti*, 101.
12. May 1, 8, and 9, 1916, *New London Day*.
13. May 9–22, 1916, *New London Day*.
14. June 3, 1916, *Cronaca Sovversiva*; May 10 and 16, 1916, and January 31, 1953, *New London Day*; 1920 US Population Census: John Turello Draft Registration Card, 1917.
15. May 24 and 27, 1916, *New London Day*.
16. Judith E. Smith, *Family Connections: A History of Italian and Jewish Immigrant Lives in Providence Rhode Island 1900–1940* (Albany: State University of New York Press, 1985), 154–55; Joseph W. Sullivan, *Marxists, Militants & Macaroni: The IWW in Providence's Little Italy* (Kingston, Rhode Island: Rhode Island Labor History Society, 2000), 30–35.
17. May 31, June 1–6, 1916, *New London Day*.
18. Raffaele Schiavina (Max Sartin), introduction to Luigi Galleani, *The End of Anarchism?* (Orkney, UK: Cienfuegos Press, 1982), iv.
19. *Cronaca Sovversiva* subscription list, seized during Bureau of Investigation raid of the paper's offices in 1917, Old German Files, BI Files, 8000–169.
20. January 4, 1913–October 29, 1917, *L'Era Nuova*.
21. "Connecticut, list of Contributors to *Umanita Novà*," BI Files, Old German Files, cases #387223 and #65998.
22. Pernicone, *Carlo Tresca*, 195.
23. October 17, 1914, December 1, 1917, *Cronaca Sovversiva*; letter to Aldo Candolfi, February 29, 1916, in Bureau of Investigation Files, Old German Files, #386976; 1920 US Population Census; Luigi Fabbri, *Life of Malatesta*, Anarchy Archives, http//dwardmac.pitzer.edu/anarchist/archives/malatesta/lifeofmalatesta.

24. Federico Sora, Archivio/Biblioteca Enrico Travaglini, dossier on Paris Carnaroli, in author's possession; May 31, 1962, *L'Adunata dei Refrattari*; May 18, 1962, *New London Day*; US and New England Naturalization Index, 1791–1906.

25. Federico Sora, Archivio/Biblioteca Enrico Travaglini, dossier on Luigi Ferri, in author's possession.

26. December 13, 1919, July 31, 1920, *La Frusta*.

27. Fraser, "Yankees at War: Social Mobilization on the Connecticut Homefront, 1917–1918," Dissertation, Columbia University, 1976, 97–115.

28. June 7, July 7, and August 24, 1917, *New London Day*; Stone, *The Day Paper*, 119–20.

29. March 31, 1917 *Cronaca Sovversiva*; Avrich, *Sacco and Vanzetti*, 59, 95–97.

30. Avrich, *Sacco and Vanzetti*, 58–66, 96, 97–99, 156–59.

31. Avrich, *Sacco and Vanzetti*, 102–3. Avrich interviewed a number of Galleanists and received confidential information from several of them about the bombing campaign. For an account of the legal frame up of the Milwaukee anarchists, see Dean A. Strang, *Worse than the Devil: Anarchists, Clarence Darrow and Justice in a Time of Terror* (Madison: University of Wisconsin Press, 2013).

32. January 13, February 3, April 7, December 17, 1917, March 9, and March 30, 1918, *Cronaca Sovversiva*.

CHAPTER EIGHT

1. June 11, 1897 *l'Agitazione*, quoted in Vernon Richards, *Malatesta*, 79.

2. Marx and Engels, *The German Ideology*, quoted in Howard Selsam and Harry Martel, *Reader in Marxist Philosophy* (New York: International Publishers, 1970), 190.

3. Aldo Valentini interview, Italians of New London Oral History Project.

4. Elissa Giommi, "The Fort," 1.

5. Connecticut Historical Preservation Commission Records, New London Surveys, 6.

6. Avrich, *Sacco and Vanzetti*, 156–57.

7. "United States Housing Corporation Historic District" (New London), National Park Service, National Register of Historic Places, https://www.livingplaces.com/CT/New_London; February 13, 1909–August 18, 1928, *Cronaca Sovversiva*; CPC, busta 1098; US Population Census, 1940.

8. United States Housing Corporation Historic District.

9. March 12, 1910–August 18, 1928, *Cronaca Sovversiva*; Draft Registration Card, 1917; CPC, dossier of Federico Sora on Paris Carnaroli, Archivio-Biblioteca Enrico Travaglini.

10. September 1, 1914, *New London Day*.

11. January 8, 1906, *La Questione Sociale*; November 17, 1906, *Cronaca Sovversiva*.
12. October 12, 2000, *New London Day*.
13. Passport application for Augusto Peroni, 1920; subscription lists for Marchegian anarchist newspapers, from Archivio-Biblioteca Enrico Travaglini.
14. August 31, 1901, *La Questione Sociale*.
15. February 20, 1904, *La Questione Sociale*.
16. April 23, 1904, *Cronaca Sovversiva*.
17. Daniel Guérin, *No Gods, No Masters*, 40–41; George Plekhanov, *Anarchism and Socialism* (Chicago, IL: Charles H. Kerr & Company, n.d.), 67.
18. New London Chamber of Commerce, *New London Connecticut: Utopia of the North Atlantic, The Ideal City Winter and Summer* (n.p/: circa 1920s); The New London Ship and Engine Company, *Why We Located in New London* (n.p.: August 1916).
19. April 25, 1901, *La Questione Sociale*.
20. October 13, 1900, *La Questione Sociale*.
21. February 29, May 3 and 17, and November 1, 1904 *New London Day*; New London and Waterford *Directory*, 1905.
22. March 12, 1904, *La Questione Sociale*.
23. July 10, 11, and 14, 1923, *New London Day*.
24. Giommi, "The Fort," 9–10; three of the articles published in the *New London Day* over the last few decades include "Clubs: Ethnic Roots that Bind," by Tim Murphy, October 25, 1981, "Neighbors Recall Italian Dramatic Club, con amore," by Jennifer Zeis, October 29, 2000, and "Where Everybody Knew Your Name," by Ann Baldelli, February 20, 2005.
25. John Johnson Jr. and Joel Selvin, *Peppermint Twist* (New York: Thomas Dunne Books, 2012), 42–43.
26. September 15, 1923, *L'Adunata dei Refrattari*; interview with Victor Frausini, 1998, Italians of New London Oral History Project Collection.
27. July 31, 1926, May 2 and November 21, 1931, and September 19, 1936 *L'Adunata dei Refrattari*; Marcella Bencevenni, *Italian Immigrant Radical Culture*, 106.
28. April 7, 1917, *Cronaca Sovversiva*.
29. March 11 and May 8, 1909, *New London Day*; July 17, 1909, August 20, 1910, and July 27, 1912, *Cronaca Sovversiva*.
30. "Interview of Italian Dramatic Club Dinner's Male Cooks & Interview of Individuals Present & Old Photos on Bulletin Board, 1997–1998." Italians of New London Oral History Project Collection.
31. March 12, July 2, and December 24, 1927, *L'Adunata dei Refrattari*.
32. September 26, 1903, *La Questione Sociale*; May 27, 1905, October 22, 1910, and December 7, 1912, *Cronaca Sovversiva*; August 31, 1901, *L'Aurora*; 1930 US Population Census. Palombaro is a town in the Abruzzo region to the south of the Marche; Broccoli, however, was born in Fano.

33. July 9, 1910, *Cronaca Sovversiva*.

34. September 1, 1923, *L'Adunata dei Refrattari*; August 7, 1909, *Cronaca Sovversiva*.

35. December 7, 1912, *Cronaca Sovversiva*; Giommi, "The Fort," 8; interview with Gaspare Casavino, 1997, Italians of New London Oral History Project Collection.

36. March 12, 1910, July 22, 1916, January 13, 1917, March 9, 1918, *Cronaca Sovversiva*; May 24, 1924, August 29, 1925, February 25, 1928, and April 7, 1928, *L'Adunata dei Refrattari*.

37. Marcella Bencevenni, *Italian Immigrant Radical Culture*, 3.

38. Eugene O'Neill, *Unfinished Plays*, 31.

CHAPTER NINE

1. September 22, 1917, *Cronaca Sovversiva*; K. W. DeBelle, Hartford, April 25, 1917, Bureau of Investigation (BI), Old German Files, 20713; Thomas C. McKone, New London, April 26, 1917, BI, Old German Files 20713.

2. December 17, 1910, *Cronaca Sovversiva*; February 23, 1915, *New London Day*.

3. November 1910, March 29, 1913, and June 12, 1914 *Cronaca Sovversiva*; see May 10, 1913 and July 15, 1916, *Cronaca Sovversiva* for Perella's two articles; Draft Registration Card, Ernesto Perella; Draft Registration Card, Fortunato Renzoni; Bureau of Investigation, Old German Files, Ernesto Perella File, 369782; Perella, as "Ernesto R. Penella," was listed as among Galleani and the others who lost their appeal to avoid deportation (June 15, 1919, *New York Times*). Perella had not joined the appeal because the government for unexplained reasons had not pursued him further. ("Cases Around and Determined in the Circuit Court of Appeals and District Courts of the United States and the Court of Appeals of the District of Columbia," October–November 1919, vol. 259, *Federal Reporter*, 734).

4. Avrich, *Sacco and Vanzetti*, 122–28.

5. BI, "Italian Anarchists," Old German Files, 194561; Sullivan, *Marxists, Militants & Macaroni* 20.

6. Avrich, *Sacco and Vanzetti*, 104–111; See also Filippo Manganaro, *Dynamite Girl, Gabriella Antolini e gli anarchici italiani in America* (Rome: Nova Delphi Libri, 2013).

7. June 19–July 17, 1919, *Solidarity*.

8. Investigative Case Files of BI 1908–1922, Old German Files, Case #374742, "Italian Radicals in America, suspect Giuseppe Ciancabilla."

9. March 6 and November 27, 1920, *Il Proletario*; June 19, 1920, *Solidarity*.

10. April 7, 1921, *Il Progresso Comunista* (Fano); October 6, 1921, January 5, March 30, and June 8, 1922, *Bandiera Rossa* (Fano).

11. May 1919, *Cronaca Sovversiva*.
12. May 1, 1920 *La Frusta*; Avrich, *Sacco and* Vanzetti, 208–9; Balsamini and Sora, *Periodici e Numeri Unici*, 549.
13. November 30, 1920, *La Frusta*.
14. May 17, 1918, *New London Day*; May 17, 1918, *New London Morning Telegraph*; May 18, 1918, *Norwich Bulletin*.
15. William Hazen report, Hartford, May 11 and 18, 1920, Old German Files, Various, 375879.
16. Bureau of Investigation, "American Anarchists," January 29, 1919, Various Case Files, 177382.
17. January 28, 1919, *New London* Day; Bureau of Investigation, "Distribution of Revolutionary Literature," Various Case Files, March 5, 1919.
18. June 5, 1919, *New London Day*.
19. June 6, 1919, *New London Day*.
20. August 4, 1927, *L'Adunata dei Refrattari*; "Anarchist Attempt to Incite Laborers to Arm [sic] Revolution," February 24–25, 1919, Case #348019, Bureau of Investigation Files; Charles H. McCormick, *Hopeless Cases*, 35.
21. August 30, 1918, *Daily Herald* (Chicago); T. T. Keliher, "Part IV: Freight-Car Robberies," *Journal of Criminal Law and Criminology* 23 (Spring 1933). That Victor Frederick is Vittorio Federici is based on the following: (1) as mentioned, Frederick lived on Smith Street and called out in Italian to his confederates when fighting with the railroad police; (2) an obituary for Viola Bonano, who was born in the Fort, states that she was the daughter of "Vittorio and Giuseppina Federici (Frederick), who immigrated from Fano, Italy" (January 27, 2014, *New London Day*); and (3) the "Find a Grave" website (http://www.findagrave.com/cgi-bin/fg) lists the grave of Victor Frederick in Jordan Cemetery in Waterford as "Victor Frederick aka Vittorio Federici."
22. Quoted in Nunzio Pernicone, "Luigi Galleani and Italian American Terrorism in the United States," *Studi Emigrazione* 3 (1993).
23. Nunzio Pernicone, "Carlo Tresca and the Sacco-Vanzetti Case," *Journal of American History* 66, no. 3 (December 1979); Avrich, "Sacco and Vanzetti's Revenge," in Cannistraro and Meyer, *The Lost World of Italian-American Radicalism*, 165; June 6, 1918, *Cronaca Sovversiva*; September 28, November 11, and December 30, 1916, *L'Era Nuova*; Bureau Section Files 1901–21, Various Files, 360086.
24. Interview with Louis Tarabelli, in Paul Avrich, *Anarchist Voices*, 131.
25. See Richard Parry, *The Bonnot Gang: The Story of the French Illegalists* (2nd ed.) (Oakland, CA: AK Press, 2016); Pietro di Paola, *The Knights Errant of Anarchy, London and the Italian Anarchist Diaspora (1880–1917)* (Oakland, CA: AK Press, 2017), 63–78.
26. September 17, 1919, *Norwich Bulletin*.
27. Herbert B. Ehrmann, *The Untried Case: The Sacco-Vanzetti Case and the Morelli Gang* (New York: Vanguard Press, 1960), 73. This book, by one of

the defense attorneys in the Sacco-Vanzetti case, offers the hypothesis that the April 15, 1920 payroll robbery in South Braintree, Massachusetts, was carried out by a criminal gang out of Providence.

28. January 6, 1921, *Norwich Bulletin*; February 1, 6, and 20, 1921, *New London Evening Day*; Draft Registration Card, Pietro Facendi, September 12, 1918.

29. February 6, 1922, *New London Evening Day*; December 20, 1924, March 14, August 29, October 3, 1925, August 20, 1927, and August 18, 1928, *L'Adunata dei Refrattari*; July 22, 1922, *Norwich Bulletin*.

30. Archivio Centrale dello Stato, Cassellario Politico Centrale, Vittorio Federici, busta 1987; BI Files, July 29, 1919, Old German Files; BI Files, Various Files, August 18, 1919, 369443, Avrich, *Sacco and Vanzetti*, 113.

31. Caminita's interview and Ravarini's reports are contained in BI Files, Section Files, 360086; Avrich, *Sacco and Vanzetti*, 178–87.

32. June 7, 1917, *New London Day*.

33. Charles H. McCormick, *Hopeless Cases, The Hunt for the Red Scare Terrorist Bombers* (Lanham, MD: University Press of America, 2005), 5.

34. Agent William P. Hazen, "Bolsheviki Activities in Mystic, Conn.," BI Files, Old German Files, 374806; Reports by Agents W. W. Grimes and William P. Hazen on Michael Angelo Crisafi, BI Files, Old German Files, 295550.

35. Report of Feri W. Weiss, October 26, 1917, Old German Files, BI Files, 303991; Avrich, *Sacco and Vanzetti*, 59–60.

36. May 20, 1910, *Cronaca Sovversiva*; Federico Sora, dossier on Romolo Baldoni, Archivio/Biblioteca Enrico Travaglini, in author's possession.

37. August 18, 1917, *Cronaca Sovversiva*; Sora, "Romolo Baldoni"; US Military Draft Registration Card, Romolo Baldoni, September 12, 1918.

38. Feri F. Weiss report, September 19, 1919 (interview held on September 15, 1918), Old German Files, BI Files, #389287.

39. Feri F. Weiss report, September 19, 1919 (interview held on September 15, 1918), Old German Files, BI Files, 389287; McCormick, *Hopeless Cases*, 18–19, 104.

40. "Romolo Baldoni" file, Old German Files, BI Files, 373120.

41. September 24, 1927 and July 7, 1956, *L'Adunata dei Refrattari*; Bureau of Investigation Files, "Paolo Rinaldoni," July 12, 1920, Old German Files.

42. Bureau letter, October 14, 1920, "Amedeo Parecchini," 202600-294-1, Bureau Section Files.

43. McCormick, *Hopeless Cases*, 23; for the background to the Wall Street Bombing, see Beverly Gage, *The Day Wall Street Exploded: A Story of America in Its First Age of Terror* (Oxford: Oxford University Press, 2009).

44. BI Files, Bureau Section Files, January 4, 1920 informers' report (Ravarini); BI Files, Old German Files, "Nicolo Recchi," 373874; Avrich, *Sacco and Vanzetti*, 217.

CHAPTER TEN

1. Ferdinando Fasce, *An American Family, The Great War and Corporate Culture in America* (Columbus, OH: Ohio State University), 119–39; "Mike Kalachuk," Bureau Section Files, 202600-1278-2.

2. "Strike at Waterbury-General Situation, 363529, Old German Files 1909–21; Warren W. Grimes, New Haven, "Strike in the Naugatuck Valley due to Bolshevism," Old German Files 1909–21, 363529.

3. Jeremy Brecher, *Banded Together: Economic Democratization in the Brass Valley* (Urbana: University of Illinois Press, 2001), 7; *Metal Industry* 18, no. 4 (April 1920).

4. July 22 and 31, 1920 *Il Proletario*. Italian radicals lapsed into racial characterizations such as this, and extended their discourse to immigrants from the southern regions of Italy. Others on the United States left were not immune to such appeals to racism. Big Bill Haywood reacted to the mass arrests of union miners in the Cour D'Alene region of Idaho in 1899 by black soldiers by emphasizing the racial makeup of the troops, and used the time-tested accusation of "the black soldiers . . . at home insulting, outraging, ravishing" the wives, mothers, and sisters of the imprisoned miners. Quoted in J. Anthony Lucas, *Big Trouble* (New York: Smith & Schuster, 1997), 151.

5. December 18,1920 *Il Proletario*.

6. October 6, 1921, *Bandiera Rossa* (Fano); Christopher M. Sterba, *Good Americans*, 144–46.

7. W. F. Hazen, "Bolshevik Activities in New London," Old German Files, Various Files, 177382; J. W. R. Chamberlain, Hartford, "Apprehension of Radicals (URofW) Raids, etc., New London, Bridgeport and Hartford, Conn." November 11, 1919, Old German Files, 381672; Agent Cooney, "I. Weske, New London, Conn." Old German Files, 383696.

8. March 21, 1925, *L'Adunata dei Refrattari*.

9. Balsamini and Sora, *Periodici e Numeri Unici*, 557.

10. J. B. S. Hardman, ed., *American Labor Dynamics in the Light of Post-War Developments* (New York: Harcourt, Brace and Company, 1928), 10.

11. February 23, March 26 and May 2, 1923, *Bridgeport Telegram*.

12. September 18, 1928 *Daily Worker*.

13. BI Files 1909–21, Various Files, 202600-2159.

14. Avrich, *Anarchist Voices*, 147–48.

15. November 29, 1921 *Norwich Bulletin*; https://www.connecticutcorps.com/corp/567481.

16. Bessie Bloom Wessel, "Ethnic Factors in the Population of New London, Connecticut," *American Journal of Sociology*" XXXV, no. 1 (July 1929).

17. January 19 and 21, February 4, and March 31, 1922 *New London Day*.

18. April 11 and May 22, 1922, August 1, 1924, and December 24, 1925, *New London Day*.

19. March 8, 1921, *New London Day*.

20. Interview with A. Matt Orsini, February 15, 1998, Italians of New London Oral History Project Collection.

21. March 31, 1922, *La Frusta*.

22. Interview with A. Matt Orsini, Italians of New London Oral History Project Collection; obituary of Orsini, May 23, 2008, https://www.neilanfuneralhome.com.

23. April 17 and 18, 1922, and June 4, 1948, *New London Day*; Giommi, "The Fort," 10; Interview with A. Matt Orsini, Italians of New London Oral History Project Collection.

24. Connecticut Historical Commission, "Historical Resources Inventory, Building and Structures"; US Population Censuses, 1930, 1940; August 2, 1913, *Cronaca Sovversiva*; May 8, 1913, *In Marcia!*

25. June 11, 1904 and January 20, 1906, *La Questione Sociale*.

26. Anthony V. Riccio, *Farms, Factories, and Families: Italian American Women of Connecticut* (Albany: State University of New York Press, 2014), 142; Anthony V. Riccio, *The Italian American Experience in New Haven* (Albany: State University of New York Press, 2006), 185; Interview with Shirley Mencarelli by author, August 4, 2016; interview with A. Matt Orsini, Italians of New London Oral History Project Collection.

27. Avrich, *Anarchist Voices*, 97; Guglielmo, *Living the Revolution*, 203; BI Files, Old German Files 1909–21, Case #315825, Various.

28. October 3, 1925, *L'Adunata dei Refrattari*; Avrich, *Sacco and Vanzetti*, 126, 156–57, 188, 209–10; Avrich, *Anarchist Voices*, 109–10, 128–29, 130, 136.

29. February 3, 1925, *New London Day*; January 31, 1925, *L'Adunata dei Refrattari*; Watson, *Sacco & Vanzetti*, 256.

30. Avrich, *Sacco and Vanzetti*, 204; Piermattei, *L'uomo del sidecar*, 56–57.

31. August 9 and 11, 1927, *New London Day*; Watson, *Sacco & Vanzetti*, 331.

32. July 15, 1919, January 11, 1927, October 29, and November 5, 1928, and August 17, 1931, *New London Day*.

33. November 15, 1925, January 17, and May 22, 1928, *Daily Worker*.

34. Coverage of strike in *New London Day* from April 29–June 3, 1926; June 11 and 25, 1926, *Textile Strike Bulletin* (Passaic, NJ).

35. June 6 and 11, 1926, *Daily Worker*; July 15 and 22, 1926, *Textile Strike Bulletin*.

36. June 3, 1926 and January 30, 1953, *New London Day*; Philip Cavoli draft registration card, June 5, 1917.

37. July 1926, December 1927, January and March 1928, *Labor Defender*; October 13, 1928, September 27, 1994, *New London Day*; 1930 and 1940 US Population Censuses; New York Passenger Arrival Lists, Ellis Island; November 17, 1931, *Daily Worker*.

CHAPTER ELEVEN

1. September 4, 1924, *New London Day*.
2. December 8, 1891 and September 20, 1916, *New London Day*.
3. Lisa McGirr, *The War on Alcohol, Prohibition and the Rise of the American State* (New York: W. W. Norton & Company, 2016), 11–12, 52, 94.
4. April 24, 1914, September 7 and October 18, 1917, *New London Day*; July 15, 1909, *Bridgeport Herald*.
5. April 23, 1910 and April 21, 1914, *Norwich Bulletin*.
6. May 24, 1913 and April 21, 1914, *Norwich Bulletin*.
7. May 17, 1908 and July 15, 1909, *Bridgeport Herald*.
8. May 5, 1915, September 20, 1916, September 7, 1917, *New London Day*.
9. February 21, 1915, May 5, 1915, and April 12, 1916, *New London Day*.
10. August 30, 1924, *New London Day*; Robert Owen Decker, *The Whaling City*, 184.
11. May 21, 1931, *New London Day*; Hansen, "The Fort," 60.
12. August 1, 1930, *New London Day*.
13. January 3, 1921, *New London Day*.
14. August 16, 1924, April 19, 1929, and August 2, 1930, *New London Day*.
15. January 4 and 6, 1930, August 23, 2015, *New London Day*.
16. Giommi, "The Fort," 12–13.
17. August 18, 1922, *New London Day*. 18. Interview with Shirley Mencarelli, August 4, 2016; December 19, 1953, *L'Adunata dei Refrattari*; April 18, 1918, *Norwich Bulletin*.
19. July 11, 1932, *New London Day*; Hansen, "The Fort," 73.
20. July 22, 1922 *Norwich Bulletin*; July 15, 2010, *New London Day*.
21. December 16, 1927, *New London Day*.
22. January 23, 1930, *New London Day*.
23. January 24 and 25, 1930, *New London Day*.
24. Vittorio Federici, ACS, CPC, busta 1987; Draft Registration Card, June 5, 1917.
25. Federici CPC file; 1920 and 1930 US Population Census; Draft Registration Card.
26. March 15, 1937, September 17, 1974, *New London Day*; August 24, 1920, *Norwich Bulletin*; December 12, 1959, *L'Adunata dei Refrattari*.
27. March 7, 1921, *New London Day*.
28. March 2, 1907, *Cronaca Sovversiva* and February 28, 1907, *Barre Daily Times*, both cited in Robin Hazard Ray, "No License to Serve: Prohibition, Anarchists, and the Italian-American Widows of Barre, Vermont, 1900–1920," *Italian Americana* 29, no. 1 (Winter 2011); Mari Tomasi, *Like Lesser Gods* (Shelburne, VT: New England Press, 1988).
29. John Vattuone interview, in Paul Avrich, *Anarchist Voices*, 152.

30. Nunzio Pernicone, "Carlo Tresca and the Sacco-Vanzetti Case," *Journal of American History* 66, no. 3 (December 1979); Paul Avrich, *Anarchist Voices*, 501.

CHAPTER TWELVE

1. June 2, 1924 and July 4, 1925, *New London Day*; Giommi, "The Fort, 11."

2. April 1984 and August 15, 1998, *New London Day*; "Maria Assunta Society," Maria Assunta Society website, https://www.church.stmichaelschoolct.com.

3. Guglielmo, *Living the Revolution*, 215; November 23, 1936, *New London Day*.

4. August 9, 1922, *New London Day*.

5. John P. Diggins, *Mussolini and Fascism: The View from America* (Princeton, NJ: Princeton University Press, 1972), 110; Philip V. Cannistraro, "The Duce and the Prominenti: Fascism and the Crisis of Italian American Leadership," July–December 2005, Altreitalie, https://www.altreitalie.it/ImagePub; Philip V. Cannistraro, *Blackshirts in Little Italy, Italian Americans and Fascism 1921–1929* (West Lafayette, IN: Bordighera Press, 1999), 4–5.

6. G. Chiodi Barberio, *Il Progresso degl'Italiani nel Connecticut* (New Haven, CT: Maturo's Printing and Publishing Co., 1933).

7. "In the Hidden History of WWII, Italian Enemy Aliens were Interned, Restricted," https://www.newenglandhistoricalsocietysite.com; Gaetano Salvemini, "Italian Fascist Activities in the United States," *Center for Migration Studies Special Issue* 3, no. 3 (May 1977); July 30, 1920, *Il Proletario*; "United States ex rel. De Cicco v. Longo, District Court, D. Connecticut, July 4, 1942," https://www.ctfindacase.com; Michael C. DiClemente, "Gaetano Salvemini: A Lesson in Thought and Action," MA thesis, University of Massachusetts, Boston, June 2012, 38; May 28, 1923, *Lewiston Daily Sun*; October 13, 1942, *New Britain Herald*; Lawrence DiStasi, *Una Storia Segreta: The Secret History of Italian American Evacuation and Internment during World War II* (Berkeley, CA: Heyday Books, 2001), 3, 137–43.

8. March 20, 1923, and October 13, 1925, *Bridgeport Telegram*.

9. October 12, 1928 and October 11, 1990, *New London Day*; Sarah Elizabeth Hansen, "The Fort: A History of Italians in the Fort Trumbull Neighborhood, New London, 1900–1938," honors thesis, Connecticut College, May 2001, 58.

10. Philip Cannistraro, *Blackshirts*, 113.

11. October 12, 1928 and October 11, 1990, *New London Day*.

12. October 19, 1936, *New London Day*; See "Fascism and the Prominenti," in *Blackshirts*.

13. New York Passenger Arrival Lists (Ellis Island); October 20, 1928, *New London Day*.

14. Interview with Anthony Basilica, 1998, Italians of New London Oral History Project Collection. Archives & Special Collections at the Thomas J. Dodd Research Center, University of Connecticut Libraries.
15. Balsamini and Sora, *Periodici e Numeri Unici*, 557.
16. Federico Sora, "5 Agosto 1922–5 Agosto 2006," https://www.biblio techaliberopensiero.it; October 12, 1928, *New London Day*; July 13, 1963, *L'Adunata dei Refrattari*.
17. October 12, 1928, *New London Day*; October 13, 1928, *Hartford Courant*; October 20, 1928, *Il Corriere del Connecticut*.
18. Interview with A. Matt Orsini, Italians of New London Oral History Project Collection; November 3, 1928, *Il Corriere del Connecticut*; October 15, 1928, *Norwich Bulletin*.
19. July 13, 1963, *L'Adunata dei Refrattari*; September 14, 1912, *Cronaca Sovversiva*; US Population Censuses, 1910 and 1930.
20. May 26, 1926, *L'Adunata dei Refrattari*; Dorothy Gallagher, *All the Right Enemies*, 137–42; Nunzio Pernicone, *Carlo Tresca*, 171.
21. October 13, 1928, *Hartford Courant*; October 13, 1928, *New London Day*.
22. October 13, 1928, *New London Day*; November 10, 1928, *Daily Worker*.
23. October 19, 1928, *New London Day*; October 18, 1928, *Daily Worker*.
24. Anita's suffering from chronic cardiovascular disease slowly removed her from political involvement. She died in 1933 at the age of sixty; Lorenzo retired and, his sons having moved out, lived alone at the location of their former bakery. Connecticut State Department of Health, Medical Certificate of Death for Anita Montali, January 12, 1933; January 14, 1933, *New London Day*.
25. Sora, "Storia degli organsimi sindicali della marineria fanese," 14n53; New York Passenger Arrival Lists (Ellis Island); July 16, 1953, *New London Day*; CPC busta 2397, https://www.bibliotecaliberopensiero.it.
26. October 28, 1928 *New Haven Register*; October 27, 1928, *Il Corriere del Connecticut*.
27. October 22 and 27, 1928, *New London Day*.
28. October 20 and 24, 1928, *New London Day*.
29. October 23, 1928, *New London Day*; November 10, 1928, *Daily Worker*; November 4, 1928, *L'Adunata dei Refrattari*.
30. October 23 and 24, 1928, *New London Day*.
31. April 27, 1952, *Bridgeport Sunday Herald*.
32. November 1 and 19, 1928, *New London Day*; November 10, 1928, *Il Corriere del Connecticut*.
33. November and December 1928 *Labor Defender*; November 4, 1928, August 24, and November 18, 1929, *L'Adunata dei Refrattari*.
34. January 2, 1929, *New London Day*.
35. March 4, 1929, *New London Day*; April 27, 1952, *Bridgeport Sunday Herald*.

36. Cannistraro, *Blackshirts*, 82–109; Diggins, *Mussolini*, 91–94.
37. February 25, April 7, July 21, August 11 and 18, 1928, *L'Adunata dei Refrattari*.
38. Nunzio Pernicone, "War among the Anarchists: The Galleanisti's Campaign against Carlo Tresca," in Cannistraro and Meyer, *The Lost World of Italian-American Radicalism*, 77–78.
39. Girolamo Grasso to Nick DiDomenico, May 14, 1928, Box 20, Folder 94, Other Correspondence, Il Fondo L'Adunata Manuscript Collection, Boston Public Library; Pernicone, "War among the Italian Anarchists," 88, 95n73; Pernicone, *Carlo Tresca*, 200.
40. August 24, November 18, 1919, *L'Adunata dei Refrattari*.
41. November 3 and 27, 1983, *New London Day*.
42. November 24 and December 29, 1950, *New London Day*.
43. October 24 and 28, 1930 and July 18 and 23, 1931, *New London Day*.
44. August 20, 1937, *L'Unita Operaia*; 1940 US Population Census.

CHAPTER THIRTEEN

1. September 8, 1908, *New London Day*.
2. 1910 US Population Census; September 10, 1908, *New London Day*.
3. November 12, 1912, *Cronaca Sovversiva*.
4. Hansen, "The Fort," 45–46; Giommi, "The Fort," 12–13.
5. Interview with Inez and Vilma Frausini, 1998, Italians of New London Oral History Collection.
6. July 10, 1898, *La Questione Sociale*.
7. Jennifer Guglielmo, *Living the Revolution*, 156–59.
8. June 6, 1902, *La Questione Sociale*.
9. June 13, 1903, *La Questione Sociale*.
10. April 11 and 18, 1903, *La Questione Sociale*.
11. November 28, 1903 *Cronaca Sovversiva*.
12. May 20, 1906, *In Marcia!*
13. February 14, 1931, July 1, 1932, *L'Adunata dei Refrattari*.
14. Guglielmo, *Living the Revolution*, 150; Bencivenni, *Italian Immigrant Radical Culture*, 146–49; Avrich, *Anarchist Voices*, 97.
15. August 5, 1939, July 12, 1941, and October 2, 1943, *L'Adunata dei Refrattari*.
16. March 21, 1925, *L'Adunata dei Refrattari*; September 8, 1917, *New Britain Herald*; Old German Files, Case #8000-30552, BI Files.
17. January 17, 1920, *Il Proletario*; November 11, 1954, and August 30, 1966, *Wallingford Post*; Interview with Marguerite Manfreda by Gerald Farrel Jr., February 13, 1990, Wallingford Public Library.

18. Richard Lenzi, "Workingmen's Order: The Granite Cutters' Union of Stony Creek, Connecticut, 1895–1900," unpublished paper, 2000; February 28, 1914 and January 30, 1915, *Cronaca Sovversiva*; August 29, 1903, *La Questione Sociale*.

19. Rudy J. Favretti, "The Twilight of Rural Life: The Dissolution of Mystic's Stanton Williams Farm," *Historical Footnotes*, May 2005, Stonington Historical Society, https://www.stoningtonhistory.org/index.php; October 19, 1900, August 21 and September 7, 1909, *New London Day*.

20. November 3, 1909, June 6, and September 21, 1910, September 30, 1912, and July 7, 1914, *New London Day*.

21. November 21, 1898, January 13, 1913, May 11, 1916, January 30, 1917, and June 9, 1917, *New London Day*; "Bolsheviki Activities in Mystic, Conn.," October 6, 1919, Old German Files, BI Files, 374806; State Committee Meeting minutes, Connecticut, 1913, Socialist Party Papers, Series III, State and Local Files, 1897–1962, Part G, Connecticut, ca. 1910–1958, reel 94.

22. Rudy J. Favretti, *Jumping the Puddle: Zoldani to America* (Dexter, Michigan: privately printed, 2002) 50, 53, 55–61, 65–66, 83–84.

23. United States Department of the Interior, National Park Service, "Rossie Velvet Mill Historic District, Stonington, New London County, CT," 2007; Favretti, "The Twilight"; Favretti, *Jumping the Puddle*, 98–99, 101–2; 1900, 1910, and 1930 US Population Censuses; US Draft Registration Card, Angelo Panciera, September 12, 1918.

24. January 12, 1901, *La Questione Sociale*.

25. February 2, 1901, *La Questione Sociale*.

26. April 27, 1901, *La Questione Sociale*.

27. November 17, 1906, *Cronaca Sovversiva*.

28. July 13, 1912, *Cronaca Sovversiva*; letter from Edward Perkins Clarke in January 9, 1904, *Appeal to Reason*; 1920 US Population Census; Favretti, *Jumping the Puddle*, 78–79.

29. December 2, 1933 and October 10, 1936, *L'Adunata dei Refrattari*.

30. April 30 and June 4, 1927, *L'Adunata dei Refrattari*; February 13, 1911, August 16, 1913, August 31, 1948, and May 10, 1955, *New London Day*.

31. Linda Smith Chaffee, John B. Coduri, and Ellen L. Madison, PhD., *Built from Stone, the Westerly Granite Story* (Westerly, RI: Babcock-Smith House Museum, 2012, 64; Paul Buhle, "Italian-American Radicals and the Labor Movement 1904–1930," Spring 1978 (17) *Radical History Review*; Anthony M. Lemenowicz Jr., "Trouble in Labor's Eden: Labor Conflict in the Quarries of Westerly, 1871–1922," February 2001, *Rhode Island History Journal* 59; Carmela E. Santoro, *The Italians in Rhode Island: The Age of Exploration to the Present, 1524–1989* (Providence: Rhode Island Heritage Commission, 1990), 17; n.a., "Rhode Island, Westerly: Italians in Westerly—The Italian Minority," and n.a., "The Ethnic Factor in the Westerly Granite Industry," in Vertical Files, Local

History Room, Westerly Public Library; Zachary Garceau, "Italian Emigration to one Rhode Island town," July 4, 2016, https://www.vita-brevis.org.

32. May 10, 1913, *Cronaca Sovversiva*.

33. January 29, 1947, *New London Day*; April 15, 1898, *La Questione Sociale*.

34. August 6, 1900 and May 29, 1941, *New London Day*.

35. May 1, 1916, *New London Day*.

36. February 23, 1901, *La Questione Sociale*.

37. March 16 and 30, 1901, *La Questione Sociale*.

38. The trial was covered in the *New London Day* from October 22 to November 11, 1904.

39. January 19, 1904, November 29, 1908, and July 31, 1911, *New London Day*.

40. March 6, 1899, January 19 and December 19, 1904, November 28, 1908, March 22, and November 16, 1909, July 31, 1911 and January 28, 1919, *New London Day*.

41. July 9, 1904, *La Questione Sociale*.

42. February 3, 1906, *Cronaca Sovversiva*.

43. December 29, 1927, *New London Day*.

CHAPTER FOURTEEN

1. February 2, 1917, and January 12 and 21, 1935, *New London Day*; Connecticut Historical Preservation Commission Records, New London Surveys.

2. September 26–29, 1934, *New London Day*; Bert Cochran, *Labor and Communism: The Conflict that Shaped American Unions* (Princeton, NJ: Princeton University Press, 1979), 86–87; Jeremy Brecher, *Strike!* (San Francisco, CA: Straight Arrow Books, 1973), 166–77.

3. November 4, 1912, *Cronaca Sovversiva*; August 18, 1928, October 6, 1934, *L'Adunata dei Refrattari*; September 28, 1934, *New London Day*; Draft Registration Card, Artimio Angeloni.

4. October, 6 and 27, 1934, *L'Adunata dei Refrattari*.

5. June 9, 1934, *L'Unita Operaia*; November 13, 1935, and February 25, 1936, *Daily Worker*.

6. February 24, 1934, *L'Unita Operaia*.

7. October 30, 1934, April 30 and May 15, 1935, *Daily Worker*; August 30, 1934, February 23 and 24, 1937, January 1, 1942, *New London Day*.

8. April 13, July, 8 and 11, 1932, November 21, 1934, May 4, 1936, *New London* Day; November 4, 1934, *L'Unita Operaia*; Gregory N. Stone, *The Day Paper*, 167–69.

9. September 23, 1933, June 2 and 9, 1934, *L'Unita Operaia*.

10. November 12, 1934, December 30, 1935, and September 11, 1986, *New London Day*.

11. December 4, 1935, January 4 and 11, 1936, *New London Day*; Pernicone, *Carlo Tresca*, 220–24.

12. Pernicone, *Carlo Tresca*, 263; Diggins, *Mussolini and Fascism*, 341.

13. February 22, 1936, *L'Adunata dei* Refrattari; October 11 and November 28, 1948, December 12, 1952, September 7 and November 22, 1954, December 1, 1979, and December 23, 1990, *New London Day*; December 8, 1957, *Bridgeport Sunday Herald*; Stefano Luconi, "Ethnic Allegiance and Class Consciousness among Italian-American Workers 1900–1941," *Socialism and Democracy* 22, no. 3 (2008).

14. March 24, 1937, June 4, 1948, *New London Day*; February 10 and April 13, 1940, *L'Adunata dei Refrattari*.

15. October 19, 1936, *New London Day*.

16. November 1933, *Cronaca Sovversiva* (numero unico).

17. Pier Carlo Masini, *Storia degli anarchici italiani* (Milan, Italy: Rizzoli Editore, 1972), 364.

18. December 2, 1933, *L'Adunata dei Refrattari*.

19. Stone, *The Day Newspaper*, 210–11; Clark van der Lyke, *New London Goes to War: New London during World War II 1941–1945* (New London, CT: New London Historical Society, 2011), 38–39.

20. January 14 and March 31, 1943, *New London Day*; Hansen, "The Fort," 64–65.

21. January 9, 1951, July 9, 1956, September 13, 1990, April 16, 1997, February 11, 2005, February 17, 2009, February 28, 2010, March 18, 2012, September 2, 2012, and February 8, 2015, *New London Day*.

22. August 3, 1946, *L'Adunata dei Refrattari*; September 13, 1990 and April 16, 1994, *New London Day*.

CHAPTER FIFTEEN

1. May 9, 1953, *L'Adunata dei Refrattari*.

2. August 3, 1946 and September 2, 1967, *L'Adunata dei Refrattari*.

3. March 24, 1948, August 28, 1954, March 11, 1980, and May 24, 1988, *New London Day*.

4. October, 8 and 11, 1948, *New London Day*.

5. November 15, 1948, *New London Day*; Stefano Luconi, "Anticommunism, Americanization, and Ethnic Identity: Italian Americans and the 1948 Parliamentary Elections in Italy," *The Historian* 62, no. 2 (December 2000).

6. John Johnson Jr. and Joel Selvin, with Dick Cami, *Peppermint Twist*, 43–45, 91–106.

7. November 15, 1948, June 3, 1953, December 21, 1974, and October 27, 1997, *New London Day*.
8. September 22, 1956 and March 29, 1958, *L'Adunata dei Refrattari*.
9. August 2, 1958 and March 28, 1959, *L'Adunata dei Refrattari*.
10. January 2, 1960, *L'Adunata dei Refrattari*; December 21, 1959, *New London Day*.
11. May 31, 1962, and April 3, 1965, *L'Adunata dei Refrattari*.
12. Raffaele Petrini, CPC busta 3905.
13. July 21, 1956, *L'Adunata dei Refrattari*; Certificate of Death, Connecticut State Department of Health.
14. July 13, 1963, *L'Adunata dei Refrattari*.
15. March 27, 1971 *L'Adunata dei Refrattari*; August 23, 1959, *Bridgeport Sunday Herald*; February 20, 2005, *New London Day*.
16. February 28, 1970, March 27, 1971, *L'Adunata dei Refrattari*.
17. December 13, 1962, *L'Adunata dei Refrattari*.
18. February 28, 1959, July 24, 1965, January 7 and November 23, 1968, and September 27, 1969, *L'Adunata dei Refrattari*.
19. October 25, 1981, *New London Day*.
20. Rachona Purohit, "Good Neighbors, Good Citizens: Redevelopment and Resistance in Fort Trumbull, New London Connecticut," thesis for BA Honors Study, Department of Anthropology, Connecticut College, May 2001, 24; February 8, 1984, *New London Day*.
21. March 3 and 31, 1975, *New London Day*; Espositi, Luigi. ALS to Angelo; New London, CT, March 3, 1965; Espositi, Luigi. ALS to Max Sartin, Box 20 Folder 28; New London, CT, February 17, 1970, Box 4, Folder 65; Other Correspondence, Il Fondo L'Adunata Manuscript Collection, Boston Public Library.
22. September 8, 1939, January 4, 1952, *New London Day*.
23. November 4, 1976, October 15, 1977; *New London Day*.

CONCLUSION

1. *Connecticut Preservation News* article cited in September 21, 2000 *New London Day*.
2. I borrow the term *hoopla* from Elissa Giommi, who wrote about the neighborhood's attitude toward Columbus Day in 1928, "this hoopla was not supported by the marchegiani." Giommi, "The Fort," 11.
3. Richard Lenzi, *Immigrant Radicalism in Rural New England: A History of the Finns of Eastern Connecticut, 1915–1945* (Canterbury, CT: Finnish American Heritage Society, 1999), 66–68; interview with Sidney Resnick, in David P. Shuldiner, *Aging Political Activists, Personal Narratives from the Old Left* (Westport, CT: Praeger, 1995), 209–10.

4. Gerald Meyer, "Italian Anarchism in America: Its Accomplishments, Its Limitations," *Science & Society* 79, no. 2 (April 2015).

5. Interviews with Victor Frausini and Aldo Valentini, 1998, Italians of New London Oral History Project Collection; interview with Shirley Mencarelli, August 4, 2016.

6. Interviews with Rita Frausini, Inez Frausini, and Vilma Frausini, 1998, Italians of New London Oral History Collection.

7. Interviews with Theodore Rocheleau and Alexander Winnick, in Biographical Sketches of Connecticut Labor Leaders, Record Group 33, Box 199, Federal Writers' Project Papers, Connecticut State Library.

8. August 28, 1920, February 4, 1922, July 15, 1935, March 15, 1936, *Il Proletario*; February 4, 1925, *Daily Worker*.

9. Michael Denning, *The Cultural Front: The Laboring of American Culture in the Twentieth Century* (London: Verso, 1996), 192–93.

10. May 1, 1934, August 18, 1937, February 28, 1938, October 13, 1942, *New Britain Herald*; Carlevale, *Who's Who*, 389; Labor Party of Connecticut, "A Vote for a Labor Party Is a Vote for . . . ," Hartford, Connecticut, 1940, Socialist Party Papers, Sterling Library, Yale University.

11. Rudolph J. Vecoli, "Italian Immigrants and Working Class Movements in the United States: A Personal Reflection on Class and Ethnicity," *Journal of the Canadian Historical Association* 4, no. 1 (1993).

12. Joanna Clapps Herman, *The Anarchist Bastard: Growing Up Italian in America* (Albany: State University of New York Press, 2011), 78, 80–83.

13. Town of Stafford, *Stafford Connecticut, 50th Anniversary* (n.p.: n.p., 1969), 70, 91; January 23, 1923, *Industrial Solidarity*.

14. Paul Buhle, "Anarchism and American Labor," *International Labor and Working Class History* 23 (Spring 1983); Upton Sinclair, *Boston: A Novel* (New York: Albert & Charles Boni, 1928), 76–78, 110–14.

BIBLIOGRAPHY

BOOKS AND PAMPHLETS

Alexander, Doris. *The Tempering of Eugene O'Neill*. New York: Harcourt, Brace & World, 1962.
Anselmi, Sergio, ed. *Le Marche*. Torino, Italy: Giulio Einaudi, 1987.
Avrich, Paul. *Anarchist Voices: An Oral History of Anarchism in America*. Princeton, NJ: Princeton University Press, 1995.
———. *The Haymarket Tragedy*. Princeton, NJ: Princeton University Press, 1984.
———. *Sacco and Vanzetti: The Anarchist Background*. Princeton, NJ: Princeton University Press, 1991.
Avrich, Paul, and Karen Avrich. *Sasha and Emma: The Anarchist Odyssey of Alexander Berkman and Emma Goldman*. Cambridge, MA: The Belknap Press of Harvard University Press, 2012.
Balsamini, Luigi, and Federico Sora, eds. *Periodici e Numeri Unici del Movimento Anarchico in Provincia di Pesaro e Urbino, Dall'Internazionale al fascismo (1873–1922)*. Fano, Italy: Edizioni dell'Archivio-Biblioteca Enrico Travaglini, 2013.
Bantman, Constance, and Bert Altena, eds. *Reassessing the Transnational Turn: Scales of Analysis in Anarchist and Syndicalist Studies*. Oakland, CA: AK Press, 2017.
Barberio, G. Chiodi. *Il Progresso degl'Italiani nel Connecticut*. New Haven, CT: Maturo's Printing and Publishing Co., 1933.
Bencivenni, Marcella. *Italian Immigrant Radical Culture: The Idealism of the Sovversivi in the United States, 1890–1940*, 2014.
Benedict, Jeff. *Little Pink House: A True Story of Defiance and Courage*. New York: Grand Central Publishing, 2009.
Brecher, Jeremy. *Banded Together: Economic Democratization in the Brass Valley*. Urbana: University of Illinois Press, 2001.
———. *Strike!* San Francisco, CA: Straight Arrow Books, 1973.

Blim, Michael L. *Made in Italy: Small-Scale Industrialization and Its Consequences.* Westport, CT: Praeger, 1990.

Bramson, Ruth Ann, Geoffrey K. Fleming, and Amy Kasuga Folk. *A World Unto Itself: The Remarkable History of Plum Island.* Southold, New York: Southold Historical Society, 2014.

Bucki, Cecelia. *Bridgeport's Socialist New Deal, 1915–1936.* Urbana: University of Illinois Press, 2001.

Buhle, Paul, and Dan Georgakas, eds. *Encyclopedia of the American Left.* Urbana: University of Illinois Press, 1992.

Cannistraro, Philip V. *Blackshirts in Little Italy, Italian Americans and Fascism 1921–1929.* West Lafayette, IN: Bordighera Press, 1999.

Cannistraro, Philip, and Gerald Meyer. *The Lost World of Italian-American Radicalism.* Westport, CT: Praeger Publishers, 2003.

Carnevale, Joseph William. *Who's Who Among Americans of Italian Descent in Connecticut.* New Haven, CT: Carnevale Publishing Co., 1942.

Carroll, Michael Christopher. *Lab 257: The Disturbing Story of the Government's Secret Germ Laboratory.* New York: William Morrow, 2005.

Chaffee, Linda Smith, John B. Coduri, and Ellen L. Madison. *Built from Stone: The Westerly Granite Story.* Westerly, RI: Babcock-Smith House Museum, 2012.

Cochran, Bert. *Labor and Communism: The Conflict that Shaped American Unions.* Princeton, NJ: Princeton University Press, 1979.

Decker, Robert Owen. *The Whaling City: A History of New London.* Chester, CT: Pequot Press, 1976.

Del Pozzo, Franca. *Alle origini del PCI: le organizzazioni marchegiane, 1919–23.* Urbino, Italy: Argalia Editore Urbino, 1971.

Denning, Michael. *The Cultural Front: The Laboring of American Culture in the Twentieth Century.* London: Verso, 1996.

Diggins, John P. *Mussolini and Fascism: The View from America.* Princeton, NJ: Princeton University Press, 1972.

DiStasi, Lawrence. *Una storia segreta: The Secret History of Italian American Evacuation and Internment during World War II.* Berkeley, CA: Heyday Books, 2001.

Dowling, Robert M. *Eugene O'Neill: A Life in Four Acts.* New Haven, CT: Yale University Press, 2014.

Draper, Theodore. *The Roots of American Communism.* New York: Viking Press, 1957.

Ealham, Chris. *Anarchism and the City: Revolution and Counter-Revolution in Barcelona, 1898–1937.* Oakland, CA: AK Press, 2010.

Ehrmann, Herbert B. *The Untried Case: The Sacco-Vanzetti Case and the Morelli Gang.* New York: Vanguard Press, 1960.

Falk, Candace, ed. *Emma Goldman: A Documentary History of the American Years.* Berkeley, CA: University of California Press, 2003.

Favretti, Rudy J. *Jumping the Puddle: Zoldani to America*. Dexter, MI: privately printed, 2002.
Fenton, Edwin. *Immigrants and Unions, a Case Study: Italians and American Labor, 1870–1920*. New York: Arno Press, 1975.
Francini, A. *Italiani nel Connecticut*. New York: Tipografia Sociale de Lucia Jorio, 1908.
Gabaccia, Donna. *Italy's Many Diasporas*. Seattle, WA: University of Washington Press, 2000.
———. *Militants and Migrants: Rural Sicilians Become American Workers*. New Brunswick, NJ: Rutgers University Press, 1988.
Gabaccia, Donna, and Frasier M. Ottanelli. *Italian Workers of the World: Labor Migration and the Formation of Multiethnic States*. Urbana: University of Illinois Press, 2001.
Gage, Beverly. *The Day Wall Street Exploded: A Story of America in Its First Age of Terror*. Oxford: Oxford University Press, 2009.
Gallagher, Dorothy. *All the Right Enemies: The Life and Murder of Carlo Tresca*. New York: Penguin Books, 1989.
Guérin, Daniel. *Anarchism*. New York: Monthly Review Press, 1970.
Guglielmo, Jennifer. *Living the Revolution: Italian Women's Resistance and Radicalism in New York City, 1880–1945*. Chapel Hill, NC: University of North Carolina Press, 2010.
Hardman, J. B. S. *American Labor Dynamics in the Light of Post-War Developments*. New York: Harcourt, Brace and Company, 1928.
Herman, Joanna Clapps. *The Italian Bastard: Growing Up Italian in America*. Albany: State University of New York Press, 2011.
Johnson Jr., John, and Joel Selvin. *Peppermint Twist*. New York: Thomas Dunne Books, 2012.
Kanzler, Carmelina Como, ed. *New London, A History of Its People*. New London: City of New London 350th Anniversary Celebration, 1996.
Koenig, Samuel. *Immigrant Settlements in Connecticut: Their Growths and Characteristics*. Works Progress Administration, Federal Writers' Project for the State of Connecticut, Hartford: Connecticut State Department of Education, 1938.
LaGumina, Salvatore J., et al., *The Italian American Experience: An Encyclopedia*. New York: Garland Publishing, 2000.
LeBlanc, Paul. *Left Americana: The Radical Heart of US History*. Chicago: Haymarket Books, 2017.
Lenzi, Richard. *Immigrant Radicalism in Rural New England: A History of the Finns of Eastern Connecticut 1915–1945*. Canterbury, CT: Finnish American Heritage Society, 1999.
McCormick, Charles H. *Hopeless Cases: The Hunt for the Red Scare Terrorist Bombers*. Lanham, MD: University Press of America, 2005.

McGirr, Lisa. *The War on Alcohol, Prohibition and the Rise of the American State.* New York: W. W. Norton & Company, 2016.

Merriman, John. *The Dynamite Club.* New Haven, CT: Yale University Press, 2016.

New London Chamber of Commerce. *New London Connecticut: Utopia of the North Atlantic: The Ideal City Winter and Summer.* N.p.: n.p., circa 1920s.

New London Ship and Engine Company. *Why We Located in New London.* N.p.: n.p., August 1916.

Nye, Robert M. "Alessandro Secchiaroli: With Eleven Dollars in His Pocket," *Alessandro Secchiaroli Barn Limited Conditions Assessment Study.* Branford, CT: Nelson Edwards Company, Architects, 2011.

O'Neill, Eugene. *Eugene O'Neill at Work: Newly Released Ideas for Plays,* edited by Virginia Floyd. New York: Frederick Ungar Publishing Co., 1981.

———. *The Unfinished Plays: Notes for The Visit of Malatesta, The Last Conquest, Blind Alley Guy,* edited by Virginia Floyd. New York: Continuum, 1988.

Di Paola, Pietro. *The Knights Errant of Anarchy: London and the Italian Anarchist Diaspora (1880–1917).* Oakland, CA: AK Press, 2017.

Parry, Richard. *The Bonnot Gang: The Story of the French Illegalists.* Oakland, CA: AK Press, 2016.

Pernicone, Nunzio. *Carlo Tresca: Portrait of a Rebel.* Oakland, CA: AK Press, 2010.

———. *Italian Anarchism, 1864–1892.* Oakland, CA: AK Press, 2009.

Piermattei, Dante. *L'uomo del sidecar: Memoria del Riccardo Orciani, un fanese con Sacco e Vanzetti tra emigrazione e anarchia.* Fano, Italy: Grapho 5 Edizioni, 2015.

Plekhanov, George. *Anarchism and Socialism.* Chicago: Charles H. Kerr & Company, n.d.

Rafferty, Pierce, and John Wilton. *Guardian of the Sound: A Pictorial History of Fort H. G. Wright, Fishers Island, N.Y.* New York: Mount Mercer Press, 1998.

Riccio, Anthony V. *Farms, Factories, and Families: Italian American Women of Connecticut.* Albany: State University of New York Press, 2014.

———. *The Italian American Experience in New Haven.* Albany: State University of New York Press, 2006.

Richter, Robert A. *Eugene O'Neill and "Dat Ole Davil Sea": Maritime Influences in the Life and Works of Eugene O'Neill.* Mystic, CT: Mystic Seaport, 2004.

Rose, Philip M. *The Italians in America.* New York: George H. Doran Company, 1922.

Santoro, Carmela E. *The Italians in Rhode Island: The Age of Exploration to the Present, 1524–1989.* Providence: Rhode Island Heritage Commission, 1990.

Sheaffer, Louis. *O'Neill, Son and Playwright,* vol. I. New York: Cooper Square Press, 2002.

Selsam, Howard, and Harry Martel. *Reader in Marxist Philosophy.* New York: International Publishers, 1970.

Schrecker, Ellen. *Many Are the Crimes: McCarthyism in America*. Princeton, NJ: Princeton University Press, 1998.
Shuldiner, David P. *Aging Political Activists, Personal Narratives from the Old Left*. Westport, CT: Praeger, 1995.
Sinclair, Upton. *Boston: A Novel*. New York: Albert and Charles Boni, 1928.
Skirda, Alexandre. *Facing the Enemy: A History of Anarchist Organization from Proudhon to May 1968*. Oakland, CA: AK Press.
Smith, Dennis Mack. *Modern Italy: A Political History*. Ann Harbor: University of Michigan Press, 1997.
Smith, Judith E. *Family Connections: A History of Italian and Jewish Immigrant Lives in Providence, Rhode Island 1900–1940*. Albany: State University of New York Press, 1985.
Stafford Library Association. *The History of the Town of Stafford*. Stafford Springs, CT, 1935.
Stone, Gregory N. *The Day Paper: The Story of One of America's Last Independent Newspapers*. New London, CT: Day Publishing Company, 2000.
Strang, Dean A. *Worse than the Devil: Anarchists, Clarence Darrow and Justice in a Time of Terror*. Madison: University of Wisconsin Press, 2013.
Sullivan, Joseph W. *Marxists, Militants & Macaroni: The IWW in Providence's Little Italy*. Kingston, RI: Rhode Island Labor History Society, 2000.
Thornton, Steve. *A Shoeleather History of the Wobblies: Stories of the Industrial Workers of the World (IWW) in Connecticut*. N.p.: Shoeleather History Project: n.d. circa 2014.
Tomasi, Mari. *Like Lesser Gods*. Shelburne, VT: New England Press, 1988.
Tomchuck, Travis. *Transnational Radicals: Italian Anarchists in Canada and the US 1915–1940*. Winnipeg, Manitoba: University of Manitoba Press, 2015.
Topp, Michael Miller. *Those without a Country: The Political Culture of Italian American Syndicalists*. Minneapolis: University of Minnesota Press, 2001.
Town of Stafford. "Stafford, CT: 50th Anniversary." Stafford, CT, 1969.
Turcato, Davide. *Making Sense of Anarchism, Errico Malatesta's Experiments with Revolution*. Oakland, CA: AK Press, 2015.
van der Lyke, Clark. *New London Goes to War: New London During World War II*. New London, CT: New London Historical Society, 2011.
van der Walt, Lucien, and Michael Schmidt. *Black Flame: The Revolutionary Class Politics of Anarchism and Syndicalism*. Oakland, CA: AK Press, 2009.
Watson, Bruce. *Sacco & Vanzetti: The Men, the Murders, and the Judgment of Mankind*. New York: Penguin Books, 2008.
Weinberg, Chaim Leib. *Forty Years in the Struggle: Memoirs of a Jewish Anarchist*. Duluth, MN: Litwin Books, 2008.
Weinstein, James. *The Decline of Socialism in America, 1912–1925*. New York: Vintage Books, 1969.

Whetten, Nathan L. *The Foreign-Born Population of Connecticut.* Bulletin 246, Storrs: University of Connecticut, 1943.
Young, William. *Stafford Illustrated: A Descriptive and Historical Sketch of Stafford, Connecticut.* N.p.: Young & Cady Publishers, 1895.
Zimmer, Kenyon. *Immigrants against the State: Yiddish and Italian Anarchism in America.* Urbana: University of Illinois Press, 2015.

ARTICLES

Baldelli, Ann. "Where Everybody Knew Your Name: Decades Ago, Fort Trumbull Was a Close-Knit Neighborhood." *New London Day* February 20, 2005.
Balsamini, Luigi. "Carta e anarchia: una collezione di giornali anarchici della provincial di Pesaro e Urbino (1873–1922)." https://www.e-review.it/balsamini-carta-e-anarchia.
Benedict, Rev. Arthur J. "Kensington." *Connecticut Magazine* 6, no. 2 (September–October 1900).
Buhle, Paul. "Italian-American Radicals and the Labor Movement, 1905–1930," *Radical History Review* Spring 17 (1978).
———. "Anarchism and American Labor." *International Labor and Working Class History* 23 (Spring 1983).
Capelli, B. "L'Emigrazione anarchia italiana negli USA." *Volontà: revista anarchia bimestrale* (November–December 6, 1971).
Cannistraro, Philip V. "The Duce and the Prominenti: Fascism and the Crisis of Italian American Leadership." *Altreitalie* (July–December 2005). https://www.altreitalie.it.
Cartosio, Bruno. "Sicilian Radicals in Two Worlds." In *In the Shadow of the Statue of Liberty: Immigrants, Workers and Citizens in the American Republic 1880–1920*, edited by Marianne Dibouzy. Paris: Presses Universitaires de Vincennes, 1988.
Davis, John A. "Italy 1796–1870: The Age of the Risorgimento," in *The Oxford History of Italy*, edited by George Holmes. Oxford, UK: Oxford University Press, 1997.
DiRenzo, Anthony. "St. Sebastian Day Is the Anniversary of the Caltavatura Massacre." January 20, 2014. https://www.thetimesofsicily.com.
Dowling, Robert M. "On O'Neill's 'Philosophical Anarchism,'" in *Eugene O'Neill and His Early Contemporaries*, edited by Eileen J. Herrmann and Robert M. Dowling. Jefferson, NC: McFarland & Company, 2011.
Favretti, Rudy J. "The Twilight of Rural Life: The Dissolution of Mystic's Stanton Williams Farm," *Historical Footnotes*, May 2005, Stonington Historical Society, https://www.stoningtonhistory.org.
Garceau, Zachary. "Italian Emigration to One Rhode Island Town." https://www.vita-brevis.org.

Gillette, Jonathon H. "Italian Workers in New Haven: Mutuality and Solidarity at the Turn of the Century," in *Support and Struggle: Italians and Italian Americans in a Comparative Perspective*, edited by Joseph L. Troper, James E. Miller, and Cheryl Beattie-Repetti. Staten Island, New York: American Italian Historical Association, 1986.

"In the Hidden History of WWII, Italian Enemy Aliens were Interned, Restricted," n.d. https://www.newenglandhistoricalsocietysite.com.

Keliher, T. T. "Part IV: Freight-Car Robberies. *Journal of Criminal Law and Criminology* 23 (Spring 1933).

LeBlanc, Paul. "Making Sense of Trotskyism in the United States: Two Memoirs." *Labor Standard*, n.d. https://www.laborstandard.org.

Lementowicz, Anthony M. "Trouble in Labor's Eden: Labor Conflict in the Quarries of Westerly 1871–1922." *Rhode Island History* 59 (February 2001).

Lenzi, Richard. "Stout Proletarian Hearts: The Socialist Labor Party in New Britain, Connecticut 1895–1900." *Connecticut History* 37, no. 1 (Spring 1996).

Levy, Carl. "Errico Malatesta and Charismatic Leadership," in *Charismatic Leadership and Social Movements: The Revolutionary Power of Ordinary Men and Women*, vol. 19, International Studies in Social History, edited by Jan Willem Stutje. Amsterdam: Berghann Books, 2012.

Luconi, Stefano. "Anticommunism, Americanization, and Ethnic Identity: Italian Americans and the 1948 Parliamentary Elections in Italy." *The Historian* 62, no. 2 (December 2000).

Maria Assunta Society. "Maria Assunta Society," n.d., https://www.church.st michaelschoolct.com.

Meyer, Gerald. "Italian Anarchism in America: Its Accomplishments, Its Limitations." *Science & Society* 79, no. 2 (April 2015).

Molinari, Augusta. "Luigi Galleani: Un anarchico italiano negli Stati Uniti." *Miscellanea Storica Ligure* VI, no's. 1–2 (1974).

Murphy, Tim. "Clubs: Ethnic Roots that Bind." *New London Day*, October 25, 1981.

Pernicone, Nunzio. "Carlo Tresca and the Sacco-Vanzetti Case." *Journal of American History* 66, no. 3 (December 1979).

Pernicone, Nunzio. "Luigi Galleani and Italian American Terrorism in the United States." *Studi Emigrazione* 3 (1993).

Ray, Robin Hazard. "No License to Serve: Prohibition, Anarchists, and the Italian Widows of Barre, Vermont, 1900–1920." *Italian Americana* 29, no. 1 (Winter 2011).

Salvemini, Gaetano. "Italian Fascist Activities in the United States," *Center for Migration Studies, Special Issue* 3, no. 3 (May 1977).

Socialist Workers Party, "Connecticut Trailblazers—Connecticut Militant Campaign." *Party Builder* 3, no. 1 (March 1946).

Sora, Federico. "Nascita e sviluppo del movemento sindicale e dei lavoratori a Fano: cronistoria e specificita," *Lavoro, diritti, memoria, La Camera del Lavoro della provincial di Pesaro e Urbino dale origine ai primi anni '70*, edited by Andrea Bianchini. Pesaro, Marche, Italy: Metauro Edizioni, 2007.

Topp, Michael Miller. "The Italian-American Left: Transnationalism and the Quest for Unity," in *The Immigrant Left in the United States* edited by Paul Buhle and Dan Georkakas. N.p.: State University of New York Press, 1996.

Turcato, Davide. "Italian Anarchism as a Transnational Movement, 1885–1915." *International Review of Social History* 52 (2007).

Vecoli, Rudolph J. "Primo Maggio: Haymarket as Seen by Italian Anarchists in America," in *Haymarket Scrapbook*, edited by Dave Roediger and Franklin Rosemont. Chicago: Charles H. Kerr Publishing Company, 1986.

———. "Italian Immigrants and Working-Class Movements in the United States: A Personal Reflection on Class and Identity." *Journal of the Canadian Historical Association* 4, no. 1 (1993).

Wessel, Bessie Bloom. "Ethnic Factors in the Population of New London, Connecticut," *American Journal of Sociology* XXXV, no. 1 (July 1929).

ANARCHIST PRIMARY SOURCES

Fabbri, Luigi. *Life of Malatesta*. Anarchy Archives. https://www.dwardmac.pitzer.edu.

Galleani, Luigi. *The End of Anarchism?* Orkney, UK: Cienfuegos Press, 1982.

———. [Mentana, pseud.]. *Faccia a Faccia col Nemico*. Boston: Gruppo Autonomo, 1914.

Guèrin, Daniel, ed. *No Gods, No Masters: An Anthology of Anarchism*. Oakland, CA: AK Press, 2005.

Kropotkin, Peter. *The Conquest of Bread*. London: Penguin Books, 2015.

Malatesta, Errico. *Il Nostro Programma*. New London, CT: Gruppo S. A. L'Avvenire, 1903.

———. "Anarchism and Organization." https://www.theanarchistlibrary.org.

Most, Johann. The Beast of Property, 2nd ed. New Haven, CT: International Workingmen's Association, n.d., circa 1887.

Richards, Vernon, ed. *Malatesta, Life and Ideas: The Anarchist Writings of Errico Malatesta*. Oakland, CA: PM Press, 2015.

Turcato, Davide, ed. *A Long and Patient Work: The Anarchist Socialism of L'Agitazione 1897–1898: The Complete Works of Errico Malatesta*, vol. Chico, CA, 2016.

Vanzetti, Bartholomeo. *The Story of a Proletarian Life*. Boston: Sacco-Vanzetti Defense Committee, 1923.

UNPUBLISHED PAPERS

Baldwin, Peter Cunningham. "The Italians in Middletown, 1893–1932: The Formation of an Ethnic Community." BA honors thesis in American Studies, Wesleyan University, 1984.
Clouette, Bruce Alan. "Getting Their Share: Irish and Italian Immigrants in Hartford, 1850–1940." PhD dissertation, University of Connecticut, 1992.
DiClemente, Michael C. "Gaetano Salvemini: A Lesson in Thought and Action." MA thesis, University of Massachusetts, Boston, 2012.
Fraser, Bruce. "Yankees at War: Social Mobilization on the Connecticut Homefront, 1917–1918." PhD dissertation, Columbia University, 1976.
Giommi, Elissa. "The Fort," n.d.
Hansen, Sarah Elizabeth. "The Fort: A History of Italians in the Fort Trumbull Neighborhood, New London, Connecticut, 1900–1938." Honors thesis, Connecticut College, May 2001.
Lenzi, Richard. "Open Shop Connecticut: Labor and Radicalism in the Nutmeg State during the 1920s." Independent graduate studies, Trinity College, 2001.
———. "Saturated with Anarchy: The Galleanist Movement in New Britain, Connecticut, 1910–1919," Eastern Connecticut State University paper, 1999.
———. "Workingmen's Order: The Granite Cutters' Union of Stony Creek, Connecticut, 1895–1900," Trinity College graduate paper, 2000.
Petriccone, Michael J. "The Immigrant City of New Haven: A Study in Italian Social Mobility 1890–1930." Senior honors thesis, University of New Haven, 1979.
Pucci, Alceo. "Socialismo Revolutionario Anarchico a Fano," Urbino, 1973–1974, tesi di laurea, https://www.sistemabiblioteca.riofano.it.
Purohit, Rachona. "Good Neighbors, Good Citizens: Redevelopment and Resistance in Fort Trumbull, New London, Connecticut." Thesis, BA honors study, Department of Anthropology, Connecticut College, May 2001.
Sora, Federico. "Storia degli organismi sindicali della marineria fanese," 2016.

SPECIAL COLLECTIONS

Archivio-Biblioteca Enrico Travaglini
Via Garibaldi, Fano, Italy
Website: https://www.bibliotecaliberopensiero.it

Investigative Reports of the Bureau of Investigation 1908–1922
Various Files
Old German Files
Bureau Section Files 1909–1921

Connecticut Historical Preservation Commission Records, New London Surveys, Archives & Special Collections, Thomas J. Dodd Research Center, University of Connecticut Libraries.

Federico Sora. Research biographies of Fanese and Marchegian anarchists compiled from: Ministero dell'Interno, Direzione Generale Pubblica Sicurezza, Casellario Politico Centrale; Tribunale di Pesaro; Pretura di Fano; Pretura di Mondavio; local anarchist and commercial press:
    Baldoni, Guido
    Baldoni, Romolo
    Bartolucci, Effisio
    Biagioni, Alberico
    Busca, Gino
    Camerini, Adolfo
    Campanella, Livio
    Cardaci, Enone
    Carnaroli, Paris
    Cecchini, Alberto
    Cicerchia, Luigi
    Cortucci, Alberto
    Del Moro, Armando
    Dondero, Federico
    Falcioni, Nazzareno
    Fazio, I.
    Fazio, S.
    Federici, Vittorio
    Ferri, Luigi

Il Fondo L'Adunata Manuscript Collection, 1917–1985. Rare Books and Manuscripts Department, Boston Public Library.

Italians of New London Oral History Project Collection. Archives & Special Collections at the Thomas J. Dodd Research Center, University of Connecticut Libraries.

National Archives, Italians to America Passenger Data File 1855–1900. https://www.aad.archives.gov/aad.

Socialist Party Papers, Series III, State and Local Files, 1897–1962, Part G, Connecticut, ca. 1910–1958, reel 94, Sterling Library, Yale University.

Street Files, New London Landmarks Society, New London, CT.

Vertical Files, Local History Room, Westerly, Rhode Island Public Library.

Works Progress Administration, Federal Writers' Project, Ethnic Group Studies, Connecticut State Library, Hartford.

DOCUMENTS

Connecticut Bureau of Labor Statistics. First Annual Report, 1885, Hartford: State of Connecticut.
———. Eighteenth Annual Report, Meriden, Connecticut: Journal Publishing Company, 1902.
———. Labor Bulletin, Connecticut Public Documents, 1908.
Libretto di Matricolazione, Sergio Mencarelli, Compartamento Marittimo, Marina Mercantile Italiana, Rimini, 1904 (copy in possession of author).
New London and Waterford Town Directories, 1905–1920.
Office of the Federal Register. *The Federal Register* 259 (October–November 1919).
"United States ex rel. De Cicco v. Longo, District Court, D. Connecticut, July 4, 1942." https://www.ctfindacase.com.
United States Housing Corporation Historic District, New London, CT, National Park Service, National Register of Historic Places, n.d. https://www.livingplaces.com.
US Population Censuses, 1900, 1910, 1920, 1930, and 1940.
United States Surgeon-General's Office. "Report of the Surgeon-General, United States Army, to the Secretary of War." Washington: 1901.
Wallingford Town Directories, 1899–1915.

NEWSPAPERS AND PERIODICALS

L'Adunata dei Refrattari
The Alarm
Appeal to Reason
L'Aurora
Bandiera Rossa (Fano)
Bridgeport Herald
Bridgeport Telegram
Chi Siamo! (Fano)
Il Corriere del Connecticut
Cronaca Sovversiva
Daily Worker
L'Era Nuova

La Frusta (Fano and Pesaro)
Granite Cutters Journal
Hartford Courant
In Marcia! (Fano and Pesaro)
New Britain Herald
New London Day
New London Morning Telegraph
New York Times
Norwich Bulletin
Il Progresso Comunista (Fano)
Il Proletario
La Questione Sociale
Regeneraçion (Los Angeles)
Solidarity
Textile Strike Bulletin (Passaic, NJ)
L'Unita Operaia

VIDEOS

Farrel, Gerald Jr., dir. "Pane e Lavoro: The Emigration of Italians to Wallingford." Wallingford, CT: Wallingford Historic Preservation Trust, April 4, 1995. Video.

INTERVIEWS

Coduri, John B., July 23, 2015, by author.
Manfreda, Marguerite, n.d., by Gerald Farrel Jr., Wallingford Public Library.
Mencarelli, Shirley, August 4, 2016, by author.

INDEX

L'Adunata dei Refrattari, 99, 116, 118, 129, 147, 159, 172, 186, 187, 222, 232
L'Agitazione (Ancona), 39, 43
Ambrosini, Ariodante, 79
American Federation of Labor (AFL), 29
Alleva, Aurora, 197
Amalgamated Clothing Workers, 148
Amalgamated Textile Workers, 239
American Relief for Italy, Inc., 227
anarchism
   anti-organizational, 14, 31–32, 44
   history of, 1–3
   organizational, 13–14, 50, 70
Angeloni, Artimio, 188, 214
L'Anonimato (Paris), 133–34
Ansonia, Connecticut, 98, 126, 145
antifa, xvii
Antolini, Ella, 125, 128, 199
Antonelli, Ettore, 10
Arace, Giuseppe, 83, 84–85, 89
Arace, Raffaele, 130
Arditi del Popolo, 127
Asci, Angelo, 136
L'Aurora, 28, 43, 44
Avrich, Paul, xiii, 103, 125, 142, 171

Bakunin, Mikhail, 1–2
   and secret revolutionary elite, 86

Baldoni, Domenico, 9
Baldoni, Guido, 62, 84
Baldoni, Romolo, 137–41
Ballestrini, Augusto, 19–20, 94
Balsamini, Luigi, xv, 147
Bandiera Rossa (Fano), 127
Bank Street (New London), 18, 19, 37, 49, 52, 119, 195, 207
Barbanet, Giovanni, 43, 51
Barbanet, Margherita, 43, 51
Bargnesi, Ruggero, 79–81
Barre, Vermont, 31, 41, 56, 170–71
Bartolucci, Alfredo, 81–82, 179
Bartolucci Brothers (contractors), 109, 114, 170
Bartolucci, Efisio, 62, 75, 81–82, 88, 106–7, 136, 153
Bartolucci, Gilda, 193
Bartolucci, Raymond, 223
Bencevenni, Marcella, 4, 117, 121
Benvenuti, Augusto, 37, 78–79
Benvenuti, Fred, 226–27, 235
Benvenuti, Nazzarene, 37, 79–81
   and government contracts, 78
Berardinelli, Peter, 68, 203
Berkman, Alexander, 31, 95
Berlin (Kensington), Connecticut, 24, 25, 27
Biagioni, Alberico, 37
Biancheria, Adimero, 179

Biancheria, Amilcare, 179
Bini, Ulderico, 93
Black International, 2
blackshirts. *See* fascism
Bloor, Ella Reeve, 158
Bodenwein, Theodore, 102
Bolshevik Revolution, 127, 143, 216
Bonnot Gang, 133
Bonucci, Alfredo, 56
bootlegging
  in Fort Trumbull, 161–71
  in New London, 164–64, 210
Booth Brothers Granite Company, 124
Boston (Upton Sinclair), 240
Brainerd & Armstrong silk mill, 16, 42, 49, 51, 180, 214
Bresci, Gaetano, 42, 48, 68
Bridgeport, Connecticut, 10, 30, 82, 148
Bridgeport Herald, 231
Broccoli, Enrico, 37, 38, 118–19, 155
  and Bargnesi affair, 78–80
  and Foschini affair, 58–60
Brown Cotton Gin Company, 51
Brucato, Nicolo, 95
Buda, Mario, 125
  and Wall Street bombing, 142
Buhle, Paul, 240
Bureau of Investigation, 136, 145–46
  and Gemma Mello, 154
Burns Detective Agency, 145
Busca, Giuseppe, 231

Cafiero, Carlo, 86
Caltavuturo, Sicily, 20
Camillo, Giuseppe, 153
Camillucci, Alba, 189, 227–28
Camillucci, Emilia, 116, 189, 227, 228
Camillucci, Dick, 228
Camillucci, Leo, 116, 228, 233

Camillucci, Luigi, 37, 43–44, 50, 62, 74, 84, 86, 116, 155, 165, 170, 179, 189, 227–28
Caminita, Ludovico, 62, 69–70, 72
  and Bureau of Investigation, 136
Candolfi, Aldo, 100, 196–97
Cannistraro, Philip, 175
Canzonetti, Aurelio, 238
Caracausa, Albert, 143
Caracausa, Antonio, 92, 208
Carboni, U., 84
Cardaci, Mario, 68, 87
Carnaroli, Paris, 62, 107, 229
Carocari, Rachele, 205
Caroti, Arturo, 55–56, 115
  debate with Galleani, 60–61
Casa del Popolo (Wallingford), 229, 231
Casselario Politico Centrale (CPC), xv, 35, 70
Cavoli, Philip, 158
Central Council of Italian Societies (New London), 219
Cesarini, Giordano, 188, 193, 214
Cesarini, Orvidia, 193, 214
Chamberlain, J. W. R., 135
Ciancabilla, Giuseppe, 28, 40, 43, 126
Ciavaglia, Enrico, 70
Circolo Cultura Operaia (New London), 215
Clarke, Edward Perkins, 201, 206
"Clean Up Campaign" (New London), 163–64
Coacci, Ferruccio, 155
Coalition to Save Fort Trumbull Neigborhood, xii
Coduri, Charles, 38, 62, 71, 131
  as secretary of Anarcho-Socialist Federation, 41
  views on debate within anarchist movement, 57, 59

Coduri, Joseph, 131
Columbus Day clash in New London. *See* fascism
Communist (Workers) Party, 236
  and 1934 textile strike in New London, 214–16
  and Bloom Silk Mill strike, 158
  labor organizing in Connecticut, 159–60, 216–17
  in New London, 157–60
  and New London Italians, 159, 216–17
  and united front with Gruppo I Liberi, 180–82
Congress of Industrial Organizations (CIO), 159, 217, 238
Connecticut Federation of Labor (CFL), 148
Cordiglia, Gino, xvi
Il Corriere di Connecticut, 95, 175, 183
Cravello, Ernestina, 42, 51
Cravello, Vittorio, 39, 42, 44, 47, 51, 209
Cronaca Sovversiva, xiii, 31, 32, 48, 56, 70, 71, 74, 85, 93, 95, 98, 99, 100, 103, 107, 112, 142, 170, 192, 204, 221, 241
  distribution in Connecticut, 123
  government attacks on, 123, 125, 127
Cross, Wilbur, 217

Daily Worker (New York), 148
D'Andrea, Virgilia, 197
Debs, Eugene, 73
De Cicco, Pasquale, 175–76, 179, 184–85
D'Elia, Angelo, 95
De Luca, Gennaro, 208–9, 211
Democratic Party (New London), 210, 218

Denning, Michael, 238, 239
Derby, Connecticut, 137
Di Domizio, Camillo, 232
Diggins, John P., 174–75
Dionisi, Gustavo, 70, 101
Dondero, Federico, 48, 50, 86–87, 99, 195–96
  as '*prominenti*,' 210
Dondero, Marta, 49, 59, 197
Dondero, Louis, 91
Le Donne Libertarie di Old Mystic, 205
Dos Passos, John, 238
Duval, Clemente, 171–72

Eastern Shipbuilding Company, 51, 79, 113
Electric Boat Company (EB), 217, 225
Enrico Travaglini Archivio/Biblioteca (Fano), xv
L'Era Nuova (Paterson), 72, 99
Espositi (Esposito), Luigi, 233
Esteve, Pedro, 37, 48, 56, 85, 193
Ettor, Joseph, 82

Fabbri, Luigi, 3
Facchini, Luigi, 188
Facchini, Nostralio, 153, 165
Facendo (Facendi), Pietro, 134
Falcioni, Nazzareno, 56, 62, 70, 210–11
Fano (Italy)
  anarchism in, xiii, xv, 7, 9–14
  arrival of fascism in, 147, 178–79
  artisans in, 9–10
  economy of, 8–9
  fishermen organizing in, 11
  immigration from, 12–13, 33, 62
  labor organizing in, 9, 11–12
  mutual benefit societies in, 9, 11
  post-WWI upsurge in, 128

fascism
  and Columbus Day parade, 177–79
  among Italian Americans, 174–75
  in New London, 177–78
Fascist League of North America (FLNA), 186
Favretti, Sofia, 205
Federazione Socialista Italiana (FSI), 28, 29, 30, 48, 60, 73–74, 82, 95, 146
Federici, Vittorio (Victor Frederick), 62, 136
  attacks 'spies,' 83
  biography of, 83–84
  as bootlegger, 167–70
  freight car robbery arrest, 134–35
  last years of, 233–34
  sentencing of, 134
Ferri, Luigi, 62, 100
Ficarra, Salvatore, 177–78
Filippetti, Joseph, 227
Fishers Island (New York), 16, 100
  and anarchists, 43, 44, 45
  and Italian laborers, 36–37, 110–12
Flynn, Elizabeth Gurley, 148
Fort H. G. Wright (Fishers Island), 36
Fort Neck (neighborhood). *See* Fort Trumbull
Fort Terry (Plum Island), 81
Fort Trumbull (neighborhood)
  anti-fascist legacy of, 236, 237
  and building trades, 77, 109–10
  during World War II, 222–23
  early conditions in, 16, 21
  economic development of, 15–16
  and eminent domain, xi–xii
  Fort/Shaw football games, 188–89
  and historians, xiii–xiv
  Italian immigration to, 18–20, 45
  and liquor smuggling, 192
  military presence in, 77, 109–10
  occupational structure of, 106–9
  and violence during Prohibition, 167
Fort Trumbull (military installation), 77
Foschini, Gennaro, 46–47, 72, 79, 182
  attacks *prominenti*, 208–9
Foschini affair, 58–60
  on women, 194
Frausini, Clotilda, 166
Frausini, Inez, 237
Frausini, Rita, 237
Frausini, Victor, 116, 237
Frederick, Otello, 222–23, 34
freight car robberies. *See* Galleanist movement
Frohsinn Society, 201
La Frusta (Fano and Pesaro), 99, 127, 147, 151, 178, 199

Gabaccia, Donna, 4
Galleani, Luigi, 1, 3–4, 28, 49, 51, 82
  antiwar position of, 95
  attack on Esteve, 85
  biography of, 30–31
  death of, 221
  and *Faccia a Faccia col Nemico*, 103
  final speaking tour in US, 127
  on Foschini, 58–59
  and *La Salute e in Voi*, 103
  in New London, 58, 61–62, 67–68, 94, 194
  publishes 'Matricolati,' 102, 137
  resumes activity in Italy, 127
Galleanist movement in US
  attacked in Milwaukee, 103

INDEX 289

expropriations and Sacco-Vanzetti
    case, 141–42
  and freight car robberies, 132–33
  issues 'Go-head' flyer, 129–30
  in New England, 129, 155
  response to repression, 129, 148
  revival in 1920s, 153
Gaudenzi, Vincenzo, 180
  biography of, 183
  criticism of Gruppo I Liberi, 216
Ghiandoni, Arturo, 70, 88, 116,
    188
Ghiglione, Ernesto, 58
Giano, Angelo, 180, 183
Giommi, Elissa, 152
Giovanitti, Arturo, 82
Giri, Giustina, 167
Giri, Mike, 233
Giustini, Louis, 223
Giustini, Renato, 93, 155
  and 1912 New London crisis, 83,
    84
  and 1928 arrest, 182, 188
  in 1934 textile strike, 214–15
  biography of, 180
  death of, 230
Goldman, Emma, xvi, 31, 48, 67,
    170, 195
Gori, Pietro, 28, 49, 211
  and *Primo Maggio*, xv–xvi, 43,
    116
Grasso, Girolamo, 123, 188, 231
Griswold Hotel (Groton), 17
Groton, Connecticut, 42, 43
Guadagni, Felice, 188
Guglielmo, Jennifer, 197
Guglielmotti, General Emilio, 146
Gull Island (New York), 36

Hamden, Connecticut, 30, 176
Hardman, J. B. S., 148

Hartford, Connecticut, 24, 25, 30
Hartford Courant, 184
Haywood, William D., 82
Herman, Joanna Clapps, 239
Hoover, J. Edgar, 136
Hopson & Chapin Company, 16

Industrial Union of Marine and
    Shipbuilding Workers, 217
Industrial Workers of the World
    (IWW, or Wobblies)
  and Lawrence strike, 73–74, 82
  in Paterson, 72
  in Torrington, 238
International Labor Defense, 158,
    185
International Workers Order, 33
International Working Peoples
    Association, 29
Isca, Valerio, 148
Italian American anarchist and
    syndicalist groups and circles
  Circolo Autonomo (Meriden), 32
  Circolo di Educazione ed Istruzione
    Sociale (New London), 37
  Circolo Filodramatico di New
    London, 69, 74–75, 116
  Circolo Francesco Ferrer (New
    Haven), 126–27
  and mass activity of, 146
  Circolo Karl Marx, 125, 148
  Circolo Libero Pensiero (Hartford),
    32
  Circolo Michele Bakunin (Derby),
    32
  Circolo di Studi Sociali (Milford,
    Massachusetts), 138
  Gruppo Alpino (Mystic), 205
  Gruppo Autonomo (East Boston),
    83, 93, 103, 231
  and Mario Buda, 142

Italian American anarchist and syndicalist groups and circles *(continued)*
  Gruppo L'Avvenire (New London), 3, 208–9
    crisis of, 74–90
    early political orientation, 43–44, 48, 50
    early propaganda of, 67–69
    evolution of views, 53, 56, 57, 71–72
    founding of, 41
    involvement in labor movement, 45–47, 52–53
    strength of, 44–46
  Gruppo Diritto all'Esistenza (Paterson), 40, 57
  Gruppo Gli Insorti (Paterson), 154
  Gruppo I Liberi (New London)
    in 1934 textile strike, 214–15
    and armed struggle, 92
    and arson attacks, 152
    birth of, 92
    building of IDC hall, 152, 155
    and clash with Communists, 181–82, 214–16
    and draft registration, 136
    early history of, 94–95
    and Gruppo di Donne, 198
    and illegalism, 131–35, 167–70, 171–72, 187
    and numeric unico of *Cronaca Sovversiva*, 221–22
    occupations of members, 109
    periphery of, 109
    and response to fascism, 178–81
    and response to Mutual Aid Society, 151–52
    and Sacco-Vanzetti campaign, 156–57
  Gruppo Libertá (Needham, Mass.), 133, 155
  Gruppo Luigi Bertoni (central Connecticut), 229, 231
  Gruppo Pietro Gori (New Haven), 32, 123
  Gruppo I Riabilitatori (New London), 56
  Gruppo La Rivolta (Milford, Mass.), 138
  Gruppo La Termite (Waterbury), 32
Italian American Citizens Club (New London), 157
Italian American Civic Association (New London), 227
Italian American Democratic Club (New London), 218
Italian Cooperative and Social Club (Stafford Springs, Conn.), 239
Italian Dramatic Club (New London), xi–xii, xiii–xiv, 115–16, 118, 196, 225
  building of hall, 152–53
  evolution of leadership, 228–29
Italian General Labor Union Labor Union of America, 66
Italian general strike in New London, 95–98, 164
Italian laborers
  in Connecticut, 24–27
  and strikes, 26–28, 65–66
Italian Mutual Aid Society (New London), 121, 216, 235, 237
  birth of, 149
  politics of, 151, 180
Italian Mutual Benefit Society (New London), 82, 207–8, 213
Ivoryton, Connecticut, 200

kitchen bars. *See* bootlegging
Knights of Labor
  in New London, 17
  in Willimantic, 27

Kropotkin, Peter, 1, 3

labor movement
　in New London, 17, 46–48, 51–53, 83, 95–98, 128
　See also American Federation of Labor; Congress of Industrial Organizations; Connecticut Federation of Labor; Industrial Workers of the World
Labor Defender (ILD), 159, 185
La Guardia, Fiorello, 220
La Penna, Donato, 231
League of Resistance of Brickyard Workers (Hamden), 30
League of Small Home Owners (New London), 218
LeBlanc, Paul, 32
Leverone, Antone, 207–8
Leverone's Grove, 228
　and anarchist functions, 117–18
Levinson, Bessie, 41–42
Levinson, David, 41–42
Librino, Padre Mario, 75
Libya, invasion of by Italy, 95
　Italians of New London and, 76–77
　reaction of Italian left to, 75–76, 83
Like Lesser Gods (Tomasi), 171
Lombardozzi, Anselmo, 89, 93, 136, 155, 230
　and 1912 New London crisis, 84, 86
　biography of, 86
Lombardozzi, Gaetano, 128
　and Benvenutis, 81
　biography of, 50, 87–88
Lombardozzi, Pia Zanghetti, 229–30
Lombardozzi, Riccardo, 119
La Lotta Elletoralle (Fano), 109
Lo Verde, Paots, 180
Luzi, Dulio, 221, 232
Luzi, Ray, 223
Lynn, Massachusetts, 32, 103

Mahan, Brian F., 16
Malatesta, Errico, 1, 9, 28, 48, 60, 99, 105, 133, 134
　in Ancona, 1890s, 11, 12, 13–14
　death of, 221
　during Red Week, Ancona, 100
　in New London, 40–41, 48, 197
　in US, 40
Manfreda, Helen, 199–200
In Marcia (Fano and Pesaro), 10–11, 62, 70, 197
　readership in New London, 89, 100
Marcucci, Vincenzo, 229
Il Martello (New York), 60, 185, 239
McGirr, Lisa, 162
Mechanics Educational Society of America (MESA), 238
Mello, Gemma, 154
Mencarelli, Alberto, 154
Mencarelli, Sergio, 167, 237
Mencarelli, Shirley, 237
Menghi, Antone, 82, 123–24, 209–10, 220–21
Menghi, Guerino, 114, 123, 209–10
Meriden, Connecticut, 23, 24, 30, 74
Merlino, Francesco, 28
Metal Trades Council (Groton), 217
Meunier, Arturo, 56
Meyer, Gerald, 237
Middletown, Connecticut, 30, 82
Milford, Massachusetts
　and Italian anarchism, 137
　ties with New London, 137–41, 155
Mine, Mill and Smelter Workers union, 217
Montali, Anita, 89, 152, 197
　at Copeland murder scene, 191–92
Montali, Lorenzo, 89, 189
　and 1928 arrest of, 180
　as bootlegger, 165
　as IDC deed signer, 153

Montalis' Bakery, 89
Montanari, Paolo, 38
Montesi, Anna Marie, 166
Morelli, Giuseppe, 179
Most, Johann, 17, 29
Muratori, Alfredo, 165, 170
Mussolini, Benito, xvii, 88, 147, 174, 186, 236
  and invasion of Ethiopia, 219
Mystic, Connecticut, 74
  FSI in, 204–5
  Galleani speaks in, 204
  and immigration from Val di Zoldo, 202
  Italian women's groups in, 205
  IWW local in, 202
  labor movement in, 201–2, 203–4
  occupation of Italian radicals in, 202
  and radical movement, 198, 200–2
  SLP in, 201
  SP in, 201, 206

National Textile Workers Union, 214–15
Naugatuck, Connecticut, 143
Naval Intelligence (US), 99, 130, 137
Naval Undersea Warfare Center (Fort Trumbull), 223, 232
Needham, Massachusetts, 226, 229
New Britain, Connecticut
  Galleanist circle in, 74, 103, 238
  Italian laborers in, 25, 27
  radicalism in, 30, 176
New England Workers Association, 126
New Haven, Connecticut, 30, 82
  German anarchists in, 29
  Italian laborers in, 24, 25, 28
New Haven Register, 183

New London
  Americanization campaign in, 149
  economic development of, 14–17, 77
  Eminent domain clash in, xi–xii
  Italian immigration to, 16, 18–21
  and moral reform campaigns, 161, 163–64
  'Plain Words' flyer mailed in, 130–31
  population of, 18
  posting of 'Go-Head' flyer, 129
  radicalism in, 30
  and Sacco-Vanzetti case, 156–57
  as 'wettest' town in Connecticut, 164
  and World War I, 102
New London Day, xiii, 42, 47, 92, 95, 102, 166, 183
  and early Italian immigrants, 18, 20–21, 207
New London Development Corporation (NLDC), xi–xii
New London Opera House, 43, 44, 48, 55, 67, 194
New London Shipyard and Engine Company, 113
New London Telegraph, 208
Newton, Massachusetts, 155
North Haven, 30
Norwich, Connecticut, 43, 68, 200
Norwich Bulletin, 183
Nossek, Ronald, 228
Il Nostro Programma (Malatesta), 40, 48, 53
Il Nuovo Mondo (New York), 188

Olivieri, Gaetano, 37
O'Neill, Eugene
  on New London, 17
  and radicalization of, 73
  registers for draft in New London, 102
  Visit of Malatesta and, xvi, 122, 221

INDEX 293

Orcciani, Riccardo, 155, 156
Orsini, A. Matt, 152, 153, 154, 227

Paci, Arthur, 120, 136
Paglia, Jennie, 154, 198
Palmer raids, 146, 147
Palombaro. *See* Broccoli, Enrico
Panciera, Angelo, 202
Paoloni, Guglielma, 116
Parreta, Jennuru, 180
Parsons, Albert, 30, 67
Pasqualini, Attilio, 93, 117, 136
  and 1912 crisis, 83, 84
Paterson, New Jersey
  Italian anarchists in, 28, 41, 43, 68
  movement of anarchists to New London, 39–40
Pawcatuck, Connecticut, 173–74, 185
Peppermint Lounge, 228
Perella, Ernesto, 124, 128, 130, 136, 206
Peretta, James, 231
Pernicone, Nunzio, 12, 74, 83
Peroni, Augusto, 95, 109
  and 1912 crisis, 84, 86
  1928 arrest of, 180, 182
  and Foschini affair, 58
  letter to A. Benvenuti, 78–79
Petrini, Arthur, 223
Petrini, Bruno, 226
Petrini, Giovanna, 88, 93, 193
Petrini, Nevio, 223
Petrini, Rafaelle, 83, 88–89, 93, 95, 136, 155, 182, 188
  biography of, 70–71
  death of, 230
  in Italian general strike, 96, 98
Petrini, Spartaco, 93, 226
Pettinari, Arturo
  1928 arrest of, 182
  and collection for ILD, 159

Pfizer Corporation, xi–xii
Philopena, Frank J., 97
Pierfederici, Attilio, 117, 227
  biography of, 213–14
  and Italian invasion of Ethiopia, 219–20
  and Italian Mutual Benefit Society, 82, 213
Pierpaoli, Guerino, 150
Pine Grove Camp (Niantic), 167
Plum Island (New York), 18, 36, 45
Postiglione, Umberto
  as Galleanist, 83
  in New London, 83, 86, 94–95, 96, 98
Progressive Citizens of America (New London), 226
Il Progresso degl'Italiani nel Connecticut, 175
Progresso Communista (Fano), 127
Il Proletario, 28, 48, 55, 60, 99, 146, 204
prominenti
  and fascism, 175
  in New Haven, 127, 146–47
  in New London, 68, 207–11
Proudhon, Pierre-Joseph, 1–2, 112–13
Providence, Rhode Island, 40, 59, 98

La Questione Sociale (Paterson) 28, 31, 38, 40, 41, 44, 45, 47, 52, 56–57, 59, 62, 66, 69, 75, 119, 208–9

radical labor subculture in US, 32–33
Raffuzzi, Maria, 194–95
Ragione Nuova (Providence), 125
Ramasco, Giuseppe, 49
Ravarini, Eugenio, 148
Raveggi, Pietro, 44, 203

Recchi, Nicola, 142–43, 155
Renzoni, Fortunato, 117, 128
  biography of, 123–24
  as bootlegger, 165, 166
  drift from anarchist movement of, 220
Renzoni, Leo, 223
Revere, Massachusetts, 88, 94
Ricciardelli, Evaristo, 155
Rinaldoni, Paolo, 137–41
Roda, Maria, 194
Rossi, Augusto, 107, 155

Sabatini, Longo, 180
Sacco, Nicola, 2–3, 103, 141
  arrested April 1920, 142, 155
  in Milford, Massachusetts, 137
Sacco-Vanzetti case
  and Communist-Galleanist rivalry, 159
  effect on Italian American radical movement, 155–56
  and New London, 156–57
St. Josephs Church (New London), 120
Salegna, Nicholas, 177, 189
Salvemini, Gaetano, 176
Sanchini, Giobbe, 103, 127, 231
Sanchini, Irma, 103, 199
Sanchioni, Aldelfo, 155
Sanchioni, Renato, 155
Santi, Tony, 231
Satti, Charles, 157
  and liquor business, 210
Satti, C. John, 147, 227
  and Rafaelle Petrini, 230
  rise of, 210, 218
Schiavina, Rafaelle, 98, 103, 124, 233
  in New London, 127, 221–22
Segata, Augusto, 125

Senigallia (Marche), 93, 193, 196
  as origin of New London anarchists, 38, 89
Serio, Guido, 159
Servadio, Alberto, 165, 170
Severini, Anselmo, 107, 136
Shandeor, Frank, 209–10
Shaw Street neighborhood, 188–89, 218, 235, 236
  and bootlegging, 162, 163
  and fascist presence in, 178, 186
Sicilians
  and fascism, 173–74
  and labor walkouts, 66, 98
  in New London, 20–21, 68, 76–77, 153–54
  New London organization building of, 157, 218–19
  support Italian involvement in World War I, 92
Siebold, Frederick, 29
Socialist Labor Party (SLP), 30, 32
  Italian branch in New London, 56
  meeting prohibited in New London, 147
Socialist Party (SP), 142, 147
  and 1912 elections, 73
Socialist Workers Party (SWP), 32
Società Siciliana (New London), 173
Sommariva, Rafaelle, 37
Sons of Italy (New London), 211, 227
Sora, Federico, xv, 147
Sormenti, Enea. See Vidali, Vittorio
Stafford Springs, Connecticut, 24, 26
  and Italian radical activity, 176
Stami, Cesare, 133
Stonington, Maine, 70–71
Stony Creek, Connecticut, 24, 26, 176, 200

strikes in New England
  1915 Italian laborers' walkout
    (Providence), 98
  1916 Naugatuck Valley brass
    industry, 98
  1919–1920 Naugatuck Valley brass
    industry, 126, 145–46
  1934 textile walkout, 214–16
  Bloom silk mill (New London),
    158–59
  Brainerd & Armstrong Company
    (New London), 83
  Central Vermont Railway (New
    London), 48, 128
  Consolidated Railway Company
    (New London), 65–66
  Eastern Shipbuilding and Brown
    Cotton Gin Company (New
    London), 51–53
  Electric Boat Company (Groton),
    217
  Lawrence textile strike of 1912, 73
  Rossie Velvet Mill (Mystic), 203–4
  Russell Manufacturing
    (Middletown), 82
  Sargents Company (New Haven), 28
  trolley strike (New London), 98

Tarabelli, Fernando, 155
Tarini, Irene, 120
Thompson, E. P., 14
Thoreau, Henry David, 1
Tomaselli, Giuseppe, 231
Tomchuk, Travis, 4, 101
Tonucci, Stephano, 150
Torrington, Connecticut, 217, 238
Tramontano, Faust, 218
transnationalism
  defined, 4–5
  and New London, 99–101
Travaglini, Enrico, 62

Tresca, Carlo, 100, 185
  and 1928 dispute with Gruppo I
    Liberi, 187–88
  in New London, 60
  in Waterbury, 148
Tudisca, Giuseppe, 180, 183–85
Turcato, Davide, xiv, 4
Turello, John, 97
Tusa (Sicily), 20, 97, 185
Tusana Society (New London), 158

Umanita Novà (Milan), 99
Union of Russian Workers, 33, 142
  in Connecticut, 145–46
  raided in New London, 147
L'Unita Operaia (New York), 215
United Electrical, Radio and
  Machine Workers, 217, 238
United Textile Workers Local 1889
  (New London), 215
Unity Club (New London), 227
Urbani, A., 84

Valentini, Aldo, 105, 214
Valentini, Giuseppe, 214
Valdinocci, Carlo, 103, 125, 142
Val di Zoldo
  immigrants from, 26
  women and radicalism in, 198–99
Vaninetti, John, 238
Vanzetti, Bartholomeo, 23, 103, 141,
  155
Vattuone, John, 171
Vecoli, Rudolph J., 239
Vescovi, Louis, 165
Vidali, Vittorio, 180–81
Volontà (Ancona), 89

Wallace, Henry, 226, 227
Wallingford, Connecticut, 239
  FSI in, 74, 126–27, 199

Wallingford, Connecticut *(continued)*
  Italian anarchists in, 176, 229
  Italian laborers in, 25
Waterbury, Connecticut, 10, 30, 145
Waterford, Connecticut, 20, 38, 43, 68, 74, 228
Weiss, Feri, 139–40
Wessel, Bessie Bloom, 149
Westerly, Rhode Island, 43, 74, 198
  Galleanist groups in, 83, 125, 206

White Star Lines, 62
Willimantic, Connecticut, 26–27
women
  economic role in Fort Trumbull of, 166–67
  and New London anarchist movement, 191–98
Worcester, Massachusetts, 23

Zandri, Napoleone, 114
Zimmer, Kenyon, 40

www.ingramcontent.com/pod-product-compliance
Lightning Source LLC
Chambersburg PA
CBHW030009240426

43672CB00007B/880